WESTPORT COUNTRY PLAYHOUSE
ANNIVERSARY SUMMER SEASON

ducing Managers Company and Dina and Alexander E. Racolin present

ON. JULY 11 thru JULY 16, 1966
rld Premiere — Prior to Broadway

EORGE GRIZZARD
RITA GAM
IN
The himking Man

BY JOHN TOBIAS
irected by RICHARD ALTMAN
and Lighting By ROBERT SOULE

YERS TAVERN ADJACENT TO THE THEATR
7-4177, P.O. BOX 629, WESTPORT, CONN.

93

WESTPORT
COUNTRY PLAYHOUSE

CONNECTICUT THEATRE FOUNDATION, INC.
Presents
THURSDAY THRU SUNDAY—NOV. 7, 8, 9, 10
THURSDAY THRU SUNDAY—NOV. 14, 15, 16, 17

The World Premiere
of
TOBACCO ROAD
A New Musical

OAN WILE
UENEWALD

4177
IN.

WESTPORT
COUNTRY PLAYHOUSE
AMERICA'S FOREMOST SUMMER THEATRE   FULLY AIR CONDITIONED
OUR 48th SUMMER THEATRE SEASON - 1978

June 19 - July 1
ARLENE FRANCIS
CAROL SWARBRICK   DAVID CHANEY   BONNIE SCHON
in
SIDE BY SIDE BY SONDHEIM
A Musical Entertainment

July 31 - August 12
KATHRYN CROSBY   TONY RUSSEL
in
SAME TIME, NEXT YEAR
by
BERNARD SLADE

August 14 - August 19
The Famous Continental Comedy
PATRICE MUNSEL   EDWARD MULHARE
in
THE PLAY'S THE THING
by
FERENC MOLNAR

August 21 - August 26
The London Smash Hit Comedy
DAVID McCALLUM   CAROLE SHELLEY
in
DONKEY'S YEARS
by
MICHAEL FRAYN

IA
DGE

JR.

August 28 - September 2
The Comedy Success of London and New York
DICK CAVETT

OT

September 4
TO BE AN

Sunday,
PRESERVA
JAZZ
8:00

CKETS BY TELEPHONE: 203 227-417
BankAmericard, American Express, Master Charge

JUNE 12 - 24, 2000
THE CONSTANT WIFE
W. SOMERSET MAUGHAM
rected by JOANNE WOODWARD
A lighthearted comedy of gossip, marriage and just desserts.

PORT
PLAYHOUSE
— September 8

rn to Broadway
TOM
M ALDREDGE
in
EN POND
can comedy
y
HOMPSON
th
Barbara Andres
Mark Bendo
ed by
NDERSON
5•227-4177

WESTPORT COUNTRY PLAYHOUSE
WHERE THEATRE ACTS LIKE THEA
CALL 203-227-
www.westportplayhouse.com
Connecticut
Radio Network

WESTPORT
COUNTRY PLAYHOUSE
Phone: 227-4177
AIR-CONDITIONED
JUNE 22 Thru JULY 4, 1992
JAMES B. McKENZIE, Executive Producer
– presents –

CAROLE SHELLEY
– in –
LETTICE & LOVAGE
by **Peter Shaffer**
– also starring –
DORIS BELACK
Directed by **LONNY PRICE**
Monday thru Fri...

WESTPOR
COUNTRY PLAYHOU
Phone: CA 7-4177
AIR-CONDITIONED
AUG. 15 Thru AUG. 2

HENRY T. WEINSTEIN and LAURENCE FELDMAN, Prod
– PRESENT –
The Theatre Guild & Joel Schenker Production

**ERIC PORTMAN · SIGNE HASS
GLORIA VANDERBILT · ALEXANDER SC**
– IN –
"THE BURNT FLOWER BED"
by
Ugo Betti
– with –
FRED ROLF – VINCENT GARDENIA
MICHAEL BENNAHUM

Directed by Eugene Lion

Monday thru Friday Evenings at 8:40
Saturday Eves. at 6 and 9   **Wednesday Mats.**

An American Theatre

THE STORY OF

Westport Country Playhouse

An American Theatre

THE STORY OF
Westport Country Playhouse
1931–2005

RICHARD SOMERSET-WARD

With a Foreword by
JOANNE WOODWARD AND PAUL NEWMAN

YALE UNIVERSITY PRESS

NEW HAVEN AND LONDON

To the memory of
Lawrence and Armina Langner

A catalogue record for this book is available from the British Library.

Library of Congress Cataloging-in-Publication Data

Somerset-Ward, Richard.
An American theatre : the story of Westport Country Playhouse,
1931–2005 / Richard Somerset-Ward ; with a foreword by Joanne
Woodward and Paul Newman.
     p. cm.
Includes bibliographical references and index.
ISBN 0-300-10648-3 (hardcover : alk. paper)
ISBN 0-300-10938-5 (boxed ed.)
1. Westport Country Playhouse (Westport, Conn.) 2. Theater—
Connecticut—Westport—History—20th century. 3. Theater—
Connecticut—Westport—History—21st century. I. Title.
PN2277.W472W478 2005
792'.09746'9—dc22

                    2005000849

The paper in this book meets the guidelines for permanence and
durability of the Committee on Production Guidelines for Book
Longevity of the Council on Library Resources.

Designed and typeset in Electra by Katy Homans, New York

Prepress by Gist and Herlin Press, Inc., West Haven, Connecticut

Printed in China by C & C Offset Printing Co., Ltd.

10 9 8 7 6 5 4 3 2 1

Contents

The circular sign, which, for many years, hung on the lobby wall between the two box-office windows, was hand-carved by Richard Edward Barrows and painted by Rita Merlet Barrows in 1974.

Foreword

JOANNE WOODWARD

AND

PAUL NEWMAN

We have been asked to write a brief history of the Westport Country Playhouse. It follows. Do not skip. Every line has its own astonishment!

Groucho Marx, Dorothy Gish, Lillian Gish, Armina Marshall, Jane Wyatt, Jane Cowl, Laurette Taylor, Helen Ford, Otis Skinner, Jessie Royce Landis, Charles Coburn, Gene and Kathleen Lockhart, Helen Menken, Kitty Carlisle, Monty Woolley, Jean Arthur, Sam Jaffe, Burgess Meredith, J. C. Nugent, Ruth Gordon, Ina Claire, Frances Fuller, George Coulouris, Eva LeGallienne, Richard Whorf, Mildred Natwick, Clarence Derwent, Myron McCormick, Frances Farmer, Anna May Wong, Henry Fonda, Uta Hagen, Ethel Barrymore, Van Heflin, Sally Rand, Glenda Farrell, Jose Ferrer, Alla Nazimova, Bramwell Fletcher, Gene Kelly, Betty Field, Paul Robeson, Tallulah Bankhead, Mary Boland, Walter Slezak, Tyrone Power, Roddy McDowell, Jean-Pierre Aumont, David Wayne, Dame May Whitty, Patricia Neal, Thornton Wilder, Frances Lederer, Olivia de Havilland, Robert Stack, Buddy Ebsen, Henry Morgan, Estelle Winwood, Fay Bainter, Alfred Drake, Jane Seymour, Roland Young, William Gaxton, Joan Caufield, Eddie Dowling, Ann Harding, Paul Lukas, Cornel Wilde, Sarah Churchill, Elaine Stritch, Kent Smith, Shirley Booth, Sidney Blackmer, Franchot Tone, Maurice Evans, Basil Rathbone, Eve Arden, Maureen Stapleton, Zachary Scott, Karl Malden, Kim Hunter, Vanessa Brown, Leo G. Carroll, Walter Abel, Edward Gargan, Claudette Colbert, Melvyn Douglas, Signe Hasso, Dane Clark, Gloria Swanson, Molly Picon, Celeste Holm, Margaret O'Brien, Claude Dauphin, Jan Sterling, Lionel Stander, William Prince, Paul Hartman, Joan Hackett, Walter Pidgeon, Eva Gabor, Sammy Davis, Jr., Hal Holbrook, Teresa Wright, Carol Channing, Ann Sothern, Hans Conried, Menasha Skulnik, Hugh O'Brian, Faye Emerson, Bert Lahr, Sir Cedric Hardwicke, Tony Randall, Shelley Winters, Jo Van Fleet, Eli Wallach, Anne Jackson, Imogene Coca, Betty Comden, Adolph Green, Jane Fonda, Eric Portman, Mike Nichols, Gloria Vanderbilt, Betty Furness, Billie Burke, Maria Riva, Terry Moore, Richard Kiley, Eva Marie Saint, Geraldine Page, Tammy Grimes, Dolores Del Rio, Arthur Treacher, Sandy Dennis, Eartha Kitt, Jessica Tandy, Hume Cronyn, Donald Cook, George Jessel, Claude Rains, Rod Steiger, Beatrice Little, Wally Cox, Rita Gam, Van Johnson, Liza Minnelli, Joel Grey, Tom Ewell, Helen Hayes, Dorothy Stickney, Joan Fontaine, Hurd Hatfield, Maureen O'Sullivan, Julie Newmar, Edward Mulhare, Sid Caesar, Mickey Rooney, Art Carney, Brian Bedford, Broderick Crawford, Lynn Redgrave, Theodore Bikel, Douglas Fairbanks, Jr., Louis Jourdan, Patrice Munsel, Dick Cavett, Sam Levene, Vincent Price, Frances Sternhagen, Orson Bean, Glynis Johns, Lucie Arnaz, Sheppard Strudwick, Timothy Bottoms, Shaun Cassidy, Cybill Shepherd, Leslie Caron, Nanette Fabray, Shelly Berman, Colleen Dewhurst, Gene Wilder, Jane Powell, Jerry Stiller and Anne Meara, to name a few.

An American Theatre

This is the story of one small theatre in southern Connecticut, a theatre that was created seventy-five years ago in a nineteenth-century cow barn.

Why would such a little theatre—and, up to now, just a summer theatre—be worth a book? And why would so many people in Westport and the neighboring townships have spent so much of their time, energy and money in preserving such a little theatre?

One reason is its past, which is a virtual mirror of the story of American theatre in the twentieth century. The Playhouse's founder, Lawrence Langner, was a seminal figure in that story because of his long involvement with the Theatre Guild and all that the Guild did to change the face of American theatre between the 1920s and the 1950s. For the first time, it provided a showcase for great plays—old and new, American and European—and it brought an astonishing array of writing, directing, designing and acting talent to its productions on Broadway. Ironically, however, it was Lawrence Langner's frustration with the Theatre Guild that caused him to create a summer theatre of his own—a theatre in which he and his wife, Armina, could make all the decisions themselves, and in which they would no longer be beholden to the opinions and prejudices of a committee of peers, however distinguished that committee might be.

So, in 1931, the Westport Country Playhouse came into being. Lawrence and Armina were consciously adding to a great American tradition of summer stock theatre, which was then at its height, but they were also creating a laboratory—what was called a "tryout house"—for plays that might later go to Broadway as Theatre Guild productions. So the Playhouse was the unlikely setting for world premieres of plays by Bernard Shaw, Noël Coward and William Inge, and later by Leonard Gershe and A. R. Gurney. It featured American playwrights like O'Neill, S. N. Behrman, Tennessee Williams, Arthur Miller and Neil Simon, and it was also one of those rare American theatres where you could see the classic works of English playwrights like Wycherley and Congreve, and Shakespeare, of course, and French playwrights like Molière and Dumas. In a small but important way it played a role in the creation of some of the greatest musicals ever produced—*Oklahoma!*, *Carousel* and *My Fair Lady*. And it was a magnet for actors. It's where Otis Skinner gave his last performance at the age of seventy-five, where Laurette Taylor, Ethel Barrymore, Jane Cowl, Ruth Gordon, Helen Hayes, Tallulah Bankhead and Eva Le Gallienne all performed, and where many of Hollywood's greatest film stars came to show off their theatrical skills, from Tyrone Power and Olivia de Havilland to Paul Robeson and Groucho Marx—and not forgetting two young stars of the 1960s, Jane Fonda and Liza Minnelli.

When the final curtain came down on the 2003 season and the cast and staff of the theatre gathered one last time in the old green room, surrounded by the posters and pictures of all those predecessors, the toast that Paul Newman offered before the construction company moved in to begin the rebuilding was "To all the ghosts who dwell in this place, may they be happy!"

So the past is important, but it's never as important as the future, and that's the real reason why so many people worked so hard, and gave so generously, to make sure the Playhouse survived—and, having survived, that it was properly equipped for the twenty-first century.

A theatre is not just an ornament; it can also be one of the most dynamic and important institutions within a community. So the Westport Country Playhouse is no longer just a summer theatre, though the summer season will always be the most important thing it does. "Performing arts center" might be a better description now, with theatre always as its first priority, but with lots of other things as possibilities—chamber opera, small-scale concerts, recitals, lecture series, folk festivals, film shows and even, perhaps, some dance.

All these things will happen within the four walls of the Playhouse, but there's another part of the theatre's mission that will take place *beyond* its walls, in schools and institutions throughout

Fairfield County. Theatre is a uniquely powerful way of involving children, of helping them communicate, of getting messages across to them, and it's another important reason why so many people worked so hard to renovate and re-equip the Playhouse.

Lawrence Langner was captivated by the magic of theatre when he was very young, and he was still captivated, joyously and unapologetically, when he died in 1962 at the age of seventy-two. For him, it began with a toy theatre given him as a child. For the two people who have trodden in his giant-sized footsteps at Westport there are similar, but different, stories: Jim McKenzie was performing his own one-act version of *Hamlet* for the citizens of Appleton, Wisconsin, by the time he was eleven years old, while Joanne Woodward was fortunate enough to grow up in a small town where there was a real children's theatre—the kind where children not only did the acting, but also built the sets, found the props and costumes, and ran the backstage operations.

For most of us, by contrast, the magic probably didn't take hold until later in life, but it doesn't matter—because, whether you're an adult or a child, that first moment when you suspend disbelief and become enthralled by the theatre is an experience you never forget. It's one that Westport Country Playhouse has already given to untold numbers of people, and it's one that it is now assured of being able to give to generations yet to come.

That's why the Westport Country Playhouse was worthy of all the time, effort, imagination and money that went into preserving it. And it's also why it's worthy of being written about as "An American Theatre," representative of a rare and precious breed.

R. S. W.
January 2005

CHAPTER ONE

The Prologue

In 1854, within a few months of arriving in America, Dionysius Lardner Boucicault found himself commuting up and down the Post Road between Boston and New York. In Boston, he was making his American acting debut, while, in New York, his play *Used Up* was in rehearsal. He was a busy man, and that was just as well because he wasn't the only person he had to look after—there was also his Scottish wife, Agnes Robertson, with whom he had eloped to America. She was a marvelously talented actress who had been a pupil and ward of one of the greatest of English actors, Charles Kean. Nothing did a Boucicault play more good than to have Agnes starring in it. But he was a pretty good actor himself—the best "stage Irishman" around—so what worked best for the family finances was to have two new Boucicault plays in production at the same time, one starring Agnes and one himself. Unfortunately, so profligate was their spending that he could never afford to stop writing—he used to complain that the epitaph on his gravestone would read, "Dion Boucicault: his first holiday."[1]

However fanciful it may be, it's fun to speculate about those journeys between Boston and New York in 1854. As the stagecoach rolled through southern Connecticut—through the outskirts of the newly incorporated town of Westport, only forty-five miles north of New York—is it possible that Boucicault may have looked up and caught a glimpse of a big brown barn standing in an apple orchard on the west side of the Post Road? Or was it perhaps the smell that got his attention (for the barn was used as a tannery then)? And, just to complete the fancy, was it perhaps the Irish in him that prompted a sudden, mysterious premonition that, a century and a half into the future, the name of Boucicault would owe a large part of its fame in America to its links with that foul-smelling barn?

That may be fanciful, but what is not in doubt is that, seventy-five years after Boucicault first passed the barn, it was seen by another transatlantic immigrant—this one a wealthy patent attorney from England with a passion for theatre. Lawrence Langner not only bought the barn, he turned it into a theatre—a country playhouse, the Westport Country Playhouse—and he opened the new theatre in the early summer of 1931 with Dion Boucicault's melodrama *The Streets of New York*. It was a success—and so was the brave little theatre in the apple orchard, where sheep grazed contentedly on the grounds, happy to give way to theatregoers and their automobiles on summer evenings.

Although much has changed in the seven decades that have come and gone since then, some things have remained constant. One of them is *The Streets of New York*. It is still the Playhouse's signature piece, brought back for all important occasions. Another is the continuing ability of Westport's little playhouse not just to survive as a summer theatre, and not just to take some of its productions to Broadway (as it did *The Streets of New York* in the fall of 1931, and as it has done on countless occasions since), but also to reflect, in its own history, the brilliant story of American theatre in the twentieth century—its triumphalism and its commercialism on the one hand, and its notable contribution to drama and dramatic invention on the other.

Betsie Brodie and Priscilla Murphy—
apprentices in the wings, 1960.

The American theatre scene Dion Boucicault encountered in the decade before the Civil War must have had little to commend it to someone who had worked successfully, as he had, in Ireland, England and France. But it had what mattered most to Boucicault at that moment, which was opportunity. In England, though he was recognized as a useful playwright and an excellent actor (especially in the parts he wrote for himself), his private life had become a liability. Ugly rumors circulated about the death of his first wife, who had conveniently disappeared while mountain climbing with him in Australia, at a time when he just happened to be having a passionate affair with another woman. Now he had run off with the adopted daughter of one of the most powerful actor-managers in Britain. The New World seemed a good option.

This was a time when most of the plays and almost all the leading actors to be seen in American theatres came from Europe. Stars like Junius Brutus Booth, Frank Chanfrau, J. W. Wallack and Laura Keene led their companies across the continent to play to the newly wealthy inhabitants of western mining towns, while resident stock companies built theatres for themselves in the more established cities of the east and south—Boston, New York, Philadelphia, New Orleans, St. Louis. By 1850, there were at least thirty-five resident companies operating around the country.

For Boucicault and his colleagues, the easiest way to satisfy this growing thirst for theatre was by adapting (which was often a nice word for plagiarizing) the work of European playwrights who had conveniently failed to make the ocean journey to protect their property in the New World. That was more or less what Boucicault was doing when he turned a French play called *Les Pauvres de Paris* into *The Poor of New York* (which was the title under which *The Streets of New York* was generally performed in its early days). Boucicault observed little magic in the operation: "I can spin out these rough-and-tumble dramas as a hen lays eggs. It's a degrading occupation, but more money has been made out of guano than out of poetry."[2] In this spirit, he later crafted the same plot, the same characters and the same poverty into *The Poor of* Boston, Philadelphia, Liverpool and London, respectively. In all, he wrote more than two hundred plays, the majority of them in America, and it somehow comes as no surprise that he was one of the leading advocates of the copyright law that was passed by the Congress in 1856—no one was going to be allowed to plagiarize *his* plays.

Boucicault was also quoted as saying: "Sensation is what the public wants and you cannot give them too much of it."[3] True to this creed, he added a sensational scene to *The Poor of New York* in which the Fairweathers were rescued from a burning building. He is said to have superintended the setting of the fire himself each night on the stage of Wallack's Theatre—until the night when he inadvertently, but spectacularly, ended the play's run by burning the theatre to the ground.[4]

Much of the "wisdom" Boucicault acquired about American theatre was learned from his observation of a true theatrical sensation. *Uncle Tom's Cabin* was one of the first plays he saw when he arrived in New York, and in the fall of 1853 it was breaking box-office records. George L. Aiken's play, which would become easily the most popular of the several dramatizations of Harriet Beecher Stowe's novel doing the rounds, had closed in the summer of 1852 after a perfunctory two-week run at New York City's grandly named National Theatre. But the production had been revived in Troy in upstate New York, and there it had clocked up a startling one hundred performances. When it returned to the National Theatre, it just ran and ran—more than three hundred consecutive performances, despite the existence of rival productions put on by P. T. Barnum at his Museum and by Thomas Dartmouth Rice at the Bowery Theatre (Rice was the original blacked-up

Dionysius Lardner Boucicault (1822–90). This lithograph was made in 1855, soon after his arrival in America.

Uncle Tom's Cabin. In this 1901 production, Eliza is about to cross the frozen river to freedom.

minstrel of the greatest single attraction of the American theatre in the mid years of the century, the minstrel show). Even then, *Uncle Tom* fever was only just beginning: the play became a touring sensation throughout the northern and western states and (in multiple languages) in almost every country of Europe. As late as 1927, there were still twelve companies that existed to tour that play and no other![5]

It escaped no one's attention—certainly not Boucicault's—that all this success was being garnered by an American play, not a European import, and that most of the cash it threw off was the result of performances given by touring companies that were rehearsed, staffed and equipped to present *Uncle Tom's Cabin* only—they had no other repertory. They were known as "combination companies" because they carried everything necessary to give performances of a single play—stars, supporting actors, sets, props and advance men to do the marketing. Resident companies, however talented, could not compete with this kind of onslaught, and they quickly collapsed before them. Thus the repertory system that had seemed to be taking root in America was suddenly and rudely displaced: the long run became the obsessive purpose of every theatre producer, and plays were invariably chosen for their potential as properties of combination touring companies headed by important stars. Henry Irving made no fewer than eight nationwide tours between 1883 and 1902; Sarah Bernhardt would eventually make nine. Long before that, Boucicault had claimed to be so impressed with the system that he had introduced it to England in the early 1860s when he sent out a company with his play *The Colleen Bawn*.[6]

However effective the combination company may have been as a commercial device, it was no way to develop an indigenous drama tradition. What it did do, however, was to establish New York as the undisputed theatre capital of America, for it was in New York that almost all these productions were put together and rehearsed. Theatrical talent migrated there, and so, too, did the producers, managers and agents who called the shots. Not surprisingly, it was in New York that the most important and the most innovative theatres were built by theatrical entrepreneurs like Edwin Booth (son of Junius Brutus Booth and older brother of the assassin John Wilkes Booth), Augustin Daly and Steele MacKaye. Theatres were beginning to cluster around the street called Broadway, and the advent of electricity would eventually transform their collective marquee into The Great White Way.

Not surprisingly, then, New York was where the greatest shows were staged and where, in the spirit of Barnum, impresarios competed for influence and groups of businessmen sought to win control. One such group, brazenly known as "The Syndicate," was able to offer superior productions to any theatre outside New York that was willing to place itself under The Syndicate's exclusive patronage. Most theatres welcomed this: it meant they could deal with one agent only, and it meant they were assured a regular supply of fine productions, many of them by Charles Frohman, the producing member of The Syndicate. So it was for almost two decades, until Frohman died in the wreck of the *Lusitania* in 1915 and The Syndicate petered out for lack of leadership. The Shuberts stepped eagerly into the vacuum.

Musical shows had always been popular in New York—the minstrel shows went on and on—but it was in the early years of the twentieth century, under the influence of Charles Frohman and later the Shuberts, that "the musical" became a New York phenomenon. No one was more closely associated with this development than Florenz Ziegfeld, Jr.—not just because he introduced the chorus line of long-legged beauties in stunning, if skimpy, costumes, and not just because he established the *Follies of 1907* (and every succeeding year), but because, in time, his work led to the flowering of the full-blown American musical that was to be one of the great glories of twentieth-century theatre.

If one moment more than any other can be isolated as the moment when the American musi-

Charles Frohman (1860–1915) on board ship. He was drowned in the wreck of the *Lusitania*.

Porgy and Bess in the original production by the Theatre Guild in 1935, directed by Rouben Mamoulian, with Todd Duncan and Ann Brown in the title roles. This is Catfish Row, as evoked by designer Sergei Soudeikine.

cal became a factor in theatre history it must be a night in December 1927 when Ziegfeld opened his production of *Show Boat*, by Jerome Kern and Oscar Hammerstein II. There was no chorus line to dance the audience into the show: instead, a somber group of black workers hefted massive cotton bales across the stage and sang of their servitude. It was a show of wonderful and memorable tunes—from "Ol' Man River" to "Make Believe"—but it was also brutally and sensationally truthful. Its themes of prejudice and racial intermixture caused shock and offense. *Show Boat* gave notice that the American musical would not always be a frothy, spectacular concoction—that sometimes, and quite often, it would have something to say.

It was in tough-minded, brilliant shows like *Show Boat* that the two ends of American theatre met and married—the flamboyance and the star-centered world of show business, on the one hand, and, on the other, the growing ideal of an indigenous American theatre built around a realistic approach to drama.

THAT DAMNED SEAGULL

Realism had come to world theatre from the Arctic tundra of the north. It happened in the last four decades of the nineteenth century, and it was the creation, very largely, of Henrik Ibsen and August Strindberg in Scandinavia, and Anton Chekhov in Russia—although, in Russia, it is perhaps important to add the name of Constantin Stanislavsky, a stage director, not a playwright, for it was Stanislavsky, more than anyone else, who found ways of producing these realistic plays in the essentially unrealistic and artificial confines of a theatre. It was his production of Chekhov's *The Seagull*—plotless, eventless and symbolic—that caused a sensation in Moscow in 1898 and set the Moscow Art Theatre, which Stanislavsky had co-founded with Vladimir Nemirovich-Danchenko, on its way to revolutionizing the arts of stage direction and acting throughout the world. *The Seagull* had been a disaster when it was first produced two years earlier—the actors hadn't known their lines, certainly hadn't understood them, and had no comprehension of what the play was about. Now, ironically, it was the playwright, Chekhov, who thought himself the injured party—he didn't enjoy having his play interpreted for him by a director.

That was the way it would often be in the twentieth century: dramatic realism unleashed the talents, great and small, of stage directors.

It was not only in the far north that these ideas were let loose. By pure coincidence, in the same year that the Moscow Art Theatre was being launched, a group of Irish dramatists led by W. B. Yeats, J. M. Synge and Lady Augusta Gregory was in the

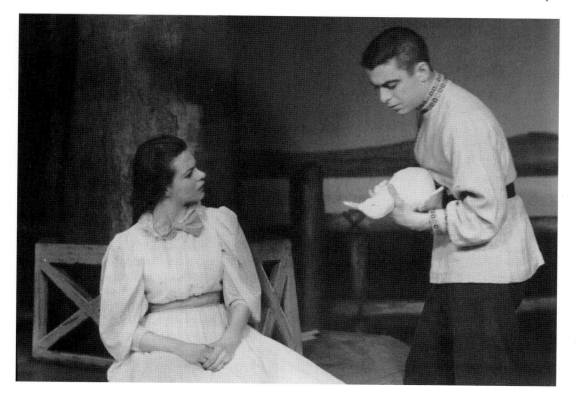

The Seagull in a 1938 production by the Theatre Guild, with Uta Hagen as Nina and Richard Whorf as Constantine.

process of creating the Abbey Theatre in Dublin. The Abbey was avowedly nonpolitical—its language was English, not Gaelic—but it was deeply nationalistic. The Irish felt, with justice, that they had too often been portrayed on the stage as comic relief. Now, in the hands of Irish playwrights and Irish actors, the record was to be put straight—too straight, many thought, for Synge's *The Playboy of the Western World* was all too frank about the poverty, cruelty and repression of Irish life: riots frequently took place when it was performed. A few years later, in 1926, Sean O'Casey's *The Plough and the Stars* caused equally bad feeling within Ireland—its satiric, sometimes mocking, portrayal of episodes of the Easter Rebellion only ten years earlier was too stinging for wounds that were still raw and open.

It was the visits to America of the Abbey Theatre in 1911 and the Moscow Art Theatre in 1923–24 that did more than anything else to sow the seeds of these new forms of theatre in the United States. Both companies brought with them something that, in America, became known as "the Method," or method acting. It had been pioneered by Stanislavsky in the early years of the century. Though it was often thought of as a style of acting, it was not. Rather, it was a method of preparing a performance in such a way that the people on the stage—the actors—would appear to the audience to be "real" people (physically and psychologically) involved in "real" situations. There would be none of the stylized, exaggerated and "unnatural" acting the theatre had relied on for centuries, with audiences being required to suspend their disbelief (a virtual impossibility in the face of such acting) if they wished to have any involvement in the drama. Many of New York's young actors were greatly struck by this method, and it was one of them, Lee Strasberg, who would eventually give it an American home when he founded the Actors Studio in the early 1940s.

Another direct result of the Abbey's 1911 visit was that it persuaded a twenty-three-year-old Princeton dropout, who had spent the last few months as a merchant seaman, that his true vocation was that of dramatist. His name was Eugene O'Neill, and he was reluctantly—certainly, in his later years, unhappily—destined to be the first great American playwright.

THE LONG DAY'S JOURNEY

In their plays, the apostles of realism had sought for some form of psychological truth, and it might be said that, however unknowingly, they had imposed the continuation of that search on twentieth century dramatists. In the case of O'Neill, the search took place, remorselessly and with ever-increasing stringency, in his own psyche, in his Catholic conscience, in the repeated exploration of a series of painful experiences in his early life—and, of course, in the very public spotlight of the performance of his plays. Writing to recommend *Strange Interlude* to his colleagues in the Theatre Guild, Lawrence Langner wrote: "This play contains in it more deep knowledge of the dark corners of the human mind than anything that has ever been written."[7] The same could be said of many of O'Neill's other plays. By the end, as he waited impatiently for death in a Boston hotel room, suffering from what he believed to be incurable Parkinson's disease, he had delivered a formidable canon that had been recognized by a Nobel Prize in 1936. Yet the most powerful and autobiographical of all his works—*Long Day's Journey into Night*—was released by his widow only after his death.

In the story of American theatre, O'Neill's plays are of seminal importance, but their existence serves to hide some of the other ways in which he shaped and influenced the course of theatrical development in the early twentieth century—ways that vitally affected what was to happen in Westport. One of these was his small but essential role in the return to "little theatres." This movement was, in some ways, a reaction against the dominance of New York and the near-monopolistic

Eugene O'Neill's *Mourning Becomes Electra*: the original 1931 production by the Theatre Guild, with Alla Nazimova as Christine and Alice Brady as her daughter, Lavinia. The sets were by Robert Edmund Jones.

power of commercial producing organizations like The Syndicate and the Shuberts; in other ways it was an attempt to imitate the artistic distinction and innovation of independent theatres in Europe. It took hold in the four or five years immediately before the United States' entry into World War I. By 1917 there were more than fifty local theatre companies, most of them in towns between Chicago and the East Coast, and by no means the least of them was the Provincetown Players of Massachusetts, founded in 1915. It was with the Players that O'Neill began his professional life the following year, writing a prolific series of one-act plays that created his national reputation — the more easily because the Provincetown Players quickly moved from the relative obscurity of Cape Cod to the bright lights of New York.

Another of the little theatre groups O'Neill wrote for on occasion was the Washington Square Players. Its life was short (1915–18) but its importance was great, because it was from among its members that the founders of the Theatre Guild were drawn.

THE THEATRE GUILD

In the years between the two world wars — and, to a somewhat lesser extent, in the two decades immediately thereafter — the Theatre Guild was the most exciting and interesting producing organization in the United States. It was founded (in the words of one of its directors, Lawrence Langner) "to produce plays of artistic merit not ordinarily produced by the commercial managers." That meant musicals as well as straight plays, old works as well as new ones, European as well as American. Beginning in 1919, it put on a number of British and European plays, most of them new to America, but in 1923, with the production of Elmer Rice's *The Adding Machine*, it began to showcase American playwrights as well. O'Neill, Maxwell Anderson, Robert Sherwood, S. N. Behrman

Original members of the Theatre Guild in 1919. From the left: Lee Simonson, Theresa Helburn, Philip Moeller, Helen Westley, Maurice Wertheim and Lawrence Langner.

and many others were the beneficiaries of this policy—as were George Bernard Shaw, Pirandello, Ferenc Molnar and other European playwrights whose work might not otherwise have crossed the Atlantic.

The Guild was designed to be a democratic organization, with all its principal directors having a say in policy and play selection. That was never easy in a directorate that included several forceful and passionate personalities—Philip Moeller, the stage director; the designers Rollo Peters and Lee Simonson (Peters was also a fine actor); and the actors Helen Westley and Dudley Digges. Moreover, the Guild attracted people of great talent and its management problems only got worse with the addition of fiery and opinionated personalities like Harold Clurman, Cheryl Crawford and Lee Strasberg. Luckily, there were some steadying hands on the tiller—Lawrence Langner, the serious English patent attorney with an even more serious passion for theatre; Theresa Helburn, who soon became executive director of the Guild and saw it through its many crises right up to her death in 1958; and the millionaire businessman Maurice Wertheim, whose financial know-how was invaluable.

The Guild was never a very profitable organization—deficits were an all too common experience—but neither did it do things by halves. In 1925, it built and opened the Guild Theatre on Broadway. The next year it founded The Acting Company and established it with an alternating repertory system. During the 1926–27 season this company was responsible for six different plays running concurrently in three different theatres in New York (one of them was Dorothy and DuBose Heyward's play *Porgy*), and it threw in a visit to Chicago as well. The next year it spun off a traveling company that visited no fewer than 132 cities. But the strain was showing, and even if the Depression had not arrived in 1929, it was clear that The Acting Company would go no further. It was disbanded and the Guild got back to first principles. Langner had finally (after many fruitless efforts) persuaded his colleagues to accept the work of O'Neill, and the 1927–28 season saw the beginning of what was to prove a great collaboration for both O'Neill and the Guild.

However artistically creditable its productions were, the Guild nevertheless had to cover its expenses and hopefully make some money as well. The 1930–31 season was particularly disastrous—a total loss of $180,000—and the divisions that had always existed between board members now threatened the future of the organization. These divisions were more political than personal. The

Depression had taken hold of America, and the more radical members of the board felt passionately that the Guild should put on plays that had something to say about the social, economic and political realities of the time. It was for that reason that *Roar China* found its way into the 1930–31 season. S. M. Tretyakov's play was (in the words of the Theatre Guild's authorized history) "a clamorous, wildly propagandistic pageant . . . a big hit in post-revolutionary Russia, it wasn't as successful in wooing Americans either into the communist philosophy or the conviction that it was dramatically worthwhile. But it was a spectacular eyeful, with its no-curtain set and the terrifying copy of a Russian tank, not to mention a British warship, on stage."[8]

All the Guild's leading directors had wanted to direct it—Rouben Mamoulian, who certainly had a claim to it after the success of *Porgy*, left the Guild when he didn't get it and went off to begin his successful career in Hollywood; Philip Moeller, who also wanted it, had to be content with Maxwell Anderson's *Elizabeth, The Queen*, starring the Lunts (greatly to the benefit of the Guild because it was the season's one major success). The director who got it was Herbert Biberman. His principal claim to it was that he had just spent several months in the Soviet Union. Lawrence Langner, with uncharacteristic distaste, later wrote of him that he "seldom talked any quieter than in a loud shout."[9] *Roar China* was certainly a loud shout, as directed by Biberman—visually very exciting, with a huge cast—but the audience recognized it for what it was—pure propaganda. It was largely responsible for the enormous deficit the Guild faced in 1931, and it brought to a head the disagreements among board members.

With Biberman removed, the subsequent conversations took place between highly civilized people, and the eventual departure of Clurman, Strasberg and Crawford to form Group Theatre was achieved with minimal acrimony—indeed, with the promise (which was honored) of financial assistance from the Guild. Those three, whose principal objection to Guild policy was that it was so rigorously apolitical, went off with their special playwrights, Clifford Odets and Irwin Shaw, to write an original and important page in American theatre history.

As for the Guild, the six directors each pitched in $10,000 to get over the immediate difficulty, and it quickly got itself back on an equilibrium. There would be several other crises in its affairs over the next thirty years—none greater than the financial crunch at the beginning of World War II, though that was happily solved by the huge success of *Oklahoma!*—but, so long as Langner and Helburn were there to guide it, the Guild never failed to make a positive (and occasionally a spectacular) contribution to American theatre.

The lesson of 1930–31, however, was clear to Lawrence Langner: while he would always remain active in the Guild, he must also find a situation for himself in which he could be the arbiter, the sole decision-maker. No more committees! Typically, Langner did not wait to find such a situation—he simply created it, in an old barn in Westport.

Because so many of America's summer stock theatres were housed in converted barns or mills—even in deconsecrated churches—and because they tended to emphasize their bucolic roots, they became known in the theatre world as "straw hats."

The idea of summer stock was almost as old as the Republic. In simplest terms, it was a theatre company that kept "in stock" all the elements (human and material) that were needed to stage a play. In the 1820s and 1830s, such companies had materialized on the edges of a few major population centers in the East—Niblo's Garden in New York was an example—and by the end of the nineteenth century there were summer playhouses to be found in the environs of most substantial towns. Elitch's Gardens Theatre in Denver opened in 1890 and is still in occasional use today; the Lake Whalom Playhouse, near Fitchburg, Massachusetts, opened in 1893; and the Lakewood Theatre at Skowhegan, Maine, in 1895. All of these were built by traction companies in an effort to stimulate traffic on their trolley lines.

THE STRAW HAT CIRCUIT

The real expansion—together with a consequent blurring of definitions—came with the "little theatre" movement immediately before World War I, but many of these companies (such as the Chicago Little Theatre, the Detroit Arts and Crafts Theatre and the Provincetown Players, with which Eugene O'Neill began to make his name) quickly became much more than stock companies and had subscription schemes that were by no means limited to the summer. Little theatres, in turn, became almost indistinguishable from community theatres, and by 1925 the Drama League of America reported more than two thousand local theatre groups across the country. Impressive though this was, it was nowhere near as impressive as the traveling tent theatres, which proliferated in the 1920s—there were said to be more than four hundred of them, together generating more productions and greater attendance than all the legitimate theatres put together.[10]

For nearly all these institutions, whether they were permanent or temporary, seasonal or full-time, the Depression and the "talkies" were the great levelers. Theatre groups fell by the wayside, and more than a thousand of their buildings were turned into movie houses. By the early 1930s the number of "legitimate" theatres existing outside New York City had been reduced to less than five hundred.

If this was a catastrophe for live theatre in America, then it was also a unique opportunity for one branch of that theatre—summer stock. The Straw Hat circuit, with its manageable economics and "can do" outlook, came into its own.

At its peak in the late 1940s, there were 125 Equity theatres on the circuit, almost all of them in the East. An Equity theatre was defined as one in which at least six actors were members of the actors' union and were protected by union rules—meaning that they were paid $20 a week for rehearsal and a minimum of $50 a week for performance.[11] By the early 1960s, the Council of Stock Theatres (COST), which operated mainly in the East and Northeast, had a membership of fifty-two theatres.[12] By 1972, it was down to twenty, and fifteen years after that, in 1987, there were only three.[13]

There was no great secret about the causes of the carnage. The original raison d'être for summer theatres outside New York had been that Broadway theatres, lacking air conditioning, generally closed in June and stayed closed through Labor Day. That had long since ceased to be true. By the 1950s, Broadway theatres, fully air-conditioned, were performing year-round, and the same was true of most professional theatres in towns across the nation.

Summer stock had survived that change without too much difficulty because, air-conditioning or no, sensible people preferred to stay out of the cities in summer, and they therefore welcomed the presence of stock theatres that provided (at affordable prices) a respectably high level of entertainment close to home. Nevertheless, Westport Country Playhouse went to great pains to advertise itself as "Air Cooled" or "Ice Cooled." What that actually meant (and would continue to mean right up to 1958) was that it had an icehouse and a blower unit that attempted to blow ice-cooled air around the building. It didn't always work well. In 1948, an alert heating and refrigeration salesman in nearby Bridgeport wrote to Lawrence Langner: "Many people have mentioned to me the uncomfortable temperatures during your summer performances."[14] Four years later, a member of the Westport management team warned Langner that the theatre's weekly bill for ice had risen to $275.40.[15]

By that time, in any case, summer stock's world was being invaded by another, and much less tractable, villain. Television was responsible not just for keeping people at home on summer evenings, but also for the ever-increasing emphasis on stars. Westport had always attracted its share of stage and movie personalities, from Ethel Barrymore and Olivia de Havilland to Groucho Marx and Tyrone Power, but now the stars people most wanted to see in the flesh were their favorite television performers—actors like Hugh O'Brian (television's Wyatt Earp), who appeared at Westport in 1958 in William Inge's play *Picnic* and sold out the house for two consecutive weeks.

So long as television stars were willing and able to appear on the stage in summer, theatres were able to compete tolerably well with television. That changed, however, in the mid-1980s, when the television companies changed their system: hiatus was moved to the spring, and current stars were no longer available in the summer. Even a relatively successful theatre like Westport had to halve the number of its annual productions—from eleven or twelve to six.

> SUMMER THEATRES . . . and some are not,
> In little hamlets that God forgot;
> Converted barns in sleepy dells,
> Disturbed by histrionic yells.
> A cast of ten; an audience of twenty,
> Mostly "in the red" for plenty;
> Loads of fun for ambitious creatures,
> Ah me! I'll stick to double features.

Some poems should remain anonymous. Throughout much of the McKenzie era, this one was displayed in the business office reception area on the wall above the door to the press office.

Television might have contributed to cutting back the number of productions summer theatres could do, but it wasn't generally responsible for putting them out of business altogether. Where that happened (which was almost everywhere) inflation was the cause. Theatre costs, like costs everywhere, soared in the 1970s and there was no way box offices could keep up. Where star actors had happily done a one-week engagement in summer stock for $500 in 1940, they were regularly demanding as much as $5,000 plus a percentage of box office by 1970. The technical unions also made demands, and the theatres could not respond.

The Council for Stock Theatres was not so much an association of summer theatres as it was an annual contract with Actors' Equity, centrally negotiated, which enabled all stock theatres to engage actors on relatively generous terms. Armed with the COST contract and a substantial network of summer theatres with which they could share productions and expenses, these theatres were able to operate on small but viable margins. Inflation chipped away at those margins until by 1987, there were only three left in the East—Ogunquit, Dennis and Westport—and the whole system became moot.

The three that survived all had safety nets—efficient subscription schemes with high rates of renewal, or impregnable tourist businesses, or both—and they were able to continue on their way, sometimes working together on joint productions, sometimes working independently. Ogunquit has specialized in musicals—sometimes five or six separate productions in a single summer—while Westport, under Joanne Woodward's artistic leadership since 2000, has developed a policy that emphasizes playwrights, new plays, directors and diversity.

circa 1931 Westport

The town in which Lawrence Langner founded his Playhouse in 1931 would be barely recognizable to twenty-first century Westporters. Its main geographical features were the same, of course—acres of wooded land on which property owners could enjoy a rare degree of privacy; rich agricultural lands with huge and hungry markets close at hand; and a grand stretch of shoreline on Long Island Sound, with the estuary of the Saugatuck River forming a grand setting for the town itself.

In 1931, Westport was approaching its centenary as an incorporated township, and its unusual combination of characteristics was already firmly rooted—its fierce Yankee independence, the determinedly democratic basis of all its institutions of governance and authority, its undoubted affluence and the emphasis it placed on all things cultural and artistic. It was true that the rich and famous were attracted to Westport. So were artists and intellectuals. So were a good many European immigrants. So was anybody who needed to be within fifty miles of New York City yet still wanted to live in a community that was more rural than urban. But the vast majority of Westport's inhabitants were genuine Westporters—people who lived and worked in the place, whose families had sometimes been there longer than the Republic. These were the people who made Westport what it was—a mature, organized and confident community.

To some extent, the railway had made Westport a dormitory town for the big city, but it could not yet be described as a commuter town. Its population in 1931 was hardly more than six thousand (compared with today's twenty-five thousand) and it had grown by little more than five hundred in ten years. The Merritt Parkway was on the drawing board and would soon be a reality, but the main north–south road was still the old Post Road, which ambled past the Playhouse entrance. The modern turnpike was years into the future.

The palatable alternative to being a commuter town was being recognized as a good summer retreat. By the early 1920s the Compo Beach area on the Sound had been developed into a summer colony of cottage dwellers, and the town was having to come to terms with problems that included "rowdiness on the beach, the need for culverts, and street signs, the movement of the sand in the winter storms and the litter in the summer."[1] Few of these summer houses had central heating— they were strictly a June-to-September phenomenon—but the Langners were not alone in buying year-round residences in Fairfield County and spending considerable amounts of time there, even though this group probably spent more time in their city apartments. There was no getting away from the fact that Westport had become "fashionable" in the 1920s. Genuine Westporters didn't mind (in fact, most of them approved), provided it was not allowed to undermine the uniquely Yankee, and cussedly independent, nature of their town.

It was not hard to see where these characteristics had come from, for Westport had been the end-result of a whole series of independent-minded revolts that stretched back more than three centuries. Over the years the revolts had become less bloody, but they had lost nothing of their

Compo Beach in the 1930s.

intensity, for what motivated them was always the determination to safeguard freedoms—freedoms of thought, religion and government, and the right to free expression.

It had begun with a discontented group in the original Massachusetts Bay Colony. The dissidents, led by the Reverend Thomas Hooker, went south and fought the Swamp War against the Pequot Indians in 1637, opening up a huge area for colonization, including much of modern Connecticut. Within ten years a group of settlers in Fairfield had broken away in search of richer lands and greater independence. They found both these things on the banks of Long Island Sound on a strip of land (now known as Green's Farms) that was home to the Indians of Machamux, with whom they made a deal. The Bankside Farmers, as they were called, prospered. Although they owed nominal allegiance to the township of Fairfield, they developed their own independent ecclesiastical society, with both religious and civil components. They used the Green's Farms Congregational Church, founded in 1711, as their

Pine Knoll, often known as the Kemper House, was Charles Kemper's home, close by the old barn. The house was demolished in 1981 to make room for the Playhouse Condominiums.

headquarters and meeting house. They elected selectmen, they taxed their members, they ran the schools, and they administered a peculiarly harsh legal system of their own devising.[2]

The townships of Fairfield and Norwalk had been incorporated in 1639 and 1651 respectively, but the area that was formally known as West Parish (and informally as Westport) remained unincorporated, subject to its own government—democratic, but decidedly ecclesiastical. This lack of formal status was increasingly seen as an anomaly, the more so because the place the settlement occupied, at the mouth of the Saugatuck River, was becoming important as a port area and as a communications crossroads. The old King's Highway, the main postal route between New York and Boston, had passed through it since 1673, and in 1807 the newly laid-out Post Road would bring a great deal more traffic. The British had paid it some unwelcome attention in the Revolutionary War. There had been a brisk engagement on Compo Hill in 1777 at the end of a three-day raid by General Tryon that had taken British troops as far inland as Danbury (they lost three hundred men on Compo Hill but managed to get back to their ships). Much worse for the people of the West Parish had been a 1779 raid in which much of Green's Farms was torched, including the meeting house, fifteen homes and eleven barns.

Eventually, in 1832, the Green's Farms Church decided it needed a meeting house closer to the center of the growing town, so Saugatuck Church was built. Three years later a group of businessmen led by Daniel Nash petitioned the state government for the incorporation of the town of Westport, including parts of Fairfield, Norwalk, Old Saugatuck and Weston—a total population of 1,800. The charter was granted, and in June, in the midst of a heat wave, a town meeting was held in Saugatuck Church to elect its officials—three selectmen, a town clerk, a treasurer, five constables, grand jurors, tithing men, hay wardens (in charge of fences and hedges), pound keepers (stray cattle) and fence viewers (to determine boundaries between properties).3 The carefully structured democracy of the Bankside Farmers was thus transferred more or less intact—but shorn of its ecclesiastical trappings—to the town of Westport.

Westport's history has been generously peppered with fine civic leaders—Roger Ludlow and John Green in the seventeenth century, Hezekiah Ripley, minister of the Congregational Church for more than fifty years, in the eighteenth century, Daniel Nash and Horace Staples in the nineteenth century and Edward T. Bedford and a succession of remarkable ladies who ran the Woman's Town Improvement Association in the early twentieth century. Horace Staples, who made separate fortunes in hardware sales, sea transportation and banking, and who was responsible for bringing the railway to Westport, was so ashamed of the town's educational institutions that he spent much of his personal fortune on building the high school and raising educational awareness—so successfully that Westport eventually developed one of the finest public education systems in the country.

    Early in the twentieth century the town's population changed quite radically as immigrants poured into the country. By 1910 one-third of Connecticut's population was foreign-born.4 Westport's percentage was somewhat lower and made up mostly of Irish and Italian, but it was sufficient to prompt the town to spend $2,750 in 1901 to buy a house on Main Street that could be used as a poorhouse. A surprisingly large element of the town's population made it known that some people—African Americans and Jews, in particular—were unwelcome: the Ku Klux Klan made its presence felt several times in 1923, and again in 1932 when four hundred people (one hundred of them in KKK robes) attended a meeting at the Little White Church on the Hill in Saugatuck.5 If they thought they could frighten away the Jews they were very much mistaken: by 1932 many of them, like Lawrence Langner, were firmly entrenched as part of the fast-growing artistic and cultural community.

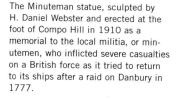

The Minuteman statue, sculpted by H. Daniel Webster and erected at the foot of Compo Hill in 1910 as a memorial to the local militia, or minutemen, who inflicted severe casualties on a British force as it tried to return to its ships after a raid on Danbury in 1777.

Westport neither looked nor felt like an industrial town. Agriculture had always been the dominant industry in the region, though the town had acquired another significant industry during the Civil War—Robert Gault's company that supplied coal, gravel and other construction materials. There were many smaller manufacturing businesses in the town—buttons and mattresses, paper and starch, embalming liquid and tanning—but nothing to compare with agriculture as an economic generator, nor even with the increasingly profitable sector of summer visitors. It meant that Westport could face the Depression without the same sense of desperation that enveloped towns more dependent on manufacturing (in much the same way that it was already enduring Prohibition with a nudge and a wink—and an awful lot of speakeasies).

In fact, in 1931, when Lawrence Langner was planning the launch of his new theatre, the town was buzzing with activity. But it wasn't the activity of manufacturing or industry. Instead, most of it was generated by the cultural and artistic community, which had grown exponentially throughout the 1920s.

There was no one reason why Westport had become a mecca for the artistic community, but there were clearly a number of contributing factors—its proximity to New York, its liberal and democratic bent, its unusual combination of semirural and seaside atmospheres, its outstanding public facilities and cultural institutions (including one of the finest public libraries in America) and its undemonstrative affluence.

To the extent that any one person could be said to be the founder of the Westport art colony it was probably George Hand Wright, who arrived in the town in 1907, but he was just one on a long list of recognizable names—people like Karl Anderson, Lowell Balcom, Hilla Rebay, James Earl Fraser, Robert Lambdin, J. Clinton Shepherd, Charles Hardy and Rose O'Neill, who was certainly the richest of them all. Even before she invented the Kewpie doll in 1909, O'Neill was well known as a prolific writer, poet, painter, illustrator and sculptor. In Westport, where she came to live in the 1920s, she was one of the most flamboyant and visible members of the artistic community. Among her fellow writers were Hugh Lofting, the creator of Dr. Doolittle; Sinclair Lewis, whose 1930 Nobel prize was celebrated with a party at the town hall; and F. Scott Fitzgerald and his wife, Zelda, whose residence in Westport during 1920 was as brief as it was memorable.

Every bit as impressive as this gathering of talent were the public institutions that Westport had accumulated by 1931. The very grand public library, named for its donor, Morris K. Jesup, whose family had lived on the Green's Farms bluff since before 1700, bore on its portal the legend "Open To All." Edith Very Sherwood, the librarian, made sure that it was especially welcoming to the artistic and intellectual community. There was also a very active historical society; the Toquet Opera House (in which opera was a rarity, but it was a good space for theatrical productions); the Fine Arts Theatre (the first Connecticut theatre to show foreign movies); the Westport Dramatics Club; and National Hall, which had been another of Horace Staples's gifts to the town.

To this collection of institutions Lawrence Langner proposed to add a summer theatre. The proud Yankee town seemed like a good prospect for such a venture. Though it was comparatively small—only six thousand residents in 1931—it was believed to have as many as three thousand

Sharon Giese was General Manager of the Playhouse, 1974–79:
I joined the Playhouse staff as the bookkeeper in 1972. A native of Chicago, I waved goodbye to my parents and drove to Westport in my used Chevy Nova. Somewhere along the road, one of the tires received a cut in it, not fatal to the drive, but it sure looked like it needed to be fixed before I drove much further. My mother had worked at J. C. Penney's for years, and I had been used to buying many things from Penney's, including tires. I looked in the Westport phone book to find the location of the local Penney's. It was on Green's Farms Road. I asked a member of the Playhouse staff where it was. She wanted to know why I wanted to go there. "To buy a tire at Penney's." "But we don't have a J. C. Penney in Westport," she said. "O, but you do," and I showed her the entry in the phone book. A puzzled silence—then "Yes, I see, but that's not a store, Sharon, that's Mr. J. C. Penney's home!"

additional summer residents, and it could draw on the much greater population of Fairfield County and the surrounding towns. The railway had made evening excursions from New York City a viable proposition, and the Merritt Parkway would soon make the road journey a reasonable alternative.

These things were important, but even more encouraging to Langner was the "feel" of the place. In the words of one of the town's historians, Woody Klein, "[The end of the 1920s] was a time when Westport underwent a cultural renaissance, a time when the town first appeared on the national scene as a beehive of achievement and creativity. It was the new—and eye-catching—Westport, as jazzy and as party-prone as any other developing suburb. Along with the cultural elite came the flappers, the Age of Dixieland, and, of course, the speakeasies that openly defied prohibition while town officials turned a blind eye."[6] To Lawrence Langner it seemed like fertile territory.

CHAPTER THREE

The Barn Becomes a Theatre

It was in the winter of 1930–31 that Rollo Peters and Lawrence Langner found the barn.[1] They knew at once that it was what they were looking for, and within days Langner was negotiating to buy it.

Peters and Langner were both deeply involved with the Theatre Guild in New York—and, at that precise moment, about as disillusioned with it as they would ever be. Their colleagues had very different ideas about the sort of plays they wanted the Guild to present, and Langner in particular wanted a place where (as he later put it) "I did not have to be subservient to the wishes of five other collaborators."[2] Finding such a place was difficult, perhaps impossible; creating it from scratch was a better solution. Hence, the barn. It was conveniently close to "Langnerlane," the farm he had purchased in Cannondale the previous year, and he already knew enough about Fairfield County and that part of Connecticut to know there was a ready-made audience of avid theatregoers.

But the barn was not a pretty sight that winter—nor had it ever been, really. It had been built in 1835 by R & H Haight as a tannery that would provide the hat-making industry (which at that time had important centers in South Norwalk, Danbury and, to a lesser extent, Westport itself) with what were called "hatters' leathers." It turned out to be a good business, and within a short time the Haights brought Charles Kemper over from Hudson, N.Y., to manage the tannery. In 1866 Kemper purchased the business from Henry Haight's widow, and it became C.H. Kemper Co.

It wasn't long before Kemper needed to expand. He moved most of the tanning business to three buildings on Riverside Avenue, and in the barn he set up a steam-powered cider mill.[3] But enough of the tannery remained in and around the barn for the smell to be pervasive. When Langner's wife, Armina Marshall, first visited it in the early spring of 1931, she recalled that "you could smell it before you saw it. But it was large and brown and, architecturally, had fine proportions."[4]

Lawrence Langner had seen its possibilities at once. It was certainly rural, sitting in the middle of an apple orchard. (Langner, however, wasn't sure what to think about apple orchards: his new property in Cannondale had boasted more than a thousand apple trees, and he had quickly found out that they, in turn, boasted more than a thousand potential diseases. By his own admission, he had "abandoned the trees to the savagery of nature.")[5] The barn had another essential quality: it sat right beside the Post Road, which, at that time, was the only north–south highway along the coast. Moreover, as Armina dryly reported, Langner was "an enthusiast for barns, . . . probably because he kept seeing them as small potential theatres."[6]

The barn in 1930, about the time Lawrence Langner first set eyes on it.

This one became a theatre in an astonishingly short time. A myth grew up—first perpetrated, it would seem, by the composer Deems Taylor, writing in the theatre's playbill on July 3, 1931—that the entire transformation was accomplished in four weeks, but that would have been impossible since the basis of it was a substantial addition to the existing barn in order to create the stage area. Much later, Armina Marshall said it had, in fact, been four months between the early spring day when Lawrence had first taken her to see the barn and the day—June 29, 1931—on which the theatre was formally dedicated by Daniel Frohman, the dean of American theatrical managers (he was the younger brother of Charles Frohman, who had done so much to revolutionize American theatre before he drowned when the *Lusitania* was torpedoed and sunk in 1915).[7] The accompaniment to Frohman's graceful speech was a crackling thunderstorm that ricocheted around the building.[8]

The Langners had taken out a mortgage of $4,000 in order to buy the property.[9] An additional $28,000 had been spent on the transformation, and that included the cost of laying water and sewage lines, clearing the surrounding shrubs to create a car park, and putting in electric wiring for the whole complex.

Langner had asked Cleon Throckmorton to design the new theatre, inside and out, and to oversee the work. "Throck," as he was known in the theatre, was a painter and scenic designer based in New York. Langner knew him best for his work as a designer with the Provincetown Players, including the early works of Eugene O'Neill, and more recently for his great success with *Porgy*, which he had designed for the Theatre

The Kemper Leather Works at Riverside Avenue.

The warranty deed, dated June 6, 1931, shows that the Langners took formal possession of the property just three weeks before opening night.

The interior of the Playhouse in 1933,
designed by Cleon Throckmorton to
resemble the puppet theatre Lawrence
Langner had owned as a boy.

Guild in 1927. But he had also seen what Throck had done to turn the old meeting house in Dennis, Massachusetts, into the Cape Playhouse, a splendid summer theatre that had opened its doors in 1927.

The model Langner gave Throck for the Westport Country Playhouse, however, was not Dennis, though it was very similar. He described to him "the toy theatre of my youth, and especially the 'tuppence colored' theatre with its gay proscenium of bright red and gold, its bright red curtain and the red-and-gold curtained side boxes," and he asked the designer to recreate it in the barn.[10] Rather than individual seats, the orchestra stalls were to be constructed as long pews, covered in red velvet, on either side of a center aisle. There would be seating for 375 downstairs, another 75 in the balcony, plus eight boxes—a total capacity of 499.

Moreover, making no secret of his ambition to transfer Westport productions to Broadway, Langner insisted that the stage have exactly the same dimensions as New York's Forty-Eighth Street Theatre. Backstage facilities were adequate, but no more than that—a fairly spacious, homely green room right beneath the stage, with cramped, decidedly "unstarry" dressing rooms leading off it. In time, the green room walls would be festooned with posters for individual plays, so that the atmosphere of the place was inevitably magnified by the ghosts of actors past (not to mention successive families of raccoons, who lived beneath the green room and found the facilities much to their liking).

An article in *Theatre Management* in September

Cover of the *New Yorker*, July 1935.

1931 waxed eloquent on the new theatre's superior design and
facilities. Although the piece was unsigned, the casual reader
could, without difficulty, deduce its principal source from the
postscript: "Mr. Throckmorton will be pleased to furnish further
information to theatre owners contemplating a similar construction. There is, of course, no obligation." Nor, as it turned out,
was there much of a market for such constructions.

The article began by explaining that "the short time allocated for the transformation made it necessary to employ seventy
men in the construction." The largest part of this was a substantial addition to the existing barn "to house the stage and equipment, including thirty sets and lines, . . . walled with asbestos
and fronted with an asbestos curtain." The article was particularly admiring of the lighting arrangements: "Four electrified
antiqued kerosene lamps are suspended from the ceiling [of the
auditorium], while rustic wall fixtures provide sufficient light at
the sides. Six spotlights are placed in the balcony and the stage
lighting equipment is complete in every detail. Two switch-
boards control the lighting arrangements. The balcony has been
built to accommodate a modern projection room, which may
be installed next year" (it wasn't).

Much effort was expended on making the decor authentic.
"An ordinary shotgun served to imbed wormholes in the lumber.
An antiquated ship-lantern adds a novel touch to the lobby." But
the designer was aggrieved that some of his vaunted facilities
were not given their due: "Although spacious restrooms have
been built beneath the lobby, the patrons, it has been found,
prefer to amble in the orchards during intermissions."

Some of Langner's own innovations added to the general
gaiety. At the end of intermissions, patrons were recalled from
the orchard by a giant cow bell, and during smaller pauses in
the action, when scene changes had to be effected backstage,
local actors entertained the audience with old songs (billed as
"elegant divertisement"). Better still, it was announced that one
of the mid-season plays, *The Bride the Sun Shines On*, would
include in its cast a number of "socially prominent" aspiring
thespians from the Westport area.[11] There was no shortage of
volunteers, for the social arbiters of Fairfield County—of whom
"Miss Annie" Burr Jennings and the dowager Mrs. Warner were
the most important—had conferred their seal of approval on the
new theatre by taking out subscriptions for Monday nights and
ensuring that their Rolls Royces delivered them to the theatre at
8:25 p.m. precisely. The curtain never went up until they were
seated.

And so the dirty, smelly old barn became a theatre. Langner
had first incorporated it in May as "Woodland Theatre, Inc.,"

but he quickly had second thoughts: on the very day of the theatre's opening, new papers were filed to rename it "Country Playhouse, Inc."

By that time flyers had already been issued bidding the people of Westport "Come One! Come All!" to see the "Sensational Hit! Stupendous Success! *The Streets of New York*, WITH A CAST OF REAL ACTORS." Seats were advertised at $1.00, $1.50 and $2.00.

The discovery of that first play (a Victorian melodrama set amid the depression and crash of 1837—a perfect choice for a 1931 audience, as it turned out) was credited to Rollo Peters, who also designed the nine scenes and took one of the leading roles. But the initial decision—to put together a repertory company for the whole season, headed by Dorothy Gish—was Langner's, and his alone. "From now on," he later wrote, "I no longer became frustrated and emotional when my ideas were turned down at the Guild. I simply took them to Westport and tried them out in our own theatre."[12]

Happy and confident though he was, it is evident from that first playbill that Langner entertained a few suspicions about his new audience. Halfway down the bill, he inserted an IMPORTANT NOTICE:

> *Men and women in the audience are requested not to crack peanuts during the performance; gentlemen and ladies will not do so. Offerings of garden produce to the actors should be made at the stage door, rather than over the footlights. While joining in the choruses, and hissing the villains, is permissible, the audience is politely requested not to stamp its feet in unison to the music for fear of bringing the house down in more senses than one.*

Cleon Throckmorton

His most tangible memorials are the Cape Playhouse in Dennis, Massachusetts, and the Westport Country Playhouse—both summer theatres he created out of existing buildings (a meeting house and a tanning barn, respectively). But in his day he was best known as a New York–based scenic and lighting designer for more than 150 plays.

CLEON THROCKMORTON
1897–1965

Although he was born in New Jersey, he spent much of his boyhood in the south. He studied to be an engineer, but he quickly got infected with the theatre bug when he met George Cram Cook of the Provincetown Players. He decided to be an actor—indeed, he was cast in a small role for the premiere of O'Neill's *The Emperor Jones*—but the Provincetown Players quickly realized that he could be of much greater use to them as a designer. So his acting career was aborted before it began and he became the celebrated creator of sets and lighting for the plays that transformed O'Neill from a local, largely unheard of, writer into the most important American playwright there had ever been. For that production of *The Emperor Jones* in 1920, he fashioned a strongly expressionist atmosphere, most memorably portrayed in a series of tableaux based on starkly backlit silhouettes, with the action being played out to the unceasing beat of a single drum.

Having established his own studio in New York, Throckmorton went on to work for all the principal producing organizations in the commercial theatre—the Theatre Guild for *Porgy* (1927), Arthur Hopkins for *Burlesque* (1927), Katherine Cornell for *Alien Corn* (1933), the Federal Theatre Project for Auden's *The Dance of Death* (1936), and many others. During these years, it was said that his name appeared on Broadway playbills with a frequency exceeded only by that of the fire commissioner.

His studio at 102 West Third Street billed itself as "Cleon Throckmorton, Inc.—Stage Settings, Design, Construction, Painting, Rigging, Lighting Hardware, Costumes, Make-Up, Properties," but he always wanted to be more than just a designer. He became an occasional producer on Broadway, he wrote several plays (though none that had any great success), and for many years he was co-owner of two theatres in Hoboken, New Jersey—the Old Rialto and the Lyric—which he largely dedicated to the revival of melodramas. He sustained his position as one of New York's premier designers into the early 1940s, but then his career began to slow, and eventually to stall. In 1948 he had to find $13,000 to avoid foreclosure. Bill Fitelson of the Theatre Guild, to which Throckmorton had appealed for help, advised his directors that there was "no good will in the business, only ill will." As a result, the Theatre Guild declined to help, and Throckmorton's theatre career was effectively ended.[13]

But another side of Throckmorton's inventive nature could not be so easily stifled. He had always enjoyed entertaining—Noël Coward was one of many friends who remembered with glee his imitation of Queen Victoria—so it was no great departure for him to become one of the pioneers in the arts of planning and designing balls, cruises, long weekend parties and community events. He executed murals for restaurants and nightclubs, he designed private homes, and he entered into the television age by designing sequences to enable news broadcasts to illustrate battles, disasters and other events that could not be filmed. He died in 1965 in Atlantic City, close to the place where he had been born sixty-eight years before.

CHAPTER FOUR

1931–32 In Repertory

Partly because of his roots in Britain, where repertory companies had flourished since time imme-
morial, and partly because he was so sick and tired of the system imposed on Broadway, first by The
Syndicate, now by the Shuberts and other commercial producers—a system that was dependent,
in almost equal parts, on undemanding drama, expensive production and the ubiquity of stars—
Lawrence Langner was determined to have a resident repertory company at Westport. And more
than that, he was determined then to take the same company, with the same plays, to Broadway.

In the theatre world, the word "repertory" is most often used in the same sense as "repertoire"—a list of the works being performed (or to be performed) by a company or an individual. But
to be playing "in repertory" means something more than that: it indicates that a number of plays—
maybe as many as five or six—are all being performed, by the same company of actors, in the same
theatre, on alternating nights. The alternation does not need to be a strict one—typically, three
plays may be offered in a single week, but sometimes as many as five. Opera companies like New
York's Metropolitan Opera work in much the same way, except that they are likely to have different
casts of singers (certainly principal singers) for each individual opera, whereas a repertory theatre
company will cast every play from the same small group of actors supported by the same small
group of backstage staff. Repertory theatre calls for most uncommon gifts of imagination, artistry
and technical competence.

THE FIRST SEASON

The task to which Lawrence Langner committed his little company at Westport in the early summer of 1931 was immensely ambitious—an eleven-week season at Westport between late June and
early September, a three-week hiatus, then a long fall and winter season in New York.

The first part of it worked well enough. Eighty performances were seen by very nearly thirty
thousand people at Westport, many of whom responded to an invitation mailed in early June "to
join the membership of the New York Repertory Company." For $10—the most expensive subscrip-
tion—they could have a seat in the first eighteen rows of the orchestra for each of six performances
("add $2.50 . . . if seats are desired in the Orchestra on Saturday nights"). The initial solicitation,
signed by Lawrence Langner, promised "a series of new plays . . . prior to their opening in New
York." It listed the names of all the actors who would be part of the repertory company, but it
notably failed to indicate what plays would be presented—nor even what sort of plays they would
be. The people of Fairfield County were asked to subscribe on trust—and they did.

The company of fourteen principal actors was led by Dorothy Gish, Rollo Peters, Armina
Marshall, Romney Brent, Winifred Lenihan and Moffat Johnston—all of them bankable names—
and included a number of others known in the profession as fine actors—people like Jessie Busley,

Dorothy Gish as Celia, and Armina
Marshall as Rosalind, in Lawrence
Langner's production of *As You Like It*,
1931.

Fania Marinoff and Frank Conlan. They would be responsible for ten of the eleven weeks, performing six plays in repertory on an erratic schedule that would be improvised as the season progressed. The missing week (which was actually the third week of August) would feature a guest company that would present Peggy Wood in Martinez Sierra's play *The Cradle Song*.

Aside from Boucicault, the playwrights were an eclectic lot—Shakespeare, Ibsen, Will Cotton, Susan Glaspell and the French comedy team of Robert de Flers and G. A. de Caillavet.

With the exception of the last-named pair, they all had considerable successes (the French comedy was, in any case, cut short after only nine performances: "Fortunately," wrote the acerbic Humphrey Doulens in Norwalk's *Evening Sentinel*, "Mr. A. P. Kaye, the chief actor, was called to England [by an illness in his family]").

Looking back on the Westport season in mid-September, the *New York Sun* noted that it had been "experimental in its nature. . . . The experiment has not, according to Mr. Langner's own testimony, been an easy one, because it was thought at first that there would not be audiences enough for any play for more than one week, as is usual with stock companies. However, each play built up its own special following, and for some of these a period of one week was found insufficient."[1]

This was especially true of *The Streets of New York*, which eventually played twenty-four times, with many people coming back more than once. Realizing that this was the case, Langner and the stage director, Knowles Entrikin, encouraged the company's music director, Dr. Sigmund Spaeth, to vary the musical content from night to night. Only one number remained constant, and that was his setting of "Whoa Emma," in which the audience joyfully joined with Sam Wren at each performance. Spaeth was not only a very competent musician and composer, he was also a well-known lecturer, humorist and authority on folk music who was currently at the height of his fame in Westport as a local personality in the new medium of radio. It was the production of *As You Like It*—the season's succès d'estime—that brought out the best in him. For it he was given what was (and, for the Playhouse, would remain) a very substantial orchestra—two violins, cello, flute, trumpet and harpsichord. He wrote an overture and a good deal of incidental music, much of it based on the sixteenth-century "Green Sleeves" theme (according to the playbill, it represented "the joyous spirit of Touchstone all through the play").[2] In addition, Spaeth provided his own choral arrangements of "It Was a Lover and His Lass" and the madrigal "Now Is the Month of Maying." He even succeeded in persuading the management to give him a chorus of eleven to sing them.

In truth, it may not have been difficult to get extra resources for *As You Like It*, for the stage director was Lawrence Langner himself. Langner had many passions, but none was greater or longer sustained than his passion for the plays of Shakespeare, and now, directing in his own

---

DION BOUCICAULT'S RENOWNED COMEDY DRAMA
IN FIVE ACTS AND ELEVEN SCENES

"The Streets of New York"

The Management has been at great PAINS to produce the drama precisely as originally performed with SENSATIONAL EFFECT in December of 1857 at Mr. Wallack's Theatre in the Broadway. For this GRAND REVIVAL they have procured ELEGANT and LAVISH SCENIC DECORATIONS from the hand of MR. ROLLO PETERS. The action of the drama has been devised by Mr. Knowles ENTRIKIN and is executed by THE FULL STRENGTH OF THE COMPANY

DRAMATIS PERSONNAE

GIDEON BLOODGOOD (The Villain)	MOFFAT JOHNSTON
CAPTAIN FAIRWEATHER	DUDLEY HAWLEY
BADGER	ROMNEY BRENT
MARK LIVINGSTONE (The Hero)	ROLLO PETERS
PAUL FAIRWEATHER	SAM WREN
PUFFY	FRANK CONLAN
DAN PUFFY	MERVIN WILLIAMS
DANIELS	RUSSELL RHODES
THE DUKE OF CALCAVELLA	ANTON BUNDSMANN
EDWARDS	ROBERT TURNEY
MRS. FAIRWEATHER	WINIFRED JOHNSTON
MRS. PUFFY	JESSIE BUSLEY
ALIDA BLOODGOOD	FANIA MARINOFF
LUCY FAIRWEATHER (The Heroine)	DOROTHY GISH

Gentlemen and Ladies, Laborers and Unemployed Persons by the Messrs. Russell Rhodes, Ronald Jones, Philip S. Graham, Jock Munro, Louis Masin, Jr., William Paine, Brooks Peters, and the Misses Barbara Child, Ann Tewksbury, Nancy McKnight and Cecilia Lenihan.

Act I. The Panic of 1837. The Office of Bloodgood, the Banker. "His hand does not tremble—not a muscle moves. What a magnificent robber!"

Act II. Scene 1. The Panic of 1857. The Park, near Fourteenth Street. "Beware, Mr. Livingstone, how you seek to renew our acquaintance."

Scene 2. Bloodgood's office. "If this panic do but last, I shall double my fortune."

Scene 3. A room in Puffy's house. "Heaven help us! I fear the worst is not come."

Act III. A room in Bloodgood's house. "Keep your gold! It would soil my poverty."

Act IV. Scene 1. Union Square. "It is my wedding ring."

Scene 2. The vestibule of The Academy of Music. "I wonder they permit such vagabonds to hang about the opera."

Scene 3. The attics at No. 19½ Cross street, Five Points. "A bullet is a good argument."

Act V. Scene 1. Brooklyn Heights. Three months later. "Look in his face and confess the infernal scheme by which Alida Bloodgood compelled you to renounce your love."

Scene 2. The exterior of No. 19½ street, Five Points. "Now Badger—do your worst! I am safe."

Scene 3. Bloodgood's house. "More than one mask must fall." VIRTUE TRIUMPHANT!

Musical Program Selected and Arranged by Dr. Sigmund Spaeth.
Orchestra under the Direction of Ruth Jenner.
Harry Shufelt—Cornetist. Mabel Benson—Violinist.
Costumes by Eaves Costume Co.

The New York Repertory Company, Inc.

All Productions Staged under the Personal Supervision of Lawrence Langner

Director	LAWRENCE LANGNER
Scenic Director	ROLLO PETERS
Producing Staff	MOFFAT JOHNSTON / WINIFRED LENIHAN
Business Manager	THOMAS C. SHIEL
Publicity and Promotion Manager	ANN GROSVENOR AYRES
Subscription Secretary	AGNES GRANT
Treasurer	KATHRYN WALSH
Stage Manager	ANTON BUNDSMANN
Assistant Stage Managers	MERVIN WILLIAMS / RONALD JONES
Casting	HOPE NEWCOMBE
Wardrobe Mistress	DOROTHY LACEY

The Streets of New York (1931), with (*from left to right*): Sam Wren, Rollo Peters, Dorothy Gish, Romney Brent, Fania Marinoff, Moffat Johnston and Will Cotton (who was the author of another successful play in the 1931 season, *The Bride the Sun Shines On*).

As You Like It (1931), in a production conceived and directed by Lawrence Langner.

The one element that never seems to have given Lawrence Langner any problem in the early years of the Playhouse was the audience. It was there, and it would be loyal.

One of the reasons it was there was because, from the very beginning, the ladies who saw themselves as the leaders of Fairfield County Society (the capital letters were pronounced) gave the Playhouse their enthusiastic support. They not only took out subscriptions themselves, but they made sure their friends and acquaintances did as well. Monday nights were when new plays opened, so it was for Monday nights that most of them had their tickets.

THE GREAT DAMES OF FAIRFIELD COUNTY

The man who most faithfully, and affectionately, chronicled the lives of these great people was Humphrey Doulens, who wrote about them in the *Norwalk Hour*. He was also the paper's drama critic, so he, too, would be in his seat at the Playhouse on Monday nights.

Doulens was a good friend of the Langners (he claimed to have been consulted by them on the location of the theatre), and he certainly played an important role in getting the word out about the new Playhouse in the mad rush of the spring of 1931, when the barn was being transformed and a company put together. Later, in 1937, Doulens joined Columbia Artists Management, where he represented many stars, including Grace Moore, André Kostelanetz, Marlene Dietrich and Lillian and Dorothy Gish.

In 1956, on the twenty-fifth anniversary of the theatre's opening, Doulens recalled the audience of those first few seasons. No one was more important, he said, than "Miss Annie" Burr Jennings, then the leader of Fairfield County Society—and the greatest heiress besides. Doulens genuflected before her "with no disrespect, rather in much admiration."

It is generally agreed [he went on] that "Miss Annie" was far too patrician a dowager to have ever admitted that she had her own "public," but I, for one, always felt that "Miss Annie" liked her role as First Lady of Fairfield County just a little bit and that if she did not play up to them, neither did she ever let her public down.

And certainly, the management would not have dreamed of parting the red and gold curtains until "Miss Annie" was safely in her downfront loge.

Not that she was ever late. All her life a devoted theatre-goer, Miss Jennings did not reserve just a pair of seats on Monday nights at Westport, she took a whole row.

Thus there was always ample room for her "court" which invariably included one or two of the "Glover Girls" and "Aunt Birdie" Mills. They would first have been invited to dine at "Sunnieholme," her residence in Fairfield, where the courses were served like clockwork.

Miss Jennings' Rolls Royce—and you could count a dozen of them on Monday nights—would deposit her at the North entrance at precisely 8:25 and she would move up the aisle like a czarina, usually in her favorite pale blue brocade, a choker of diamonds flashing on her neck. Often the points of these diamonds would come in handy when the proceedings upon the stage ran down and "Miss Annie" began to nod. . . .

But Miss Jennings was not the only attraction in the audience. Mrs. I. deVer Warner held her own, too, inevitably in black velvet and handsome furs, slipping in a side door with her son Ira and his beautiful bride Hazel.

The other ranking woman in society, Mrs. Nathaniel Bishop, Sr., was in frail health and could only attend infrequently at matinees. But her kin, the senior Mrs. Henry Bishop, sometimes came, though never on Mondays, with her sister, the imposing Mrs. Virgil Gibney, who still lived in high style in Seaside Park.

The late Mrs. Henry Budington Stoddard was another Monday Nighter, always arousing the awe that was due a Stoddard, and Mrs. Henry H. Rennell was another regular, occupying the same downfront loge for many seasons until her lamented passing.

Mrs. Alfred Levy, one of the handsomest Bridgeport ladies in our time, was another ornament, along with Mrs. Elmer Beardsley and Mrs. James Mizer, who knew the theatre and loved it.

The indomitable Miss Annie Ferguson Segee, great-granddaughter of the remarkable Hessian soldier who deserted to the Yankee troops in Bridgeport in the Revolutionary War and later built the Segee Opera House, was also too frail to make Monday nights, but she often attended the matinees. . . .

Alas [Humphrey Doulens concluded his 1956 column], the next level of Bridgeport elite shunned the stage and its people, devoting itself to bowling and yachting and, at this particular epoch, skiing. Only Mrs. Bradford Warner, beautiful now and beautiful then, made an effort to support the lively new theatre, with an occasional, if furtive, assist from Mrs. Ira Warner, Mrs. "Edie" Talbot, and Mrs. Becky Grabeau.[3]

"Miss Annie" Burr Jennings.

Lawrence Langner's sole partner in the Playhouse venture was his wife, Armina. But to the extent that he had a close and trusted colleague with whom he planned, plotted and executed the venture, it was Rollo Peters.

ROLLO PETERS
1892–1967

Look, Edwin! Do you see that boy
Talking to the other boy?
No, over there by those two men—
Wait, don't look now—now look again.
No, not the one in navy-blue;
That's the one he's talking to.
Sure you see him? Stripèd pants?
Well, *he was born in Paris, France.*

The man who wore stripèd pants and (more importantly) *was born in Paris, France,* was Charles Rollo Peters III. The verse was written by his longtime friend and sometime colleague, Edna St. Vincent Millay.[4] In the years during and immediately after World War I they had been two of Greenwich Village's most talented residents, both in their late twenties. He was a promising painter, apparently following in the footsteps of his famous father, while she was a published poet, already well on her way to the Pulitzer prize for poetry she would win in 1923. But what brought them together was not their chosen professions as much as their shared obsession with theatre—specifically, the birth pangs of the Theatre Guild, for they had both, quite willingly, become enmeshed in Lawrence Langner's web. In 1919 they appeared together in the Guild's very first production, *Bonds of Interest,* and it was also the year when Peters asked Edna to marry him—she gently, but firmly, repulsed him.[5] Ten years later, when "Look, Edwin!" was published, what she apparently remembered best about her old friend—and envied most—was that he had been *born in Paris, France.*

Rollo Peters's life started in the shadow of his father, who was in the process of becoming one of California's most admired painters. It was true that young Rollo was born while his father was studying in Paris, but he was brought up in Monterey, California, and it was there that he began to discover his own talents as an artist. By the time he was seventeen he was back in Europe, studying successively in London, Munich and Paris, before his life was interrupted, as it was for all people of that generation, by the First World War. In 1914 he returned to the United States and opened a studio in New York City.

His studies had equipped him to be a portrait painter, but in Europe he had discovered another interest—scenic design—and that was the one he chose to pursue in New York. In 1917 he even managed to combine the gentlemanly requirements of officer's training school in Virginia with the much more demanding pressures of New York theatre life.

His talents, his energy and his cosmopolitan personality gave him entrée to the artistic and intellectual circles of Greenwich Village, and it was there that he met Edna St. Vincent Millay, the actress Helen Westley, the designer Lee Simonson, the director Philip Moeller—as well as the inevitable Lawrence Langner. In 1917–18 he worked with both the Provincetown Players and the Washington Square Players as a designer. As was normal with such companies, he was quickly co-opted as a walk-on actor as well. Though untrained, he had considerable acting talents, and it was not long before he was being cast in featured roles.

By the time the Washington Square Players had been disbanded and the Theatre Guild was being formed out of its ashes in late 1918, Peters was already recognized as a leader. Almost automatically, he became one of the Guild's formative influences—the one who insisted most fiercely that it must be a professional organization, not open to amateur participants, and the one who helped Langner persuade Otto Kahn to lease the Garrick Theatre to the Guild on remarkably easy terms ("When you make the rent, you will pay the rent. When you do not make it, you need not pay it.").[6] Peters was, however, canny enough to decline an appointment as one of the Guild's co-managers.

Many people felt that Peters deserved a lot of the credit for keeping the Guild afloat during its rather desperate first year. The play chosen to launch the new company was *Bonds of Interest*. It had been translated from the original Spanish of Jacinto Benavente, and the cast included Peters as Leander. Although *Bonds of Interest* did not exactly knock the socks off either the audience or the critics, the one thing they all agreed upon was that the sets and costumes, devised by Peters and Lee Simonson from bits and pieces cast off by other productions, were stunning (and so recently executed that on opening night an actress wearing a splendidly painted "cloth of gold" dress made her first exit with a chair firmly attached to her gilded posterior).

By the time a second play was found, only $19 remained in the Theatre Guild's bank account. The good news, however, was that the new play was set in a poverty-stricken cottage. The critics praised the peeling paint of the second-hand scenery as highly realistic. *John Ferguson*, by the British dramatist St. John Ervine, who happened to have been an early acquaintance of Langner's in London, turned out to be a most unlikely hit—a heavy, tragic, religious drama playing on Broadway in late May, a time of year when it was well known that only frothy musicals could survive the lack of air conditioning. (It has to be said that a small part of the play's success might, just possibly, have been due to the fact that Broadway actors went on strike that summer. Because it cooperated with the union, the Theatre Guild was the only company not affected, so *John Ferguson*—"the hit play at the Garrick Theatre"—was actually the *only* entertainment available to New York's summer visitors. They flocked to the theatre and were rewarded with Peters's "brilliantly realistic" sets, not to mention his performance in one of the leading roles.)

Peters worked with the Theatre Guild throughout the 1920s, but never as a manager —he was convinced that the form of group management espoused by the Guild could not, and would not, work. Nevertheless, that was the way the Guild continued to be governed, though many of its worst tensions were blunted by the appointment of Theresa Helburn as executive director. And as the

Rollo Peters with Armina Marshall in *As You Like It* at Westport Country Playhouse, 1931.

Edward Thayer Monroe

Guild prospered on Broadway and in several forays outside New York, so Peters's profile grew in the world of theatre. By 1923 he was not only designing the sets for the Guild's *Romeo and Juliet* but he was playing Romeo opposite Jane Cowl's acclaimed Juliet. Later he would play Anthony to her Cleopatra and would have leading roles in many other Guild successes, including *Trelawny of the Wells* (1927), *The Age of Innocence* (1928) and *The Rivals* (1930).

But Peters (and it was increasingly true of Lawrence Langner as well) felt imprisoned by the Guild's wildly democratic way of deciding on repertory. The company came to include a number of people whose radical politics were alien to Peters and Langner, and divisive to the Guild as a whole. Things came to a head with the "directors' season" of 1930–31—a season that lost $180,000. As a result, the radicals split away to write a brave new chapter with their Group Theatre, while Rollo Peters and Lawrence Langner started driving around Fairfield County looking for a building they could turn into their own theatre.

Just as Peters had been largely responsible for getting the Theatre Guild through its first season, so it was with the Westport Country Playhouse. Not only did he find the barn and help Langner and Cleon Throckmorton transform it into a theatre, he then designed five of the first six productions, and acted in five of them as well (including the one he did not design—*As You Like It*).

After that 1931 season, Rollo Peters never again played at Westport—not (so far as is known) because there was any falling out or animosity with the Langners, but because Peters was essentially a free spirit who needed new challenges, new mountains to climb. The particular challenge he found—inspired, no doubt, by the experience of finding and transforming the old barn with Lawrence Langner—was in real estate development around the town of Nyack, New York, on the Hudson River not far from Westport. It wasn't the realtor aspect of the business that attracted him, but rather the opportunities it presented for redesigning and remodeling old houses.[7]

Rollo Peters, Armina Marshall, Knowles Entrikin, Dorothy Gish and Romney Brent on the front porch of the Playhouse, 1931.

At the same time, he found time to experiment with the new "talking pictures" in Hollywood, where he did a spell as assistant director to George Cukor. And he kept up his theatre work, though erratically, choosing his acting assignments so that each of them provided him with a new challenge—*Peter Ibbetson* in Detroit, *Autumn Crocus* in Chicago, *The Shining Hour* in Milwaukee, *Home Chat* in Philadelphia and (most memorably) two productions from the Greek Theatre in Berkeley that he produced, designed and starred in—*Within the Gates* and *The Taming of the Shrew* (with Peggy Wood). All these productions went on tour, some of them in summer stock, but never to Westport. His last tour—perhaps the most challenging and rewarding of his life—was a USO Camp Shows tour of England in 1944–45. Performing night after night in front of members of the armed services, he played Charles Condamine in Coward's *Blithe Spirit*.

That was the end of his active career on the stage. He returned home to Monterey, California, to paint in that spectacular light and to make occasional excursions to lecture on theatre at the Santa Barbara branch of the University of California. He died in 1967.

theatre (something he would never have dared do at the Theatre Guild in New York—nor would anyone have dreamed of asking him to), he was able to experiment to his heart's content. He devised an Elizabethan set on a deep apron stage "which enabled us to bring the actors out among the audience, so that they were out of focus with the scenery . . . almost the same effect as a 'close up' in the movies. I was impressed with what I discovered about the fluidity of the Shakespearian stage, which enables the play to be played continuously without any interruption or dipping of the curtain, one group of characters going off stage as another comes on, thus giving the same continuity as a motion picture."[8]

Though it joined the repertory late in the season—the last week of August—and therefore had only eight performances, *As You Like It* was a critical success—with Armina Marshall as Rosalind, Dorothy Gish as Celia, Rollo Peters as Orlando, and Moffat Johnston as Jacques. Originally Langner had also planned to include one of his own plays in the season, but the amount of time involved in the preparation of *As You Like It* forced him to postpone *Lady Godiva* to a future season (1933). The late substitute was Ibsen's *The Pillars of Society*—"not a choice substitute," according to Humphrey Doulens in the Norwalk *Evening Sentinel*, who, as always, had his ear close to opinion in the upper echelons of Fairfield County, "though the owners are proud of it."

The surprise success of the season was a new play by Will Cotton, *The Bride the Sun Shines On,* a comedy set in Westchester on the wedding day of a "pathetic but determinedly modern bride" played by Dorothy Gish. Rehearsals had been interrupted for what was to be the first of many happy events hosted over the years by the Langners at their farmhouse—the wedding reception of two members of the company, Virginia Volland and Mervin Williams (the groom was, in fact, the best man on stage). The local press noted that the play was "bubbling with gaiety and light madness" and that it had been received "with gales of laughter."[9] It had fourteen performances in Westport and seemed likely to play well on Broadway—even though it would be necessary to replace the flock of (non-Equity) Westport social beauties who had so gracefully portrayed the bridesmaids and flower girls on the Playhouse stage. In contrast, Susan Glaspell's play *The Comic*

The unexpected success of the 1931 season: Will Cotton's *The Bride the Sun Shines On*, directed by Philip Loeb, designed by Rollo Peters, with Dorothy Gish in the title role and "socially prominent" members of Fairfield County Society playing the bridesmaids.

Artist (co-written with her new husband, the novelist Norman Matson) was not a great success with the Westport audience, even though it had previously received acclaim in Europe. It was, in any case, a sentimental choice—Glaspell, like Eugene O'Neill and Cleon Throckmorton, had been an original member of the Provincetown Players and had become a friend of both Rollo Peters and Lawrence Langner in pre–World War I days: she was a literate, somewhat cerebral, writer, and her play—about a cartoonist who learns that real life can be as violent as his cartoons—was not exactly prime fare for a summer audience.

Nevertheless, by the time the season ended with a final performance of *The Streets of New York* on September 12, Langner and his team had every reason to be pleased. Only the French comedy *Come What May* had been a clear failure, and there was no question of its going to Broadway since its leading actor was home in England, tending to his family. The Ibsen and Glaspell plays could be pointed to with pride, even if the audience had greeted them with something less than rapture, and *The Streets of New York*, *The Bride the Sun Shines On* and *As You Like It* were all unmitigated successes. Prospects for Broadway seemed good—but first, Langner had to persuade the actors that the repertory system should be continued beyond the end of the Playhouse season.

Since arriving at Westport in mid-June, the actors had performed prodigiously. They had learned, rehearsed and staged six plays, presenting them in an alternating rotation throughout the season. There was no chance of learning one play, performing it, and then forgetting it while you got on with the next assignment—you had to have them all in your head, all of the time. Think of it from Dorothy Gish's point of view: she had to remember the words, characterizations, blocking, direction and, in some cases, music, of no fewer than six roles—Boucicault's Lucy Fairweather; Shakespeare's Celia; Ibsen's Dina Dorf; Cotton's Psyche Marbury; Gaspell's Nina; and Flers and Caillavet's Celeste. Three of these were leading roles; all of them were substantial. Langner had chosen the actors because they were all fine troupers, people to whom acting was innate—yet there must have been nights during that Westport season when Dorothy Gish had to remind herself that her name was Lucy, not Psyche (or Nina or Celeste or Celia or Dina), and that this was a night when she was going to have a narrow escape from a burning warehouse, not get married to a cad in a society wedding up Westchester way.

The actors did not have a problem with the hard work. Rather, it was their instinctive knowledge that they had, among their six plays, one undeniable hit: *The Streets of New York*. All actors dream of long runs on Broadway, and Langner's Westport troupers were no different; they did not want to jeopardize the chances of *Streets* by having it erratically scheduled as part of a repertory. Langner, who was bubbling over with confidence, disagreed: he planned to open at the Forty-Eighth Street Theatre with the Boucicault play, then introduce the other four at intervals of two weeks until they were all running in repertory. He convinced the actors there was nothing to worry about. But he was wrong.

The Streets of New York was greeted with delight by critics and audiences alike. Gilbert Gabriel, writing in the *New York American*, reported that the actors "know how to do it. Last night they knew how to make the most social and official audience of the year unbend entirely, having an increasingly jolly time—and even how to make Al Smith and Jimmie Walker put their heads together,

down in Row B, and sing in affectionate honor of the Streets of New York."[10] The problems began a week later with the introduction of the Ibsen play, *The Pillars of Society*, with Armina Marshall as Lona Hessel and Rollo Peters as Johan Tonnesen. This time the *New York American* slugged its review "An Earnest Addition to Mr. Langner's Repertory,"[11] and the *New York Evening Journal* was even more pointed: "Ibsen Play Seriously Revived."[12] John Mason Brown concluded his review in the *Evening Post* with a crushing summary: "In short, by all means see *The Streets of New York*, but be sure to see the Boucicault version and not the Ibsen version."[13]

Worse still, ticket agents, hotel ticket offices and potential ticket buyers, unfamiliar with the repertory idea, assumed that *The Streets of New York* had closed and that *The Pillars of Society* had opened in its place. Within days, Langner was addressing a desperate letter to ticket buyers: "Because of the opening of *The Pillars of Society*, many of our friends are under

Moffatt Johnston as the odious Gideon Bloodgood in *The Streets of New York* (1931).

the impression that *The Streets of New York* has been withdrawn. This is not the case, and as it is a necessary part of our repertory plan that *The Streets of New York* shall continue in our program, we are asking if you will help us to counteract this misunderstanding by recommending this play to your friends, if you enjoyed it."[14]

There were other problems, and not the least of them was the attitude of the unions, whose rules made no provision for repertory. There was no problem with Equity, the actors' union—Langner had recognized it from the start at Westport, in the same spirit that the Theatre Guild had been the first major producing organization to recognize it in New York (which was why, for seventy-five years, the Guild would be given the privilege of not having to put up an Equity bond for its plays). But the technical unions were a problem: *The Streets of New York* had nine separate sets; *Pillars* had only one—yet the union insisted that the two plays must use the same number of stage-hands. Even if all else had been fine, Langner would have found the economics of this hard to bear.

As You Like It was postponed, then cancelled (Langner officially announced that he had been called on to superintend another production for the Theatre Guild and would be unable to give sufficient time to the restaging of his Westport production). *Pillars* was taken off in face of an

Ibsen's *The Pillars of Society* (1931), with Armina Marshall as Lona Hessel and Rollo Peters as Johan Tonnesen.

increasing number of empty seats. Only the Will Cotton play, *The Bride the Sun Shines On*, seemed to work, and that did eventually run at the Fulton Theatre for twenty-two weeks in repertory with *The Streets of New York*. Artistically, these successes could be said to have salvaged the season, but no one was talking about the financial consequences.

IF AT FIRST YOU DON'T SUCCEED . . .

Nothing daunted, the summer of 1932 found Lawrence Langner trying again. The pattern was to be same—a resident company of actors

performing a group of plays in repertory, and then (hopefully) transferring the season to Broadway. Armina Marshall was again in the company, but all the other names were new. They included Osgood Perkins, June Walker, Elizabeth Risdon, Hugh Buckler and an interesting ingénue named Jane Wyatt. Although the subscription flyer issued in the spring assured patrons that "the six plays are all comedies," the three that were listed looked challenging, to say the least. Two of them were English adaptations of foreign plays—"a comedy of the recent Spanish revolution" called *The Devil's Elbow*, and a Swedish play called *The Nobel Prize*. The third play, by contrast, was to be a world premiere—*For Husbands Only*, described as "a modern comedy by Basil Lawrence."

Things were a little clearer when the posters went out at the end of May. *The Devil's Elbow*, it turned out, was really called *The Devil's Album*; the Basil Lawrence who claimed to have written *For Husbands Only* was actually Lawrence Langner himself; and there were two new titles now on offer—*Thoroughbred* and *Chrysalis* (though, since the titles were printed on the same line, most patrons must have thought they were booking for a single play called *Thoroughbred Chrysalis*).

Ultimately, neither of the two foreign plays was performed (though *The Nobel Prize* would become a vehicle for Otis Skinner in 1933). The season led off with Doty Hobart's comedy *Thoroughbred* ("a horsey comedy," the critics noted) and it was soon running in harness with *For Husbands Only*.

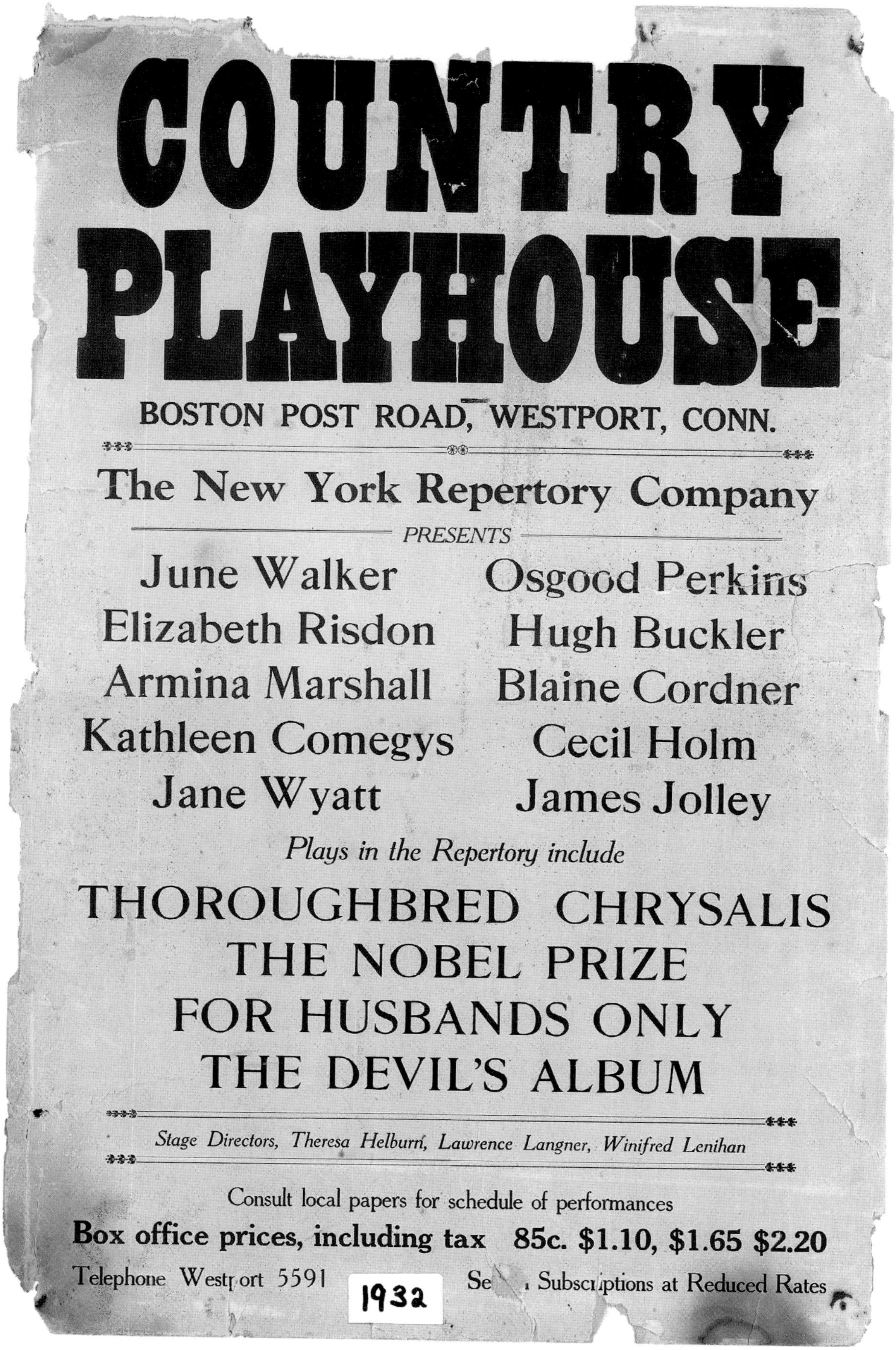

COUNTRY PLAYHOUSE

BOSTON POST ROAD, WESTPORT, CONN.

The New York Repertory Company

PRESENTS

June Walker	Osgood Perkins
Elizabeth Risdon	Hugh Buckler
Armina Marshall	Blaine Cordner
Kathleen Comegys	Cecil Holm
Jane Wyatt	James Jolley

Plays in the Repertory include

THOROUGHBRED CHRYSALIS
THE NOBEL PRIZE
FOR HUSBANDS ONLY
THE DEVIL'S ALBUM

Stage Directors, Theresa Helburn, Lawrence Langner, Winifred Lenihan

Consult local papers for schedule of performances

Box office prices, including tax   85c. $1.10, $1.65 $2.20

Telephone Westport 5591   Se   Subscriptions at Reduced Rates

1932

49   1931–32

They worked in vaudeville, in tent theatres, in touring theatre companies, in silent movies, on Broadway, in summer stock, in live radio and television, even on video. Few performers have spanned such a busy era of change and invention—and managed to keep up with it all.

It was D. W. Griffith who made the Gish sisters famous. They came from Springfield, Ohio, and started performing with touring companies as early as 1902. As they later told the story, putting them on the stage had been the last resort of their mother when she was abandoned by their alcoholic father. The girls were

THE GISH SISTERS
LILLIAN 1893–1993
DOROTHY 1898–1968

known as Lillian and Dorothy de Guiche (though Dorothy was occasionally billed on her own as "The Dimpled Darling"), but by the time they made their film debut together in *The Unseen Enemy*, a 1912 Biograph one-reeler, they were simply Gish.

Lillian quickly became a protégée of Griffith: she starred in some of his greatest films—*Birth of a Nation* (1915), *Intolerance* (1916), *Broken Blossoms* (1919) and *Way Down East* (1920). Silent filmgoers knew her, and loved her, as the brave little waif who never gave up. Dorothy, meanwhile, had her own independent career in films, not as starry as Lillian's but including a number of D. W. Griffith roles, of which the most famous was the hilarious "little disturber" of *Hearts of the World* (1918). Griffith brought the sisters together again in *Orphans of the Storm* in 1922. In the meantime, Lillian had used an assignment from Griffith to supervise the remodeling of his studio on Long Island to make a film herself. It was called *Remodeling Her Husband*; it starred sister Dorothy, and it was Lillian's only attempt at directing. She later wrote an autobiographical volume that may be the best thing ever written about Griffith—*The Movies, Mr. Griffith, and Me* (1969).

Dorothy was the first to forsake Hollywood for the theatre world. She took the train east in 1928 and quickly became a Broadway star as the enterprising Fay Hilary, who specialized in mate-swapping, in *Young Love*. During the next quarter century she performed in some twenty Broadway productions, many of them produced by the Theatre Guild, and made occasional forays to strut her stuff in summer stock. After her Herculean efforts in the repertory company of 1931, she returned to the Playhouse in 1933 for Frank Mandel's *Understanding Women*, and again in 1936 for *Russet Mantle*, a Lynn Riggs play. Thereafter, as a resident of Westport, she was frequently seen in the theatre as a member of the audience.

Lillian left Hollywood two years after her sister, having apparently decided she had no future in talking films. Her first Broadway role, in 1930, was Helena in *Uncle Vanya*, and she went on to play Marguerite Gautier in *Camille* two years later. By 1936 she was Ophelia to John Gielgud's celebrated Hamlet, and the following year she created the role of Martha Minch in Max Anderson's play *The Star Wagon*. Like her sister, Lillian was not too grand to play summer stock, and in 1950 she followed her sister to the Westport Playhouse as R. C. Sherriff's *Miss Mabel*.

It was also at Westport, in 1956 in *The Chalk Garden*, that the sisters performed together for the last time. It was actually the first time they had appeared together on stage since *Her First False Step!*—when they were four and nine, respectively.[15]

Dorothy died in 1968, but Lillian, who lived into her hundredth year, never really stopped working. She played many supporting roles in the theatre and on television, and in 1987 she returned to major screen work in *The Whales of August*, after which she happily went out on tour to lecture on the silent film era.

Lillian is credited with one of the wisest statements ever made by an actor: "Never get caught acting."[16]

Lillian and Dorothy Gish—as teenage
film stars and at the time of their last
performance together, which was in
The Chalk Garden at Westport in 1956.

The repertory company for the 1932 season poses on one of the theatre's outside staircases. At far left is the season's ingénue, Jane Wyatt; Armina Marshall is on the next step above her.

At this point (it was the Fourth of July weekend), Robert Garland, the august but gossipy critic of the *World Telegram*, found his way to Westport. "It is in Connecticut," he informed his readers. "There are fine old houses, charming inhabitants and the Country Playhouse which, according to Mr. Langner, has made his life a hell on earth ever since he bought it." Garland found "the owner-impresario" in his barn, "undismayed by apple trees, thunder storms and an open-air bar where the near-beer is little short of calamitous."[17]

Langner was probably not pleased to see Garland, who had been the lone New York critic to deride *The Streets of New York* on Broadway the previous fall. He had disliked "its stilted dialogue, its machine-made story and its sophomoric sobriety," all of which, he had complained, "puts me in mind of Mr. Eugene O'Neill's *Strange Interlude*. Only, of course, *Strange Interlude* is funnier."[18] Langner, who had been the proud producer of the 1928 world premiere of *Strange Interlude*—a Pulitzer Prize winner and one of the least funny plays ever to be presented on Broadway (it had actually been banned in Boston)—could not have been thrilled to see the critic in the theatre for the premiere of his own modest offering. Indeed, it is clear from Garland's review that the real identity of Basil Lawrence was not disclosed to him. But no matter—he liked the play.

In fact, other than the beer, he liked almost everything he saw in Westport, and that included

Elizabeth Risdon, Osgood Perkins and Jane Wyatt in Rose Albert Porter's *Chrysalis* (1932).

Thoroughbred, in which Elizabeth Risdon gave "a perfectly swell performance" in the leading role. *For Husbands Only* he characterized as "a domestic quadrangle with a sophisticated accent on the wrangle," and he praised the four principals—Armina Marshall, Osgood Perkins, June Walker and Hugh Buckler. Even the "unknown" playwright was offered words of encouragement: "Marking, as it did, a declaration of independence in marriage, the little comedy was an apt presentation for the fourth day of July. Apt enough, I mean. Anyway, the summer citizens of Connecticut gave evidences of enjoyment."[19]

In 1932, Armina Marshall Langner was a member of the New York Repertory Theatre company that performed five plays during the season. In *School for Lovers*, her husband's adaptation of Molière's *The School for Husbands*, Armina's role required her to be locked in a boudoir offstage and to bang loudly on the door demanding to be let out. At one performance this part of the action was accompanied by a loud wailing from the fifth row and six-year-old Philip Langner's pleading voice: "Let my mother out!"

In 1932 Jane Cowl appeared in Ashley Dukes's play *The Man with a Load of Mischief*. The inexperienced director was Lawrence Langner himself. But it made no difference to Miss Cowl, who believed in directing herself. To this end (Lawrence Langner remembered), "She brought her own electrician with her in all her plays, and he in turn carried a large mirror which he held at the footlights so that she could see herself at the lighting rehearsals, and in this way, right up to her last appearance, she was always lighted to look young and beautiful to her audience."

Thoroughbred and *For Husbands Only* were soon joined in the repertory by Rose Albert Porter's play *Chrysalis*—another world premiere and an altogether more distinguished piece that earned a run on Broadway (though a rather brief one, with the young Margaret Sullavan in the lead). Its Westport production, designed by Cleon Throckmorton, marked the directing debut of Theresa Helburn.

Then there was an embarrassing silence. Many patrons, in good faith, had subscribed for six plays: they needed to know what, and when, the last three would be. Not until July 25 was Langner in a position to announce the fourth production, which would open on August 1, and once again he was delving into his bottom drawer. Some time before, he and Arthur Guiterman had written an adaptation of Molière's *The School for Husbands*. They rewrote it in rhyming verse, added some songs, and renamed it *School for Lovers*. The audience loved it! Whatever the other headaches of the Westport season, this was not one of them: it was an unmitigated success and went on to have a Theatre Guild production on Broadway and a national tour.

The fifth spot on the rotation was eventually filled by *Dear Mistress*, a new play by Kathryn McClure, but it was clear by this time that the repertory scheme wasn't working. They simply couldn't get enough productions up and running on time.

Ever the pragmatist, Langner abandoned repertory there

and then, in mid-season. Conscious that he owed his subscribers a sixth play, he quickly arranged for a very great star, Jane Cowl—now in her late forties but still the slim, dark-haired, dark-eyed beauty who had been the darling of Broadway through much of the 1920s—to appear in the Ashley Dukes play *The Man with a Load of Mischief*. It had been a success in London during the 1930–31 season, but now, directed by Lawrence Langner himself, it was seen in a "completely revised" version. The people of Fairfield County responded by establishing a box-office record that would not

be broken until Paul Robeson starred in O'Neill's *The Emperor Jones* eight years later.

Finally—and perhaps to cement his alliance with the Westport public—Langner brought to the theatre the woman whom many people thought was the greatest American actress then living. Laurette Taylor was, in many ways, a tragic figure. At this stage of her career (she was the same age as Cowl), in the aftermath of her second husband's death, she was reclusive and often alcoholic. But Taylor could communicate with an audience to a degree that almost no one else ever dreamed of. It was Theresa Helburn, many years later, who wrote of her:

> Laurette, helpless and loving. Her inner radiance fell like moonlight on an audience without the use of any stage tricks that I could detect. In my day there has been no other such radiant personality as hers. She had a quality— oh, call it an ability to love, for I can't think of anything closer to it—which got across the footlights and aroused an immediate response.[20]

The play she appeared in at Westport—*Finale* by S. K. Lauren—was not much to write home about, but it served a purpose, which henceforward would be Langner's purpose: it brought to Westport the best in American theatre. What's more, he gave his subscribers a 15 percent discount!

Happily, *Finale* was not the end of the road for Laurette Taylor. In time, she returned to the stage for two legendary performances—Mrs. Midgit in the 1938 revival of Sutton Vane's

School for Lovers (1932) was an adaptation by Lawrence Langner and Arthur Guiterman, written in rhyming verse, of Molière's *The School for Husbands*. It later transferred to Broadway, where it reverted to its original title. In the Westport cast were (*left to right*) Blaine Cordner, June Walker and Osgood Perkins.

Outward Bound, which she brought triumphantly to Westport the following year; and then, in the last months of her life, in 1945–46, she created Amanda Wingfield in Tennessee Williams's *The Glass Menagerie*—an assumption that was spoken of with reverence and awe by all who saw it.

So, with two seasons completed—both of them fairly successful so far as the Westport audience was concerned—Langner retired to lick his wounds and reconsider the strategy for his little theatre. "I abandoned my plan for a Repertory Company," he later wrote, "and found myself with a loss of over $100,000 in cash and a substantial gain in experience."[21] Even for someone earning considerable fees as a patent attorney, this was a massive loss, and it came in the depths of the Depression, at a time when he was discovering just how much he had lost in the bond market.

Perhaps it wasn't just time to rethink the venture. Perhaps it was time to restore sanity by closing it down altogether?

"Helpless and loving"—Laurette Taylor
as she looked in 1903.

CHAPTER FIVE

1933–41 "Doing the Plays We Really Want to Do"

During the winter of 1932–33 Lawrence Langner did a lot of hard thinking. The idea of running a repertory company at Westport was clearly dead, a victim of economic and logistical realities—it would not be attempted again until Ralph Roseman and Jim McKenzie put together a repertory company for a short season of Shaw plays in the spring of 1965. But the winter was not without its compensations for Langner: two of Westport's 1932 productions opened on Broadway. *Chrysalis* was not very successful, but *School for Lovers* (which happened to be his own production, co-written with Arthur Guiterman) did very well and went on a national tour.

More important, perhaps, Langner was very aware of the way the Westport public had responded to the two little extras he had presented at the end of the previous summer when he had abandoned the repertory idea—first, Jane Cowl's two week box-office sell-out, then the briefer, but equally spectacular, appearance of Laurette Taylor. If he hadn't known it before, Langner could now be certain that star names would always work at the Playhouse.

The next nine seasons—1933 through 1941, when the theatre closed for the duration of the war—mined this seam. And it worked. That didn't mean the Playhouse made a profit (Langner reckoned on a loss of between $3,000 and $9,000 a season), but he was presenting plays he wanted to present, and generally with casts he was proud of. There was a steady supply of big names— Ruth Gordon, Ina Claire, Otis Skinner, Eva Le Gallienne, Frances Farmer, Henry Fonda, Ethel Barrymore, Uta Hagen, Alla Nazimova, Jane Cowl, Dorothy Gish, Laurette Taylor, Paul Robeson, Haila Stoddard, Gene Kelly, Tallulah Bankhead and Tyrone Power (to name just a few). There were also some very demanding plays by playwrights like O'Neill, Shaw, Ibsen, Dumas—and yes, Aristophanes. There were modern plays by important writers like Robert Sherwood, S. N. Behrman and Noël Coward. And there were musicals by Offenbach, Novello, Johann Strauss and the new team of Comden and Green. It was a rich mix.

ONE SEASON AT A TIME

With the exception of 1935, which had only six productions, each running two weeks, these Westport seasons all boasted between eight and eleven different plays. Putting together seasons such as these was never easy—the more so because the Playhouse was closed for eight months of the year and had no permanent staff. It did, however, have the advantage of being closely linked to the Theatre Guild through Lawrence Langner, and there is no doubt that much of its business was

A relaxing moment for staff and actors during the 1941 season. Elaine Anderson, the Playhouse's stage manager, is standing behind the umbrella. Her husband, Zachary Scott, is reclining on the grass at front.

"Sheep may safely graze"—the Playhouse in the 1930s.

conducted from his office at the Guild's theatre in New York (whereas he maintained a rigorous separation between his theatrical ventures and his patent firm).

Despite this, there is abundant evidence that Westport operated most of the time by the seat of its pants—and that was true of summer theatres in general. Most years the first subscription letter in the early spring was vague (sometimes downright misleading) about the season's offerings, but it didn't seem to matter: the leaders of Fairfield County Society sent in their checks as promptly as ever—indeed, with increasing promptness, because it seems to have become a matter of some importance to individual families to retain the same seats from year to year (in time, subscription rights were willed from generation to generation and were known to have featured in divorce settlements).

As Harry Wagstaff Gribble, the author of *March Hares*, was entering the Playhouse, a jolly-looking inmate of the sanitarium [next door to the Playhouse] called over the wall and asked "Are you Lawrence Langner?", to which Harry answered "No". "I know that", was the happy response from the inmate, "because I am."

Clearly, Westport could not produce all these plays on its own, nor was there any need for it to do so. In the 1930s many summer theatres were still operating in the northeast corridor, and all of them needed productions. Because actors were unlikely to commit to engagements that resulted in only one or two weeks' fees, it made sense to tour each production around a number of different theatres. Sometimes they would originate in a particular theatre, sometimes they would be independent productions originating in New York, but however they came into being, they would normally travel the circuit with actors, costumes (particularly if they were period), specially designed props (an exploding suitcase, perhaps) and a supervising stage manager who had overseen rehearsals and would guide the production into each new theatre before leaving it for the local staff to operate. The one thing that was unfailingly required of individual theatres was that they make their own scenery. Scene docks and paint shops were necessary adjuncts to stock theatres, and often the busiest parts of them.

In a July week in 1935 the *New York Times* published a list of thirty-one theatres it defined as "summer playhouses," all of them operating that week between Maine and eastern Pennsylvania:[1]

New York: Ridgeway Theatre, White Plains; Westchester Playhouse, Mount Kisco; Rockridge Theatre, Carmel; New Rochelle Playhouse; North Shore Playhouse, Whitestone, Long Island; County Theatre, Suffern; Phelps Players, Phelps; Maverick Theatre, Woodstock
Massachusetts: South Shore Players, Cohasset; Berkshire Playhouse, Stockbridge; Cape Playhouse, Dennis; Oak Bluffs, Martha's Vineyard; Beach Theatre, West Falmouth; Marshfield Hills, Gloucester
Rhode Island: Kingston Playhouse, Kingston; Theatre-by-the-Sea, Matunuck
Maine: Ogunquit Playhouse; Garrick Players, Kennebunkport
New Jersey: Cape Playhouse, Cape May; Old Mill Playhouse, Shrewsbury
Connecticut: Westport Country Playhouse; The Summer Theatre, Stamford; Anhalt Players, Old Saybrook; New York Players, Ivorytown; Stony Creek Theatre; Chapel Playhouse, Guilford
New Hampshire: Repertory Playhouse, Keene; Chase Barn Playhouse, Whitefield
Pennsylvania: Grove Theatre, Nuangola; Paula Shay Players, Shawnee-on-Delaware

It's clear from this list that, in the mid-1930s, at a time when Broadway theatres still lacked air-conditioning, summer stock was a thriving business. Any production worth playing (and a few that were not) could find a place on the circuit. In 1933, *Variety* reported that a total of eighty-seven different plays had been presented in summer stock that summer, and that fifteen of them were likely to get Broadway productions. The other principal trade paper, *The Stage*, was more optimistic: it listed twenty-five candidates for Broadway, but only half a dozen of them were also on the *Variety* list.[2] As it happened, the half dozen would have been a more realistic prediction, with Westport claiming two of them—*The Pursuit of Happiness* and *Champagne Sec*, both of which included Lawrence Langner's name as co-author.

Westport had two additional advantages over the other summer theatres—its proximity to New York, and its known links to Broadway and the Theatre Guild. The forty-two miles that separated Westport from the theatre district of New York was a very manageable distance—

SUBSCRIPTION BLANK, 1934

REDUCED PRICES FOR THE SIX PLAYS

Class A $9.90   One orchestra seat for entire six productions, $9.00, plus tax 90c — $9.90. (Established Box Office price, $13.20.) For Friday or Saturday nights, add to Class A $3.30.

Class B $6.60   One orchestra or front balcony seat for entire six productions, $6.00, plus tax 60c — 6.60. (Established Box Office price, $9.90.) For Friday or Saturday nights, add to Class B $3.30.

Class C $4.95   One balcony seat for entire six productions, $4.50, plus tax 45c — $4.95. (Established Box Office price, $6.60.) For Friday or Saturday nights, add to Class C $1.65.

The subscription prices for Wednesday matinees are Class A, $7.92, and Class B, $5.50.

I desire CLASS A, B or C Membership for the Subscription

Season, and enclose check for $..

for...................... orchestra / balcony   seats for...................... matinee. / evening.

Please make cheques payable to Westport Season of 1934, Inc.

I desire a year's subscription to The Stage (magazine), and enclose cheque for $1.50 made payable to "The Stage."

NAME..

PERMANENT WINTER ADDRESS..

SUMMER ADDRESS..

TELEPHONE NUMBER..

WESTPORT COUNTRY PLAYHOUSE

Six subscription plays will be produced with Visiting Stars and Featured Players.

Each Play Will Be Presented For One Week Only.

SUMMER SEASON 1934

SUBSCRIPTION PRICES SAVE
BETWEEN 20% TO 33⅓%

Westport-based staff could commute to and from rehearsals in the city, while actors felt they were performing somewhere close to civilization rather than way out in the boondocks. More importantly, perhaps, the local audience could be bolstered by visitors from New York. Early playbills contain an announcement on the Coming Attractions page: "A train leaves Grand Central for New York nightly at 7:00 D.S.T. A train leaves Westport for New York nightly at 11:23 D.S.T. A taxi is available to and from the station at special rates to Playhouse patrons."

Transferring a summer production to Broadway, which was what all actors and producers dreamed of, seemed more likely to happen via Westport than any other summer theatre. That was certainly one reason Westport tended to originate more productions than the other theatres. Moreover, beginning in 1935, the collective leadership of the Theatre Guild began to use Westport to try out what Lawrence Langner called "some of its more doubtful items"—that is, plays the co-directors couldn't agree on. Among them were the controversial *If This Be Treason* in 1935, and several plays that were thought by some directors to be "difficult," including Shaw's *The Millionairess* and André Birabeau's *Dame Nature*, both in 1938.[3]

Westport was generally considered to have "class." When Bosley Crowther of the *New York Times* visited the Playhouse in 1935 he wrote of an institution, still only in its fifth season, that "has become . . . an exceptional theatrical institution, notable for its ingenious dramatic experiments." Crowther went on: "The most striking thing about the Westport theatre to an exhaustively questing visitor is the elaborate organization which is functioning from morn to midnight out there on a pastoral hillside, and the air of professional seriousness with which a lot of people go about doing lots of things. . . . With a new play being offered each week, and each play being rehearsed for two weeks, there are regularly two companies in rehearsal around the place, morning and afternoon. Then there is scenery to be built and painted in the scene-dock (a sort of barn) adjacent to the theatre; reams of publicity to be written and sent out, accounts to be kept and such in the offices (really a barn) hard by, not to mention the ultimate job of performing a play when the night eventually falls."[4]

LANGNER AS PLAYWRIGHT

1933 was rightly remembered as Lawrence Langner's year. The previous season, in the desperate search for suitable plays to make up the Playhouse repertory, he had twice raided his bottom drawer—first for the "Basil Lawrence" play *For Husbands Only*, then for the Molière adaptation *School for Lovers*. Rewarded by a Broadway run for the latter, he was less bashful when it came to planning the eleven-play schedule for 1933: he included no fewer than three examples of his own work, two of which made it to Broadway. In fact, in the fall of 1933 he had the extraordinary experience of seeing three plays of which he had been author or co-author all running on Broadway at the same time. It was, he wrote, "a record which I have never since approached, and never will again."[5] In the entire history of Broadway the number of people who have had such an experience can probably be counted on the fingers of two hands.

Writing plays was a private hobby for Langner—it wasn't something he talked about much in the 1920s when he did most of it. He knew he was no Shaw or O'Neill, nor even a Robert Sherwood or a Philip Barry. He recognized that his particular talent was producing—not even directing, though Westport showed he was pretty handy at that, too. Nevertheless, he had read so many plays, good and bad, that he knew something about writing and structuring them, and it was perhaps inevitable that his restless intelligence would want to see if he could do it, too—if only to find a productive use for the long hours he spent traveling in the patent business, and for the hours "between 3 a.m. and 5 a.m.," which he once admitted was when much of the writing was done.[6]

His 1933 offerings at Westport included two undoubted successes and one equally certain failure. *Lady Godiva* was the one that went down with all hands. Langner had written it to honor a "very modern" eleventh century English noblewoman who rode naked through the streets of Coventry in order to persuade her husband, the Earl of Chester, to reduce the taxes he had imposed on the people. In some way that was not altogether clear to either reviewers or audience, the play attempted to emphasize what Langner characterized as "the importance of wearing clothes

Violet Heming as a fully clothed Lady Godiva (1933).

in order that Man might claim kinship with God." But that hardly mattered compared to the big moment when Violet Heming, in the title role, made her appearance to ride through the streets of Coventry. The play's Broadway prospects, if they had ever existed, disappeared forever when Ms. Heming, who (it was said) had political ambitions, appeared unsuitably (and very fully) clothed.

Champagne Sec, on the other hand, was an instant and predictable success. It was a simple rewriting (by Langner) of everyone's favorite operetta, *Die Fledermaus*. With lyrics by Bob Simon, and an outstanding cast that included Peggy Wood, Kitty Carlisle and Helen Ford, it more or less made its own way down the Post Road to Broadway.

By contrast, *The Pursuit of Happiness* was one of Broadway's most unexpected successes, and it began the brief but very interesting husband-and-wife writing partnership of Lawrence and Armina Langner. In the decade before World War II, they wrote several plays together, of which *The Pursuit of Happiness* was much the most notable, before the collaboration became (in Lawrence's words) "too argumentative and difficult to contemplate."[7]

The Pursuit of Happiness was Armina's idea. She had learned from an astrologer (the kind you consult through the mail) that it was her destiny to write, and about the same time she had found

Champagne Sec *was an adaptation (by Lawrence Langner and Robert Simon) of Johann Strauss's* **Die Fledermaus**. *It had its premiere at the Playhouse in 1933 and went on to Broadway. It starred Peggy Wood and Helen Ford, and the young Kitty Carlisle, who remembers it with affection:*

My first job was in Westport, in summer stock. I played Prince Orlovsky. I had made friends with the press agent, a lady of enormous savvy. As we were walking up the hill to the first performance, I asked her: "How do you become a star?"

On the way back down the hill after the performance, she said to me: "That's how you become a star."

As a reward, I went straight to Hollywood, which turned out to be no reward at all!

in Lawrence's desk a very serious and rather pretentious draft for a play about the Declaration of Independence. She suggested they make it into a comedy—and that turned out to be exactly what it needed. It became famous as "the Bundling Play" because it featured a scene in which a young Hessian officer, recently deserted from the British army, is introduced to a technique of wooing that appears to have been popular in the rural districts of colonial New England and Pennsylvania. In those permissive times (authoritative sources agree) the use of the family bed was sanctioned for the

Two ways of "bundling." Tonio Selwart with Peggy Conklin (1934) and Alfred Drake with Mary Hatcher (1947) in Westport productions of *The Pursuit of Happiness* by Lawrence and Armina Langner.

purposes of courtship. Two young people seriously contemplating matrimony would be allowed to conduct their wooing while snuggled up together in the bed, fully clothed (other than their boots) and firmly separated by a center board. The couple of the Langners's play had the misfortune to be discovered with the center board out of place.

At Westport, the Hessian was admirably played by a young man named Tonio Selwart, who had recently come to America from Bavaria and found himself Broadway-bound almost before he had collected his visa. His co-star was the twenty-one-year-old Peggy Conklin, who was in the process of making the leap from chorus girl to Broadway star. *The Pursuit of Happiness* ran a full season on Broadway and subsequently became a perennial favorite in theatres throughout America. It was the only real success of the husband-and-wife writing partnership (which, to begin with, coyly hid its identity behind the names of Alan Childs and Isabelle Loudon), but it was a very substantial success. It eventually became the source for the 1950 musical *Arms and the Girl*.

That Broadway season of 1933–34 must have given Lawrence Langner a great deal of satisfaction—and his bank manager, too. *Champage Sec* and *The Pursuit of Happiness* were joined by *School for Lovers*, the adaptation of Molière's play that Langner and Arthur Guiterman had presented at Westport the previous year. Langner later told an interviewer that it was *The Pursuit of Happiness* that "paid for the building of the Westport Country Playhouse, with enough left over to finance . . . the extensive alterations [of 1949]."[8] And if the financial benefits were not, in themselves, of great importance (which, in the middle of the Depression, they probably were), then the theatrical soul of this very unglamorous patent attorney from South Wales must have had a lot of fun seeing his name in lights almost everywhere he turned.

THE PLAY'S THE THING

The 1933 season set a pattern to which Langner would adhere for most of the remaining seasons that he personally controlled the Playhouse, which was up to 1958. Beginning in 1937 he relieved himself of most of the day to day administration by bringing in managers for each individual season, but he never ceased to be the arbiter of which plays were performed—because for Lawrence Langner, the play *was* the thing. In the summer of 1935 he wrote to Theresa Helburn: "Westport has been a wonderful thing this summer for me because we are really running it as an Art Theatre now—and to hell with Broadway tryouts, none of which ever seem to amount to anything, anyway."[9] The "Art Theatre" analogy was certainly true of the 1935 season—it contained some very strong meat—but, for the most part, Langner was careful to give his Westport audience a sufficient supply of the stars and comedies he knew they really wanted. Again and again, you can see him luring his audience to "difficult" plays by casting them with major stars.

That was what he was doing when he opened the 1933 season with *The Nobel Prize*. This was the Swedish play he had wisely postponed from the opening season—wisely, because in 1933 he

Otis Skinner in *The Nobel Prize* (1933).

was able to make a major event of it by persuading a true legend of the American theatre to head up the cast. Otis Skinner was seventy-five years old, and this would be his last appearance on the stage. He had first appeared professionally in Philadelphia in 1877, and he would be forever associated with the role of the beggar Hajj in *Kismet*, which he played for four years right before World War I, and with the role of Falstaff in Shakespeare's *Henry IV* and *The Merry Wives of Windsor*. Having undertaken 325 different roles in fifty-two years, he had made his farewell appearance on Broadway in *A Hundred Years Old* in 1929. Now Lawrence Langner persuaded him to make his final appearance on any stage in the humble surroundings of Westport Country Playhouse, and the Fairfield County audience willingly turned out (however difficult the play) to show their appreciation. Much later, in 1951, when Langner came to list the twelve most important productions staged at Westport in its first twenty years, Otis Skinner in *The Nobel Prize* was right up there at number two, topped only by the memory of Ethel Barrymore in *The School for Scandal*.

Langner loved the great English comedies of the seventeenth and eighteenth centuries, and he wanted his audience to enjoy them, too. Ethel Barrymore had first come to the Westport Playhouse in 1938 in Somerset Maugham's *The Constant Wife*, but when she came back two years later it was to star in one of the greatest of all the English comedies—Richard Sheridan's *The School for Scandal*, first performed in 1777. Barrymore was sixty-one years old in 1940, but the low, resonant voice, the perfect timing and the electric presence that had always been her hallmarks were still there. Indeed, after several years of semi-retirement, her Westport appearance came only a few weeks before she would once again take Broadway by storm as the Welsh teacher Miss Moffat in Emlyn Williams's *The Corn Is Green*.

Skinner and Barrymore were legends when they came to the Playhouse. Ruth Gordon was hardly that, though she was certainly a famous actress and a name that drew an audience. She had spent many years in the shadow of Helen Hayes, whose roles she seemed fated to take over on Broadway, but in 1934 she had dramatically changed her type by playing a prostitute in *They Shall Not Die*. Suddenly she was perceived as a great star in her own right, and one who could choose her plays. What she chose for the Westport season of 1935 (with a good deal of prompting from Langner, no doubt) was an English comedy of the Restoration era—William Wycherley's *The Country Wife*, first performed in 1675. The Westport audience loved it, and they loved Gordon, too—she became a frequent visitor to the Playhouse, and always a sell-out.

The Country Wife, as Lawrence Langner later wrote, "had some strange vicissitudes." The Westport production and Ruth Gordon's performance were greatly enjoyed by a visitor to Westport that summer, Helen Hayes. She offered to back its production on Broadway. Unfortunately, it got entwined in the grip of an impresario "whose exotic genius," as Langner put it, "blossomed in the theatre like deadly nightshade." When the impresario backed out at the last moment, Gordon sailed for London and got an English impresario to back its production by the Old Vic company. The Old Vic thought it could improve on the version of the play Langner had arranged for Westport, and it commissioned the English playwright Ashley Dukes to do it. Try as he might, he couldn't do so without making use of some, at least, of Langner's version. So when the play eventually came to Broadway, generously backed by Helen Hayes and still starring Ruth Gordon, an agreement was made: Langner was paid (in his own words) "a royalty of 1% for the use of the Westport version. Wycherley must have turned in his grave at the thought of my being paid. Alas, the story ends sadly. The play failed, and Helen lost a good deal of money. She told me years later she liked it better at Westport."[10]

Ruth Gordon in the letter-writing scene of Wycherley's *The Country Wife* (1935).

Wycherley was not the only Restoration playwright Langner tinkered with. He also had his wicked way with Congreve. In 1936 he combined two of that playwright's most famous works—*Love for Love* and *The Way of the World*—into a play called *The Way To Love*, and he invited another of America's great actresses to star in it. Eva Le Gallienne never needed an introduction to Westport—she was a long-time resident—and she would become a frequent and very popular performer at the Playhouse. Aside from the fact that they both hailed from Britain and had spent much of their early years in London, she and Langner had a natural affinity—they both abominated the "serial quality" of the commercial theatre and they had both taken steps to break away from it. In 1936 Le Gallienne had just finished winding up her Civic Repertory Theatre, which, in its eight-year existence, had brought great drama into the lives of thousands of Americans, and always at rock bottom prices. The closing of the company in the middle of the Depression was the nation's loss, but it was also, in an ironic way, Westport's gain, because the Congreve play with which she opened the 1936 season, and Dumas's *Camille* with which she closed it, were the first of many memorable Le Gallienne performances at the Playhouse.

Having so many great actresses around the place was not always an advantage. In 1937, when Langner adapted Gozzi's play *Princess Turandot* as a vehicle for the young actress Anna May Wong, she was unfortunately told on opening night that Ethel Barrymore, Ina Claire, Eva Le Gallienne and Alla Nazimova were all in the audience. In a blind funk, she overplayed with disastrous results, and the play sank without trace.[11]

One of the reasons great actors came to Westport was the knowledge (which traveled fast in the world of theatre) that production standards at the Playhouse were high. In New York in the 1920s, the Theatre Guild had quickly acquired a reputation for innovative and interesting design. In Westport, where budgets were necessarily lower, Langner could not achieve the same lavishness of costuming and decor, but he could (and he did) insist that each production was put in the hands of a highly competent designer. Summer stock it might be, but Lawrence Langner's heart had long since grown accustomed to beating in time to Broadway's, and he believed that each play he presented at Westport should have a chance, however slim, of making it to the Great White Way. To that end, he employed resident designers of ability, and often brilliance. In 1931 Rollo Peters had filled the position (as well as several major acting roles), and in subsequent seasons he was followed by designers as distinguished as Charles Stepanek (1932–33), Stewart Chaney (1934) and Tom Adrian Cracraft (1935). For the most part, these men still had their reputations to make, but they had already established themselves as bright hopes for the future. At Westport, they designed five or six plays in as many weeks, oversaw the process of turning their drawings into actual sets and costumes and then had the satisfaction of seeing some of the world's finest actors inhabit their designs and turn them into great drama. For a few weeks each summer the Playhouse was a high pressure laboratory where artists and technicians showed off their skills alongside the aristocracy of the theatre.

Few plays have ever brought Westport so much attention as *If This Be Treason* in 1935. Written by Dr. John Haynes Holmes, pastor of the Community Church of New York, it was, without doubt,

McKay Morris as the President in *If This Be Treason* (1935).

pacifist propaganda, but it also made extremely good theatre — witness the reception it got in conservative Westport: "There was curtain call after curtain call at the end," reported the *World Telegram*, "and the audience shouted and pounded their feet until the author was dragged in front of the footlights."[12] The play depicted a President of the United States who arrives in office to find that his predecessor has made it all but certain that the United States will go to war with Japan. Refusing to accept this, and flying in the faces of his cabinet and the Congress, the President sails to Japan and averts war by persuading the Japanese people to confront their leaders and demand peace. The conservative press thundered against the play: "The regrettable infusion of Japan into such a dramatically crude plot is bad enough," wrote columnist Ogler Quiller, "but then there is the equally reprehensible inclusion of the 'munitions manu-facturers' as the American *villains*." Quiller and others tried to stop the play being presented on Broadway in the fall: "I hope my very good friend Mr. Cordell Hull, as Secretary of State of the United States, will see to it that no such thing happens, for the sake of American good manners and fair play."[13] But the play had been, all along, a Theatre Guild tryout, and it duly appeared on Broadway to quieter, but very respectful, reviews.

If This Be Treason has to be seen in the context of its times, because it was a context that greatly concerned Lawrence Langner. Throughout the 1920s and 1930s he had been traveling regularly in Europe on his patent business, and particularly in Germany. He saw what was happening there, and he was concerned. He also kept himself informed about what was happening in the Soviet Union, and he was appalled. Like many others, he feared that the idealism exhibited by pacifists and young people in America and Europe might expand into an endorsement of communism. In 1937–38 he and Armina set out to write a play that would, gently and without being propagandistic, explore this theme. They chose to set it in an American community that was fueled by a communist ideology. Several such communities existed in the 1930s, though they were steadily deteriorating as practice turned to failure. The Langners did their first-hand research at the Oneida Community in upstate New York, where they greatly admired the fortitude and determination of the remaining members, but the message of their play, *Susannah and the Elders*, was clearly the failure of communism as a practical ideology. Somewhat daringly, they dedicated it to their friend George Bernard Shaw. Even more daringly, they allowed another friend, Theresa Helburn, to play a small part in it—her first venture into acting since 1916, and certainly her last. As she herself later described the outcome: "The dramatic critic of *Variety* got pleasantly intoxicated after the opening and headlined his review the next day 'Theresa Helburn was dynamic in the leading role'. This caused a slight difficulty as Uta Hagen . . . was playing the lead. My part was small to start with. I managed to get it cut in half during the two weeks of the run."[14] Despite this, *Susannah and the Elders* did very well at Westport in the summer of 1938, but on Broadway, where the producers ludicrously turned it into some sort of comedy, it failed quickly and quietly.

While his writing efforts kept him amused, and occasionally brought him a certain amount of fame, if not fortune, it was the writing efforts of others, more talented, that kept Langner most involved. These were years when he was frequently in touch with Eugene O'Neill and George Bernard Shaw, both of whom he had successfully wooed on behalf of the Theatre Guild, and both of whom he was proud to call a friend, and it was a time when he tried to get as many living playwrights as possible into his Westport seasons. Shaw made his first appearance with *You Never Can Tell* in 1935 and quickly became a regular (*Fanny's First Play* in 1936, *The Millionairess* in 1938, Jose Ferrer in *Arms and the Man* in 1939, Jane Cowl in *Captain Brassbound's Conversion* in 1940, and many more after the war). O'Neill first appeared in 1939 with *Anna Christie*, and again in 1940 with Paul Robeson's memorable *The Emperor Jones*, but Langner made sure that other playwrights he regarded as important—Robert E. Sherwood and S. N. Behrman were certainly two of them—were also well represented.

In the late 1930s he was on the trail of another. Early one summer the guest pagoda at Langnerlane was occupied by a young man with a distinctly southern accent. Lawrence's son, Philip, remembers that the young man "was writing a play for the Guild. My father introduced him as a shoe salesman to all our visitors, most of whom found the name 'Tennessee' laugh-out-loud funny."[15] Tennessee Williams was, in fact, writing *Battle of Angels*, a play that was destined to run into awful trouble with the censorship laws in Boston in 1940 and would be abandoned by the Guild before it reached New York, much to Langner's distress (and even more to Williams's). Many years later, in 1957, much rewritten, it would emerge as *Orpheus Descending* and take its rightful place in the Williams pantheon, although, even then, it failed to convince audiences. For Langner, Tennessee Williams was the one that got away—he never gave the Theatre Guild another play—but he would, in time, become a staple at the Playhouse, as in every other theatre in the English-speaking world.

A STRATEGY THAT WORKS

As the 1930s drew to a close, the pattern of Westport seasons became established. Writing in the Playhouse *Bulletin* in June 1935, Langner compared the two systems with which he had experimented at the Playhouse. He confessed that he had found the least dissatisfaction with the resident repertory company system of the first two seasons (he tried it again in 1935 in a somewhat diluted form, using a basic team of resident actors headed by Tom Powers and Frances Fuller, but augmenting them with visiting stars for most plays: this was also the season he scheduled only six plays, each running for two weeks). But in his heart of hearts Langner knew he was never going to revert to the idea of a resident repertory company—it had certainly worked well enough in 1931 and the early part of 1932, but the pressure it had placed on everyone (including himself, having to find the plays) was too great to contemplate ever again.

It was the second of the two systems—he called it "the Visiting Star system"—that would inevitably become the norm, because it was the one the audience really wanted. Of the 1933 and 1934 seasons, when the star system was in the ascendant, he told readers of the *Bulletin*: "When we were able to secure good plays, well cast and well directed, the system worked excellently. However, it was impossible to secure enough good manuscripts for summer tryout purposes." The next stage, therefore, was to shed the compulsion for every play to be a Broadway tryout, and to concentrate on finding enough plays—new and old, American and European—to guarantee the audience a twelve-week season that had enough variety, enough stars and enough quality to ensure that subscriptions would be renewed. The other condition (unstated but just as important to Langner) was that each Westport season must be something he could be proud of. The moment he felt ashamed he would close the theatre.

The six pre-war seasons between 1936 and 1941 proved that this prescription would work. Langner found the plays—partly by dipping into the riches of British and European theatrical history (the Restoration comedies, Molière, Dumas and others in translation), and partly by reviving modern American and European plays that had already been successfully presented on Broadway, and that people were glad to see again in new productions. Thus, Robert Sherwood's *Petrified Forest*, so successful on Broadway in 1935, was mounted at Westport in 1937 with Frances Farmer and Philips Holmes in the Bogart role; and Noël Coward's *Private Lives* came to Westport in a highly polished production with Eva Le Gallienne and Rex O'Malley nine years after its New York premiere. And, occasionally, there were new plays that might, indeed, have a Broadway date ahead of them, though that was no longer of enormous importance to Langner. Nevertheless, Westport was the place where director/writers George Abbot and Philip Dunning most often brought their new creations for tryout in the 1930s, and it was increasingly the place where the Theatre Guild tested plays about which it was doubtful.

There were occasional guest productions, like the well-known drama about China, *The Yellow Jacket*, which Mr. and Mrs. Charles Coburn had been performing all over the world since 1916, and which sold out the house when it came to Westport. And Langner tried to include a musical each season. Among those were Planquette's *The Chimes of Corneville*, Offenbach's *La Belle Hélène* and a 1939 review called *Magazine Page* by a brash young group of Greenwich Village writers who called themselves *The Revuers*: they

In the winter of 1935–36, Lawrence Langner purchased a considerable amount of additional land in order to expand the theatre's facilities—and paid a great deal more than he had in 1931.

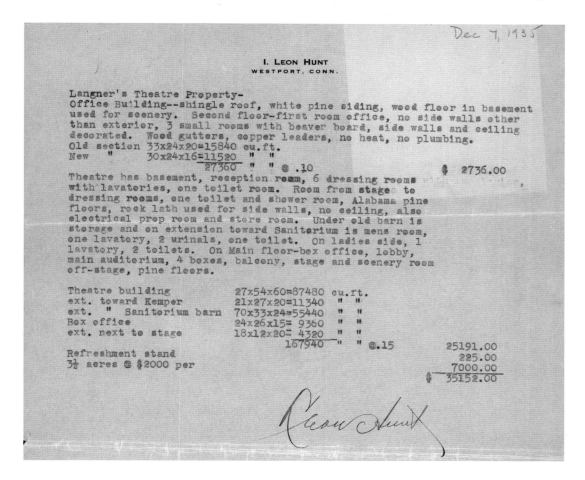

COUNTRY » » PLAYHOUSE
Boston Post Road, Westport, Connecticut

LAWRENCE LANGNER IN ASSOCIATION
WITH DWIGHT DEERE WIMAN PRESENTS

HELEN MENKEN
IN A NEW COMEDY
"GAILY I SIN"
BY GUIDO NADZO
WITH A CAST OF DISTINGUISHED PLAYERS
DIRECTED BY ANTOINETTE PERRY
SPECIAL MUSICAL ARRANGEMENT

FOR ONE WEEK ONLY
Week of September 4th to 9th
RESERVE BY PHONE WESTPORT 5591
PRICES—Eves., $2.00, $1.50, $1.00, 75c and 50c, Plus Tax
Mats $1.50, $1.00, 75c, 50c—Curtains 2:30 and 8:45

Country « « » » Playhouse
Boston Post Road, Westport, Connecticut

LAWRENCE LANGNER presents

CHARLES COBURN   LOUISE GROODY

Mr. and Mrs. Coburn
in the Chinese Fantasy
"THE YELLOW JACKET"
By George C. Hazelton and Benrimo
with
LOUISE GROODY
REX O'MALLEY   SCHUYLER LADD
MARY HUTCHINSON   KATHLEEN COMEGYS
and others
With Special Musical Arrangement

"THE PLAY THAT HAS GONE 'ROUND THE WORLD"
SPECIAL CHILDREN'S MATINEE FRIDAY

FOR ONE WEEK ONLY
Week of July 17th - 22nd
Reserve by Phone Westport 5591
PRICES—Eves., $2.00, $1.50, $1.00, 75c and 50c, Plus Tax
Mats $1.50, $1.00, 75c, 50c—Curtains 2:30 and 8:45

Westport Country Playhouse
Boston Post Road, Westport, Connecticut

LAWRENCE LANGNER in association with
GILBERT MILLER
presents

Jean ARTHUR and Sam JAFFE
in a comedy adapted by RUTH LANGNER
from the Hungarian of Otto Indig
"The Bride of Torozko"
Directed by
Herman Shumlin
director and producer of "Grand Hotel"

—ONE WEEK ONLY—
Mon., July 9 - Sat., July 14
Reserve by Phone Westport 5591
PRICES—Eves. 50c to $2.00 plus tax. Wed. Mat. 50c to $1.50 plus tax.
Curtain — 2:30 and 8:45

Westport Country Playhouse
Boston Post Road, Westport, Connecticut

Helen Ford
in
THE COMIC OPERA
"The Chimes of Corneville"
with
George Meader
and
A. P. KAYE   JOHN CHERRY
JAMES JOLLEY   LUCY MONROE
and Special Ensemble

Music by   Directed by
PLANQUETTE   LINA ABARBANELL
Book and Lyrics by
Arthur Guiterman

—TEN DAYS ONLY—
Thurs., June 28 - Sat., July 7
Reserve by Phone Westport 5591
PRICES—Eves. 50c to $2.00 plus tax. Wed. Mat. 50c to $1.50 plus tax.
Curtain — 2:30 and 8:45

COUNTRY « « » » PLAYHOUSE
Boston Post Road, Westport, Connecticut

LAWRENCE LANGNER Presents

GEORGE ABBOTT'S
AND
PHILIP DUNNING'S
PRODUCTION OF
"HEAT LIGHTNING"
BY LEON ABRAMS AND GEORGE ABBOTT
A New Play of the Great Southwest with
JEAN DIXON
(From the original casts of "Once in a Lifetime"
and "Dangerous Corner")
ROBERT GLECKLER
(From the original cast of "Take a Chance")
EMILY LOWRY   ROBERT SLOANE
ROSAMUND PINCHOT COBURN GOODWIN
PRIOR TO BROADWAY

FOR ONE WEEK ONLY
Week of Aug. 28 to Sept. 2
RESERVE BY PHONE WESTPORT 5591
PRICES—Eves., $2.00, $1.50, $1.00, 75c and 50c, Plus Tax
Mats $1.50, $1.00, 75c, 50c—Curtains 2:30 and 8:45

Westport Country Playhouse
Boston Post Road, Westport, Connecticut

PRIOR TO NEW YORK OPENING
ARCH SELWYN and HAROLD B. FRANKLIN
in association with ARTHUR HOPKINS

presents

Frances STARR
in
"LADY JANE"
A New COMEDY by H. M. HARWOOD
(Co-author of "Cynara")
WITH
LILA LEE   FRIEDA INESCORT
PAUL McGRATH   REGINALD MASON
FRANK ELLIOT   ALAN MARSHALL
LOWELL GILMORE   HENRY VINCENT
FLORENCE SELWYN
Staged by MR. HARWOOD
Settings by Woodman Thompson

—ONE WEEK ONLY—
Mon., Sept. 3 - Sat., Sept. 8
Reserve by Phone Westport 5591
PRICES:—Eves. 50c to $2.00 plus tax. Wed. Mat. 50c to $1.50 plus tax.
Curtain — 2:30 and 8:45

included Betty Comden and Adolph Green, who would have a distinguished role to play in the future of the Playhouse, and it also introduced the talents of a young woman named Judith Tuvim—later known as Judy Holliday—and a young man named Gene Kelly.

And there were stars galore, of course: Henry Fonda in *The Virginian*, Tyrone Power in *Liliom*, Paul Robeson in *The Emperor Jones*, and all those great ladies of the theatre—Ethel Barrymore, Laurette Taylor, Ilka Chase, Alla Nazimova, Jane Cowl, Eva Le Gallienne, Ruth Gordon, Dorothy Gish . . . the list went on and on. Inevitably, there were some stars who never got to Westport, and Humphrey Bogart was one of them: he was announced as the lead in Strindberg's *There Are Crimes and Crimes* in 1935, only to be withdrawn a week or two later.

For the audience, the system clearly worked—you could see that from the subscription list, which was based on a solid core of renewals and grew bigger from year to year. And it worked for Lawrence Langner, too, so long as production standards were maintained at a high enough level to satisfy his demanding nature. At any rate, he felt sufficiently confident about the system to step back a bit at the start of the 1937 season and to bring in professionals to help him run the theatre. Day Tuttle and Richard Skinner were veterans of summer theatre. Since 1932 they had been running the Westchester Playhouse at Mount Kisco, and in the 1937 and 1938 seasons they helped in the running of Westport as well. Importantly, this included sharing several productions (and their costs) with Mount Kisco. In 1939 and 1940, John Haggott and John Cornell (Langner's son-in-law) were entrusted with the management of the theatre, and they were responsible for seasons that broke even financially, and may even have made a little money (Langner was uncharacteristically coy on the subject).

The last play of the 1938 season was an adaptation of a Somerset Maugham story by John Colton and Clemence Randolph. The play, sometimes known as Sadie Thompson, was called Rain at Westport—and it proved to be prophetic.

Shortly after the season ended, on September 21, Westport was engulfed by what was then the largest hurricane to hit the town since records had been kept—it triggered a cyclone and a tidal wave, which surged in from Long Island Sound. The swollen waters of the Saugatuck River caused widespread flooding on both banks, including most of the shops on Main Street. The high winds brought down trees all over town, including the huge elm tree on the corner of Old Mill Road and Hillspoint Road that had long been a landmark—it was almost 100 feet tall, and it was completely uprooted by the storm, falling across the electricity and power lines. Amazingly, there were no reports of damage to the Playhouse, and because it had happened after the end of the season, no interruption to the schedule. The previous year, 1937, a somewhat smaller hurricane had hit the town while the season was still in progress, causing a power outage that lasted several days. During this time, the Playhouse continued to perform with the help of car headlights shining into the auditorium from the back doors.

These were years when Lawrence Langner was seriously preoccupied with other things. From afar, he was watching his homeland absorb the full might of Nazi aggression, and he feared for the outcome. He never doubted that the United States would eventually be compelled to enter the war, and he believed that, in preparation for that moment, he could make an important contribution. Throughout 1940 and 1941 he spent more and more of his time in Washington, D.C., as he first conceived, then (in July 1940) launched and helped to operate the National Inventors Council, which would, indeed, make a major contribution to the eventual victory.

By the beginning of 1941, although the United States was still not at war, it was apparent that Langner was not going to be around Westport a great deal that summer. Naturally enough, it was Armina who stepped up to take charge, and she and Lawrence persuaded a resident of Fairfield, John C. Wilson, to join the two of them as one-third owner of the 1941 season. Wilson was a theatre professional, most closely associated, personally and professionally, with Noël Coward, and also with Alfred Lunt and Lynn Fontanne, who at that time were the most glamorous acting partnership in the world. All the accounts of Wilson in the 1940s speak of an extremely difficult man, but what he had to offer the Playhouse were his contacts and his stature in the theatre world on both sides of the Atlantic. In the twelve seasons he worked alongside the Langners at the Playhouse he was responsible for bringing in many of the most popular plays and most important stars, and he personally directed some of the finest productions in the theatre's history.

For most Americans, the end of 1941 was the end of an era—after Pearl Harbor, things would never be the same again. In many ways, that had to be true for the Playhouse, too—it was mothballed for four seasons and did not open its doors again until the spring of 1946. But Lawrence and Armina Langner and their partner, Jack Wilson, perfectly understood the importance of theatre in giving continuity and purpose to the life of a community. So when they reopened the Playhouse in 1946 they determined to do so in such a way that it would seem as though it had never closed. They intended to pick up exactly where they had been so rudely interrupted at the end of 1941—with the same quality and quantity of summer theatre, with the same "visiting star system" and with the same mix of froth, tough meat and strong, demanding theatre.

The yardstick against which they would have to measure themselves was provided by the 1940 and 1941 seasons. In retrospect, it is possible to see these years as the zenith of summer stock. It was a time when television sets had not yet arrived in living rooms but when Hollywood had made actors and actresses into household names. Writing from Westport in August 1941 the columnist Tom Wolf observed: "This year mid-season reports from a great majority of the nation's 70-odd summer theatres are monotonously similar: record business, extra matinees, standing room only. A few straw hat impresarios may net as much as $30,000 profits." Wolf admitted that "the migration of stars to summer stock is . . . undoubtedly an important factor," but it was not the only one—"the tryout earlier this season of a new musical here at Westport actually made money without a well-known player in the cast" (he was referring to a production of Offenbach's *La Belle Hélène* that had been presented "in a new swing version").[16]

By any standard, the 1940 and 1941 seasons at Westport were memorable.

1940—AN ALMOST PERFECT SEASON

It was the Playhouse's tenth season. It started late, on July 1, by which time the other summer theatres in the area—in Ridgefield, Milford and Stamford—were already a week or two into their seasons. But the Westport season started with a great deal of excitement. The *Bridgeport Post* listed almost forty ladies who would be hosting social functions for opening night, and the *Norwalk Hour* reported

For a boy from the streets of Pittsburgh (and aggressively proud of it, too), it was ironic that his first real break in show business happened in the "toniest" of summer theatres, the Westport Country Playhouse. It was August 1939. The show was a musical review called *Magazine Page*, and Kelly was part of a group called *The Revuers*.

There was a lot of talent on stage that week. It included a young singer called Judith Tuvim (who would soon be much better known as Judy Holliday) and a pair of writer-performers called Betty Comden and Adolph Green. But Gene Kelly stole the show.

FIRST STEPS: GENE KELLY'S BEGINNINGS IN SHOWBIZ

He celebrated his twenty-seventh birthday while he was in Westport, and it may have been the first birthday of his life that was truly worth celebrating. He'd had to work his way toward his goal of being a choreographer through a lot of dead-end jobs, like bricklaying, and even after he and his brother Fred had started giving dance concerts in Pittsburgh, and he'd finally made his way to New York in 1937, he had to wait more than a year before he was finally offered a chorus dancer's job on a Mary Martin show, *Leave It to Me*. It was the next summer that he wound up in Westport—and he made a lot of friends at the Playhouse in a short time, witness the events that followed.

The first obvious result of *Magazine Page* in Kelly's life was that it sent him back to Broadway in short order. He spent the 1939–40 season at the Booth Theatre creating the role of Harry in the Theatre Guild's production of William Saroyan's play *The Time of Your Life*. (The lesson was that it never hurts to steal a show in a summer theatre when the owner of the theatre happens to be the head of the Theatre Guild, and when the Theatre Guild's executive director is also an habituée of that theatre.)

Which explains why Kelly was not slow to drop everything and dash up to Westport again when they put out an emergency call for him the following summer. It was 1940 and the Playhouse was doing Lynn Riggs's *Green Grow the Lilacs*, with music specially written by Bethell Long. Some choreography was needed in a hurry. John Haggott, John Ford's substitute director, ran Kelly to earth at the Ridgeway Theatre in White Plains where he was doing a summer musical called *Two Weeks with Pay*—which suddenly turned into at least one week with double pay.

Whether Richard Rodgers, who lived in Westport, first saw Gene Kelly in *Magazine Page* at the Playhouse or in *The Time of Your Life* on Broadway is not known—but Kelly's next engagement (other than a brief appearance in one of the Westport productions that followed *Lilacs*, O'Neill's *The Emperor Jones* with Paul Robeson)[17] was his first great starring role in the Broadway premiere of Rodgers's *Pal Joey* in the fall of 1940.

Gene Kelly in the 1940s.

that "first night reservations have been made by Edna Ferber, Joan Crawford, Grace Moore, Lily Pons, Fanny Hurst, Faith Baldwin, Eva Le Gallienne, Armina Marshall, Theresa Helburn, Arthur Bodansky, Cleon Throckmorton, . . . and many other people of prominence."[18] The opening night performance would be followed by a birthday bash in and around the theatre, and the *Westporter Herald* confided to its readers that "Mrs. Erwin Jennings is entertaining for dinner a party of fourteen" before the Children's Aid Benefit performance later in the week.

Ina Claire as Marion Froude in S. N. Behrman's *Biography* (1940). Eight years earlier, on Broadway, Claire had created the role of Froude, the celebrated artist who has lovers all over the world, but no husband.

And there was a lot to be excited about. The season began with Ina Claire as the portrait painter Marion Froude in S. N. Behrman's *Biography*, a role she had created on Broadway eight years before. Along with Philip Barry, Behrman was generally thought of as America's finest writer of stage comedies, and *Biography* had been acclaimed by the critics as his best—even Robert Garland had been moved to describe it as "adult and provocative . . . an evening of rare playgoing felicity."[19] And Ina Claire, "the svelte, blonde-haired, hazel-eyed beauty with the tipped-up nose and weak chin," who was returning to the Playhouse after a five year absence, was everyone's favorite comedienne—John Mason Brown would later call her "the Comic Spirit incarnate."[20]

Hot on the heels of Miss Claire came another great actress making a welcome return to Westport. Jane Cowl, now in her late fifties, was magnificent as Lady Cicely Waynefleet in Shaw's *Captain Brassbound's Conversion*. Opening night brought her an unexpected and joyous reunion, for in the audience was Bayard Veiller, the playwright who had written *Within the Law*. That was the play that had catapulted Cowl to fame in 1912. She had started out with the intention of becoming a journalist in Boston, but she had come under the influence of David Belasco and been persuaded by him that she should become an actress. Ten years later, with not a great deal to show for it, she had found in Mary Turner, the falsely imprisoned woman of *Within the Law*, the role of her dreams.

While these first two productions had been going on, a lot of frenetic activity had been taking place backstage. The season's third production, according to the posters, was due to be a revival of a play the Theatre Guild had put on in 1931. It hadn't caught on with the audience then, right at the bottom of the Depression, and it had only run for sixty-four performances. But Langner had liked Lynn Riggs's play *Green Grow the Lilacs*, and so had Terry Helburn. Where better to try it again than Westport, with a marquee director—John Ford, no less— and a young man who was becoming quite well known in films, John Wayne?

The frenzy had begun in the first week of July and was fully reported in the *Bridgeport Post*: "Mr. Wayne last week received an offer of $25,000 from a Hollywood studio to play one picture with Marlene Dietrich. John Haggott and John Cornell, operators of the Westport Country Playhouse, released Mr. Wayne from his contract. The play will be presented as scheduled, but another male lead will be engaged."[21] John Haggott later said that he released Wayne because the actor had made it clear he would honor the Westport contract (and turn down the film, which was *Seven Sinners*, directed by Joe Pasternak) if Haggott asked him to do so.

Ward Bond, the burly actor who was another John Ford favorite (and who would finally be made a star by television's *Wagon Train*) was engaged to take over the role—or, as *Variety* elegantly put it, "was billed for the heavy." But Bond, too, failed to show and the part was eventually played by Arthur Hunnicutt. The rest of the story was reported by Jeeter Fry in *Variety*: "Although John Ford had agreed to stage *Lilacs* here and was expected right up to opening night, he never appeared. Reached by phone several times by John Haggott, co-director of the Playhouse, he explained that he was detained by film commitments, but expected to get away in a day or two. Actual direction, which was generally praised, was handled by Haggott who explained he followed ideas he and Ford mapped out together in Hollywood last spring."[22]

Music for *Green Grow the Lilacs* had been specially written by Bethell Long—"lively old cowboy songs and the square sets at 'Old Man Peck's Party' had members of the audience jiggling their feet," wrote the *Norwalk Hour*.[23] There was also some pretty good choreography. The assistant stage manager for the production was twenty-six-year-old Elaine Anderson Scott, a Texan who was then married to the actor Zachary Scott (and later to John Steinbeck). Fifty years later, she still recalled the production vividly: "Johnny Haggott had found Gene Kelly, who was working around the neighborhood doing a summer musical called *Two Weeks with Pay* down at the Ridgeway Theatre in White Plains, to come up and stage some square dances for us. . . . Since John Ford hadn't showed up, Haggott directed, and it was a smashing evening. I was backstage, but naturally, being a Texan, I had to dance in the square dances!"[24]

And that, of course, wasn't the end of it. After the opening night performance Terry Helburn went backstage to congratulate the cast and crew, and (as Elaine Anderson Scott remembered) "I was there when it happened, and I remember, it was strictly *her* idea. She said to us all 'This would make a good musical'."[25] Getting Dick Rodgers to see the play wasn't difficult—after all, he lived in Fairfield. "He was called, and he came down, and he sat through *Green Grow the Lilacs*, and I was also there afterwards, at the discussion with Terry and Lawrence. Dick said 'Yes, it's a good idea'."[26] And that's how *Oklahoma!*, and an important page of theatre history, came to be written.

After all the excitement of *Green Grow the Lilacs*, the 1940 season continued more sedately with a revival of Mary Roberts Rinehart's much-loved mystery play, *The Bat*. Truth to tell, it caused more excitement among the Westport patrons than *Green Grow the Lilacs* had. Some of them had very likely

The Theatre Guild gave the world premiere of *Oklahoma!* in 1943, less than three years after Richard Rodgers saw *Green Grow the Lilacs* at Westport.

seen it during its record-breaking Broadway run twenty years before; many more of them would have known the Rinehart novel on which it was based, *The Circular Staircase*. And it featured yet another well loved actress, Claudia Morgan, who was returning to the Playhouse for the first time since she had appeared in Shaw's *Fanny's First Play* in 1936.

Next came the aristocracy of the theatre—first Ethel Barrymore as Sheridan's Lady Teazle in *The School for Scandal*, then Paul Robeson in the title role of O'Neill's *The Emperor Jones*. Both Barrymore and Robeson were familiar with their parts. Barrymore had played Lady Teazle twice before—once in the early 1920s with John Drew as Sir Peter, and again in 1932–33 when she had taken the play on an eighty-five-week coast-to-coast tour. This time, far from having to undertake an exhausting tour, Miss Barrymore was able to commute nightly from her home in Mamaroneck, New York. As for Robeson, he had first played Brutus Jones, O'Neill's former Pullman porter who sets himself up as a Caribbean dictator, as early as 1923 when the play was virtually unknown and sometimes still bore its earlier name, *The Silver Bullet*.

Paul Robeson in O'Neill's *The Emperor Jones* (1940).

Haila Stoddard wasn't an aristocrat of the theatre—she was only twenty-seven in 1940. She had already made her mark on Broadway when she succeeded Peggy Conklin as Ellen Murray in *Yes, My Darling Daughter* in the fall of 1937, but she wasn't too proud to spend her summers learning her trade the hard way—in stock companies. The summer of 1940 she was spending at the Bucks County Playhouse in New Hope, Pennsylvania, and it was one of their successful plays that she brought to Westport—Allan Scott's *Good-Bye Again*. In a way, it was an audition because it gave Lawrence and Armina Langner a chance to see her before she returned to Broadway to play Sister Susannah in their play *Susannah and the Elders* (it crashed on Broadway, but through no fault of Haila Stoddard's).

The season ended, as it had begun, with a Behrman play. Whereas *Biography* had belonged to the period when Behrman's writing had been strongly influenced by his left-wing views, which gave his comedies a particular bite and tension, *Serena Blandish*, based on an Enid Bagnold novel, was a straightforward comedy about a wide-eyed innocent in upper-class London. It had played successfully on Broadway in 1929; now it was revived with a young Viennese actress named Greta Maren in the lead.

It was typical of Lawrence Langner (and indicative of his real concerns in the hot summer of 1940) that the box-office take for the last week of the season was donated to the Allied Relief Fund to buy clothing, food and medicine for victims of the war in Europe.[27]

1941—TALLULAH AND TYRONE

With Lawrence Langner increasingly in Washington, the 1941 season saw Armina in control of the Playhouse for the first time, with Jack Wilson installed as her co-producer and partner. In addition, it was announced that Jose Ferrer and Richard Skinner, respectively star and producer of the hugely successful revival of *Charley's Aunt* on Broadway, would be "prominently associated with the theatre." The experienced Skinner, who had managed the Playhouse with Day Tuttle in 1937 and 1938, was appointed general manager.

Jack Wilson's first contribution was to deliver Tallulah Bankhead. She came hot-foot from

Broadway where she had enjoyed a long run and a major-league success in Lillian Hellman's *Little Foxes*. This would not be her first visit to the Playhouse, she informed the Westport press when they were invited to watch her rehearse in New York: "I sat in the right proscenium box of your theatre many times several seasons ago, you know, and I often wondered what the 'feel' of the Playhouse stage would be. And now I'm to find out for myself."[28] The visits to the theatre she referred to were in 1937 when she had come to see Dorothy Sayers's *Busman's Honeymoon*. The attraction was John Emery, one of the stars of that show. They had married six weeks later.[29]

The play Wilson and Bankhead selected for her was not exactly a difficult choice: it was one in which she had had a long run in London several seasons back—Jacques Deval's French farce, *Her Cardboard Lover*, substantially revised by P. G. Wodehouse. Robert Garland of the *World Telegram*, once again ignoring the unwritten convention that New York critics did not review summer stock productions (how Langner wished he would stay away!), pointed out that the play was severely dated. "Is it now such stale stuff? Sure it is, but what difference should that make to Tallulah? It has been a long time since she has been allowed to wear a coiffure that compliments her stunning blonde hair, or to display her ever-shapely figger [sic] in so becoming a negligee. . . ."[30] Mr. Garland, it seemed, was a fan, and so was all of Westport—there wasn't even standing room available.

A few weeks later, the Playhouse was once again besieged, this time for the visit of Tyrone Power and his wife, Annabella. They came to perform Ferenc Molnar's *Liliom*, a play that had done very well for the Theatre Guild in 1921—it had run for 300 performances with Joseph Schildkraut and Eva Le Gallienne (in 1945, of course, it would be the source for the musical *Carousel*).

In 1941, Tyrone Power was the Crown Prince of Hollywood —in his late twenties, dashingly handsome, and married to a very beautiful French woman. But he was much more than a pin-up: he was the latest (and, as it turned out, the last) in a long line of Irish actors who bore the name Tyrone Power. He had been born in Connecticut, and his earliest jobs in the entertainment business had been in summer stock in West Falmouth, Massachusetts. He had gone on to play Shakespeare in Chicago with his father. Now, eight years into his film career (he was under contract to Twentieth Century Fox), he was determined to get back on the stage whenever he could—and since he couldn't undertake extended runs, that meant summer stock. Darryl Zanuck, his boss at Twentieth Century Fox, had thwarted his first attempt in 1940, but in the summer of 1941 Tyrone and Annabella successfully escaped to Westport—or so they thought.

"I've wanted to come back to summer theatre," Tyrone told

Tallulah Bankhead opened the 1941 season in Her Cardboard Lover by Jacques Deval and P. G. Wodehouse. Lawrence Langner recalled that she arrived for rehearsals with a lion cub she had found in a circus in the wilds of Nevada.

On the opening night at the Playhouse, after romping around the stage in a particularly alluring negligée, Tallulah took her first curtain call alone. The next curtain call she appeared with the baby lion in her arms, her tawny hair picking up the color from his, or vice versa, but in any event making a pleasing picture of "actress and lion meet audience." Naturally, the curtain calls multiplied; for each call Tallulah displayed her lion in a more imaginative manner. Tallulah carried the lion on stage with her as she toured from one summer theatre to another, until by the end of the season the lion had grown almost as large as a St. Bernard and weighed over thirty pounds, and under these conditions he was led, not carried, to the footlights.

NEXT WEEK

Monday, July 16th through Saturday, July 21st

The Incomparable

TALLULAH BANKHEAD

in

"WELCOME DARLING'S"

A REVUE

with

JAMES KIRKWOOD

SHEILA SMITH   DON CRICHTON   BURNELL DIETSCH

and

THE MARTINS

Musical Direction by
PETER HOWARD &
TED GRAHAM

Settings and Lighting by
MARVIN REISS

the syndicated columnist Tom Wolf, "because it's relaxing and because it gives you a new perspective. Everyone has fun doing his work in stock. Here there's nothing of the huge, inhuman machine atmosphere that dominates Hollywood. And you get a chance to see yourself in better, truer perspective."[31]

Anabella explained why they had chosen *Liliom*. "It's a play that gives us each good parts; it's a play in which my accent doesn't matter; and mostly, because we both love it. Tyrone and I have been reading plays—old and new—for nearly two years and we came back to *Liliom* again and again."[32]

To judge by the local newspapers, everyone who was anyone in the world of New York showbiz (and a few who weren't) came out to Westport to see the Powers and to be photographed with them. On opening night, the *World Telegram* sent its drama editor, Frank Farrell, and he managed to find himself a vantage point in the wings where he could not only see the action and follow the script but could also monitor the backstage drama. Tyrone proved himself a real trouper, he reported, when, in the second scene of Act II, Eustace Wyatt, who was playing the magistrate, forgot his lines and got hopelessly lost. For about two minutes, Power and Wyatt gamely improvised, until Wyatt finally repeated the line at which he had departed from the text. "You just said that," Power ad libbed, and quickly led the grateful Wyatt into the next section of the script. As Farrell reported: "Not an indication of this did the audience have. I asked several persons on the first night list, which had more celebrated names than one would find at a Gilbert Miller premiere. They had no idea anything had gone wrong onstage."[33]

Aside from that, Farrell and the other critics thought it was a fine show (directed by Lee Strasberg) and that Tyrone and Anabella were both outstanding. The audience agreed: on opening night, the *Norwalk Hour* reported, the Powers took "a dozen-and-a-half curtain calls." But what the audience didn't know was that there had very nearly not been an opening night.

Tyrone Power and his wife, Annabella, during the run of *Liliom* at Westport (1941).

The weekend before the Monday opening, Power had received a cable from Twentieth Century Fox. They wanted him to pull out of the play and fly back to Hollywood at once for urgent reshoots on the film he had recently made with Betty Grable, *A Yank in the RAF*. It seemed that he had no option—his contract with Zanuck made it clear that the studio owned him body and soul. Nevertheless, Langner consulted the theatre's lawyer in Bridgeport, Ken Bradley (husband of Ina Bradley, who would become one of the most important forces in the Playhouse's affairs for the next fifty years). Bradley came up with a 300-year-old Connecticut Blue Law, which enabled the local authorities to prevent a man leaving the state if he tried to do so before fulfilling a contract. Langner asked the local sheriff to come to the Playhouse to make sure Power (who had no intention of leaving) stayed exactly where he was. Mr. Zanuck was thereupon informed by telephone that the forces of law and order in the great State of Connecticut stood ready to enforce the law. Zanuck caved.

In the end, of course, a compromise was crafted, but one that distinctly favored Westport. It was agreed that *Liliom* would be performed on the Monday and Tuesday, then Power would fly to Hollywood and back, causing performances for the remainder of the week to be cancelled—but he would return in time to reopen the production at the beginning of the next week and would then perform uninterrupted for two weeks. Despite the inconvenience to its box office and patrons who had booked tickets for later in the first week, the Playhouse gained two extra performances of a show that was sold out from start to finish.

By the time the 1941 Westport season ended with Jack Wilson directing one of America's truly great comediennes, sixty-one-year-old Grace George, in Laurence Eyre's *Mis' Nelly of N'Orleans*, both audience and management were well pleased. The season had included other highlights beside the visits of Tallulah and the Powers: there had been a seminal performance by the fifty-six-year-old American actress Mary Boland in Lynn Starling's *Meet the Wife*, a production of Offenbach's *La Belle Hélène*, and an Ivor Novello play—*Curtain Going Up!*—with Constance Collier and Violet Heming. Although nothing was said publicly, it seemed likely that the Playhouse was in profit for the season, and there was no reason to think the next few seasons would be any different.

By year's end, however, it was clear that there wouldn't be any more seasons in the immediate future.

Jack Wilson had a house in Fairfield, but the Langners knew him more as a professional colleague in the theatre than as a neighbor. In particular, they knew him as the manager of Noël Coward and the Lunts, and as a well-established theatrical producer who was uniquely well connected on both sides of the Atlantic.

Recalling the man he and Armina invited to be their partner at the Playhouse in 1941 (and who remained their partner there until May 1957), Lawrence Langner wrote: "Jack Wilson, tall and handsome, not only brought an air of distinction to our theatre, but his friends gave our playhouse a cachet enjoyed by no other summer theatre of its kind. Thanks to Jack, it was not unusual to meet at the Playhouse Noël Coward, Tallulah Bankhead, Terence Rattigan, Anita Loos, Pamela Brown, Bea Lillie. . . ."[34]

JOHN C. WILSON
1899–1961

As a manager, Wilson was no great shakes—in fact, Coward sometimes felt he was a disaster—but it turned out that he had real talents for producing and directing. Cole Porter's *Kiss Me Kate*, the premiere of which he directed on Broadway in 1948, was testimony to his abilities as a director, and the long list of plays and musicals he produced in New York and London (where he worked with H. M. Tennent Ltd.) leaves no doubt about his effectiveness as a producer and impresario. So far as the Westport Playhouse was concerned, he brought to it a lot of stars, he arranged for a lot of good and interesting plays to be tried out there, and he himself directed at least one play most seasons.

Wilson had been born in Trenton, New Jersey, and given an Ivy League upbringing—Andover and Yale. His interest in theatre was fed by Monty Woolley at Yale, and it was while he was a student that he came to know Thornton Wilder. But the career prospects lined up for him by his father were on Wall Street, not Broadway. Dutifully, he spent a few years selling securities for C. D. Barney & Co., but he stayed involved in amateur theatre and he never ceased to dream of making it his full-time career. He tried his luck writing screenplays; he worked briefly for Paramount; and he experienced London theatre for the first time during two trips to Europe.

It was while he was in London, on his way home to New York, that he met Noël Coward. They were both in their mid-twenties—the improbably handsome American with a passion for theatre, and the playwright who was enjoying his first success with a play of his own, *The Vortex*. Their meeting quickly led to a personal relationship that was illegal in the eyes of the law, and a professional relationship that would involve Wilson in managing virtually all Coward's interests and activities in the United States.

To begin with, Wilson's Wall Street firm did a good job of managing Coward's assets. The Crash found him fully invested in gilts and as immune as one could be from the chaos of the markets. In 1934 Coward joined Wilson and the Lunts in establishing a company called Trans-Atlantic Presentations, granting it exclusive rights to produce future Coward shows in the United States. *Point Valaine*, a Coward play that starred the Lunts, was the first of a long line of plays "presented by John C. Wilson." They included all Coward's American productions, most notably the celebrated *Private Lives* with Tallulah Bankhead in 1948, but there were a great many plays by other people, as well as Theatre Guild productions starring John Gielgud, the Lunts and most of the greatest stars of the day. Wilson quickly became an important producer on both sides of the Atlantic.

In 1937 he did something much more unexpected—he married Natasha Paley, the morganatic grand-daughter of Tsar Alexander II. She was a woman of stunning beauty, much celebrated by Cecil Beaton in pictures that "posed her against upturned bedsprings, her blonde hair scraped into a black hat and a bunch of freesias at her neck."[35] Coward was best man at the wedding and appears to have genuinely liked Natasha, to whom he was always very good. By this time, in any case, it was clear that the personal relationship between Coward and Wilson had changed. They continued doing business with each other for another fourteen years, and they collaborated on numerous productions. Wilson and Natasha regularly hosted Coward in Fairfield, and they accepted his winter invitations to join him in Jamaica, but Coward's diaries make it clear that the confidence and trust he had previously placed in Wilson's judgment was no longer always present. Most of all, he hated Wilson's increasing dependence on alcohol.

The last straw, in all probability, was Wilson's production of Coward's play *Home and Colonial* at Westport Country Playhouse in 1951. It was actually the world premiere production—under the title *Island Fling* and starring Claudette Colbert—and Coward genially cabled that he would sail the Atlantic to see it. Wilson told him not to come—quite why is not known since the production appears to have been very successful. At any rate, Coward assumed he had "bitched the play . . . and doesn't want me to see for myself." The next month—August 1951—he wrote to confirm the end of their association. They continued to meet occasionally, and Coward remained a family friend, but the closeness of the relationship, both professional and personal, was gone.

In an unpublished memoir, written in 1958, Wilson looked back on his association with the Playhouse: "My twelve summers spent at Westport have proved a valuable and rewarding experience, as has my subsequent association with the Langners."[36] From the Playhouse's point of view, they were even more valuable and rewarding, for not only did Wilson bring a succession of great stars to the little theatre but he also directed some very superior productions there—*Her Cardboard Lover* with Tallulah Bankhead (1941), *Angel Street* with Frances Lederer and Bramwell Fletcher (1946), Rattigan's *French Without Tears* and Otis Bigelow's *My Fair Lady* (both in 1947), Thornton Wilder and Armina Marshall in Wilder's *The Skin of Our Teeth* (1948), Claudia Morgan in *What About Maisie?* (1953), Anita Loos's *Darling, Darling* with Gypsy Rose Lee (1954), and several others—all with fine ensemble casts, all meticulously prepared, and all staged with the sort of panache that made summer stock, at its best, very good indeed.

Jack Wilson ceased to be a co-director of the Playhouse in May 1957, but he continued his association with the Langners and the Theatre Guild, and it was his production of Coward's *Fallen Angels* with Hermione Gingold and Carol Bruce (though he did not direct it himself) that was one of the crowning glories of the Langners' final season in 1958. Wilson died of heart failure in 1961.

Natasha Wilson, Lawrence Langner, Theresa Helburn, Armina Marshall, John C. Wilson and Tallulah Bankhead at Westport, 1941.

New York World-Telegram

NEW YORK, WEDNESDAY, JULY 18, 1934. (Copyright, 1934, by New York

Manhattan Summer

SEYMOUR

Lawrence Langner and (right) his famous playhouse at Westport, Conn.

CHAPTER SIX

1890–1962 Lawrence Langner

Very few people in Westport knew the reason Lawrence Langner was so often absent from the Playhouse in the summers of 1940 and 1941. In their wildest imaginings they would never have guessed that he was making frequent visits to the Department of Defense, that he sat on top secret Washington committees that included some of the most powerful men in the nation, and that he had even been known to have meetings at the White House.

Because people like to know where their neighbors' wealth comes from, some Westporters probably took the trouble to find out that Langner was a successful patent attorney in New York, but, for most of them, he was no more and no less than their genial, portly host at the Playhouse—a shy and diffident man on the surface, yet one who seemed to be on first name terms with every star who ever trod the theatre's boards, and with every famous personality who ever came visiting.

Though he neither sought nor received much credit for it, in 1940–41 Langner was already playing a crucial role in the United States' secret preparations for war. He had watched in agony—but with great pride—as his native country stood alone in the hot summer of 1940, and fought, and won, the Battle of Britain. Because he had traveled extensively in Germany throughout the inter-war years, he knew about some of the terrible things that were happening to his fellow Jews in Germany—and he had written passionate and angry letters to people (like George Bernard Shaw) who seemed to be misrepresenting them. He knew better than most that the United States could not, in the long run, remain neutral about Nazism, and he found a lot of people in Washington who agreed with him. That is why, in July 1940, President Roosevelt endorsed his plan to create a National Inventors Council, and why Langner was immediately asked to become its (unpaid) secretary.

The National Inventors Council's contribution to victory is one of those intangibles of the war years, something that is impossible to calculate or measure. Writing of it much later in a brief fragment of autobiography, Langner dismissed it in two sentences: "My efforts resulted in the formation of the National Inventors Council, under the chairmanship of Dr. Charles F. Kettering, which performed the job of examining inventions for the Army and Navy during World War II. During the period of the war, this council evaluated over 210,000 inventions and submitted over 11,000 files as including worthwhile suggestions to the war agencies."[1] This makes it sound a much more bureaucratic organization than it was. In many vital fields, reflecting the characters of its chairman and its secretary, it was proactive. It was largely responsible for introducing dry batteries that proved invaluable in tropical climes, gyroscopic stabilizers for tank turrets that made cannon fire from tanks more effective and more deadly than ever before and the Stiles-Hedden land mine detector that saved untold numbers of lives in every theatre of the war and contributed most greatly to the defeat of Rommel in the North African desert.[2] A much bigger example, which ultimately, of course, was given its own very secret organization, was brought to Langner's notice in 1940 when Dr. Vannevar

The first meeting of the National Inventors Council, 1940. Dr. Charles F. Kettering sits at the head of the table with Lawrence Langner standing to his left.

Bush, head of the National Research Council, showed him a letter President Roosevelt had sent him on June 14 of that year: "I noted in it," Langner later wrote, "the instruction to continue research in the field of fissionable uranium, indicating that from the very beginning Roosevelt was fully conscious of the importance of this research. This information, which I kept locked in my bosom, was a source of constant apprehension to me during the war, for I knew that the Germans were working on this fissionable material."[3]

THE MAKING OF A PATENT ATTORNEY

Langner had been born in Swansea, in South Wales, the son of a jewel merchant, but his parents had divorced when he was seven and his father had died very soon afterwards leaving the family poorly provided for. They moved to London, and Lawrence went to work at the age of thirteen after a perfunctory education. His first employment was as a clerk in a theatrical office (eight shillings a week). It was there that he met, and even spoke to, Ellen Terry, and then saw her on the stage, and it was there that he became stage-struck—a condition from which he never recovered. But his mother didn't think the theatrical milieu was good for him, and she soon had him working in a patent agent's office (ten shillings a week).

Just as he had loved his toy theatre as a boy, so now he fell in love with the real thing, but he was wise enough, even as a teenager, to know that theatre must—for now, at least—play a secondary role in his life. At seventeen he transferred to the foreign department of one of the biggest patent law firms in the world, Haseltine Lake & Co. (one pound a week), and he determined that he would take the exams of the British Chartered Institute of Patent Agents in order to become properly qualified in his own right. He took them in 1910 and placed first, thus assuring himself of fulfilling what had been his ulterior motive all along—a posting to Haseltine Lake's New York office. He arrived there in 1911 with a violent toothache, and immediately began work as a technical assistant ($18 a week).

In little more than two years he had left Haseltine Lake and established his own firm. For a twenty-three-year-old beginner with no formal education beyond eighth grade, and with only two years' residence in the United States, that was an enormous leap. Yet he did it with a great deal of confidence because his travels for Haseltine Lake had taken him to Dayton, Ohio, and introduced him to the most important inventor then living in America, Charles F. Kettering. Kettering had already invented the electric cash register, and he had now come up with something even more important—an electric self-starter for automobiles. He was looking for someone who could arrange patent protection for the starter in Europe. He took to Langner immediately and entrusted him with the project ($200 a week plus expenses), despite his youth. In business terms, Kettering was the most important contact Langner ever made, for he was a prolific inventor—he went on to patent the high compression automobile engine, fast-drying lacquer finishes, engine oil coolers, leaded gasoline and high octane fuels and variable speed transmissions. His name is most proudly remembered in the title of the Sloan-Kettering Institute for Cancer Research in New York City, of which he was a co-founder.

Initially the new firm consisted just of Langner and his younger brother Herbert (who had swiftly followed him across the Atlantic), together with a single clerk, but within a year or two it was joined by two of his friends from Haseltine Lake and became Langner, Parry, Card & Langner. Over the years it would be spectacularly successful with a client list that included Delco (Kettering's company), Duso, Diesel, Ethyl Gas, American Tobacco, Bethlehem Steel, General Foods, General Motors, IBM, General Electric, Coca Cola, Aluminum Company of America, and many more.

During World War I Langner acted as a munitions adviser to the U.S. Army, and he was on the spot, in Europe, when the continent got under way again after the war. So successful was his firm that, by 1920, he was able to arrange half-year status for himself, dividing his time evenly between his profession and his hobby, the theatre. Though he observed the strictest division between these two parts of his life—he never conducted theatre business from the firm's offices, and he never conducted the firm's business from his theatre office (he even used a pen name, "Basil Lawrence," for his early plays so as to avoid the risk of giving offence to business contacts who might happen to visit a theatre where one of them was playing)—he continued to keep himself abreast of the patent business and made sure his clients saw him frequently. This was particularly the case in the mid-1930s when he began to realize that what was happening in Germany would have important consequences far beyond Germany's borders. It was then that he conceived the idea of the National Inventors Council and began to gear up Charles Kettering and many of his other clients and business associates for the role they were going to have to play in it. It was, without doubt, the greatest service he did for his adopted country, and probably for his homeland as well.

THE THEATRE BUG

Lawrence caught the bug when he was very young, and his father was the one most responsible. Langner Sr. was a fiery man with a short fuse, and he was a great deal more than a jewel merchant: he was also a fine amateur musician, a keen cyclist and the proud owner of one of Swansea's first automobiles. Lawrence knew him for a very short time: the thing he remembered disliking about him was his insistence that he practice the cello, and the thing he liked most about him, and blessed him for all his life, was the gift of that toy theatre. In it, he staged performances of *The Sleeping Beauty, Cox and Box* and *The Corsican Brothers*, and it was also the place where he first let his imagination take hold and transport him into worlds far beyond his own. More than thirty-five years later, when he created his own theatre in Westport, he would instruct Cleon Throckmorton, the designer, to reproduce the red-and-gold decor of the original toy theatre.

Young Lawrence also had proof that the real theatre would be every bit as exciting as he thought. When he was six he was taken to a pantomime at Swansea's Wine Street Theatre, and afterwards his father took him backstage. He never forgot the thrill of it.

A few years later, in London, when he watched Ellen Terry as Portia in rehearsals of *The Merchant of Venice*, he was ready and willing to be captivated, and he was. In time, he would discover there were no limits to his interest in theatre, and very few limits to his ability to take part in

Helen Westley and José Ruben in The Washington Square Players' production of Lawrence Langner's play *Another Way Out*, 1916.

it—though acting, he learned, was never going to be part of his résumé: the first time he went on the stage was in the role of a "girl singer" while he was a blushing schoolboy, and the last time was in a production of one of Floyd Dell's plays at the Liberal Club in New York—Dell accused him of lacking "glamour."[4] But all other avenues were open to him—proprietor, producer, playwright, "play doctor" and even director.

The theatre bug became a lot worse when he settled in New York and became part of a group of young people that included the future columnist Walter Lippmann, the painter Robert Henri, the novelist Frank Waldo and "a wild-looking, highly educated young woman" called Theresa Helburn. The group would meet in the evenings for play readings. At this time, too, Langner began traveling in Europe, and it was in Berlin that he became acquainted with—and very excited by—the productions of Max Reinhardt. Back in New York he decided that an "uptown" existence was not for him: he moved to Greenwich Village, joined the Liberal Club, and became first a friend, then a colleague, of real theatre people like Susan Glaspell and her husband George Cram Cook, Edna St. Vincent Millay, Zoë Atkins, Eugene O'Neill and Theodore Dreiser.

It was with these and other Liberal Club members that he formed the Washington Square Players in February 1915—a troupe whose manifesto portentously announced that it intended to promote "the birth and healthy growth of an artistic theatre in this country" based on "ability and the absence of purely commercial considerations." In their two years of existence before America's entry into World War I shut them down, the Players performed sixty-two one-act plays, several of them by O'Neill, Glaspell and Dreiser, and one or two by Lawrence Langner, including the very first play they ever performed, which was called *Licensed* and would have featured Theresa Helburn in the role of a young woman who discovers she is pregnant on her wedding day, had not her parents made her withdraw because they thought the play immoral. The Players performed at the Bandbox Theatre on Fifty-seventh Street; they included in their casts a number of very talented actors, including Katharine Cornell, who made her stage debut with the Players; and they mounted two nationwide tours. It was a serious enterprise by serious people who were *very* serious about creating an alternative to the commercial theatre.

Even while all this was going on, Langner was aggressively growing his international patent business, constantly traveling in Europe and the United States. He was in Berlin at the outbreak of war in 1914, and he would be in Europe again as soon as it was over in 1918. He went regularly to

Chicago on business, spending evenings with a group of theatrical and literary personalities who would have been part of the Greenwich Village/Liberal Club "gang" had they lived in New York—people like Ben Hecht, Sherwood Anderson and the writers associated with the *Little Review*. Back in New York he somehow found time to start the Washington Square Bookshop with Charles and Albert Boni—a Greenwich Village landmark that lasted many years—and he took an enthusiastic interest (but no active part) in the Provincetown Playhouse, a summer theatre that was founded on Cape Cod in 1916 by some of his friends in the Village. The Provincetown Players very soon moved to New York and ceased to be just a summer theatre company. Indeed, they become a major force in American theatre and were responsible for staging many of O'Neill's early plays—including, in 1920, *The Emperor Jones*, which made its sensational debut with a curtain-raiser called *Matinata* by Lawrence Langner, a.k.a. Basil Lawrence.

FOUNDING FATHER OF THE GUILD

One day at the beginning of 1919 Langner ran into Helen Westley and Philip Moeller in the Brevoort, and "what started as a wake for the dear dead pre-war theatre turned into a 'borning-party' for the Theatre Guild."[5] Within a few weeks a declaration of policy had been drawn up, 135 subscribers had been signed up, and $500 had been put up—by Lawrence Langner. Otto Kahn made the Garrick Theatre available, and the Theatre Guild began its life with a play that perfectly represented its policy of putting on works that were beyond the ken of New York's commercial theatre. *Bonds of Interest* was translated from the original Spanish of Jacinto Benavente (who would win a Nobel Prize for Literature in 1922) and it was given a fine production. Trouble was, the critics didn't much like the play, and the public didn't much want to see it. Langner continued to put up $500 a week for four weeks, until Maurice Wertheim attended a performance and agreed to help out with the funds. Luckily, Langner quickly found, in Brentano's bookshop, a play by a man he had once known in London, St. John Ervine. Mr. Ervine waived his right to an advance payment and *John Ferguson* turned out to be a most unlikely and surprising hit, and it set the Theatre Guild on its way.

Administratively, the first important action the directors took was to invite Theresa Helburn to become executive director. At thirty-two, she was three years older than Langner, and her arrival at the Guild marked the beginning of a long partnership between the two of them, lasting right up to Helburn's death thirty-eight years later. Perhaps it would be more accurate to describe them as co-conspirators rather than partners, for they were as likely to join forces against recalcitrant Guild directors as they were to form a two-pronged attack on a playwright who was reluctant to cut a few minutes out of his latest play. For both of them, it was the most important professional relationship of their lives.

The patent business had made Langner a relatively rich man, but not rich enough to support the Theatre Guild indefinitely. Although it was often referred to as "an art theatre," it was still very definitely a commercial enterprise—it was always dependent on its own box office. Certainly, it endured a number of financial crises, and there were times when its directors had to bail it out with temporary loans, but for a lot of the time it did very well and made profits (though never huge ones, except in the case of *Oklahoma!*). As early as 1925 it was able to build its own theatre right in the middle of New York's theatre district, in head to head competition with the Shuberts and all the other Broadway producers. By 1930 the original subscriber list of 135 had grown to 35,000 in the New York area and 45,000 nationwide.[6] And this had been achieved by sticking to the prescription that had been drafted in 1919—"to produce plays of artistic merit not ordinarily produced by the commercial managers"—and by producing them under the same rules and regulations (and therefore with the same costs) as other commercial producers. The only exception was a small but important one with Actors' Equity. Because the Guild was the first theatre organization to recognize Equity and to abide by its rules, for seventy-five years it was given the exceptional privilege of not having to post a bond for each of its productions.

For the first twenty years of its existence—at least until the 1939 season when it presented Katharine Hepburn in *The Philadelphia Story*, and maybe beyond into the 1943 season when it first staged *Oklahoma!*—the Guild was genuinely a revolutionary organization and its prestige was enormous. It brought to American theatre a dimension that had been missing—meticulous productions of the best of European theatre, old and new, along with premieres of new plays by easily the finest generation of American playwrights that had yet appeared—O'Neill, Elmer Rice, Robert E. Sherwood, Philip Barry, S. N. Behrman and several others. It presented a succession of challenging, demanding plays such as this country had not seen before, and Lawrence Langner's association with it gave him a unique position in the world of theatre.

In 1958 John Gassner, the Sterling Professor of Dramatic Writing and Literature at Yale, who had been the Guild's all-important play-reader from 1929 until 1944, concluded a review of the Guild's history up to that moment by remarking that it had now (in the 1950s) become customary among the young to regard the Theatre Guild as a bastion of conservatism: "The Guild ceased to be revolutionary because its cause had triumphed. Largely as a result of the example set by the Theatre Guild, Broadway managements became hospitable to plays of intellectual caliber and unconventional dramaturgy. It became possible to produce any kind of drama in New York. In time, the gap between a typical 'Guild play' and a typical 'Broadway play' became narrower and in the case of literate and sophisticated comedy, often imperceptible."[7]

Lawrence Langner lecturing on Elizabethan Theatre to apprentices, 1952. He was largely responsible for the creation of the Shakespeare Festival Theatre and Academy at Stratford, Connecticut, in 1955.

By then Langner had long settled for the fact that the Guild had lost its revolutionary zeal, and he was not sorry for it because he knew it had been a job well done. In the 1950s theatrical experimentation had returned to Off-Broadway from whence it had come at the time of the Theatre Guild's interference in New York's theatre scene (for that was how the commercial producers saw it). Of the original directors, only Langner and Helburn remained, and they were content to see the Guild pay the penalty for its large and increasingly conservative subscription list—a steady move toward more commercial productions.

In the early years Langner and Helburn had normally been seen as the conciliators among their fellow directors, but that disguised the fact that they held very strong views of their own. That, more than anything else, was why Langner needed the Westport Playhouse in the early 1930s—not just as a place where he could do the plays he wanted to do without having to apply for permission to his co-directors, but also because he needed somewhere to experiment. He told Helburn: "All my [patent] clients have research departments to develop new products. The summer theatre must serve the same function for new plays and for playwrights, for actors and technicians, for directors and stage designers."[8]

THE ART OF MIDWIFERY

In an age before e-mail and cell phones, Langner was the ultimate "multi-tasker." When he came to write his autobiography, *The Magic Curtain*, he subtitled it *The Story of a Life in Two Fields, Theatre and Invention*. But the multi-tasking went much further than that: his powers of concentration were phenomenal. When he was reading or writing he was capable of shutting out everything else—Armina once said: "When I wanted to tell him something I'd yell and stamp my feet, but nothing could penetrate when he was deep in thought or work on a project. Finally, when he was finished, he'd look up and ask: 'What did you say?' He had learned to concentrate when studying patent law while working as a novice in England. He could shut off everything else from his consciousness."[9] Writing a profile of him for the *New Yorker* in 1949, Robert Rice observed: "Perhaps it is Langner's absorption in something else at times when another man would be giving his full attention to ordering dinner, discussing the weather or tying his shoelaces that has enabled him to carry out his formidable dual program of law and theatre without visible strain. He has spent most of his life thinking furiously, and by now his power of concentration is extraordinarily developed."[10] It was this power to "think furiously" and to concentrate tremendously that enabled Langner to do so many things so productively.

Nevertheless, his form of multi-tasking, unlike that often espoused by a younger generation, recognized that there was a difference between doing a number of things one at a time and trying to do them all at once. It was while he was attempting to do the latter—demonstrating the beauties of the Elizabethan stage whilst driving a car—that he came to grief. The car accident wasn't serious, but he never drove a car again—whereas he spent a great deal of time extolling the Elizabethan stage.

Langner was a Jew, and he was immensely proud of it. The playwright S. N. Behrman, writing an affectionate eulogy shortly after his death, noted that this pride in his religion and his race "was implicit—a part of his mystical temperament. It was beyond ritual and it was beyond the necessity for assertion. It was simply part of him—an air that he breathed. But when this race and this religion were aspersed, the response was automatic and dignified and proud."[11]

By all accounts, Langner wasn't the easiest person to be around. He was a workaholic, a man who couldn't bear to have a free moment; he was absent minded to a remarkable degree, frequently failing to recall the names of even his oldest associates and acquaintances; he was rarely on time for an appointment because he refused to wear a watch; he drove colleagues (and most of all employees) crazy with his endless prevarications; and he could sometimes be dismissive of other people's ideas. Yet everyone recognized in him an altruism that was extraordinary—almost everything he did, he did for the theatre. He could also be extremely generous: when Richard Rodgers's wife showed him something she had invented, a "jonny mop," he wrote up the paperwork for her so that she could apply for a patent and sell it to Johnson & Johnson, which she did.[12]

It helped that he never needed much more than six hours' sleep a night, but it is nevertheless remarkable that he was able to juggle so many unrelated projects. In his patent firm he had very capable partners and colleagues, but he was always the key person, the one around whom the business revolved. At the National Inventors Council and the National Advisory Council to the Committee on Patents of the House of Representatives, to both of which he was secretary before and during the war, he accepted responsibility for oversight and management of a huge body of work, much of which was highly secret and all of which was extremely sensitive—yet he still managed to maintain his influence, and even to some extent his presence, at both the Theatre Guild and Westport. There was Terry Helburn at the Theatre Guild, of course, as hyperactive as he was himself and much more narrowly focused, and at Westport he increasingly looked for, and found, capable managers, of whom Martin Manulis was the archetype, but his fertile mind was forever coming up with new projects—a Negro Ballet Theatre, the Shakespeare Festival Theatre and Academy at Stratford, which he brought to fruition in 1955, and many more. In 1941 he admitted to an interviewer: "perhaps I have started too many things. My wife makes me count to twenty now before I leap."[13]

All this was "real world" activity. Yet the most fascinating side of the man was the other, entirely separate life he led—the life of the imagination. In all, he wrote some twenty plays, most of them original, a few of them adaptations of existing works in various languages. His most important writing partnership was with his wife, Armina, because it produced far and away the most successful play he was ever involved with as an author, *The Pursuit of Happiness* (the "bundling play"), but several of his other works had success, and he would always be able to look back on that fall season of 1933 when he had three plays running on Broadway simultaneously.

The first of his plays to be given a professional (or near-professional) production was the one-act *Licensed*, performed by the Washington Square Players in 1915 (the play in which Terry Helburn's parents refused to let her play the role of a woman who finds herself pregnant on her wedding day). It was probably no coincidence that he was at his most prolific in the 1920s, the time when he traveled the most. One of the ways in which he made the long train and boat trips productive was by writing plays, and it was something from which Westport would profit in the 1930s—every time an embarrassing gap appeared in the schedule, Lawrence would dip into his bottom drawer and bring out another play. The writing went on through the 1930s, though the husband-and-wife team found it harder and harder to work at it together and finally gave it up for the sake of the harmony of their marriage. But by that time it had brought in a nice little income (though none of it from the Theatre Guild, which had always had a very sensible rule that it would not produce works written by any of its own directors), and *The Pursuit of Happiness* would continue to pay royalties for many years to come.

Lawrence Langner knew so much about playwriting that he would never, by any stretch of the imagination, have described himself as a great playwright—he had read and studied far too many plays to entertain any such fantasies. Partly because he had read so many plays, good and bad, and

Westport
Country
Playhouse
Boston Post Road, Westport, Connecticut

PHOEBE FOSTER

in
A NEW COMEDY
by
LAWRENCE LANGNER
and
ARMINA MARSHALL
(Authors of
"The Pursuit of Happiness")

"FOR LOVE OR MONEY"

WITH

WILLIAM HARRIGAN   CAROL STONE
PERCY KILBRIDE   CLAIRE WOODBURY
LOUIS JEAN HEYDT   EDWARD MacNAMARA

STAGED BY
WORTHINGTON MINER
(Director of "REUNION IN VIENNA")

—ONE WEEK ONLY—
Mon., Aug. 27 - Sat., Sept. 1
Reserve by Phone Westport 5591

PRICES:—Eves. 50c to $2.00 plus tax. Wed. Mat. 50c to $1.50 plus tax.
Curtain — 2:30 and 8:45

partly because he had spent so many hours tackling these problems in his own plays, he understood the technical aspects of playwriting better than most producers—storytelling, structure, plot lines, dialogue. That is what made him such a good "play doctor," or midwife, and it helps to explain why he won, and retained, the confidence of some of the best playwrights of his time.

His relationships with Eugene O'Neill and George Bernard Shaw are fascinating examples of the intermingling of personal and professional friendship—and how hard it would have been to achieve the latter without the former. These relationships had little or nothing to do with Langner's expertise as a play doctor—he knew better than to try and tell those two men how to do their jobs! —but they had a great deal to do with the trust the playwrights reposed in him to be an honest and faithful producer, one who would always honor his word.

O'Neill, in particular, had reason to be grateful for a producer who could read a new play and recognize its potential at a time when other people—professionals where he was a mere amateur— were writing it off. That was certainly the case with *Strange Interlude*, which the directors of the Guild were very loathe to accept, having turned down much of O'Neill's earlier work. It was also the case with S. N. Behrman's *Second Man*, which the Guild's play-reader had formally rejected when Langner got hold of it and insisted that it be produced. It became the cornerstone of Behrman's career. In the case of Shaw, it was more a case of persuading a crotchety and difficult old man to allow his work to be produced in a place, Broadway, and in a country, the United States, for which he had no great esteem. But Shaw, the great Socialist, loved his royalty statements, and by the time he died it was estimated that he had earned $350,000 in fees from the Theatre Guild—almost exactly the same sum the Guild had lost on the production of his plays!

THE OPTIMIST

In any discussion of the creative side of Langner's life it is perhaps unfair to introduce his song poems, but they are a neat reflection of a man who often looked rather solemn in his photographs, but who was generally bubbling away with amusement or enthusiasm, or some other emotion, underneath. He wrote these song poems to celebrate a number of phenomena, as and when they occurred to him—things like "interior decorators" and "the joys of married life"—but there is one in particular that could well have been written at the beginning of the twenty-first century and would need comparatively little amendment to make it topical. It is called "The Air Is Busy (celebration of GE-Marconi wireless phone)," and it begins:

> *You can call up New York*
> *And hear all your friends talk*
> *On the new GE-Marconi*
> *Wireless phone that isn't "phoney."*
> *So don't travel alone,*
> *Take your wireless phone*
> *Wherever you roam:*
> *You can always call home*
> *For you talk through the air*
> *From almost anywhere.*

Such light-hearted scribblings were prone to happen at serious moments when he probably should have been thinking about other things. It is true that he carefully separated his theatre life from the patent and government work, but the two could get embarrassingly mixed up without warning. John C. Green, who was a colleague of Langner's on the National Inventors Council, remembered an incident when the two of them were visiting the Pentagon: "On entering, we were provided with passes to be surrendered on departure. When we were ready to leave, Lawrence couldn't find his pass. We stood at the guard's desk, with a line growing behind us, as Lawrence went through his overcoat, jacket, vest and trousers, divesting himself of old theatre programs, instructions to actors, scripts, drafts of proposed patents . . . everything but his pass. Finally, as the file grew and the line lengthened behind us, the exasperated guard said 'O, the hell with it! You can pass'."[14]

Domestically, he was a contented man. He had been married twice—the first marriage, to Estelle Roege in 1915, ended in divorce in 1923. It was then that he married Armina Marshall and enjoyed with her a partnership of almost forty years that brought them both great joy. Looking back on it in 1980, when she herself was eighty-three and Lawrence had been dead for eighteen years, Armina, a straight-shooting daughter of the West when it was still the Wild, Wild West, summed it up very frankly: "Our marriage was happy because Lawrence was married to someone else first. He was married to a perfectly charming woman and they lived in Greenwich Village where all kinds of wild things were going on. I, on the other hand, didn't know anything. I didn't know what a lesbian or a gay was: I was pure and square. I just loved the theatre so much, and he was exactly the kind of man who interested me because he was so different from anyone else I had ever met."[15] Their marriage was very much a working partnership, centered on the theatre where Armina had interlocking careers as an actress, a co-writer with her husband, an official of the Theatre Guild, a producer, an impresario and co-owner of the Westport Playhouse.

From the toy theatre in Swansea to having his name on a Broadway marquee—even to owning his own theatre for real—was quite a large step. So was the transformation from the boy who left school at thirteen to the man who shared some of Washington's most closely guarded secrets during the war. But then, Lawrence Langner lived in turbulent times. Born into the empire of Queen Victoria, he lived through two world wars and witnessed many of their appalling consequences in Europe. Then he lived his senior years against the backdrop of an unstable nuclear balance and the Cold War. Yet he never ceased to be an optimist. He was optimistic that the world's leaders would come to their senses, and he was optimistic that theatre—American theatre, in particular—would have an important role to play in the future civilizations of America and the world. He never ceased to make plans for his own little theatre in Westport. Writing about his friendship with George Bernard Shaw in 1951, he said: "With the development of a Westport Theatre Arts Center devoted to the playing of comedy, and the possible home of a Bernard Shaw Repertory Company, who knows what the future may bring forth?"[16]

Nowhere is this optimism better displayed than in a letter he wrote the day after Christmas 1962. It must have been on his mind for a long time, for the words to which it was effectively a riposte were written in October 1946. They were written by Eugene O'Neill on the fly sheet of the first edition of *The Iceman Cometh*, which he had dedicated to Langner:

"To Lawrence—What can I write after all these years in which we have tried to create a theatre? I can't write the truth that it's ten times more rotten than when we started—in so many ways. And we must live in that pipe dream—or die—(as I believe I've said in this play) Love remains (once in a while); friendship remains (and this is rare, too). The rest is ashes in the wind! Well, we have friendship, so what the hell! Gene, Oct '46."

So, on December 26, 1962, Langner sat down and wrote to the university librarian at Yale— because it was to that library that all his own papers had been left.[17]

Langnerlane, the farm in Weston purchased by the Langners in 1929–30, was the scene of a great deal of entertaining on behalf of both the Theatre Guild and the Playhouse.

Dear Mr. Babb:

These two copies of *The Iceman Cometh* written by Eugene O'Neill, and published by Random House, are unique. Both Lawrence Langner and Armina Marshall worked on the production of this play for New York City, and it was during this time that O'Neill felt quite pessimistic about the conditions of the theatre. I did not agree with his pessimism except to the extent that we had not developed sufficient good playwrights to take his place. However, there was a good crop coming up, and there still is.

I write these words in the year 1962, when many others are pessimistic about the American theatre. Pessimism and optimism are merely states of mind. Gene was usually pessimistic, but then he wanted the millennium to happen in the 1940s. I knew it would not happen and never expected it to happen. I knew things would go up and down, according as we had great writers to write the plays, and great actors and organizations to put them on the stage.

Gene expected the world to be better than it was—so did I, but I was glad that it was good enough to breed people such as Eugene O'Neill and the other wonderful playwrights of this period, such as Bernard Shaw. I was thankful and also optimistic in believing that such times will appear in the theatre again, and indeed, may be just around the corner.

Will you please place this letter in the book *The Iceman Cometh*, which was dedicated to me.

Thanking you, I remain,

Cordially yours,

Lawrence Langner

The letter has the unmistakable feel of valediction—a hopeful, optimistic man putting on record his true beliefs at the end.

He died suddenly that night.

A FRIENDSHIP AGAINST THE ODDS:
LAWRENCE LANGNER AND EUGENE O'NEILL

In the summer of 1917, with the Washington Square Players hoping to give the premiere of O'Neill's one-act play *In the Zone*, Langner traveled to Cape Cod to seek out the playwright and ask his permission. He found him living on the edge of the ocean in an abandoned coastguard station that was formerly the home of the writer Mabel Dodge. "The resounding surf, the background of a wrecked sailing ship, and the lithe, muscular body of O'Neill, his dark Irish eyes set deep in his sun-tanned face, made an appropriate O'Neill setting for my first meeting with our foremost playwright, with whose destiny my own was later linked for so many years."[18]

Portrait of Eugene O'Neill in 1921 by William Zorbach.

By the time of that meeting, Langner had already seen a number of O'Neill's one-act plays performed by the Provincetown Players, and he had begun to realize that this really might be America's great playwright in the making. The realization became certainty in 1920 when the Provincetown Players produced *Beyond the Horizon*, the bleak and unremitting story of two New England brothers. After that, as Langner later said, "his great plays crashed into the American theatre like giants crashing through an undergrowth of lesser plays."[19]

Langner's purpose throughout the 1920s was to persuade O'Neill to allow the Theatre Guild to be the producer—preferably the first producer—of all his major plays. It involved Langner, generally accompanied by Armina or Terry Helburn, in hundreds of hours of travel to Bermuda or Sea Island, Georgia—

or (after the war) to France, Washington State, California or Boston, in all of which the O'Neills lived for a time without ever finding a permanent home. Early on, it became clear that the two men liked each other and trusted each other, so it was by no means impossible that the Guild would be given the rights it sought. What turned out to be far harder for Langner was persuading his fellow directors that the plays were worthy of the Guild's time and effort. Even when it was finally agreed that the Guild would give the premieres of *Marco Millions* and *Strange Interlude* in 1927, one of the directors still wanted to take out all the "asides" which were such an integral part of *Strange Interlude*. Langner wrote: "I wanted to choke him, but restrained myself."[20]

Eugene O'Neill and Lawrence Langner

In the end, the Guild produced nine consecutive plays by O'Neill, all of them shepherded through the rehearsal and production process by Lawrence Langner and O'Neill himself. O'Neill was very private about his writing—only Carlotta, his wife, really knew what he was up to—but the Langners were generally let into the secret during the later stages of writing, or very soon after it was finished. Then it was a matter of guaranteeing the playwright sufficient rehearsal time for him to be certain he could go on working at the play alongside the director as it began to emerge on the stage.

Throughout these years O'Neill regarded the Theatre Guild as his spiritual home. This was so during the successes of *Strange Interlude* and *Mourning Becomes Electra* (both of them at Wagnerian length), as well as the comedy *Ah, Wilderness!* (with George M. Cohan), and even during the failure of *Days Without End*, when the New York critics predictably shied away from the play's strong religious connotations.

The friendship between Langner and O'Neill survived the long years during which O'Neill worked on what he intended to be an eleven-play cycle, *A Touch of the Poet*, and it survived the out-of-town failure of *Moon for the Misbegotten* in 1947. It even survived the onset of his crippling battle with Parkinson's disease (as he always referred to it: in actual fact, it may not have been

Parkinson's, but some variant).[21] But his illness meant he could no longer be present at rehearsals, and that, though not fatal to the plays, was a problem that was insurmountable. O'Neill had always enjoyed and excelled at the rehearsal process when one of his newborn plays was put on the stage for the first time, tested, tautened and very often shortened here and there to give it the necessary dramatic tension. He would allow no one else, however much he trusted them, to change a word.

The Iceman Cometh, which was dedicated to Langner, was a case in point. Even though it was quite successful in its original Theatre Guild production, Langner told O'Neill immediately after the first performance that *"The Iceman Cometh*, like [Shaw's] *St. Joan*, would never be properly presented until after the expiration of the copyright, when it might be possible to cut it. Gene smiled at me in his usual disarming way and said it would have to wait for just that. Later on I asked Gene if he would mark my copy of the play with the places where he would agree to cut and where he would not. It was astonishing to see how boldly he wrote the word 'No' in blue pencil against most of my proposed cuts and how tremulously he wrote his infrequent 'Yes'. Then he wrote on the front page of the manuscript: 'To Lawrence Langner, The Hell with your cuts! Eugene O'Neill.'"[22]

O'Neill's plays would certainly have been produced without Lawrence Langner, but they might have had to wait quite a long time. It is hard to imagine that he would have had the patience or forbearance to deal with New York's commercial theatre. By the time he died, in 1953, Broadway had changed for the better, and it had done so, in large part, because the Theatre Guild had prompted it to do so. Be that as it may, writing to Terry Helburn after the war, O'Neill put his relationship with the Guild (and therefore with Langner) in its proper perspective: "[*Mourning Becomes Electra* in 1931] was a splendid production—your high spot as a theatre, I think—a great Guild achievement against great odds—an event that was a high example of the combined acting, producing and writing art of the American theatre—so compelling that in the depths of the depression the tragic trilogy brought packed houses to the theatre in late afternoon for weeks at a six dollar top! And to me it is also a high spot. It did more than any other single play to win the Nobel Prize. . . . Well, all that belongs to the Guild, too. And whether people of this country give a damn about it or not—and they don't—it belongs to them."[23]

BEARDING "THE GENIUS" IN HIS DEN: LAWRENCE LANGNER AND GEORGE BERNARD SHAW

Writing in 1951, Lawrence Langner explained what must seem, to a twenty-first century audience, a baffling reliance on the plays of George Bernard Shaw during the early years of the Theatre Guild and the Westport Country Playhouse. In thirty years the Guild had presented thirteen of them; in twenty years the Playhouse had presented seven. Langner computed that these twenty productions had racked up a combined loss of $350,000. "But had it cost the Guild ten times that amount, it would have been more than worth it to us. Our presentation of his plays to American audiences gained us a following which benefited all the other writers whose plays we produced during this period. But more than that, we counted his plays amongst the most precious contributions to modern theatre, and in presenting them, we fulfilled one of our best reasons for existing."[24]

While no one other than Shaw himself (and he only mischievously) would seriously compare him with Shakespeare, there were a great many people in the first half of the twentieth century who thought he might be the closest the English theatre had yet come to producing another Shakespeare. Langner's rationalization was not out of kilter with respectable academic opinion at the time, though even he may have been unduly pessimistic about the ability of Shaw's plays to endure. "No writer for the theatre has affected his times as much as Shaw has done, and for this very reason, many of his plays have become obsolete because the social customs against which they were directed also have become obsolete."[25] That was an overly optimistic assessment of the future of such established customs as prostitution, religious hypocrisy, slum landlordism, profiteering and the other evils against which Shaw fulminated. Even a play that Langner argued (to Shaw himself) was already obsolete—*John Bull's Other Island*, written in 1904 about what was then called "the Irish Question"—was rendered relevant, if not topical, by events of the 1970s and subsequent decades. By and large, it is not the subject matter of the plays that has militated against them, so much as their style (a lot of debate, not much drama, very little characterization) and their length.

Langner's last visit to Ayot St. Lawrence in 1950. Shaw died later that year, aged 94.

In the 1920s, however, Shaw was still relatively uncharted territory in the United States. At the end of the nineteenth century, Richard Mansfield had starred in *Arms and the Man* and *The Devil's Disciple*, but there had been few, if any, performances of his other plays. Moreover, Shaw—as prolific as ever—was still writing.

In those days Broadway theatres had an 8:30 curtain time, and most of the "last trains" to the suburbs left between 11:30 and midnight. That was not enough time for an average Shaw play—unless "the Genius" (as Mrs. Shaw deprecatingly and lovingly referred to her husband) would agree to cuts. He wouldn't. When Armina pointed out to him that cut versions of Shakespeare were being successfully presented on radio, he replied "My dear girl, it's bad enough to do that to Shakespeare, but it's sacrilege to cut Shaw!"[26] Nevertheless, the Langners never stopped trying to get him to make cuts, and occasionally they were rewarded.

Lawrence's first sight of GBS was when he was fifteen and was given a ticket to one of Shaw's lectures. It was entitled "The Position of the Artist under Socialism." Shaw informed his audience that artists would be "capitalist millionaires" in a socialist society. "My income as a state dramatist," he said, "would be enormous." "And serve you right!" shouted a member of the audience.[27]

Instead, Shaw lived in a capitalist country—one that deplored and resented his attitude to World War I which he had made public in 1914 in a pamphlet, *Common Sense About the War*. For several years his plays were rarely, if ever, performed and he was, by his own admission, close to bankruptcy when the newly founded Theatre Guild approached him. He gave them a new play, as yet unperformed, called *Heartbreak House*, and it was the success of that play that not only rehabilitated Shaw but formed the basis of the Theatre Guild's reputation as an important force on Broadway. The play, with its Chekhovian overtones and what seemed to be its prediction that "this house without foundations" will once again run aground or blow itself up through lack of direction, touched a nerve in the post-war world (one that it quickly forgot about as the 1920s progressed). What it proved to Shaw, in the short term, was that the Theatre Guild was made up of serious people and had great potential for him—and that Lawrence Langner could be trusted. He came to this last conclusion despite the fact that photographs of the Guild production showed Captain Shotover clearly made up as the spitting image of Shaw himself—beard and all—and despite the fact that the actress playing Hesione Hushabye had blonde hair, not the "beautiful black hair" spoken of in the play. When Shaw demanded to know if they had changed the line (a capital offense) Langner came clean and said: "Well, not exactly. We just mumbled it—what would you have done?"[28]

What it came down to in the end was that they liked one another. As a result, between 1920 and 1935 all Shaw's new plays were given their world premieres in America by either the Theatre Guild or, in the case of *The Millionairess*, the Westport Playhouse. The only major exception was *The Apple Cart*, which began its life in London.

Over the years, Langner—sometimes accompanied by his wife, sometimes by Terry Helburn—met Shaw many times. They met at his London apartment, at his summer holiday house at Stresa on Lake Maggiore and at his country home at Ayot St. Lawrence. These meetings were clearly a source of joy to Shaw as much as to Langner. Their correspondence—increasingly unin-

"GBS and the Lunatic" at Stresa, Italy, in 1929.

hibited as the years went by—was easily able to absorb their disagreements. In 1938 it was even able to absorb Langner's fury, and the extreme hurt to his Jewish soul, when he read the first draft of Shaw's play *Geneva*, which was nothing like as condemnatory of Hitler and Mussolini as the facts—the known facts—required. "I do not believe that you will want future generations of Jew-baiters to quote you as part-authority for a program of torturing, starving, and driving to suicide of Jews all over the world. . . . [Y]ou justify Hitler as though he had merely opened his doors and allowed the Jews to depart. . . ."[29] Partly as a result of this outburst, Shaw made substantial changes to the third act of the play and somewhat changed the character of the play's protagonist, The Jew. *Geneva* was not produced by the Theatre Guild, nor was it produced in England, and it failed in a 1940 New York production by another organization.

Shortening and editing the plays was the constant refrain of the Langner-Shaw relationship. At the outset, at the time of *Heartbreak House*, Langner had been informed by Shaw's lawyer that cuts were never allowed, under any circumstances, and he was warned that Shaw had an amazing ability to find out exactly what went on in theatres, even as far away as Broadway. Once, he was told, he had denied an impresario permission to put on a play at a Fortieth Street theatre because he had been informed that the street was under repair (which it was). Much later Shaw told Langner that most of his information was derived from a lady admirer who attended performances of his plays in New York with a copy of the book on her lap. Shaw was informed by mail of the slightest deviation from the authorized text or the stage directions. He was presumably also informed of such phenomena as street repairs and (in one case) an impending presidential election—he sent instructions that *Heartbreak House* could not open until the 1920 election was over, apparently because he feared that election rallies and parades would be bad for the box office.[30]

Immediately after *Heartbreak House* Shaw gave the Guild another brand new and unperformed script. *Back to Methuselah*, he told Langner, was not only the best play ever written but also, very probably, the longest (it was really five plays in one and the Theatre Guild eventually presented it in three separate evenings). When Langner inquired about a contract he was told: "Don't bother about a contract. It isn't as if any other lunatic will want to produce *Back to Methuselah*."[31] The lunatic had the chutzpah to go back to the playwright a few weeks later and implore him to shorten *The Tragedy of the Elderly Gentleman*, which was the second of the five plays that made up the *Back to Methuselah* cycle. This time Langner conscripted Mrs. Shaw as his ally, and together, in a frontal attack, they persuaded the Genius to shorten the play by even more than had originally been hoped. But it didn't always work: when *St. Joan* was about to have its premiere in New York the Guild was so desperate to make some cuts that it persuaded Winifred Lenihan, who was playing Joan, to cable Shaw herself. He cabled back to her: THE GUILD IS SENDING ME TELEGRAMS IN YOUR NAME. PAY NO ATTENTION TO THEM. SHAW.[32]

Just as they had decided not to produce *Geneva* (but for very different reasons) the directors of the Guild decided to turn down Shaw's offer of *The Millionairess* in 1938. Langner, finding himself outvoted, made use of his ownership of the Westport Playhouse to stage the premiere there. Jessie Royce Landis played the millionairess, Epithania Fitzfassenden, and Westport had, by its local standards, a considerable success. Few people (certainly, few critics) agreed with Langner's assessment of the play—until Katharine Hepburn played the title role in the Theatre Guild's 1952 production. Then, overnight, *The Millionairess* became an accepted part of the Shaw canon.

Langner belonged to that generation of theatre-goers to which Shaw came, not as a long-winded preacher of social fables, but as a breath of fresh air. "Where Ibsen was solemn and dour," Langner wrote, "Shaw was humorous and gay. He destroyed with laughter where Ibsen had destroyed with tragedy. Shaw's major contribution was to provide a galaxy of brilliant theatrical experiences which both entertained and stimulated his audiences. His ideas flowed in an ebullient stream out of the theatre into the lives of the intelligent public of his day. Before his advent, the theatre of ideas was like a dreary church in which the congregation took itself so seriously that its influence was confined to a coterie which regarded itself as the custodian of modern thought."[33]

Shaw himself, of course, was never satisfied. In 1950, on his last visit to Ayot St. Lawrence (Shaw died later that year, aged ninety-four), Langner reminded him that, between them, the Theatre Guild and the Westport Playhouse had performed twenty of his plays.

"I've written fifty. Why don't you do the other thirty?" asked the Genius.

Armina Marshall was in her mid-twenties—a girl from Oklahoma with a dream of playing on Broadway—and the dream was fading fast. She had spent several weeks in New York, going from office to office in a fruitless search for a casting agent who might have something to offer her. With her money almost gone, she was becoming resigned to the long journey home and the admission that the dream was just that—a dream.

"Then I remembered a letter of introduction I had to Lawrence Langner, the head of the Theatre Guild. He was extremely nice to me. He explained that they were doing a play that had six nuns in it. It was a walk-on for $15 a week. When the casting director said that they already had six nuns, Lawrence said 'Put in a seventh.'"[34]

THE SEVENTH NUN: ARMINA MARSHALL LANGNER
1895–1991

The Oklahoma in which the Seventh Nun had been brought up was still a territory, not even a state. "My father was the sheriff, which was more important than being the mayor because he handled desperadoes. When we lived under the jail in Pawnee, he had a collection of guns. Every time he'd say 'Hand over your gun' he'd get another one. I slept with a gun under my pillow from age seven—and I could shoot straight."[35]

The sheriff's daughter somehow developed a passion for theatre. "Two plays used to come to our town. One was *Faust* and the other was *Uncle Tom's Cabin*. When I saw Little Eva join Uncle Tom in heaven after he was beaten to death and everyone cried, I said 'That's for me: I'm going to be Little Eva.'"[36] She started putting on plays in the barn—"We charged a penny for admission. I never had the slightest interest in anything but acting, and New York was the place to go."[37] The family moved to California where she finished high school, spent two years at UCLA, did some teaching to earn money, and played small parts in local theatres. Then it was time for New York and the Academy of Dramatic Arts.

Her family was bitterly opposed to a career in the theatre, especially if it was in New York. When he saw her off on the train, her father told her "Now listen, sister, don't get mixed up with any of those Jewish theatrical producers." A few years later, when she became Mrs. Lawrence Langner, she wired him: "Dear Papa, I've just married a lovely Jewish New York producer." By return came his reply: "You made your bed, now you lie in it."[38]

The play in which the Seventh Nun made her New York debut was *The Tidings Brought to Mary*, a Theatre Guild offering over the Christmas season of 1922. She and Lawrence were married in 1923, and it wasn't long before she was playing featured parts on Broadway, mostly (but not entirely) in Guild productions. In 1925, she was Germaine in *Merchants of Glory*, in 1927 Signora Ponza in Pirandello's mystery play, *Right You Are if You Think You Are*. In 1931 and 1932, she joined the repertory company for the summer seasons at the Westport Playhouse, and that brought her two roles on Broadway—Lona Hessel in Ibsen's *The Pillars of Society* and Dorine in Will Cotton's *The Bride the Sun Shines On*—as well as a national tour of *The Nobel Prize*. In 1935, another Westport transfer brought her back to Broadway in the controversial *If This Be Treason*, but after that she concentrated her career on producing and writing with her husband. He didn't want her going off on tour—or, as she recalled him putting it: "You go on the road and someone else will be in this house."[39] What acting she did thereafter was almost entirely at Westport, most notably opposite Thornton Wilder in his play *The Skin of Our Teeth* in 1948.

All this time, of course, she was regularly traveling with her husband, as well as writing seven plays with him (and enjoying the sensation of having her name in lights on Broadway marquees during the remarkable success of their play *The Pursuit of Happiness*). She was also beginning to take a bigger role in the management of first the Westport Playhouse and then the Theatre Guild, where she was the enormously successful director of the radio and television department that worked with U.S. Steel as its sponsor for sixteen years. When Lawrence died in 1962 she became Co-Director of the Theatre Guild as well as principal owner of the Westport Playhouse and director and trustee of the Shakespeare Festival Theatre and

Academy at Stratford, Connecticut. She died in 1991 at the age of ninety-six, having outlived her husband by more than twenty-eight years.

It was the combination of her Wild West upbringing with his Old World inclinations and manners—and their coming together in the electric atmosphere of New York—that made Lawrence and Armina's such a formidable and accomplished partnership. And typically, it was these opposite inclinations that led them to Westport in 1930: "Lawrence felt the Theatre Guild needed to do musicals, Shakespeare and Restoration comedy. He wanted to find a little theatre to do them in. I, being from the West, wanted land. I was playing summer stock in Darien, and I began looking at houses. I looked at fifty houses before we found one."[40]

Armina at the Playhouse's 25th
anniversary party, 1955.

CHAPTER SEVEN

1946–58 Happily Losing a Little Money

It was by no means certain the Playhouse would open again after the war. At the beginning of 1944 (which was about the time the success of Allied forces began to prompt thoughts of a post-war world), Lawrence Langner's secretary sent him a note:

> Reminder: Ask for a conference regarding Westport Country
> Playhouse which has been losing money steadily and which, in your
> opinion, should be wound up.
>   What will be the effect of this loss on your 1944 income?
>
>   K.S.

Certainly, the theatre was losing money during the war. Even though it was idle, there were still fixed charges to pay, and Langner had obtained permission to pay them out of his own pocket since the Playhouse bank account was empty.[1] It seems likely that the "reminder" of 1944 was prompted more by the wishful thinking of Langner's advisers and accountants than it was by his own intentions. He had always been careless of the way he lavished money on the Playhouse—he said that he treated it as an investment in his own education and enjoyment. In 1951, when his son Philip became general manager and Armina and Jack Wilson were at least as active in the theatre as he was himself, he wrote: "As long as I am in a minority [of the directorate] I believe it will continue to be solvent," and that was probably an accurate perception.[2]

CHESKA AND THE SUBSCRIPTION SCHEME

Something else had happened during the war years that suggested that Langner had every intention of reopening the theatre as soon as possible. He had begun conversations with another Westport resident, Francesca Braggiotti Lodge, about instituting a more thorough-going subscription system after the war. Mrs. Lodge, known as "Cheska" to her friends, was a dancer, choreographer and occasional actress who had run the Braggiotti-Denishawn dance studio in Boston with over a thousand pupils, and now had more than forty dance classes for private students in the New York–Connecticut region. One of the keys to her success was the innovative way in which she had expanded the traditional idea of subscription so that it became a sort of snowball, getting bigger and bigger the more you rolled it. Purely incidental was the fact that Cheska was married to John Davis Lodge, a glamorous film actor who was the grandson of Henry Cabot Lodge and the brother of Henry Cabot Lodge, Jr., both of them U.S. senators from Massachusetts.

The box office, 1951. Madison Myers (*left*) with Tatiana Gillette and Joanne Atkins.

Francesca Braggiotti Lodge rehearsing
A Midsummer Night's Dream for an
open-air dance recital in 1941. She is
Titania, and her daughter Lily, who
became an actress and frequently performed at the Playhouse in the 1950s,
is Puck.

Francesca Lodge in the late 1950s—
former First Lady of Connecticut, now
wife of the U.S. Ambassador to Spain.

In 1943, at the time of her meeting with the Langners, John Lodge was on active duty with the U.S. Navy and Cheska was continuing to run her dance business. Thirty years later she recalled the meeting in a note she wrote for the Playhouse playbill: "At this important meeting we discussed the reopening of the Playhouse—when?—how?, etc. . . . . We discussed a method I had devised with success for my many (over forty) private classes—*Subscription!* It worked with our dance school in Boston: could it work for the Westport Playhouse? Shall we try? We did! Lawrence and Armina gave a sensational lunch at the Longshore Club [in 1946], filling the head table with outstanding theatrical luminaries who gave us their support. We introduced the 'scheme' by representing each town in Fairfield County with a table headed by a sparkling personality as chairman (or should I say chairperson?) and each one in turn presented their committees."[3]

Of course, the Westport Playhouse had had a subscription scheme long before Cheska appeared on the scene—indeed, from its very inception—but the scheme she invented and ran was much more effective, for it consisted of committees of socially ambitious ladies, each of them representing a single town, and all of them competing frenetically for the honor of standing up at Cheska's annual luncheon to announce they had sold more subscriptions than any other town.

As the Playhouse's General Subscription Chairman, Cheska ran the scheme from what was (literally) the commanding height of Connecticut—the Governor's Mansion in Hartford. Her husband, who entered politics on his return from the war and served one term in the U.S. Congress representing Fairfield County, was elected governor in 1947. From the Mansion, Cheska oversaw her legion of committees, running a unique subscription scheme that effectively made a civic project out of a private enterprise. Nor was she above using incentives to encourage her ladies—in 1955, Mrs. James Cochrane of Westport won the prize (an all-expenses-paid winter trip for two to Jamaica) for bringing in the most subscriptions that year—seventy of them![4]

What Cheska's enterprise meant for Lawrence Langner and his colleagues was that, in each season of Cheska's chairmanship, 85–90 percent of the subscription was sold before the end of May—a very solid basis on which to begin box-office sales for the remaining seats.

Of course, it couldn't last. In itself, Cheska's departure for Madrid, where her husband was installed as U.S. Ambassador to Spain in 1955, did not slow the success of the scheme—her chosen successor, Ina Bradley, who had been the champion committee chairperson for several years, took her place and became a Playhouse institution in her own right for almost four decades—but outside influences had a deleterious effect, television being the most obvious of them. Nevertheless, as late as the 1980s the subscription scheme was still accounting for 35–40 percent of each season's capacity (in a house that had, by then, increased its seating capacity by more than half), and that was a remarkable testament to the system Cheska had invented and literally hundreds of Connecticut ladies had given their time and prestige to operate.

WASHING THE ELEPHANT

Visiting the Playhouse in the summer of 1949, Gordon Allison of the *New York Herald Tribune* observed that there was an ancient theatrical maxim that goes "If you want to know what it's like to wash an elephant, go find an elephant and wash it." That's what he was doing in Westport—he had got himself a small part ("eighteen words, and each one of them full of substance") in one of the plays and he had spent two weeks "discovering just how a summer theatre ticks." What he had discovered, chiefly, "was that summer theatre is a complicated operation and that people who do it regularly for a living have a supernatural energy and a reckless disregard for the nervous system." In short, he had found out that washing the elephant is very hard work indeed, and especially at

Westport because Lawrence Langner's theatre "is what's known as a 'prestige house.' It is efficiently operated and highly successful. Playwrights, directors, actors, technicians and apprentices want to be associated with it because it's a showcase. Consequently, the activity is greater."[5]

The new element was the apprentice system. Like much else that was good, it had been introduced to Westport by Martin Manulis, the managing director who was brought on board by Jack Wilson as soon as the theatre reopened in 1946. As producer, director, impresario and adminis-

trator, Manulis was the ideal person to run the theatre; he was young, energetic and a splendid manager of talent. He would only be at the Playhouse five years before television called and he went off to become CBS's star drama producer during the great years of "live" television drama, but they were the five years immediately after the war when, from small beginnings, he was able to devise an operating system that would be the Playhouse's model for seasons far into the future.

The apprentice system was not new—some summer theatres had used it before the war—but its introduction at Westport solved many of the problems that had seemed intractable in the 1930s. To begin with, of course, it gave the theatre a very cheap supply of labor—in a normal year, eight to twelve extra pairs of hands, in some years as many as twenty. They were expected to do anything and everything—and that, of course, was part of the joy of it for them: they got to experience many different aspects of theatre, and although there was no formal teaching element involved they probably learned more about the stage in twelve weeks than they did in all their college courses. They painted scenery, they scavenged for props, they helped shift scenes, they did walk-on parts (and sometimes small speaking parts), they acted as costume assistants, as assistant stage managers, as parking valets . . . best of all, perhaps, they got to do "showcase" performances of their own, many of which resulted in professional jobs in touring companies or, if they were very fortunate, on Broadway.

What everyone who has ever been an apprentice at Westport remembers most graphically are the hard work and the long hours. The flyer that was traditionally sent out early in the year called for young people (sixteen or older) who were prepared to work seven days a week throughout the season. "We are professionals who expect professional dedication from those apprentices accepted into the program," said the flyer, and it added: "For those questioning whether theatre is for them, this may give them the answer."[6] And for many, it did—it's no secret that, in any summer, there are apprentices who leave before the season is over, normally by "mutual agreement."

From that day to this, apprentices and interns have been the backbone of the Westport system. They have included people from all parts of the nation and as far afield as Pakistan, though a great many of them have come from Westport and the New York region. They have included people who have gone on to fame and fortune in the entertainment world—Stephen Sondheim, Tammy Grimes, Frank Perry, Sally Jessy Raphael, Christina Crawford. And they have included a great many more who have decided that, while "theatre *is* for them," the role they will play is backstage, or certainly beyond the reach of the spotlight.

If apprentices are the backbone of the system, then the local labor market is no less important. To this day Westport and its environs are full of people (of several generations, from grandparents to teenagers) who have spent summers at the Playhouse—ushering, helping in the box office, operating concession stands, parking cars, even managing the house. And they have done it all for precious little remuneration, if any.

As Gordon Allison found out for himself in that summer of 1949, the elephant takes a lot of washing, and it needs a small army of willing helpers to get it done.

BACK TO BUSINESS

With Jack Wilson and Lawrence and Armina Langner back in harness, and with Martin Manulis now added to the team, the Playhouse got straight back to work in the summer of 1946. It opened with a Sidney Howard play that had been a Theatre Guild premiere in 1924, *They Knew What They Wanted* (it was the play that was later made into the musical *The Most Happy Fella*). It was memorable in Westport annals because it brought to the Playhouse for the first time a woman who would become one of its pillars—as an actress, a director and a long-time Wilton resident. In the summer of 1946 June Havoc was twenty-nine years old and already a veteran of the entertainment industry—

June Havoc and Lawrence Langner going over the script of *Lysistrata '48*. Langner directed the play, which opened the 1948 season. It was a modern adaptation by Gilbert Seldes of Aristophanes' play *Lysistrata*, which is about a sex strike imposed by the women of Greece on their husbands in an attempt to get them to end the long-running Peloponnesian War.

like her sister, Gypsy Rose Lee, she had begun appearing in silent movies at the age of two! For all the great career that still lay ahead of her—on Broadway, in films and in television—the Westport audience laid claim to her in 1946, and it would not give up its claim until her final appearance on the Playhouse stage in 1983.

What was laughingly known as "the star dressing room" had some interesting occupants that summer. Miss Havoc was succeeded by the boy wonder from England—eighteen-year-old Roddy McDowall, already a film star for ten years and now making his stage debut as Roger in *Young Woodley*. Two weeks later came McDowall's antithesis—Dame May Whitty, in her eighty-first year—to play a supporting role in Emlyn Williams's gruesome play of criminal psychology, *Night Must Fall*. Then there was Thornton Wilder, the playwright, visiting Westport to play the Stage Manager in his 1938 play, *Our Town*—a role that would be taken, fifty-six years later, by Paul Newman in another Westport production that would go to Broadway and, eventually, be seen on nationwide television.

Other fine actors would use the star dressing room that summer of 1946—Bramwell Fletcher, Peggy Conklin and nineteen-year-old Patricia Neal, whose "Daisy Mae–style hot mama" in *The Devil Take a Whittler* got a lot of attention—but none of them would have quite the star power of the woman who arrived in August to play the Maude Adams/Helen Hayes role in J. M. Barrie's *What Every Woman Knows*. She was the oldest of the de Havilland sisters (Joan Fontaine was the younger one) and her name was Olivia. Like Lawrence Langner, her father had been a British patent attorney: he had practiced in Japan and had represented Langner's firm there. Olivia was paid $500 for a week's work on the stage of the Playhouse, but no one was left in any doubt that her most important piece of business that week took place in Lawrence and Armina's garden a few hours before the play opened on Monday night (see next page).

In retrospect, that summer of 1946 was a sort of miracle. It wasn't just that the Playhouse had reopened on time and apparently without missing a beat, and it wasn't just that ten plays had been presented, all of them with fine casts. More important for the future were the things that had taken place offstage—the establishment of Cheska's subscription scheme (she had also found time to make an appearance onstage in the production of Noël Coward's *Design for Living*), the arrival of the first apprentices and the leadership of Martin Manulis, which was probably more responsible than anything else for putting an end to Lawrence Langner's recurring thoughts about closing down the Playhouse. From henceforward, so far as he was concerned, it was there to stay!

The bride and groom are pictured between J. Kenneth Bradley, who officiated, and Lawrence Langner, who gave the bride in marriage.

The day Olivia de Havilland made her debut at the Playhouse—August 26, 1946—was a more than usually hectic day for the actress. That afternoon, at 12.30 p.m., she was married to the novelist and journalist Marcus Goodrich. The wedding ceremony took place on the island in the middle of the swimming pool at Langnerlane, the Westport property owned by Lawrence and Armina Langner. Immediately after the ceremony, the bride left for the Playhouse where she opened that evening in Barrie's *What Every Woman Knows*.

De Havilland was thirty and this was her first marriage. Goodrich was forty-eight and this was his fifth. The bride was given away by Lawrence Langner. He had been a friend of her late father, who, like Langner, was a patent attorney and had acted for Langner's firm in Japan. The ceremony was performed by the Rector of Christ and Holy Trinity Church, Westport, and the license was arranged (at twenty-four hours' notice) by Judge J. Kenneth Bradley. Escorted by Lawrence Langner, the bride crossed the bridge to the island to the strains of Mendelssohn's *Wedding March* played by a lady harpist from the *Oklahoma!* orchestra in New York, who had been brought to the farm on the back of a truck.

At her own request, the bride promised to "obey." She wore a paisley print dress of blue and rose figures on a white background, a large royal blue crownless hat trimmed with a matching blue veil and band of green velvet. She carried an old-fashioned nosegay of white hydrangea florets, tiny pink rosebuds and blue delphinium buds, tied with white satin streamers, and wore long white gloves and blue slippers. Her only ornaments were a triple strand of pearls, pearl earrings and her ruby and diamond engagement ring. Her wedding ring was a plain gold wedding band.

THE MANULIS YEARS

In the five years that Martin Manulis ran the theatre, the Playhouse season was gradually extended from ten to fourteen productions. In most seasons one or two of them were generally labeled "under the supervision of Lawrence Langner and Theresa Helburn"—that meant they were Theatre Guild tryouts and were headed for Broadway. The 1948 contract with the Guild, which was typical, guaranteed the Playhouse a budget of $6,815.84 for staging a tryout (which was a very good budget by Playhouse standards—and it would be higher if the production was to go on tour). More importantly, it guaranteed the Playhouse "a profit of $750 for the week's operation" out of what was then a maximum weekly gross at the box office of $7,987.35.[7]

The Manulis years were, on the whole, very good years. There were moments of tremendous triumph, like the success of William Inge's first play, *Come Back, Little Sheba*, which made Shirley Booth a great star on Broadway and eventually won both a Tony and an Oscar. And there were moments of insupportable sadness—like the death of Mary MacArthur, Helen Hayes's daughter, less than six weeks after they had played together on the Westport stage in *Good Housekeeping*.

There were moments of great tension, as when the Playhouse scheduled Arnold Schulman's play *My Fiddle Has Three Strings*, directed by Lee Strasberg, at a time when its star, J. Edward

Bromberg, the plump, wide-eyed Hungarian-American actor, had been blacklisted in the McCarthy witch-hunt. And there were moments of considerable pride, as when the theatre presented Winston Churchill's daughter, Sarah, in Philip Barry's *The Philadelphia Story*, the play in which Katharine Hepburn had first starred for the Theatre Guild in 1939.

There were a lot of return appearances—Eva Le Gallienne in *The Corn is Green*; Thornton Wilder in his own *The Skin of Our Teeth* (with Armina Marshall, making her last appearance on the stage); Tallulah Bankhead in Coward's *Private Lives* (directed by Martin Manulis); Ruth Gordon in *A Month in the Country*; Jessie Royce Landis in *Papa Is All*; June Havoc in three magnificent title roles—Belasco's Girl of the Golden West, Aristophanes' Lysistrata (updated to 1948 and directed by Lawrence Langner) and O'Neill's Anna Christie; and Jose Ferrer in Robert McEnroe's *The Silver Whistle*, which went on to have a great success on Broadway as well as a national tour, though the

The saddest picture in the Playhouse's archive. It shows Helen Hayes and her nineteen-year-old daughter, Mary MacArthur, during the week in 1949 when they played together in William McCleery's *Good Housekeeping*. Six weeks later, Mary died of polio.

Basil Rathbone and Meg Mundy, co-stars of Rattigan's *The Winslow Boy* (1950).

critics generally credited its success to Ferrer's acting talents rather than the quality of the play ("It ain't what you do, it's the way that you do it," commented William Hawkins in his review for the *World Telegram*). One actor appeared more than any other—in 1948 and 1949 E. G. Marshall was in four or five shows each season.

Just occasionally a play would make a return appearance. In 1947 the Playhouse brought back "the bundling play"—Lawrence and Armina's *The Pursuit of Happiness*, which had had so much success in 1933. This time it starred Alfred Drake, making an auspicious Westport debut, with Mary Hatcher.

Few people have had a greater influence on the Playhouse then Martin Manulis. He was managing director for only five seasons, 1946 through 1950, but they were the seasons immediately after World War II when the theatre was given the basic structures and mechanisms that enabled it to survive the remainder of the century, and beyond. He was responsible for introducing the apprentice system to Westport, and it was on his watch that the subscription scheme was created by Francesca Braggiotti Lodge and developed into such a powerful instrument by the Playhouse staff and its network of volunteers. He was also responsible for producing five highly successful summer seasons, each of which must rank among the best seasons ever produced at the Playhouse.

MARTIN MANULIS
BORN 1915

He arrived in Westport (with his wife, the beautiful actress Katherine Bard) as a relatively experienced producer and director in his early thirties. His introduction had been through John C. Wilson, for whom he had worked as head of production before the war, and for whom he continued to work while he was at Westport. Along with the Langners, Wilson was a co-director of the Playhouse.

Manulis had begun his career by managing small theatres in East Hampton and Gloucester, Massachusetts, and he had then served three and a half years in the U.S. Navy as a lieutenant in the ETO, for which he wrote and staged an all-sailor show that toured the South Pacific. But it was Jack Wilson who opened the doors for him and gave him the sort of assignments a young person in the theatre must have dreamed of. He directed *The Philadelphia Story* with Diana Barrymore, *Pygmalion* with Ruth Chatterton and *Twentieth Century* with Lenore Ulric. He was Wilson's assistant director on the original production of Coward's *Blithe Spirit*, and he was sole director of the celebrated 1947 Westport production of *Private Lives* that starred Tallulah Bankhead. He usually directed one or two plays a year at Westport, in addition to his duties as managing director—which meant, basically, running the theatre artistically and administratively.

When he left Westport at the end of 1950, it was to become a staff producer for CBS Television. He soon found himself producing shows like *Crime Photographer*, *The Best of Broadway* and *Climax!* It was on *Climax!* that he first worked with the director John Frankenheimer, and when he was appointed producer of *Playhouse 90* in 1956 he took Frankenheimer with him.

These were the high days of live television drama, and *Playhouse 90* was probably the most ambitious and celebrated exponent of it—a live 90-minute drama every week for three seasons, followed by another season of specials and reruns. Manulis produced it for the first two seasons, winning a series of Emmys and leaving the show eventually because he was simply too exhausted to go on. Among the famous titles were *Requiem for a Heavyweight* with Jack Palance; *Eloise* with Ethel Barrymore, Kay Thompson and Louis Jourdan; *The Miracle Worker* directed by Arthur Penn; *Charley's Aunt* with Jeanette MacDonald; *Without Incident* with Errol Flynn; and *The Eighty Yard Run* with Paul Newman and Joanne Woodward.

Doing live drama on television was about as terrifying as being on the receiving end of carpet bombing. Frankenheimer said it was like going from one catastrophe to another. And Bill Paley, CBS's owner, made it even more hazardous by ordering that advertisements should be bunched at the beginning and end of *Playhouse 90* presentations so that nothing would interrupt the action of the play. Yet these were the conditions under which some of the best television drama of all time was produced. Adrenalin was the fuel that made it happen, and it is incredible to think of someone producing a different play each week for two seasons. That is what Manulis did!

He went on to be head of production for Twentieth Century Fox Television and to run his own production company, for which his most famous and accomplished film was *The Days of Wine and Roses* (1963). Much later in his life, in the late 1980s, he briefly returned to the world of theatre as artistic director of the Ahmanson Theatre at the Music Center in Los Angeles, but he quickly concluded that that was an organization in need of someone younger than him (he was in his seventies by that time), so Westport remained his last significant adventure in live theatre.

His place of honor in entertainment history, which he will certainly have, will be as one of the princes of television drama in that brief, but spectacular, interval before videotape and electronic editing took the spontaneity and risk out of television drama. But the Westport Playhouse owes him a debt as well. He was the man who set it on its way after World War II and convinced Lawrence Langner that, far from closing it down, he should invest money in it so that it could be enlarged and modernized and made viable for what turned out to be the remainder of the twentieth century.

Martin Manulis and his wife, the actress Katherine Bard, at Westport in the late 1940s.

Brodkin was the Playhouse's resident set designer for four seasons immediately after World War II. These were the Manulis years when production standards at the Playhouse were about as high as they have ever been, and Brodkin was one of those who was most responsible for that state of affairs. He had come to Westport at the end of a five year stint in the U.S. Army during which he had produced a number of training films for the Signal Corps. Although he picked up his career where it had been broken off by the outbreak of war—as a theatrical set designer—theatre was no longer his long-term objective. He had been bitten by the film bug, and he increasingly saw television as the medium in which he would make his mark.

HERBERT BRODKIN
1912–90

Everyone who worked with Brodkin at Westport—actors, directors and especially the apprentices—benefited from the experience because he was more than just a very good designer: he was a man of the theatre who knew a great deal about production and direction as well as design. It was at Westport that he directed for the first time—including a production of *The Philadelphia Story* with Sarah Churchill. But it was inevitable that he would depart sooner or later for television, and his opportunity came in 1950 when he was hired as a set painter for Philco Theatre. Later that year he was promoted to set designer for CBS's *Charlie Wild, Private Detective*, and the next year he made the much more difficult step to become producer of the series. "I became a producer almost out of self defense," he later recalled. "We had to get a show on every week and no one really knew how to do that—so we just did it."[8]

From there, Brodkin's career blossomed. He quickly became one of television's most important drama producers on series like *The Alcoa Hour*, *Studio One*, *Playhouse 90*, *The Defenders*, *Brenner*, *Espionage* and *Shane*. Even series that sounded, for all the world, like typical commercial programming aimed at the mass market were often given, in Brodkin's hands, a serious core of content. *The Nurses* was one such series. It ran on CBS for three seasons in the early 1960s, and tackled (among many other issues) abortion, euthanasia, substance abuse among physicians and nurses, domestic violence, Nazi medical experiments on Jews, the impact of racism on successful African American professionals and parent rejection of babies born with disabilities. None of these were issues you would expect to see dealt with by commercial television at that time.

Herbert Brodkin.

Later in the 1960s, Brodkin and Robert Berger formed an independent company, Titus Productions, and made a number of groundbreaking programs for the networks—the 1978 mini-series *Holocaust*, *Skokie* (with Danny Kaye), *Pueblo*, *The Missiles of October*, *Sakharov* and (in 1987) *Mandela*. Few American television producers have a résumé as distinguished as that.

But Brodkin came to hate the medium of television. As early as the 1950s, he felt, it had given in to all the lowest common denominators associated with crass commercialism. "Largely, people have been trained by the networks to be morons," he said in a 1985 interview. "Instead of giving them anything good, the networks claim to be giving them what they want. They have reduced the audience's level of receptivity to a bunch of monkeys asking for the same peanuts. And they are the same organ grinders giving it to them."[9] Predictably, Brodkin was not much loved in the television industry. But he was greatly respected.

Wilder's first encounter with the Westport Country Playhouse was not a very happy one. It was in 1932 and he was already a famous novelist with a Pulitzer prize for *The Bridge of San Luis Rey*. He was also a playwright, but not, at that stage, a successful one. In 1917, when he was only twenty, he had written *The Trumpet Shall Sound*, a play about a Christ-like figure in New York. It had been staged by the American Laboratory Theatre in 1926, but not very successfully. His shorter, one-act plays, including *The Long Christmas Dinner,* were generally thought to be more promising.

THORNTON WILDER AT WESTPORT

Armina Marshall, Thornton Wilder and Betty Field in Wilder's *The Skin of Our Teeth* (1948)

Nevertheless, Thornton Wilder was a person of consequence in the American literary firmament and he was known to have ambitions in the theatre. He was also a considerable linguist. So in 1931–32 he was given parallel commissions that required him to translate and adapt foreign language plays—*Lucrèce* for Katharine Cornell, and Otto Indig's play *The Bride of Torozko* for Westport. He delivered both commissions, but the Indig play was deemed to need some further "bulking," and Wilder, who had an exploratory trip to Hollywood on his schedule, didn't have the time (nor perhaps the inclination) to do it. In the end, it was done by Lawrence Langner's sister-in-law, Ruth, and *The Bride of Torozko* was performed as part of the 1934 Westport season, with Jean Arthur and Sam Jaffe in the principal roles.

By the time Wilder and Westport got involved again he was a famous man of the theatre with two more Pulitzer prizes to his name, both of them for plays. *Our Town* had made its historic debut on Broadway in 1938, and Wilder had proved himself a formidable actor by standing in as the Stage Manager in early 1939 when Frank Craven was absent. He later took the play to several summer stock theatres, though they did not include Westport. The second Pulitzer winner—*The Skin of Our Teeth*, with Frederic March as Antrobus and Tallulah Bankhead as the maid, Sabina—had its premiere in 1942 and ran on Broadway for more than a year, at a time when Lieutenant Colonel Wilder was serving in his second world war (he had been a corporal in the Coast Guard in World War I).

These two plays, innovative and wildly unexpected in terms of what had happened, and was happening, in American drama, are the basis of Wilder's claim to greatness in the theatre. Not everyone has agreed—there were those like Harold Clurman on the political left who dismissed him as a sentimentalist—but posterity has had fewer doubts, about *Our Town*, at least. Westport has presented it twice—the first time, in 1946, with Wilder himself as the Stage Manager; the second time, in 2002, with Paul Newman leading a talented cast of his Westport neighbors in a production, directed by James Naughton, that went on to have a limited, and entirely sold-out, run on Broadway.

The Skin of Our Teeth, as groundbreaking in its day as *Our Town*, though it has traveled less well, was successful at Westport in 1948, with Wilder as Antrobus and Armina Marshall making what turned out to be her last appearance on the stage. But Westport has never staged Wilder's other major play—what started as *The Merchant of Yonkers* in 1938, became *The Matchmaker* in 1954, and was adapted into the musical *Hello, Dolly!* in 1964.

There were lots of other debuts—Basil Rathbone, Elaine Stritch, Robert Stack, Franchot Tone, Lillian Gish, Cornel Wilde (then hugely famous as Chopin in the film *A Song to Remember*) and the young Julie Harris, who appeared in a 1948 Actors Studio production of *Sundown Beach* directed by Elia Kazan. Gertrude Lawrence also came to Westport for the first time. In 1950 she brought Arthur Macrae's *Traveller's Joy* from the Cape Playhouse in Dennis where she was the resident star—in 1940 she had married the theatre's owner, Richard Aldrich. Sadly, she never came back to Westport: two years later, aged only fifty-four, she died while playing Anna in *The King and I*—one of the few really great stars for whom both New York's Broadway and London's West End darkened their marquees on the night of her death.

Martin Manulis (*right*) directs a 1949 rehearsal of *Western Wind*, with John Baragrey (*left*), Cornel Wilde, Patricia Knight and the author Charlotte Francis.

Not all debuts are either memorable in theatre history or even marginally successful. Westport witnessed one such in the summer of 1947. Philip Langner, Lawrence and Armina's son, had graduated from Yale in June. He was cast as The Pony Express Rider in *The Girl of the Golden West*. Terrified of forgetting his line ("Big hold-up down at the Forks. Ramirez is on the trail"), he managed to make his entrance on cue but forgot his saddlebags. He didn't do much better in a later scene with June Havoc—"She used to take my arm in an iron grip and drag me down to the footlights," he recalled.[10]

Literally hundreds of similar stories are told by former apprentices who took their first (and, in many cases, their last) faltering steps on stage at the Westport Playhouse. Unlike them, Philip Langner was an engineering graduate from Yale, and he had no designs on an acting career, but he would shortly play an important part in the theatre's governance and management.

THE BARN IS TOO SMALL

If the Westport Country Playhouse was anything to go by, inflation could be measured at very nearly 100 percent since 1931. In that year, you could buy a subscription for six performances in the front twelve rows of the orchestra for $10.00. In 1948 it was $19.80. In truth, the actual price was not a great issue—they could probably have doubled the cost of seats and still sold out—but Langner was determined that his theatre was to remain accessible to everyone, whether they were members of the Yacht Club or penniless college students. What was much more of an issue in the summer of 1948 was the size of the house. In 1931 capacity had been estimated at 499; since then, fire regulations and various small alterations had reduced it to 448. Langner determined it must be increased by at least 200.

Aside from some patching and necessary repairs, nothing of substance had been done to the barn since Cleon Throckmorton's makeover of 1931. Lawrence and Armina decided that the summer of 1949 was the right time to do something about it, and Armina wrote a blithely overstated memorandum to the Westport planning authorities:

> The costs have gone up so greatly that we cannot operate with a sufficient margin of profit with the expected increased expenses of the new season. We may, therefore, ultimately have to close down if we are not allowed to enlarge.[11]

The reference to "a sufficient margin of profit" is probably the first recorded mention of profit in connection with the Playhouse, though it seems likely that it had been (at the very least) covering its expenses since 1940. The threat to close down, of course, was pure blarney, but the Langners were right that the immediate post-war period was the time to tackle the question of enlargement. As early as the summer of 1947 Lawrence and his architect, Edwin Howard of Westport, had talked to an engineering consultant about the structural considerations that might be involved "in widening the main auditorium and removing certain column obstructions."[12] That particular project was quickly abandoned, but it was decided to do necessary work on the masonry and foundations in the spring of 1948. An estimate of $600 was reportedly exceeded by more than 400 percent.[13]

Nevertheless, Howard was given the go-ahead to proceed with plans to enlarge and remodel the auditorium. A Redding builder, Theodore Dachenhausen, was engaged, and in March/April 1949 the necessary work was done, with Philip Langner overseeing the project on his father's behalf. Working with an estimate of $16,635, he brought this one in under budget. The lower four boxes were removed, the orchestra seating area was substantially enlarged, and the theatre's capacity was increased by very nearly 50 percent to 675. Three years later, on a budget of "about $5,000," the balcony seating capacity was increased by another fifty.[14] Eventually, with the addition of various new benches and chairs, the theatre was said to be able to seat 798—but the official figure usually quoted was "just over 700."

Still there were the questions of air conditioning and heating. The theatre was officially advertised as "air cooled." What this meant was that there was a room in the basement with a heavy door to which, once or twice a week depending on how hot it was, the ice company delivered several 300-pound blocks of ice, each of them six feet high and two feet wide. Powerful fans whirred away above the ice and blew cold air through ducts into the auditorium. Lawrence Langner clearly didn't think that air conditioning was as urgent as increasing the theatre's seating capacity, and he hoped eventually to be able to install a "combined heating and air conditioning plant."[15] The air conditioning was added in 1958, virtually of necessity, but heating for the winter months was not yet a priority.

Various other building projects were contemplated at various times. One of them was the addition of a warehouse and a large studio, which Lawrence discussed with his son Philip in the summer of 1951. Though it came to nothing, it illustrates the expansionist feelings that Lawrence then harbored for the Playhouse. He saw it as a year-round rehearsal facility for the Theatre Guild, on the one hand, and for productions he himself might be interested in, on the other. In a letter to Philip in which he discussed the need for heating in such a facility, he bluntly stated the order of priorities: "It is definitely understood that I have the first call on the time of the studio for shows in which I am interested or the Theatre Guild is interested."[16]

The other expansion project, which did indeed come to fruition and which effectively

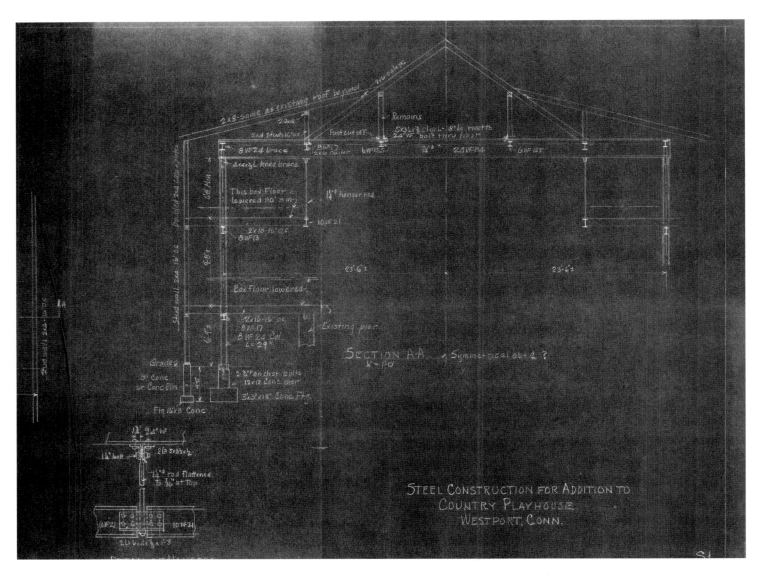

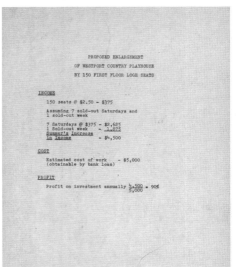

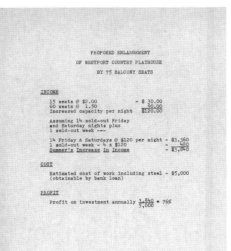

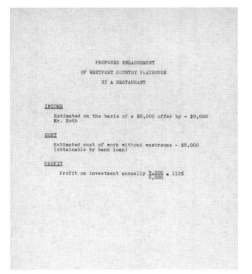

Blueprint for the Playhouse refurbishment, 1949.

After the refurbishment.

changed and upgraded the Playhouse as a facility, was the introduction of a restaurant adjacent to the theatre. The Player's Tavern opened in 1954 and proved to be a very popular addition—partly, perhaps, because a former apprentice named Tammy Grimes was installed as hostess at $20 a week (her stage debut at the Playhouse would happen two years later, in 1956, in *The Gimmick*).[17]

BY THE SEAT OF THEIR PANTS

With two hundred more seats to sell for every performance, the Playhouse's marketing was ramped up for the 1949 season. It came under the general direction of the theatre's press representative, Ralph Lycett, who not only looked after the Playhouse's publicity and media promotion but oversaw the subscription office as well. Since 1946 he had worked effectively with Cheska Lodge to organize her subscription drives, and in 1947 he had brought in a subscription manager—Lorraine Hansberry—who was to run that office for thirty-six years and who brought to it a gift for detail and caring that perfectly complemented the upfront approaches of Mrs. Lodge, and later Ina Bradley, with their committees of Connecticut ladies.

But this was summer stock. The theatre was shut down for eight months of every year, and it really wasn't until late in the winter that the Langners and Jack Wilson and Martin Manulis began to take soundings with other summer theatres and with leading producers, actors, directors and agents on both coasts. Even then, very little was certain. So running a subscription system was a bit of a nightmare—or it should have been.

Early in May a confident-sounding letter went out from the Playhouse's directors to the patrons. It told of unimaginably wonderful things that were going to happen on the theatre's stage that summer and asked them to renew their subscriptions immediately. Some of the promised happenings did take place, of course, but "truth in advertising" was not much of an issue. The 1949 letter was right about three shows—Helen Hayes in *Good Housekeeping*, Eva Le Gallienne and Richard Waring in *The Corn Is Green* and the George S. Kaufman musical show *Pretty Penny*. But the other stars it hinted were on their way ("have expressed interest and may come to Westport") were "no-shows"—among them Louis Jourdan, William Bendix, Boris Karloff, Sir Cedric Hardwicke, Bert Lahr, Groucho Marx.[18]

Caricature of Ralph Lycett. In the years immediately after World War II, Lycett was the influential director of marketing and press relations for the Playhouse, as well as heading up the subscription and box-office departments.

It didn't seem to matter. The patrons of the Country Playhouse had cottoned on years before to the way it was done—and they'd also discovered that what was delivered (however late in the day) was almost always as good as, if not better than, the promises of early May. No one told them in 1949 that Ruth Gordon was coming back, or Elaine Stritch and Kenny Delmar, or Sarah Churchill, or E. G. Marshall. But they subscribed in faith, and their faith was amply rewarded.

Nevertheless, it was often scary for the management, and in 1948 it was thought politic to add another pair of hands. Paul Crabtree, who was a budding playwright, actor and manager, and a protégé of the Theatre Guild, was appointed associate director and stayed two years before going on to run the Famous Actors Playhouse in East Rochester. One of Crabtree's own plays, *A Story for Sunday Evening*, was produced in 1949, with Cloris Leachman in the cast, but the announcement of his appointment the previous year had said only that he would "direct and act in some of the Theatre Guild tryouts."

Tryouts were very important to the Playhouse. By 1950 twenty-five brand new plays had begun their lives at Westport, and a great many more had had important revivals inaugurated at Westport in preparation for a Broadway run or a national tour.[19] Both Lawrence Langner and Theresa Helburn, the executive director of the Guild, had every intention that this use of Westport as a tryout theatre and laboratory should continue. But there was an annoying impediment that had to be removed. Robert Garland continued to come up to Westport each summer to review plays in defiance of the convention that the New York press did not subject summer stock productions to Broadway-style criticism. He had now moved from the *World Telegram* to the *New York Journal-American*, and it was there that Lawrence Langner addressed a revealing letter to him in the summer of 1949:

> We get a lot of fun out of running our theatre at Westport, where we are free to use it as an incubator to give youngsters a chance to try out plays, or others who wish to experiment. They use the theatre, knowing that what they are doing is not for the great theatre-going public of New York, and, in fact, catching them at Westport is really catching them with their pants down. Years ago, some critics criticized the tryouts in the New York papers, and it resulted in authors and play agents refusing to try out plays at Westport. They went some other place, fur-

ther away, like Skowhegan, and we had nothing but the dull, routine job of running a summer stock company, which we leased out to somebody else. We think that Westport is really an opportunity for some young playwrights to try out their wares, and, God knows, that's what the theatre needs, but they cannot do this in the full glare of New York publicity.

We are always happy to have you at the Playhouse, and I know you will appreciate our problem and cooperate with us. Thanks in anticipation.[20]

What sort of reception the letter got is not known, but the Theatre Guild tryouts went on, so authors and agents were clearly not frightened away again. Indeed, within a month of the letter being written the Playhouse staged two of the most important tryouts it ever staged—William Inge's *Come Back, Little Sheba* and the Johnny Mercer/Robert Dolan musical *Texas L'il Darlin'*, starring Elaine Stritch and Kenny Delmar. Just how important these tryouts were for the Playhouse was made clear in an article in the *Bridgeport Sunday Post* the following year: "*Come Back, Little Sheba* has more than justified, by its Broadway run, the $3,000 loss of the Westport tryout, and *Texas L'il Darlin*'s year on Broadway has justified the $6,000 loss encountered in its Westport launching." The article was based on a long interview with Lawrence Langner during which he told the reporter that the money he and Armina had made from the massive (and continuing) success of *The Pursuit of Happiness* (the so-called "bundling play"), following its staging by the Playhouse in 1933, had "paid for the building of the Westport Country Playhouse, with enough left over to finance last season's extensive alterations."[21]

Buddy Ebsen appeared in *The Male Animal* by Elliott Nugent and James Thurber in 1947. John Braithwaite, who was a 15-year-old usher that season, remembers: "Buddy was known for his tap dancing in Shirley Temple films (*above*). After the curtain came down on the first night, he returned carrying his brown and white tap shoes. He sat on the apron, put on his shoes, and tap danced for about ten minutes to the audience's happy applause."

And lest it be thought that Robert Garland had been banished from the Playhouse—or had decided to boycott it in the future—the *Bridgeport Post* noted that he was in the audience the following summer for the premiere of Lawrence Langner's own play, *The Life of the Party*.[22] This was a piece in which Langner, ever aware of the dangerous world around him, took satiric aim at Stalin's Soviet Union. It wasn't a great critical success with the reviewers. "Mr. Langner has succeeded in making the folks who bow to the Kremlin look stupid—perhaps too stupid," wrote Fred Russell in the *Bridgeport Post*.[23] *Variety* was even more dismissive: "[*The Life of the Party*] is a good title for a bad play, unhappily timed in these post-Korea weeks when Soviet Russia can't easily be taken any way but seriously."[24] Tallulah Bankhead, who was in the audience for several performances, laughed uproariously (the play's star, John Emery, was her former husband), but the audience, as a whole, seemed to share the opinion of the critics—Act II was noticeably harder to hear in the auditorium because of the sound of cars noisily departing the parking lot.[25]

Although no one knew it when the 1950 season ended, the Manulis years were over. He went off with Phillip Langner to Nassau in the Bahamas, where they planned to run a winter theatre season, and it was there, on December 15, 1950 (Philip remembers the date very precisely), that Manulis received the phone call that summoned him to CBS Television and the beginning of his storied career as a drama producer in the great days of live television. The decision was quickly made that Philip would succeed him at Westport.

Bill Inge was a Midwesterner from Kansas, a tall, shy man who made his living first as a teacher, then as an actor, and eventually, in 1943, as drama critic of the St. Louis *Star-Times*. It was in that capacity that he was sent to interview one of St. Louis's former inhabitants, Tennessee Williams, in the fall of 1944. They got along well—indeed, it was the beginning of a friendship. A few weeks later, Inge went to Chicago to see Williams's new play, *The Glass Menagerie*, which was trying out there on its historic road to Broadway. Aside from being very moved by Laurette Taylor's depiction of Amanda Wingfield, Inge learned something essential from the play, and he wrote about it in his (unpublished) journal:

> Tennessee had shown me a dynamic example of the connection between art and life. I could see, from what he had told me of his youth and family life, how he had converted the raw material of his life into drama. I had been wanting to write plays myself, but I had never known where to look for material. I always tried to write like Noël Coward, with each attempt an embarrassing failure. Now I knew where to look for a play—inside myself.[26]

The play he wrote was *Farther Off from Heaven*, a comedy based on his memories of his own family and relatives. He sent it to someone else he had met on that visit to Chicago—Margo Jones, who was then assisting in the direction of *The Glass Menagerie* and was now (in 1947) about to open her own arena the-

COME BACK, LITTLE SHEBA
1949

atre in Dallas. She read Inge's play and decided to make it her very first production in Dallas. Tennessee Williams, who was visiting Jones at the time, also read the play and sent it to his agent, Audrey Wood.

Though it was reasonably successful in the new theatre at Dallas, Miss Wood (who was Mrs. William Liebling of Westport, Connecticut, in real life) didn't think it would work on Broadway and

didn't pursue it.[27] But Inge, nothing daunted, and with Williams's strong support, wrote another play, *Come Back, Little Sheba*. Williams again sent it to Audrey Wood, with his own strong recommendation, and this time Miss Wood knew it was the real thing.

She took it to the Theatre Guild and had the good fortune to get it into the hands of Phyllis Anderson, who quickly became the play's most ardent champion. Lawrence Langner and Theresa Helburn were less sure, but they eventually agreed that the Guild should present the play at Westport as an add-on to the 1949 season—that is, in the week after Labor Day. If it worked there, then it would go to Broadway.

The portents were not good. The second week of September in 1949 was exceptionally cold throughout the Northeast and the actors found themselves rehearsing in a diabolically frigid theatre with no heating. The director, Daniel Mann, had a number of B film credits to his name in Hollywood, and he had spent time at the Actors Studio in New York, but he had done nothing of substance on Broadway. Both Audrey Wood and the Theatre Guild knew they would be taking something of a gamble on him.

The cast, on the other hand, was full of experience. Sidney Blackmer, who played Doc, had been on the New York stage since 1917—tall, dark and handsome, everyone's idea of a leading man—and he had done well in Hollywood, too, mostly as suave politicians and high-class crooks (often indistinguishable). But it was also true that in all his years of acting (he was fifty-four in 1949) he had never yet had a major hit. Shirley Booth, on the other hand, twelve years younger, was a real catch for the part of Lola, the slovenly housewife who spends so much time dreaming of Little Sheba, the cute little puppy who ran away from their home long ago, that she never seems to get her housework done. She had won a Tony Award in 1948 for her performance as Grace Woods, the secretary who talks back all the time in Fay Kanin's *Goodbye, My Fancy*, and before that she had come close to stealing shows like *The Philadelphia Story* (as the wisecracking photographer) and *My Sister Eileen* (as the would-be authoress). It was Langner's idea that she should be approached, but it was Audrey Wood who finally persuaded her to take the part.

In her memoirs, with remembered horror, Audrey Wood recalled the dress rehearsal in front of a papered audience of Westport businessmen and friendly locals—"never have I been so chilled as I was in that drafty auditorium"—but she also recalled the audience's reaction to the climactic scene when Doc, having come off the wagon and now in a drunken rage, threatens to kill his wife with a hatchet—"you couldn't hear a sound from anywhere in the drafty theatre. We knew: *Sheba* worked!"[28]

The local critics knew it, too. They loved the play, they thought well of the production, and they heaped praise on the cast. The *Norwalk Hour* predicted (accurately) that the role of Lola—"a wonderfully etched character drawing"—might bring Shirley Booth an Oscar, and it picked out Cloris Leachman and Lonny Chapman, the two younger co-stars, for particular praise.[29] The *Bridgeport Post* put the spotlight on Sidney Blackmer's performance—"he really shines in the third act when he comes home intoxicated. His portrayal of the role makes the scene gripping and exciting as in his drunken mind he thinks of all the things that might have been. He blames his wife for what is really his own weakness."[30]

Because Shirley Booth had a prior commitment, *Come Back, Little Sheba* could not open on Broadway until more than halfway through the 1949–50 season, but no one had any doubts about it there—Shirley Booth and Sidney Blackmer both won Tonys. Two years later, Shirley Booth won her Oscar for the film, but Blackmer was crassly overlooked by the producers—the part went to Burt Lancaster.

As for the original hero of *Come Back, Little Sheba*—the author, William Inge—he was spectacularly successful for almost a decade. He won a Pulitzer for *Picnic*, which starred Ralph Meeker, Peggy Conklin, Eileen Heckart and Paul Newman on Broadway in 1953. Two years later, he returned to his roots in Kansas for *Bus Stop*, which tells the story of a bus's enforced stopover during a blizzard: Cherie, a nightclub singer, gets swept off her feet by

Shirley Booth and Sidney Blackmer in William Inge's *Come Back, Little Sheba* (1949).

a randy cowboy named Bo, while the other passengers keep a critical eye on them. Harold Clurman directed the play on Broadway where it ran for almost 500 performances, but it was as a film that it was best known—because the role of Cherie was taken over by Marilyn Monroe in one of her finest performances.

The Dark at the Top of the Stairs (the rewrite of *Farther Off from Heaven*) was also successful in 1957, but thereafter Inge knew nothing but failure. It was as though the life he was drawing on—his own—had run out of steam; all it could do was repeat itself, and that was more or less what his later plays were doing.

Alcohol had been a problem for Inge during the production of *Sheba*, and depression was never far away.[31] Sadly, in 1973 he committed suicide—a major playwright of the Midwest who had a shining hour that was all too brief, but who nevertheless created four of the best and strongest dramas of twentieth century American theatre.

Philip Langner had been five years old when his parents purchased the old barn and made it into a theatre. He knew it intimately, and he knew his parents' ambitions for it. He had an engineering degree from Yale and had spent the summer of 1947 as an apprentice at Westport. He had gone on to receive a rigorous and highly practical training at the Theatre Guild, where he had been moved around from department to department, getting to know many different aspects of the profession, as well as working summers at the Playhouse. In the spring of 1951 he was about as well prepared as it was possible to be to run a summer stock company. And that is what he did between 1951 and 1958, spending eight months of the year with the Theatre Guild in New York or London, and four months at Westport, where he shared the management with Windsor Lewis, Peter Turgeon and Henry Weinstein, but mainly with Charles Bowden. Bowden, who was married to the actress Paula Laurence, had forsaken an acting career for the army, where he had risen to the rank of major, but he had returned to his roots the previous summer—as a stage manager at Westport. In 1951 he was named head of production.

1951: THE TWENTIETH ANNIVERSARY SEASON

The initial subscription flyer was, as usual, way over the top. Half of Hollywood was on its way to Westport, it seemed, and the season would include "an INTERNATIONAL DRAMA FESTIVAL featuring one each of the finest plays of BERNARD SHAW, EUGENE O'NEILL, JULES ROMAINS, PIRANDELLO, WILLIAM SHAKESPEARE and HENRIK IBSEN" (quite definite would be "THE MERCHANT OF VENICE" with BASIL RATHBONE as "SHYLOCK").[32] In the event, Mr. Rathbone, who had appeared at Westport in Rattigan's *The Winslow Boy* the previous summer, did not appear, nor did the plays of Messrs O'Neill, Romains, Pirandello, Shakespeare and Ibsen. There was, however, a double helping of Shaw.

For all that, it was a memorable season. Opening on June 4, earlier than ever before ("due to many hundreds of requests from our subscribers who would like their summer theatre-going to begin earlier"), it consisted of thirteen productions—and it would have been fourteen had not the world premiere of Noël Coward's *Island Fling* with Claudette Colbert been extended for a second week, causing a new play by Leon Stein, *Go, Catch a Falling Star*, to be cancelled at the last minute. No matter—Miss Colbert established a new box-office record of $12,403 in the first week, then bettered it with $12,819 in the unscheduled second week (with a top ticket price of $3.60).

Hugh Herbert's *For Love or Money* (1951) with nineteen-year-old Betsy von Furstenberg and the British star John Loder.

The black tie audience on the season's opening night included "the young stage, radio and television star" Grace Kelly. There were a great many late arrivals, for the curtain once again coincided with a cloudburst. Because of the machine-gun noise of the rain on the roof, those who managed to find their seats in time had the greatest difficulty in hearing any of the words in the first scene, and some of those who did manage to hear the words were not too pleased with them. Philip Barry's play *The Animal Kingdom* was a daring choice for opening night. It argued (in the words of the critic Brendan Gill) "that a man may be more truly married to his mistress than to his wife, and in that case an adulterous relation[ship] is more honorable than monogamy."³³ But before the press could wax too indignant at this assault on values doubtless held dear by Fairfield County's populace, Olivia de Havilland was on the boards once again, and there was nobody else to write about.

In contrast to the J. M. Barrie play in which she had appeared in 1946, de Havilland's vehicle this time was Shaw's *Candida*, and although the local reviewers gave her a slightly tepid reception (Helen Deegan's story in *The Stratford News* was slugged "Olivia Good as Candida, But She's Overshadowed by Cast"), the audience in the theatre just loved her—she was called back to take ovation after ovation.³⁴ The British star John Loder was next in, with Hugh Herbert's *For Love or Money*, and he, too, was somewhat overshadowed—in this case by the appearance of a nineteen-year-old ingénue called Betsy von Furstenberg.

Curiously, the stars of the next piece—which was the premiere of a romantic comedy by Robert Anderson called *Love Revisited*—had much the same experience: Richard Kendrick and Helen Claire were generally overwhelmed by the audience's obvious interest in Douglas Watson, who had lately played Romeo to Olivia de Havilland's Juliet on Broadway.

All of a sudden, on July 2, with virtually no warning to subscribers, a second Shaw play was on

Claudette Colbert and Edith Meiser in the world première of Noël Coward's *Island Fling* (1951).

the stage—this one a sixty-year-old work called *The Philanderer*. For whatever reason, it filled a week before *The Holly and the Ivy* came in. This was a play about a clergyman and his three children that had run for a full year in London. In Westport it bored the critics to distraction but got an enthusiastic reception from the audience. It was followed by a much tougher piece—Walt Anderson's *The Little Screwball*, which dealt with the Puerto Rican community in New York City. With what was, for summer stock, a huge cast of twenty-one, and with nine separate sets, it told the story of attempts by three different men to adopt a Puerto Rican boy in order to make him "legal" and therefore able to go to public school in New York. It got six curtain calls on opening night and even the critics were cautiously optimistic that it might have a future on Broadway.

And then, the Main Event. Jack Wilson, whose personal relationship with Noël Coward had long since run its course, had gone to London in the spring to talk with Coward (as the subscription flyer had put it) "regarding the possibility of world-premiering Mr. Coward's new comedy, *South Sea Bubble*, at Westport if a suitable star can be found for the leading role." Like many of Coward's works at this time, it had been written for Gertrude Lawrence, but she wasn't available and Coward was unwilling to wait until she was. Instead, Wilson persuaded Claudette Colbert to do it, and Coward approved. The role was that of Lady Shotter, wife of a British colonial governor, in a play (now retitled *Island Fling*) that was really a satirical jab at the efforts of Britain's post-war Socialist government to decolonize. But whatever else it was, it was a star vehicle and Colbert took full advantage of it. It was the first time since Tyrone Power's *Liliom* in 1941 that the Playhouse had extended a run beyond its advertised duration, and it used the pages of a cooperative local press to communicate with its subscribers about the necessary changes. All the world, it seemed, came to visit Colbert in her dressing room. Marlene Dietrich came, so did Charles Laughton, Danny Kaye,

Richard Rodgers and Otto Preminger, among others. After the final performance Colbert herself gave a supper for the theatre's staff and apprentices at Westport's Bantam restaurant.

By rights, it should have been downhill after that, especially since one of the remaining offerings, the season's only musical, was rumored to be in trouble both in rehearsal and during its first week on the stage in Clinton (the sort of trouble where the director insists that his name be removed from the credits). It was *Alice in Wonderland*, with music by John Charles Sacco and book by his wife, Frances Pole, but if it was in trouble, the Westport audience didn't seem to notice. The reviewers picked up most of the adjectives of the press release—"light-hearted," "tuneful," "delightful"—and heaped extravagant praise on the costumes.

But there were also some good strong plays with fine casts at the end of the season. Edward Mabley's *Glad Tidings* starred Melvyn Douglas, Signe Hasso and Joan Bennett and was directed by Haila Stoddard's husband, Harald Bromley. "Like champagne," said the *Greenwich Time*, "there's not a great deal of substance here, but it sure is fun."[35] Then came one of America's best known playwrights (and a New Canaan resident besides), S. N. Behrman, with a play that had been running in London for a year but had not yet been seen in the United States. Directed by Charles Bowden and starring Edna Best and James Lipton, *A Foreign Language* was based on W. Somerset Maugham's novel *Jane*, and it brought the critics back, rather uncomfortably, to the theme they had briefly touched on at the beginning of the season with *The Animal Kingdom*. Helen Deegan,

Edward Mabley's *Glad Tidings* (1951) with (*from the left*) Joan Bennett, Melvyn Douglas, Signe Hasso.

writing in the *Town Crier*, said she "couldn't care less" about the plot of Berhrman's comedy ("marital hedgehopping," she called it), though she allowed that the audience had enjoyed it a whole lot more than she had: "We find it difficult to join in the fun when the apparently accepted theme behind it all is that marriages are made to be broken."[36] Somewhat rewritten, and reverting to its original title, *Jane*, the play had a respectable run on Broadway that winter, winning high praise for Edna Best as the drab Liverpool woman who is transformed into an enchantress.

Finally came two new plays officially tagged as Broadway tryouts. Both of them were praised more for their casts than for their dramatic content. Philip Lewis's *A Case of Scotch* had two young stars with fast-growing reputations—John Forsythe and Margaret Phillips. Phillips was required to speak in a Scottish accent throughout the play—a test the reviewers agreed she passed with flying colors. Lawrence Riley's comedy *Kin Hubbard*, directed by Jack Wilson, boasted a quartet of fine American actors—Tom Ewell, Josephine Hull, John Alexander and June Lockhart—and was based on the life of Frank McKinney Hubbard, "our country's foremost cracker-barrel philosopher." June Lockhart, playing Hubbard's wife, Tiny, had the challenging experience of playing the opening night in front of the lady she portrayed, Hubbard's widow, who was present in the audience. Like Margaret Phillips before her, Lockhart passed the critics' test—one of them, clearly smitten, described her as gracing the stage "with a winning person, charm, characterization and captivating delight that is refreshing and wholly delectable."[37]

By any standard, it was a pretty good season. It had clearly pleased the audience more than it had pleased the critics, but no one was going to worry much about that. What was more interesting was the deep divide between the weight and seriousness of the original plan and the relatively lightweight outcome. Admittedly, there is nothing very lightweight about Shaw's *Candida* and *Philanderer* almost back to back, but the season previews published in the local press in late May and early June had clearly given the impression that the projected "International Drama Festival" would be the centerpiece of the season, and that it would include (in addition to *Candida* and the promised *Merchant of Venice* with Basil Rathbone) productions of Pirandello's *Six Characters in Search of an Author*, Jules Romains's *Dr. Knock* and O'Neill's *Desire Under the Elms*.

Writing in his autobiography, *The Magic Curtain*, which was published in 1951, Lawrence Langner acknowledged that the Playhouse now had a particular brief for new plays and new authors, and that it was, to some extent, a laboratory. If that was so (and there were certainly a lot of new plays and tryouts over the next few years), then it was also true that the theatre's first priority was its subscription list. That was the foundation on which it stood, and there was a clear reluctance on the part of management to do anything that might dilute the subscribers' faith by moving too far away from the sort of mix provided in 1951.

Jackets, ties, calf-length dresses. A summer audience at the Playhouse, 1950.

The 1952 season began with yet another production of a George Bernard Shaw play, but this one was special (in retrospect) because, on the last night of its run, Theresa Helburn brought two guests to see it—Alan Jay Lerner and Frederick Loewe. They saw Tom Helmore and Dolores Gray in Jack Wilson's production of *Pygmalion* . . . and four years later they created a musical version on Broadway. *My Fair Lady*, of course, had little to do with Westport—any more than *Oklahoma!* really did—but it is a source of pride, to this day, that those two great shows were both "seeded" at the Playhouse.

With Philip in charge, Lawrence and Armina did something they hadn't done for a great many years—they left the United States in June for a holiday in Italy. Before leaving, Lawrence noted that *Pygmalion* had made a loss and that the theatre had what might (and did) turn into an horrendous problem with skunks in its cooling system. Besides the skunk threat, there was the usual quota of problems at Westport that summer—a display of backstage prima donna behavior by one of the stars (she threatened to withdraw because her dressing room wasn't air-conditioned); recurring problems with the playbill printer; and so on—but nothing that made Lawrence and Armina regret their absence.[38] There was an emphasis on musicals—no less than four of them, of which one was a ballet evening with Alexandra Danilova, Mia Slavenska and Frederic Franklin. Another innovation was a lecture series—four lectures on the theme of Shakespeare and the Elizabethan Theatre. One of the lecturers was Basil Rathbone (doubtless in compensation for the fact that the subscription flyer had once again duplicitously announced him as a certainty, this time to open the season in *Libel*), and another of the lecturers was Lawrence

Robert Sherwood's play about Hannibal, *The Road to Rome* (1953), with Arlene Francis (*left*) as Amytis, the wife of Rome's ruler, Fabius Maximus. When it was first produced in 1927, Charles Brackett described the play as "a hymn of hate against militarism—disguised, ever so gaily, as a love song."

himself, fresh from Italy, speaking on his plans to establish an American Shakespeare Festival Theatre and Academy at Stratford, Connecticut, which he finally succeeded in doing in 1955.

Each season in the fifties had its highlights—Claude Rains in *Jezebel's Husband*, Eva Gabor and Ezio Pinza in Ferenc Molnar's *The Play's the Thing*, Lillian Gish and Eva Marie Saint in *The Trip to Bountiful*; a performance of Leonard Bernstein's little opera *Trouble in Tahiti*; Jessica Tandy and Hume Cronyn in a triple bill that included two Sean O'Casey plays and Chekhov's monologue "On the Harmful Effects of Tobacco"; the Gish sisters together in *The Chalk Garden*; and Sir Cedric Hardwicke in Priestley's *An Inspector Calls*. Every now and again the box office was genuinely overwhelmed, and that was spectacularly the case for William Inge's play *Picnic*, which opened the 1958 season with Hugh O'Brian (television's Wyatt Earp) as Hal Carter—a vivid illustration of the new power of television in people's lives.

Old friends returned—Tallulah Bankhead in a revue called *Welcome Darlings*; Franchot Tone and Betsy von Furstenberg together in *Oh, Men! Oh, Women!*; John Forsythe, Haila Stoddard, Alfred Drake, Eva Le Gallienne, Claudia Morgan, Ben Gazarra, Elaine Stritch, Bramwell Fletcher, Celeste Holm, Melvyn Douglas and many more.

And there was an impressive list of newcomers—Beatrice Lillie, Rod Steiger, Leslie Nielsen, Bert Lahr, Arlene Francis, Gypsy Rose Lee, Eartha Kitt, Tammy Grimes (who had been an apprentice at the theatre and had more recently worked in the restaurant) and Christopher Plummer not far behind, then Shelley Winters, Gloria Vanderbilt, Betsy Palmer, Hal Holbrooke, Imogene Coca, Hermione Gingold, Carol Bruce, Don Ameche and Groucho Marx in his own play (with the nightly bonus of an extemporized Groucho speech at the final curtain). Of all these, it was Betsy Palmer and Arlene Francis who were destined to be the most frequent visitors to the Playhouse over the years. Bert Lahr was generally acknowledged to be the bravest actor ever to appear on the Westport stage—had he not agreed to take part in Gore Vidal's play *A Visit to a Small Planet*, despite knowing that he would have to play alongside "the fabulous acting cat, Grenadier Saadi," who was the ultimate scene-stealer? (Mr. Lahr's award was generously shared with the ingénue Kathern Shaw, who was allergic to cats but soldiered on nonetheless.)[39] The funniest people to appear, according to both audience members and theatre staff, were Groucho Marx and Hermione Gingold, both of whom would make return appearances. On seeing the Playhouse for the first time, Miss Gingold was quoted as saying "My lord, it's positively m-e-d-i-e-v-a-l."[40]

But Lawrence Langner was never satisfied—he was always trying to lure actors into his theatre. In 1953 he read that Alec Guinness was going to be at the Shakespeare Festival in Stratford, Ontario, that summer: could he not bring one of the productions to Westport? When Guinness

The Doctor In Spite of Himself (1956). Molière's play was adapted and directed by James Lipton, with (*left to right*) Marilyn Clark Langner, Jules Munshin and James Ambandos.

pleaded, among other things, that the Stratford productions would be "in the round" and therefore unsuitable for a proscenium theatre, Langner got back to him by return: "We can build a forestage at Westport so that you can practically restage in one day. Won't you write your Canadian friends and see whether they will send the company to Westport after the Canadian Stratford season?" Guinness managed to fend him off.[41]

History does not relate whether Lawrence Langner was in the theatre on a certain day in August 1956. The play was Marcelle Maurette's *Anastasia*, in an adaptation by Guy Noble. Dolores Del Rio was in the title role. Sitting in the audience, and making her very first visit to the Playhouse, was a twenty-six-year-old actress who was just beginning what promised to be a major career in films and theatre. Joanne Woodward was not yet a resident of Westport—that wouldn't happen until 1961—but

Langner would have recognized her all right, for she had understudied Kim Stanley in the Theatre Guild production of *Picnic* in 1953. No one could possibly have foreseen it on that day—least of all Miss Woodward herself—but this was the person who, one day, forty-four years into the future, would ride to the rescue of Lawrence Langner's theatre and carry it into the twenty-first century.[42]

In the meantime Westport continued to send occasional shows to Broadway. Walter Macken's play *Home Is the Hero* was one of them, in 1955. The author, a former member of the Abbey

Alice Ghostly and Richard Eastham in Leonard Bernstein's opera *Trouble in Tahiti* (1954). This was one of many fine sets designed for the Playhouse by its scenic designer at the time, Marvin Reiss.

Theatre in Dublin, played the role of the bullying Irishman who returns home after serving a five-year prison term for murder. Macken took with him to Broadway the very talented cast of colleagues the Theatre Guild had assembled at Westport, including Peggy Ann Garner, Glenda Farrell and Christopher Plummer, who was making his debut in a theatre where, many years later, he would become a board member.

Home Is the Hero was also a good example of the sort of talent the Westport Playhouse could bring to the creative and backstage operations of its productions. The designer in this case was Marvin Reiss, a marvelously talented scenic, costume and lighting designer who later took two more Westport productions to Broadway (*Back to Methuselah* in 1957 and *Third Best Sport* in 1958), as well as taking one in the opposite direction—*A Party with Betty Comden and Adolph Green* arrived at Westport in the summer of 1959 after a five month run in New York.

Reiss was not the only outstanding designer at Westport in the 1950s: Peter Larkin went on to design some of Broadway's most famous productions (*The Tea House of the August Moon*, which ran for almost three years in the mid-1950s, was one of them), and Eldon Elder was another Westport designer who would amass distinguished credits on Broadway and elsewhere. So would Elliot Martin, though he was not a designer. He was the stage manager of *Home Is the Hero*, as he was of many of the best shows produced at Westport in these years (*Texas L'il Darlin'* was another one he took to Broadway, as early as 1949), and for much of the time he combined his stage managing duties with the day-to-day running of the theatre.

Underpinning and guaranteeing all of this was the continuing success of Mrs. Lodge's subscription scheme. Each year, it seemed, the number of subscribers was up and the percentage of the total subscription sold before opening day (however uncertain the plans for the season) varied between 85 and 90 percent. The key to this effort was the annual luncheon party held at Cobb's Mill Inn to launch the subscription. In 1953 it was attended by 250 members of Cheska's subscription committees, plus members of the radio, press and television, plus (what was most important) a substantial group of theatre personalities who lived in and around Fairfield County—among them

Lillian Gish, Raymond Massey, Ezio Pinza, Carol Channing, Jessie Royce Landis, Peggy Conklin, Jean Dalrymple, Eileen Heckart, Romney Brent and Paula Laurence. Even the enforced departure of Mrs. Lodge herself, bound for Madrid where her husband was appointed U.S. Ambassador in 1955, did not put a crimp in the subscription scheme. Ina Bradley, wife of the theatre's Bridgeport attorney, took over "as though to the manor born," and she would continue to run it—and eventually the theatre's governing board as well—for almost forty years. She quickly became, in effect, the theatre's "hostess," heading up all its public events and appearing on stage on Monday nights to introduce the new play that was opening that night. Since Mrs. Bradley was a person of awesome beauty and was never known to appear twice in the same ensemble, there were inevitably actors who felt they were being upstaged. They were—and the audience loved it!

There were other changes at the Playhouse during the 1950s. Midway through the decade the Players Tavern had been opened adjacent to the building so that, for the first time, dining was included among the theatre's services. 1955 was also the Playhouse's silver jubilee, and (as was the tradition) the season's opening night was made memorable by a gigantic hailstorm that rendered the play inaudible and the parking area impassable. It was a guilty remembrance of the mud heap on which patrons had sloshed and slithered to their cars after that performance that persuaded the Langners to have the parking lot properly paved in the spring of 1958.

Important as these changes were, everyone agreed that far and away the most important change made to the theatre in the 1950s, or at any other time, was the installation of the theatre's first real air-conditioning system in 1958. The ice house in the basement was finally put to other uses.[43]

Just as the physical plant was being improved, so, too, were the theatre's drama programs. In the 1930s the Playhouse had occasionally put on plays especially for children, but the practice had lapsed after the war. In 1955 the management decided to venture back into the field "somewhat apprehensively." A single performance of a play about Davy Crockett was put on, and the house

NEXT ATTRACTION
Monday, July 29th through Saturday, August 3rd
"A highly delectable comedy . . . Seems destined for Broadway . . ." VARIETY

PRIOR TO BROADWAY

Jessica Tandy
and
Hume Cronyn

in

"The Man in the Dog Suit"
with
ISOBEL ELSOM
A Comedy by William H. Wright and Albert Beich
From a Novel by Edwin Corle
Directed by MELVYN DOUGLAS
Settings by MARVIN REISS

NEXT ATTRACTION

MONDAY, JULY 15th through JULY 20th

Dynamic!
Vibrant!
Provocative!

EARTHA KITT

in

"MRS. PATTERSON"

TALES OF THE FIFTIES

Paul Heller was assistant set designer in 1948 and 1949:

A very colorful carpenter, Bill McGirr, built all the scenery with his local crew, and I painted it with the designers . . . McGirr was a wonderful old-time union guy. He brought in union guys, and he was a genius. I remember his tool box, his road box (he used to go out with shows on the road). Inside his tool box he had written: "Them that can brag without lying, let 'em brag—Abe Lincoln."

The first weekend I was there, we were painting scenery. We'd have this tiny corner that was the paint shop. The arrangement was that McGirr had the whole shop from Sunday through Wednesday, then we had the shop from Wednesday night on for the painting. He'd lay out all the sets for us to paint, and he was meticulous. So that first week, on our last night we worked all night, and I left everything hanging around. The next morning I came in and everything that could be moved had been moved to my little corner. Bill looked at me and said, "You mess up my shop, I mess up your shop." That was his lesson to me. We became great friends, but you couldn't leave so much as a paint can anywhere. When we left that shop we had to leave it clean. And when he left it, he left it perfect for us. It was a wonderful discipline.

We painted in the shop. Sometimes we painted structural parts outside. In those days, we used horse glue and dry pigment. The colors were marvelous because you were using real pigment. It was an art. You had to mix up the sizing, basically glue and water, and add the color. There was a real skill to get the paint thick enough to cover and thin enough to flow. It would go on the flats. Sizing kept the paint from falling off. It's the bonding agent that holds the pigment to the surface. So there was always this hot glue pot going. It was a real experience!

We worked interminable hours. That year, most of us lived in a little rooming house next to the theatre. We'd walk over in the morning and go to work, and late at night I'd crawl back into bed. . . .

I remember that I got $25 per week (unlimited hours) and made another $16 helping to park cars ($2 per performance). They were good days. I went up to Lawrence Langner after the second season because they wanted me to come back. I said: "I've been working here and I get $25 a week. Don't you think it's time I got some more money?" Langner replied: "You know what, Paul? When the time comes that you ask for more money, you graduated from Westport."

It's true. I got to be more than they needed.

Lillian Ross spent much of the summer of 1949 on the Straw Hat Circuit preparing an article for the New Yorker.

At the Falmouth Playhouse [in Coonamessett-on-Cape Cod], a nineteen-year-old veteran apprentice known to one and all as Susie, who had spent the summer of 1948 at the Westport Country Playhouse, invited me to lunch with her at a nearby inn. We were joined by the Falmouth's Resident Manager, a young man named Herman Krawitz [destined to be General Manager of the Metropolitan Opera], and by Sir Cedric Hardwicke, who had just arrived to begin rehearsing *The Winslow Boy*—his first experience in a summer theatre.

"You two can eat together and get to know each other real well," said Krawitz . . . to Susie and Sir Cedric.

"Jolly good!" said Sir Cedric gallantly.

Susie turned to Sir Cedric, measuring him solemnly. "The trouble with eating with Westport actors was that they always talked about themselves," she said. "It was *so* boring!"

Sir Cedric glanced uncertainly at Krawitz, who gave him a jovial pat on the back and said, "Never pay special attention to stars is my theory. Around here they get treated just like anyone else."

"Jolly good!" Sir Cedric said, sounding puzzled but vaguely reassured.

After a few moments of silence, Krawitz asked Sir Cedric what he planned to do in the fall. The actor told him he expected to direct and act in a Broadway presentation of Shaw's *Caesar and Cleopatra*, and that after his engagement at the Falmouth he was flying to England to have a talk with Shaw about the production. "If I may say so, I am rather looking forward to seeing Shaw," said Sir Cedric. "We worked together when I was rehearsing to play Caesar in the London production in 1925." He paused and looked dubiously at Susie.

"Girl I know at Vassar likes Shaw, too," she said blandly.

As we were leaving, the bartender waved cordially to Sir Cedric and called, "I *heard* you was up on the Cape, Mr. Rathbone!"

When Gertrude Lawrence came to Westport in 1950 with Arthur Macrae's Traveller's Joy, she impressed everyone with her acting skills. Chilton Ryan was a production assistant that year:

There was a scene in the play when they drank champagne, and Miss Lawrence insisted on real champagne, not ginger ale. So I got a case of cheap (New York) champagne and kept it in the ice room down below. There were 300-pound blocks of ice there, with fans above them that blew cool air through the ducts into the auditorium. That was why the Playhouse was advertised as "air-cooled." Each evening I'd bring up another bottle, until the Friday evening when I went down to the ice room at 7:45 and found someone had made off with my

horde. In those days, liquor stores closed at 8, so I leaped into a car and raced to Calise's Liquor, grabbed three bottles ("pay you later"), and got back to the Playhouse just in time. Unfortunately, in my haste I had picked up three bottles of some sort of sparkling burgundy. When Miss Lawrence was offered a glass onstage that night she picked it up and said, "O goody! Pink champagne—my favorite."

Phoebe Hopkins Burston was an apprentice that year. She recalled another example of Gertrude Lawrence's skill:

Traveller's Joy was set on a ship. A tray of canapés was passed around. Most of the canapés were fake and glued to the tray so they wouldn't slip off. There were two or three canapés that were real. Gertrude was to pick up a real one and eat it. But toward the end of the run, some of the fake canapés came unglued. At one performance, she mistakenly picked up a fake one and popped it in her mouth. She never missed a beat—I'm not sure what she did with it, but I distinctly remember that she never missed a beat.

In 1950, Gertrude Lawrence and Dennis King, stars of *Traveller's Joy*, posed on the steps of the Jolly Fisherman restaurant in Westport with one of the most impressive groups of staff and apprentices ever assembled at the Playhouse. *Front, from left*: Frank Perry, King, Lawrence, Prudence Truesdell. *Second row, from left*: Dorothy Herr, King Sinanian, Peg Henry, Mary Rodgers (daughter of Richard). *Third row, from left*: Chase Stoltez, Neal Wilder, Phoebe Hopkins, Sam Wilson, Conard Fowkes, Chilton Ryan. *Back*: Stephen Sondheim.

In her autobiography, the actress Patricia Neal wrote:

"*Devil Take a Whittler* had only a two-week run in Westport [in 1946], but those two weeks may have been the most important of my entire life, because Richard Rodgers and Lillian Hellman came to see the play."

MORE TALES FROM THE FIFTIES

The "breakthrough" productions in Ms. Neal's career were Hellman's *Another Part of the Forest* in 1946, right after her Westport appearance, and the film of Rodgers's *John Loves Mary* with Ronald Reagan and Jack Carson in 1949.

June Havoc was Minnie, the Girl of the Golden West, in Belasco's play, and she remembers the 1947 production with glee:

Armina and Lawrence Langner produced, from the vault, the original Belasco script for us to peruse, and we were true to Belasco's directions, even so far as using corn flakes for snow. There was no room backstage for the offstage dancing, so we used the loading dock, whooping it up and dancing away happily, despite the July heat and despite no air-conditioning. And mind you, we wore heavy garments, for we were supposed to be dancing in the mountains of California—bearskin coats, raccoon hats. No one complained about the lack of comforts.

One afternoon, we struggled through a dress rehearsal without the leading man. Armina was directing this one, so when the leading man nonchalantly appeared at the end of the dress rehearsal, there was a deadly silence. He had been attending a cocktail party and felt he had done nothing wrong. With trembling voice, Armina stepped down to the edge of the stage: "You are a disgrace to the theatre," she said hoarsely (for she had lost her voice during rehearsals). Whereupon Lawrence came to her aid and in stentorian tones announced: "Sir, you will never again appear in a Theatre Guild production. Rehearsal is over!"

On opening night, we had our revenge on the gentleman. All of us appropriated his speeches into our own, getting through quite nicely. No one seemed to notice that he was practically mute throughout the entire performance!

John Braithwaite was a fifteen-year-old usher in 1947, before the theatre was air-conditioned:

We had to arrive at 7 p.m. When I asked why we had to arrive a full hour before the show started, I was told our responsibility was to open the doors at 7 p.m. to air out the musty smell. Lots of people smoked in that era. Many had asthma. The musty smell bothered them, and often made them cough during the performance. There was a lot of dust in the basement, under the house. If interns were moving furniture in the basement during the day, the dust would rise up into the house—another annoyance.

The doors on both sides of the house would remain open during the entire show to create an air flow on hot evenings. The actors often complained that the Post Road traffic noise was distracting, so we had to close the doors on one side of the house. Then the audience members would complain they were too hot!

A proper air-conditioning system was not installed at the Playhouse until 1958. In the meantime, there were frequent problems with wild animals who were, understandably, attracted to the cooler atmosphere of the theatre's ice house and its whirring fans. Paula Laurence, the actress who was married to Chuck Bowden, the Playhouse's co-general manager, recalls a night early in the 1951 season:

John Wilson's wife, Natasha, who was a famous beauty, used to bring starry guests to the Playhouse. On the night she was bringing Tyrone and Anabella Power—and, I think, Maggie Chase, the editor of *Vogue*—the auditorium was filled with the most awful stench. It turned out that a skunk had got itself trapped in one of the air vents and was spraying profusely in its terror. Chuck came in and escorted Natasha and her guests to their seats. Like the well-bred people they were, they gave no sign of having noticed the smell—until Natasha drew in a deep breath and said: "Skunk! Dee-licious!"

The next summer, Baboo Smiles (née Fritzsche) was one of the apprentices:

I remember one night when a mother skunk had given birth to her babies under the theatre, and was very protective of them . . . with the spray to go with it. The audience was getting *very* annoyed. As a solution, they decided to send me, the smallest of the apprentices, to crawl under the theatre floor on my belly while dragging a case of Air-Wick in order to open a bottle every few feet. It was not a significant solution!

Peter Levin was an apprentice in 1949. As such, he made a small contribution to A Month in the Country, adapted and directed by Garson Kanin and starring Kanin's wife, Ruth Gordon:

At the end of the run of *A Month in the Country*, Gar Kanin gave every apprentice a gift. Mine was an autographed copy of [his play] *Born Yesterday*. It is open on my desk now. That he would bother to see the apprentices as contributing members of the theatre community was astonishing to me. I thought we were pretty much invisible. But Gar saw us all. Six years later, he cast me as Peter Van Daan in the original Broadway production of *The Diary of Anne Frank*.

June Lockhart was in the cast of Kin Hubbard *in 1951, along with Josephine Hull and Tom Ewell:*

Josephine Hull was the tiniest little lady. So all the chairs on the set had to have short legs so that she could sit on them. Dead center was a chair with very, very short legs which was sort of her chair where she would sit most of the time. . . . My parents, Kathleen and Gene Lockhart, were both actors and close friends of Josephine, so they were pleased I was able to work with her. One night she went up.* It was during a scene when she was supposed to be decorating the room with smilax [a decorative draping vine] for a party that was about to happen. She and I are alone on stage and she's got all this dialogue to do while she's hanging this smilax around the set. And she goes up.*

It was hilarious. It became a five-minute bit. The stage manager is offstage trying to cue her, and she finally figured out what she was supposed to be saying. But the audience just collapsed because they could see what was happening, and by now I was flat-out laughing,

too. And it's Josephine Hull! Who cares if she can't remember her dialogue? Really, that was how we all looked at it!

Tammy Grimes was an apprentice in 1954:

I was fired from the box office in my first week because I was unable to work out the proper change to give to ticket buyers. Instead, they sent me to work backstage, and that was where I longed to be, among the stars and the other apprentices. I was appointed to press Richard Kiley's pants to his approval for each performance. This made me happy.

Then along came Apprentice Night when we were allowed to "show off our wares." I donned Lawrence Langner's full-length raccoon coat, which I had found in a trunk in the costume department. When my turn came, I descended the stairs to the stage and sang "They call the wind Mariah," finishing to exuberant applause. At the end of the show, I once again descended the stairs for the company call—but this time I tripped over the coat and rolled down the stairs, giving myself a concussion. The ambulance men arrived and took me to hospital, though I was awake by the time we got there. The next day I was back to pressing pants.

But then they had an audition for a member of the jury in *Libel* and I got the part. What bliss!

Tom Ewell, Josephine Hull and June Lockhart in *Kin Hubbard* (1951).

*"Going up" is the theatrical term for forgetting one's lines.

Conard Fowkes, a 1950 apprentice who went on to become secretary/ treasurer of Actors' Equity Association, recalls the "Westport Culture and Birdwatching Club":

The club was a creation of two other apprentices that year, Frank Perry and Chilton Ryan. Its membership met nightly in Frank's mother's house just in back of the Playhouse. It was, in fact, a nightly poker game (nickel, dime and quarter) masterminded by Sondheim, who was adamant that the game be played, not only according to Hoyle, but straight in the extreme—no joking around, no wild card games and no betting out of turn. Frank had at hand a bottle of cheap booze that he peddled at 35 cents a shot, but he had few takers because Stephen frowned on drinking during the game. Occasionally, members of the current cast would sit in, but more often they would watch for a while and then retire to Frank's living room to chew the fat . . . there was, you see, nowhere in Westport other than Frank's living room for these actors to retire to after the show, a complaint that was renewed with each cast. I do have a clear memory of leaving the game once at 3 a.m. and encountering . . . Frank Perry, well saturated with gin, lying on the floor attempting to get through by phone to the Pope.

Lily Lodge, daughter of Governor and Mrs. (Francesca) Lodge, found herself playing alongside Maureen Stapleton in Tin Wedding, *a play by Hager Wilde and Judson O'Donnell that was given a pre-Broadway tryout at Westport in 1952:*

There was a scene in which Maureen had to drop everything—crockery all over the place—and I had to pick it all up for her. I was very young and only just out of Actors Studio where I had been trained in Method acting. I assumed there would be a minutely rehearsed way of picking it all up—my big moment. You can imagine how shocked I was when I discovered there would be no rehearsal at all of that section. "Just pick it all up!" Maureen told me.

Sally Jessy Raphaël was an apprentice at the Playhouse in 1955. In her autobiography, Sally: Unconventional Success, *she described one of her early acting experiences:*

At Westport I appeared in a play with Geraldine Page. It was called *The Empress* [by Elaine Carrington], and I had to dye my hair black for the role. The only trouble was that when my blond roots began to grow in, the stage lights gave me a surreal appearance: to the audience, I looked completely bald.

Christina Crawford was an apprentice in 1957. In her book Mommie Dearest *she recalled the experience:*

Since Mother and Daddy were going to be away for most of the summer, first in Los Angeles, then touring Europe and Africa in preparation for the opening of international bottling plants, it was decided that I would spend just a few days with them in New York and then go to Westport, Connecticut, to work as an apprentice in the summer stock theatre there.

I was in New York on my eighteenth birthday. As a surprise, Daddy gave me his 1957 Thunderbird convertible. We went down to the street in front of their Sutton Place apartment and there it was, parked at the curb, all shiny and unbelievable. It was really gorgeous. I hugged and kissed both of them and cried.

Westport Country Playhouse was a jewel among summer stock theatres, run by the Theatre Guild in New York. Because it was only

fifty miles from the city, everyone wanted to play Westport. We had the best shows and stars of the season.

There were about ten apprentices that summer. At first I was an anomaly to the rest of the group. But after a few weeks, everyone had too much work to spend any extra energy on someone else. We were welded into a team by the work itself and I liked the theatre very much. Each week a new show brought a new cast of people, problems, and challenges.

(Above) Frank Perry in *Detective Story* (1955).

(Below) Apprentice Sally Jessy in *The Empress* (1955)

was full. Clearly there was an audience, so in 1956 a full-scale program of Children's Theatre was begun with Friday morning performances of four entertainments—a magic show, a puppet show, a children's ballet and a bravura staging of *Robin Hood's Treasure* by the Mae Desmond Children's Theatre.[44] It was the beginning of a tradition that has never lapsed and that is still, in an age of cell phones and computer games, a popular feature of summers in Westport.

Slightly more controversial was the introduction in 1956 of a weekly fashion show before the Wednesday matinee. Models from the Dress Box of Westport came to show off the latest fashions on the patio of the Players Tavern, sometimes accompanied by "narrative comments" from Ina Bradley. Matinees were better attended than ever.

The next year the Playhouse tried out a very different kind of innovation—a poetry reading series. The first poet to be featured, on a Thursday afternoon in July, was Robert Frost. "The playhouse was jammed to capacity," reported the *Norwalk Hour*, "and additional seating had to be arranged at the last minute. The curtain was delayed a short time due to the fact that at 4 p.m. the box office was besieged by a line estimated at one hundred feet. Mr. Frost was applauded continuously for five full minutes at the end of the readings and finally consented to read five more poems."[46] Unlike children's theatre, poetry readings did not become a tradition at the Playhouse—because it turned out there was only one Robert Frost.

> ## THE BEST OF THE FIRST QUARTER CENTURY
>
> *Writing in the theatre's playbill at the beginning of the twenty-fifth season in 1955, an anonymous correspondent listed what were, in his or her view, the fifteen most memorable productions that had yet been seen on the Playhouse's stage. In chronological order, they were:*[45]
>
> William Wycherley's *The Country Wife* with Ruth Gordon (1935)
> Sidney Howard's *Ode to Liberty* with Ina Claire (1935)
> Henrik Ibsen's *Ghosts* with Alla Nazimova (1939)
> S. N. Behrman's *Biography* with Ina Claire (1940)
> Lynn Starling's *Meet the Wife* with Mary Boland (1941)
> Ferenc Molnar's *Liliom* with Tyrone Power and Annabella (1941)
> Emlyn Williams's *Night Must Fall* with Dame May Whitty (1946)
> Noël Coward's *Private Lives* with Tallulah Bankhead (1947)
> Robert McEnroe's *The Silver Whistle* with Jose Ferrer (1948)
> Emlyn Williams's *The Corn Is Green* with Eva Le Gallienne (1949)
> William Inge's *Come Back, Little Sheba* with Shirley Booth (1949)
> Arthur Macrae's *Traveller's Joy* with Gertrude Lawrence (1950)
> Bernard Shaw's *Candida* with Olivia de Havilland (1951)
> Edward Mabley's *Glad Tidings* with Melvyn Douglas and Signe Hasso (1951)
> Horton Foote's *The Trip to Bountiful* with Lillian Gish (1953)

HARNESSING THE NEW MEDIA

One of the reasons the staff of the Playhouse was so gratified by the success of the "extra curricula" programming was because, ever since the end of World War II and the introduction of television services, it had been assumed that Americans had too much ready-made entertainment coming into their homes to be bothered with taking their children to see live theatre shows, or going out to hear a poetry reading. It was true that television did not seem to have cut into the Playhouse's evening audience yet, but it was also apparent that the arrival of a real, eighteen-carat television star like Hugh O'Brian had greater drawing power than even Groucho Marx or Bert Lahr.

The Theatre Guild had addressed itself to the new media at an early stage. Before the war, Lawrence Langner and Terry Helburn had proposed to NBC Radio that they should mount a regular series of Guild plays. They were rebuffed by an NBC executive who told them, "The name of the Theatre Guild is the kiss of death in radio." In a typical Langner/Helburn coup, however, they reversed the positions immediately after the war by signing their own contract with a radio sponsor—U.S. Steel. Observing that "the standards of radio were mediocre at best," they made the decision to produce the programs themselves ("live") and to lease them to a radio network. "The Theatre Guild on the Air" came into being in September 1945 and ran successfully for eight years.[47]

Langner and Helburn saw no reason why they shouldn't do the same in television. Visiting London for the opening there of *Oklahoma!* in April 1947, they went to the BBC to observe the production of some dramas. "Though technically imperfect," Armina wrote, "they gave evidence that the medium would ultimately be capable of bringing the finest works of the theatre into homes even to a greater degree than radio."[48] When they got home they made an agreement with the nascent NBC Television company by which the Guild and NBC would share the costs of producing seven plays at the rate of one a month, all of them to be transmitted "live." The first play was St. John Ervine's *John Ferguson*, fondly remembered by Langner and Helburn as the play that had established the Guild on Broadway in 1919. Next morning, the newspaper reviewer Jack Gould summed up the fiasco in a memorable sentence: "The Theatre Guild entered into the field of TV last night and fell flat on its art."[49] But lessons were learned and things got a lot better. Gertrude Lawrence starred in Shaw's *The Great Catherine*, and the seventh and last production was Wilder's *Our Town* with Raymond Massey as the Stage Manager. Writing in *The Forum*, John Gassner expressed the opinion that the production "will go down in history as the day when television drama was really born."[50]

For the next five years, until 1953, the Guild had to be content with its radio contract. But television was becoming well established—*Omnibus*, presented by Alistair Cooke early on Sunday evenings and about to begin its second season in the fall of 1953, had shown what could be done with "live" drama. U.S. Steel decided it would like to switch its contract with the Theatre Guild from radio to television, and for the next eight years the Guild, with its own television production department under Armina Marshall, produced a sixty-minute play for television every other week throughout the year—a massive undertaking.

It was natural, therefore, that the Westport Playhouse should be eyeing television as well. In 1955 Philip Langner produced a discussion paper entitled "Festival of Comedy Presentation." He proposed that each summer a group of Westport plays should be televised "live" (whether from the stage or in a television studio was not decided), with the Playhouse providing the production. In this way, Langner pointed out, television would be able "to take care of some of its summer problems," and Westport would be able to attract more star performers by being able to offer them a (small) Westport fee and a (very large) television fee. Nothing came of the proposal, but it is indicative of the way theatres like Westport were looking to promote themselves by jumping on the new media bandwagon—in this case, by allowing their summer presentations to be tryouts for television, in much the same way that many of them were tryouts for Broadway.

As though to prove the soundness of Philip Langner's premise, it wouldn't be long before the Playhouse was staging a tryout for Hollywood. The second presentation of the 1959 season was a production of Shaw's *Arms and the Man*, starring Tony Randall. "Within two months of the exclusive one-week Westport engagement," reported the *New York Herald Tribune*, "Abner L. Greshler Productions of Hollywood will start shooting the film with Mr. Randall again in the starring role." The tryout appears to have been unsuccessful (for Mr. Greshler, though not for the Playhouse) for the film was never made.[51]

1958 — THE LANGNERS' FAREWELL

When the year began, no one—not even the Langners—knew this would be Lawrence and Armina's last season in control of the Playhouse. Nor was any announcement made at the end of the season, and for good reason: the subscribers knew and trusted the Langners; if they thought they were withdrawing, they might decide not to renew their subscriptions while they waited to see what the new management would do. In any event, the Langners had no intention of disappearing completely, for they would continue to own the Playhouse and they would continue to live close by—though no longer at Langnerlane: in 1952 they had bought a smaller property, Apple Hill, and the Langnerlane farm, which they had owned since 1930, would eventually (though not quite yet) be sold. With Apple Hill, the Langners acquired a new neighbor—June Havoc lived next door.

For several years past Lawrence and Armina had, in effect, rented the season to a new company formed each year and called "Westport Season, Inc." Most recently, these companies had always included Philip Langner, so it was kept very much within the family. In 1958 Philip was partnered

Three of the popular attractions of the 1958 season: Faye Emerson in *Tonight at 8:30*; Groucho Marx in *Time for Elizabeth*; and Hugh O'Brian (television's Wyatt Earp) meeting the press with his co-star Susan Oliver during the run of *Picnic*.

with Henry T. Weinstein, who had come to Westport after two years as general manager of the Falmouth Playhouse on Cape Cod (where he had been responsible, among other things, for the world premiere of Arthur Miller's *A View from the Bridge*). Philip was increasingly involved in the production company he ran with Weinstein (over and above their responsibilities at Westport). They were "packagers" of shows for the circuit of summer stock theatres, which included Westport and which was now as large as it ever got—nationwide, there were as many as fifty theatres in the circuit, of which thirty were located in the northeast corridor.[52] Having their own showcase theatre at Westport helped, but, even so, Langner and Weinstein were unusually successful in the business, with several of their productions in line for potentially profitable Broadway runs or national tours. At the same time, Philip had been an associate director of the Theatre Guild since 1956, on his way to becoming co-director in 1961. For all these reasons, it made sense for him to shed his summer responsibilities at Westport. It would therefore be necessary to find new lessees for 1959, going outside the family for the first time.

But no one knew this when the 1958 season got under way. Prophetically (but for no very good reason), they billed it as "The 1958 Gala Season," and they began it with what was, for Westport and all other summer stock theatres, a "first"—a complete season, booked, signed and cast before opening night. Philip Langner and Henry Weinstein proudly announced it in the first playbill of the season:

> The 1958 Season at the Westport Country Playhouse is unique in the annals of Summer Theatre. Never before has it been possible to gather together such a galaxy of stars in such a medley of Summer Theatre entertainment. Read this astonishing list of stars who will make your summer theatre-going at Westport a memorable experience: DON AMECHE, JESSICA TANDY, HUME CRONYN, MELVYN DOUGLAS, ALFRED DRAKE, FAYE EMERSON, HERMIONE GINGOLD & CAROL BRUCE, DODY GOODMAN, SIR CEDRIC HARDWICKE, CELESTE HOLM, BERT LAHR, GROUCHO MARX, BURGESS MEREDITH, AND HUGH O'BRIAN (WYATT EARP).
>
> Such a program of stars could not be achieved on Broadway for an investment of under a million dollars. Thanks to Summer Theatre economics, and the pleasure the stars derive in treading the boards of the better theatres, it is possible for you to see these players in parts which most of them have made famous at box office prices which will fit every theatre lover's purse.
>
> This is the first time, as far as we know, that any summer theatre has been able to publish at the beginning of its season, the names of all the plays and stars who will appear.
>
> The plays are mostly comedies and have been especially selected for variety and contrast. Among the lighter of these are Noël Coward's *Fallen Angels* starring Hermione Gingold and Carol Bruce, *The Remarkable Mister Pennypacker* starring Burgess Meredith, *Time for Elizabeth* starring Groucho Marx, *Visit to a Small Planet* starring Bert Lahr, and *Dulcy* starring Dody Goodman.
>
> Equally amusing, but with a deeper tone, are *Picnic* starring Hugh O'Brian, *Tonight at 8:30* starring Faye Emerson and *Triple Play* starring Jessica Tandy and Hume Cronyn.
>
> Romantic tragic-comedy returns with *He Who Gets Slapped* starring Alfred Drake and *Holiday for Lovers* starring Don Ameche, while English comedy is given full play in *An Inspector Calls* with Sir Cedric Hardwicke.
>
> The new plays, both comedies, are *Strange Partners* starring Melvyn Douglas and *Third Best Sport* starring Celeste Holm. Both of these are Theatre Guild Broadway possibilities.
>
> This will be the first appearance at Westport of the two greatest American comedians, Groucho Marx and Bert Lahr, also Sir Cedric Hardwicke, Don Ameche, Hermione Gingold, Carol Bruce, and Dody Goodman.[53]

For some years past, the Playhouse had billed itself as "America's Outstanding Summer Theatre," and it had never been shy of claiming to be the classiest of all the "straw hat" theatres. If ever a season set out to prove it, it was the 1958 season.

It was not a bad moment for Lawrence Langner to step back and admire his handiwork.

The musical had long been recognized as Broadway's greatest contribution to the art of theatre, and Lawrence Langner, Theresa Helburn and the Theatre Guild had done more than most to make it an enduring contribution. In 1935 they had produced George Gershwin's *Porgy and Bess*, the first great American opera (though it was not called an opera then: it was not until fifty years later, when the Metropolitan Opera first produced it, that it was recognized for what it truly was). In 1943, they had brought *Oklahoma!* to the stage of the St. James's Theatre, and only two years after that they had brought *Carousel* to the Majestic. But now, as the 1950s dawned, they were not alone in thinking they had found the perfect vehicle for the next one.

THE ONE THAT GOT AWAY:
THE STRANGE CASE OF
"MY FAIR LADY"

Ever since it had first been seen in New York, in 1914, American producers had talked about the potential of Shaw's *Pygmalion* as a musical. That first production had starred Mrs. Patrick Campbell as Eliza Doolittle, the role she had created in London earlier that year. In 1926 the Theatre Guild had revived the play with Lynn Fontanne as a not-very-Cockney Eliza; and in 1945 Gertrude Lawrence had played the role in a long-running production, despite the fact that she was forty-seven years old at the time.

Theresa Helburn of the Theatre Guild was one producer with very definite ambitions to make *Pygmalion* into a musical—and the Guild had the inestimable advantage of a long and close relationship with Shaw. But that, on its own, was not enough: it was also necessary to be in partnership with a Hungarian film producer named Gabriel Pascal. He had emigrated to Britain in the 1930s and had succeeded in winning the confidence of Shaw, who had allowed him to make films of several of his major plays. He had also given him the motion picture rights to *Pygmalion* and—more importantly—had written an additional scene for the film. This was the spectacular royal party scene. No one was going to do a musical version without that scene, and Pascal held the rights.

Shaw died in 1950, and Pascal failed to persuade the Shaw Estate to let him make a musical version of *Pygmalion*. Not unnaturally, he turned to Helburn and Langner for help. They formed a partnership, convinced the Estate, and set out to find a creative team willing to do the hardest part. Richard Rodgers and Oscar Hammerstein, who had written both *Oklahoma!* and *Carousel*, turned them down, so they approached Alan Jay Lerner and Frederick Loewe, who had been responsible for both *Brigadoon* (1947) and *Paint Your Wagon* (1951). Lerner and Loewe accepted enthusiastically, but for the role of Eliza Doolittle they set their hearts on Mary Martin, who had had such a success in *South Pacific*. Whether she could have pulled it off at the age of forty-three was as doubtful to her as it was to others, but it was in order to persuade Lerner and Loewe that Eliza was capable of being played by someone other than Mary Martin, if necessary, that Langner decided to put on a production of Shaw's original *Pygmalion* at Westport Country Playhouse at the beginning of the 1952 summer season.

Terry Helburn invited Lerner and Loewe to attend the last performance of the run as her guest. The Eliza they saw was the American actress Dolores Gray, who had only recently finished a three-year run in London as Annie Oakley in *Annie, Get Your Gun*. Lerner and Loewe loved the play and were convinced. On October 28, 1952, they signed a letter of agreement with the Theatre Guild to make a musical version of *Pygmalion* "in association with Gabriel Pascal."

Lawrence Langner, who admitted that he had put on the play at Westport "especially for their benefit," later discovered that the Playhouse had made a loss of $1,376.99 for the week of June 16, 1952, when *Pygmalion* was playing. "Never in theatre history did so small a loss help to produce so huge a series of fortunes," he wrote.[54]

As it turned out, the fortunes did not include one for the Theatre Guild.

Only weeks after the signing of the agreement, the Guild was informed that Lerner would not be able to proceed with the project and the deal was off. For Langner and Helburn, it was a tremendous disappointment; for Pascal, who had invested money he could ill afford in order to buy the rights from the Shaw Estate, it was a disaster. He died less than two years later, with no further efforts having been made to interest other creative teams. It seemed to be the end of the trail.

Then, three months after Pascal's death, Langner and Helburn read in the *New York Times* that Lerner and Loewe had secured the rights to make a musical version of *Pygmalion* with another manager, Herman Levy. They were thunderstruck, and furious. There was an exchange of "sharply worded" letters.

Then Langner and Helburn did something that was typical of them. In Langner's words: "Throughout our long careers in the theatre we had never taken any action, legal or otherwise, which would inhibit the creativity of authors. Despite our feelings, we therefore decided that whatever rights we might have should be dropped. . . . In art, and especially in theatre, the end usually justifies the means. The end in this case was to create a beautiful musical from *Pygmalion*. . . . The enormous amount of work and travel performed by Pascal and the Guild in the year 1952, and the production of the play in Westport, all helped to get the project started. But these were merely the preliminaries to the artistic work—the composing, the writing, the scenic investiture, the casting, the direction, the costuming—all these are what mostly mattered, and for these the world is indebted to the group of artists including Alan Lerner, Fritz Loewe, Moss Hart [the director], Oliver Smith [set designer], Cecil Beaton [costumes] and all the others."[55]

Better than almost anything else, that sums up the extraordinary and selfless devotion to the theatre of Lawrence Langner and Theresa Helburn.

Dolores Gray as Eliza in Shaw's *Pygmalion* at Westport (1952)

It was Oscar Hammerstein who likened her to Hercules in his funeral eulogy of her. "A tiny woman with a wise little smile on her face, an alert, brisk, bustling little woman—a kind of small Hercules—without the great man's muscles, but surely having as much energy and stubbornness as he could have possessed. No Augean stables would have been too big for her to clean if she had had to clean it to get a show on."

She was never part of the Westport Playhouse, yet she was a huge presence there for twenty-nine seasons, right up to her death. Like the Langners, she and her husband, the writer John Baker Opdycke, came

"A KIND OF SMALL HERCULES": THERESA HELBURN
1887–1959

to live in Westport, and she was often to be seen at the Playhouse. More importantly, she ran the Theatre Guild, which was where many Westport productions were conceived, rehearsed and brought to life, and it was always part of her happy conspiracy with Lawrence Langner that Westport should be a place where Theatre Guild productions could be tried out on their way to Broadway.

They had known each other a long time—ever since Langner first came to New York as a twenty-one-year-old in 1911. She was three years older than him, the youngest daughter of an intellectual New England family that lived on the Upper West Side—her German-educated father was a leather merchant who spent most of the working week in Boston, while her mother was an activist in educational and artistic circles. Theresa graduated from Bryn Mawr in 1908 and promptly had her first nervous collapse. Throughout her life, this was to be a recurring pattern—periods of frenetic activity followed by exhaustion—but it was rarely, if ever, apparent to outside observers, nor did it seem to interfere with her amazing productivity.

After Bryn Mawr, she recuperated on a farm in Massachusetts, and began to write. She did postgraduate work at Radcliffe, and took part in George Pierce Baker's legendary 47 Workshop at Harvard. Among her fellow graduates from the workshop were a group of people who would be important to her later on—Eugene O'Neill, Philip Barry, Lee Simonson, Robert Edmund Jones and Maurice Wertheim. She returned to New York and supported herself in a number of ways—writing poetry in *Century*, *Harper's* and *New Republic*; teaching drama at Miss Merrill's Finishing School in Mamaroneck (where Katharine Cornell was one of her pupils); and serving as governess to the Herter family. It was with the Herters that she spent a year in Paris in 1913–14, returning to New York only when the opening shots of World War I forced her to.

In New York, she wrote plays, two of which were produced unsuccessfully on Broadway—though one of them, *Enter the Hero*, subsequently became very popular with amateur troupes—and she became drama critic of *The Nation*. By this time, Lawrence Langner was both a friend and associate. He had got her involved first in the Washington Square Players, and then as a play reader for the newly formed Theatre Guild. It was not long before he and his colleagues in the Guild were asking her assistance in a much bigger way—"I was made executive secretary pro tem," she recalled. "Pro tem" turned out to be almost forty years.

The first twenty of those years were difficult, not just because making good theatre is a constant battle to create the conditions and atmosphere in which a lot of different people's talents can blossom simultaneously, but also because the Theatre Guild had been established as a cooperative venture between its six directors, and the rule was that they must all have a say at all stages of all productions. It was the job of the executive secretary to make sure that this happened—and to pick up the pieces afterwards. The firm yet unobtrusive way in which she constantly did this was described in a 1930 *New Yorker* profile as "a chronic miracle. . . . Compact and dynamic of figure, this woman of the iron-gray shingle and the pertinent chin, the keen eye and the stubborn back, is the terror of actors, the bane of playwrights, and the thorn of agents, managers, and kindred mortals."[56]

Her last twenty years at the Theatre Guild were much easier because the other directors all went off to pursue their own projects in the late 1930s, leaving Terry Helburn and Lawrence Langner to run the Guild on their own. Armina joined them as an associate director, then as the head of the radio and television departments and eventually, in the early 1950s, as a full director, but between 1939 and 1959 it was essentially a collaboration between longtime friends who shared each other's enthusiasms—or, as Lawrence Langner put it, "we are tolerant of each other's lunacies."

Helburn claimed they had never had a quarrel—just "differences of opinion."[57] She described Langner as "by profession, an international patent attorney, and by avocation, a kind of Benjamin Franklin with ideas

Opening night party for *The Girl of the Golden West* (1947): (*left to right*) Lawrence Langner, Armina Marshall, Theresa Helburn, June Havoc.

about everything under the sun. He not only had ideas, he was prepared to implement them. When he saw something that should be done, he brushed aside obstacles as though they weren't there, and set out to do it regardless. Sometimes, when I think how often I've been the bulldozer to push aside obstacles in the path of Lawrence's ideas, I think I would have been wiser to take to my heels. But what a lot of fun I would have missed!"[58]

"The fun she would have missed" was perhaps best summed up by the title of the autobiography she was working on when she died—*The Wayward Quest*. The quest was theatre—that was her whole life, she admitted—and it had led her and her colleagues in the Guild to a number of conclusions: "We discovered in the long run that much of the public was weary of tired formulas and standardized productions, that the thinking few had become many, that there were enough of them to constitute an important theatrical audience. . . . We discovered that when we believed in a play the audience was apt to believe in it, and the box-office draw, on which we had not counted, was greater than we had dared to hope. We discovered that the more firmly you stick to your ideal the more staunchly the public will support you."[59]

Not everyone agreed. In its profile of Theresa Helburn the *New Yorker* claimed the Guild had often been guilty of producing dull plays, and for that "the answer lies . . . with Theresa Helburn, or fundamentally with the misbegotten intellectualism of her college years that exalted literature and excluded life."[60]

Terry Helburn may have smiled to herself when she read that, and she may have reflected that it was the way most of New York's "traditional" theatre people—from producers to critics—tried to cover up the influence the Theatre Guild had had, and was having, in changing the commercial theatre's "lowest common denominator" approach to its audience. She put it into words when she spoke at the laying of the cornerstone of the Guild Theatre in 1924:

"[T]he function of the theatre is not only to entertain but to stimulate, not only to make you feel but to make you think. . . . The greatest advance in the thinking public is brought about by plays that crash the barriers, that leave their audiences quivering, uncomfortable, sometimes disgusted, but always asking: *Why?* These plays are the Guild's most precious failures, they are its realest successes, even though their success is only apparent in the seasons that come after; for the theatre moves rapidly, and the dynamite of one decade is the building stone of the next."[61]

THE SILO CIRCUIT BRUSHES UP ITS LINES AND SETTINGS

Once again summer playhouses and tents along the Atlantic seaboard prepare for the new season. Typical of the straw-hat theatres that are now painting their sets and rehearsing their casts is the Westport (Conn.) Country Playhouse depicted below. Details on plays and dates can be found on Page Five.

CHAPTER EIGHT

1959–72 Under New Management

The changing of the guard was smoothly accomplished. A week before the opening of the 1959 season, Lawrence and Armina Langner gave a party at Langnerlane to introduce the new management to the press. Henry Weinstein was not new—he had been Philip Langner's co-manager at Westport the previous season and would remain at the Playhouse until 1961 when he joined public television to run its new drama strand. It was Weinstein who did the deal with the Langners to take over the management of the theatre, and it was Weinstein who brought in Laurence Feldman as his partner and co-producer, as well as James B. McKenzie to be the general manager.[1]

McKenzie was thirty-three years old, a handsome and charming man from Wisconsin and no stranger to summer theatre. When he arrived in Westport that summer he estimated he had already been responsible for 197 weeks of Equity (i.e., professional) stock at various theatres around the country, from Wisconsin and Illinois to upper New York State. He had been a stage manager, producer and director; he had worked in theatres, arenas and under canvas; he had done shows in proscenium arches and "in the round," indoors as well as outdoors . . . he knew a lot about theatre.

Jim McKenzie would spend the next forty-one summers at Westport, and he would make it his home. He would be greatly loved and widely respected. And the Playhouse would owe its survival to him.

Laurence Feldman would not be so lucky. He was a year younger than McKenzie, and he had not previously been involved directly with a theatre, though he and Weinstein had for many years been respectively managing director and director of the Theatre Fund. Feldman was, in fact, an attorney who had operated a one-man office in New York since graduating from Columbia Law School in 1954. In the Westport playbill he was described as "a well known trial lawyer throughout the United States,"[2] but less than two years later, in 1962, five justices of the Appellate Division of the State Supreme Court found him guilty of misconduct and suspended him from practicing law for two years. They found he had engaged in "systematic solicitation" of personal injury negligence cases, which composed about half his law practice.[3] In short, he was an ambulance chaser.

Feldman was a large man—about six feet tall and 220 pounds. Always impeccably dressed, he walked with a cane as a result of an automobile accident in 1958 that had laid him up for the better part of a year. "It was then," the New York Times later reported, "that he first conceived the theatre career that was, briefly but spectacularly, to make him one of the most successful operators of suburban stage theatres in the New York area."[4] He operated the Westport Playhouse for five years— 1959 through 1963—and he continued to have an impact on it thereafter as one of the owners, with

1959 apprentices at work in the scene shop.

Henry Weinstein, of a producing and packaging company that bore their first names in its title—the Laurence Henry Company.

In March 1967, aged forty, Feldman was murdered—bludgeoned to death in the middle of the night while he was in bed in his penthouse apartment on East 38th Street. The police reported no evidence of robbery—and no one was arrested for the crime.

In June 1959, when the Langners introduced the new team to the press, all this was far away in the future. What was much more to the point at that moment was the announcement of two very positive developments for the Playhouse.

The first was the opening of the new Connecticut Turnpike. The Bronx line was now only thirty-five minutes away.

The second was another remarkable growth in the subscription list. Ina Bradley announced it was up to 1,250—a 25 percent increase since the previous season.

The olio curtain at a 1960s children's performance.

1959—BUSINESS AS USUAL

As he was happily moving into his new home at Owenoke Park on the Westport shore, Henry Weinstein unwarily told a reporter that the original concept for the 1959 Playhouse season had been "a festival contrasting Tennessee Williams (the decadent society) and Shaw (the forecaster of the decadence)."[5] Perhaps fortunately, the festival never really materialized. There were two Shaw productions—Tony Randall in *Arms and the Man* (the Hollywood tryout) and a large and very expensive production of *Caesar and Cleopatra* with Franchot Tone and Susan Strasberg—and one Tennessee Williams—Eli Wallach, Anne Jackson and Jo Van Fleet (stepping into Laurette Taylor's shoes as Amanda) in *The Glass Menagerie*. There was also a John Osborne play from Britain that faithfully reflected the decadent society—*Epitaph for George Dillon*. It was a play that had failed on Broadway the previous season, but had been brought back to life by the young actor Ben Gazzara. He had seen it in New York and had thought it deserved a longer life, so he had mounted a new production and brought it out on the summer circuit. Of the new plays, Frank Corsaro's *A Piece of Blue Sky* was set in the Depression and might be said to portray a different sort of decadence.

For the rest, it was business as usual. There were three musicals (two of them from the Comden and Green team) that brought Imogene Coca and Celeste Holm back to the house; there were new plays by William Gunn, Andrew Rosenthal and Harry Kurnitz, whose recent Hollywood credits included *Witness for the Prosecution* and *How to Steal a Million*; and there were a number of star vehicles—good and not so good—for Gloria Swanson, Arlene Francis, Shelley Winters, Joan

Shaw's *Caesar and Cleopatra* (1959) was launched with a toga party—(*left to right*) Henry Weinstein, Ina Bradley and her husband, Judge Kenneth Bradley.

Jim McKenzie recalled Caesar and Cleopatra as a particularly fraught production:

There is always a lot of nervous energy during the rehearsal period, but it has rarely gotten out of hand. The occasion that I remember most vividly occurred during rehearsals for our production of *Caesar and Cleopatra*, with Franchot Tone and Susan Strasberg. Susan was given a velvet cloak with a silk lining, so she would look like a real Cleopatra. Franchot insisted he would not go on unless he got a velvet cloak, too. This really wasn't in our budget, but we managed to comply. Nonetheless, antipathy was rampant. Franchot kept hinting that he wouldn't go on. Finally, we engaged a very good actor whom Franchot particularly disliked to be his standby. The sight of that actor, backstage in full costume, script in hand, turned the trick. Franchot made every performance.

Fontaine, Shirley Booth (a triumphant return to the stage where she had first played *Little Sheba* ten years before) and David Wayne.

At the end of the summer, the new management announced record receipts of $213,000. The next year, with a mix of plays that was somewhat lighter and just as starry, they pushed the record to $236,000.[6]

The recipe seemed to work, and Lawrence Langner, who had told the press at the beginning of the 1959 season that he and his wife would "exercise a supervisory interest in the Playhouse as regards the plays selected," was well pleased.[7]

Jim McKenzie recalled sitting with Langner on a park bench in front of the Playhouse in the late summer of 1959, and realizing that Langner, who was now in his seventieth year, was comfortable with having turned over the management of his theatre to a younger generation.

THE PACKAGERS

Gloria Swanson's appearance at the Playhouse in July 1959 was cause for celebration at the box office. The sixty-year-old actress was appearing in *Red Letter Day* by Andrew Rosenthal, billed as "a pre-Broadway try-out," with Mary Pickford's husband, Buddy Rogers, as her co-star. It was Standing Room Only.

It was also terrible. With uncharacteristic acerbity the *Stratford News* reported: "Miss Swanson, of course, is the main reason for the show, and she gives quite a performance. It is doubtful that any gesture she acquired in the history of motion pictures is not sandwiched into one fortunately short evening. She certainly does convince the audience that she is amazingly well preserved for her 60 years and that her hair will not come out regardless of how hard she pulls and tugs. Outside of that, Miss Swanson conveys little. For Rogers, this week's engagement is the first stage work he has had in 29 years. The reasons for the lay-off are fairly obvious. . . ."[8]

There were very few productions as bad as this one—most of them (be it said) were pretty good—but there had to be a reason why such excrescences got on to any respectable stage. That reason, most critics would tell you in the 1950s, was "the packager." Unless they were deaf and blind, those same critics would also recognize that the packager was an economic necessity—costs had risen to such an extent that it was simply not viable for a summer theatre to cast, rehearse and present a play for a single six- or twelve-night engagement without its going on to other theatres. In the 1930s and 1940s great stars had happily appeared in summer stock for between $250 and $500 a week—though it was true that, as early as 1939, Richard Aldrich, who was by then in effective charge of the Cape Playhouse in Dennis, even though its founder, Raymond Moore, was still alive, had offered Jane Cowl $1,000 for a one-week engagement.[9] In the 1960s, by contrast, stars were regularly getting $3,000 a week, and some were demanding $5,000 *and* a share of the theatre's gross.[10]

"The packager created himself about ten years ago," wrote Frederic Morton in a 1959 edition of the magazine *Holiday*, "when rehearsal costs reached the ulcer-producing stage. The knack he dreamed up at that time has been brought to perfection today: delivering a ready-made, smoothly rehearsed company, complete from bit parts to big star and even including an absentee director and an absentee stage manager. It's the packager who decides what posters will be tacked up in general stores from Bennington to Baltimore, who passes on which summer houses will have to feed Tallulah's rhesus monkey or James Mason's eleven cats, who pronounces judgment on the resuscitability of old plays or the barn-worthiness of new ones. He is the alpha, omega, and of course the ogre, of the off-New York theatre between June and September."[11]

It was easy to make the packager into an ogre. "What's become of the good old days of summer stock?" asked Arthur Gelb in an article in the *New York Times Magazine*. "This summer some thirty playhouses and about a dozen tents will share in the dubious privilege of unwrapping about thirty-five circulating 'packages,' priced at anywhere from $4,000 to $10,000. When opened and displayed for one-week stands in theatres seating between 600 and 1,200 patrons, and in tents that can seat up to 3,000, these will be found to contain such durable and/or delectable items as *Bells Are Ringing*, *Harvey*, *Babes in Arms*, *Biography* and *The Glass Menagerie*."[12]

Aside from the supporting cast, rehearsal time, props and costumes, Gelb pointed out that far and away the most expensive item was the star. "The term 'star' in summer theatre parlance is generic and applies to anyone from a solidly established Broadway actor such as Eli Wallach, through such movie and television entertainers as Gloria Swanson and Groucho Marx, to such 'personalities' as Maxie Rosenbloom. The growth of the star package is as distressing to the cultivated theatre-goer as frozen hollandaise sauce is to the gourmet . . . [T]he expanding trend toward summer theatre packaging represents a threat to imagination and self-expression in most of the better-known playhouses. For packages tend to stifle the creativity of producers and directors, curtail the opportunity for young actors to gain experience, rob the community of the old-time sense of participation in a cultural effort, and limit the horizons of all audiences, educated or not."[13]

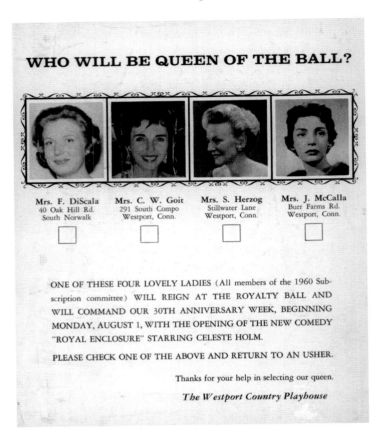

WHO WILL BE QUEEN OF THE BALL?

Mrs. F. DiScala	Mrs. C. W. Goit	Mrs. S. Herzog	Mrs. J. McCalla
40 Oak Hill Rd.	291 South Compo	Stillwater Lane	Burr Farms Rd.
South Norwalk	Westport, Conn.	Westport, Conn.	Westport, Conn.

ONE OF THESE FOUR LOVELY LADIES (All members of the 1960 Subscription committee) WILL REIGN AT THE ROYALTY BALL AND WILL COMMAND OUR 30TH ANNIVERSARY WEEK, BEGINNING MONDAY, AUGUST 1, WITH THE OPENING OF THE NEW COMEDY "ROYAL ENCLOSURE" STARRING CELESTE HOLM.

PLEASE CHECK ONE OF THE ABOVE AND RETURN TO AN USHER.

Thanks for your help in selecting our queen.

The Westport Country Playhouse

Answer:
The winner was Mrs. Seymour Herzog.

It wasn't all bad, of course. The drawing power of the stars might well bring in people who would never otherwise go near a theatre; it gave the stars important exposure to a live audience; it enabled theatres to present big, and sometimes quite expensive, productions they could never have produced on their own; and it gave playwrights and producers a very good "laboratory" in which to try out new plays and new productions. But the real beneficiaries were the stars. In the worst cases it even gave them virtual control. Playhouse managements and owners were reduced to ciphers, paying court to the stars, surrendering artistic control and anxiously counting the takings at the box office.

Was it really as bad as that? Sometimes, yes, it was—but not often, because stars were not all that mattered to packagers. Indeed, if they could do without one, they would, because the packagers' ideal was to create a production that would have a life beyond summer theatre, perhaps on

Broadway, perhaps on tour, perhaps both. That was the pot of gold, and it was not something that could be achieved with a legendary Hollywood star who would need to get back to the studio lot as soon as the Labor Day holiday was over, nor even with a television star who would have to be back in front of the cameras as soon as the network's summer hiatus was over.

Star-ridden summer stock productions were worth a packager's time if they were going to lead to a long-term future, but, on their own, they were not very profitable. A typical summer package was the one put together by Henry Weinstein and Laurence Feldman for their 1959 production of a musical review called *What A Day!* It played six theatres that summer, including Westport. Its initial production costs—covering rehearsal expenses in New York, director's and designer's fees, music copying and other basic expenses—came to $3,300. This would eventually be split equally between the six theatres. Then there were the weekly costs of presenting the play, which came to $3,600, almost entirely made up of salaries. To that, each theatre would have to add its own over-head, and a $150 booking fee for the packager.[14]

If just one theatre had mounted this production on its own for a six-day run, and that was all, it would have cost over $7,000. But with each theatre paying its own expenses and one-sixth of the

Margaret O'Brien, a stunningly talented child actress in the 1940s, came to the Playhouse in 1961 to star in Lawrence Roman's play, *Under The Yum Yum Tree*. She learned her lines side-saddle in the Playhouse grounds.

initial production costs, it would come to no more than $4,300 per theatre, plus the normal weekly overhead of that theatre. And all the packager got was that slender booking fee! It hardly seemed worth the packager's time and effort—unless the production had potential for more than a brief outing on the summer circuit, and that, of course, was what the packagers were generally hoping for.

THE PRODUCING MANAGERS COMPANY

By 1959 the packagers had become central to summer stock. Westport was in an enviable position compared to other theatres because most of the major packagers were its own people— Philip Langner, Henry Weinstein, Laurence Feldman. Moreover, Westport continued to believe it was different from other summer theatres, and it set out to prove it by taking exclusive positions in certain productions.[15] In 1959, for example, the production of Shaw's *Caesar and Cleopatra* with Franchot Tone and Susan Strasberg was exclusive to Westport on the East Coast—the only other places it played were Chicago and Detroit—and Tony Randall's *Arms and the Man* and *A Party with Betty Comden and Adolph Green* (which had been a Theatre Guild production on Broadway the previous winter) were completely exclusive to Westport that summer. In addition, Arlene Francis, who opened the season with the Harry Kurnitz play *Once More with Feeling*, was exclusive to Westport though the production wasn't— elsewhere on the summer circuit it starred Joan Bennett, Betsy Palmer and others—and William Gunn's new play, *Marcus in the High Grass*, being a Theatre Guild tryout, was also exclusive. The Guild continued to make use of its contract with the Playhouse to stage one (and sometimes more than one) tryout each season.

For the rest the Playhouse depended on the packagers, with the Laurence Henry Company being the principal one. It seemed to work well enough. In 1960, in addition to the lease they already had at the Westport Playhouse, Feldman and Weinstein purchased the lease of the Paper Mill Playhouse in Millburn, New Jersey. In 1962 and 1963 respectively, they added the Mineola Playhouse on Long Island and the Brown Theatre in Louisville.

A solid basis of four leased and operated theatres seemed like a good foundation for a packaging business, but the growing complications of Laurence Feldman's life—most notably his suspension from the practice of law in 1962—undermined it. It was difficult to imagine Lawrence Langner putting up with such a situation for long. But, as it happened, it was left to Armina to take the necessary action, for Lawrence died suddenly on the night after Christmas in 1962.

The death of such a man as Lawrence Langner inevitably leaves a great void in the affairs of all those organizations with which he has been involved—but, curiously (and certainly as Lawrence intended), that did not apply to the Playhouse. Armina had been co-owner of the theatre from the beginning: she knew as much about its workings as her husband, and she was perfectly aware that her theatre (as it now was, jointly held with her son, Philip) could not long sustain its classy reputation with a connection such as Feldman. As the 1963 summer season drew to its close, she therefore informed Feldman that his lease would not be renewed.

The announcement set off a furious act of retribution by Feldman, who proceeded to auction practically every item of furniture or decoration that was not actually nailed down, including practically the entire contents of the prop room. The famous red cushions that lined the theatre's pews were later found to have been removed to the Mineola Playhouse, where Feldman still held sway, and had to be recovered by legal action.[16] It was all very ugly but mercifully brief, because Armina already had new management in place—and not only in place but actually prepared to go straight into an unprecedented fall season of six plays, which they proceeded to do with singular success.

Laurence Feldman (*center*) posed at the launch party for the 1961 season with the stars of the opening production, Samuel Taylor's *The Pleasure of His Company*. Cornelia Otis Skinner was following in the footsteps of her father, who had made his farewell performance on the Westport stage in 1933. Hans Conried (*left*), a familiar television personality, was one of Westport's best loved and most regular actors during the 1960s.

Armina might very well have invited Henry Weinstein to become the new lessee, but he had already departed for public television in 1961,[17] so she had no hesitation in offering the lease to Jim McKenzie, who already had broad and deep experience in summer stock, and whom she (and everyone else, including her late husband) instinctively liked and trusted.

McKenzie had originally been appointed house manager at Westport in 1959, alongside Feldman and Weinstein who styled themselves "The Producers." But it quickly became clear that McKenzie was the only member of the management team who really understood summer stock production, so he, too, was hastily promoted to producer. And in 1963, doubtless seeing the way things were going with Feldman, McKenzie founded his own packaging company with two of his friends, Ralph Roseman and Spofford Beadle. The Producing Managers Company, as it was called, quickly became the most successful and dependable of all the packagers, and Roseman and Beadle joined McKenzie as producers and managers at Westport—with McKenzie as executive producer, a title he would hold for the remainder of the century.

The fall season they put on within a few weeks of their official appointment at Westport was strongly cast and well received by the critics. It kicked off with the ever-popular Hermione Gingold in Arthur Kopit's *Oh Dad, Poor Dad, Mamma's Hung You in the Closet and I'm Feelin' So Sad*, and continued with James Lipton directing *The Innocents* with Betsy Palmer. Then came an Emlyn Williams play, *The Wind of Heaven*, and a debut by a

Westport playwright, David Rogers, whose family would go on to play a significant part in the future of the Playhouse, both onstage and off. Rogers's play, *The Moments of Love*, brought the veteran actress Ann Harding to Westport, and she was followed into the No. 1 dressing room by an even greater name—Cornelia Otis Skinner, who came to perform on the stage where her father had given the final performance of his great career in 1933. She appeared with Jane Wyatt (who was returning to the theatre for the first time since her ingénue season in 1932), Constance Cummings and Peggy Conklin in Andrew Rosenthal's *The Strangers*. Finally, to cap the season, came Lucille Lortel's production of Weill's *The Threepenny Opera*—but that, alas, was marred by the terrible events of that November week when President Kennedy was assassinated in Dallas.

McKenzie, Roseman and Beadle (a.k.a. the Producing Managers Company) had had a baptism of fire, and they had more than just survived it. Even though the season was not successful financially, it nevertheless showed that they were first-class producers of quality fare. As a result, they quickly found themselves in demand. They soon ran three summer theatres—Westport, Millburn and Mineola, all of which they took over from the Laurence Henry Company. They produced and packaged shows for both this "subway circuit," as they called it, and for the much larger summer circuit of stock theatres east of the Alleghenies; they planned to develop a similar circuit for "winter stock" in Florida and warmer parts of the country; they started to build a bus and truck business to tour small-scale productions; and they set out to get one or two productions a year on to Broadway, perhaps with national tours to follow. The Producing Managers Company was nothing if not ambitious.

> **Leo B. Meyer was resident designer at the Playhouse in 1963:**
>
> The fall season included a lovely play by Westport playwright David Rogers, *The Moments of Love*. The setting was a verdant garden with a pretty gazebo center stage. In this gazebo Ann Harding, the production's aging star, would reenact love scenes from her past, using hired actors as her past amours. I designed a domed pavilion with steps up the front and a pair of large urns flanking the stairway. I'd asked the prop person to scout up two urns. The next morning two exquisite metal urns graced the stage and were filled with lush blossoms. Both David and I were delighted with the stage picture. The following morning the local papers and the local radio newscasts screamed headlines about vandalism at a local cemetery along Route 33 in Westport. The apprentices and the prop assistant had done their deadly work in the gloom of night.
>
> The play, and the setting with the urns in full view, were both well received . . . and at the end of the week the two urns mysteriously reappeared at the graveyard! To this day, they stand proudly at the side of the road, waiting to receive their membership in Actors' Equity Association.

THE SIXTIES

Many people might have thought the 1960s was the wrong time to be ambitious in the theatre business. By 1958 there were 50 million television sets in the United States and 512 stations blanketing the country. It was widely assumed that most Americans stayed home in the evenings to watch free entertainment in their own living rooms. But that wasn't entirely the case: the 1960s was a time of expansion in American theatre—in fact, it saw the greatest expansion of theatre outside New York since the nineteenth century. The Ford Foundation was partly responsible. At the same time that it was funding and organizing the development of educational broadcasting in the United States (and, in the process, turning it into "public broadcasting"), Ford started making substantial grants to small not-for-profit theatre companies that had established toeholds in cities like Houston, San Francisco and Washington, D.C. By 1966 there were thirty-five regional theatres firmly established outside New York, and for the first time in the twentieth century there were more actors employed outside New York than inside.[18]

There were other encouraging signs in the early 1960s—a veritable explosion of summer festivals (to which, in 1955, the Langners contributed the Shakespeare Festival in Stratford, Connecticut); fifty-two stock theatres in operation as members of the Council of Summer Theatres—down from seventy in 1940 but still a substantial number;[19] and as many as 1,500 universities and colleges offering theatre courses and productions.[20]

At the very least, all this posed a challenge to the creative side of American theatre. With actors, directors, designers and other creative people being offered significantly more opportunity, at much higher rates of pay, for work in television and movies, there was legitimate reason to wonder if the efforts of the Ford Foundation and the other enablers would be properly rewarded. On the whole, they were—and that was largely because it was a time when two generations of playwrights crossed paths. In the late 1950s, O'Neill's posthumous works were being seen for the first time and were arousing new-found interest in his whole canon; Maxwell Anderson's post-war work had a strong following, as did those of Lillian Hellman and William Saroyan. And coming from the other direction was a new group of young playwrights—most notably Arthur Miller, Tennessee Williams, Edward Albee, Arthur Kopit and Neil Simon.

But there were equally ominous signs to be seen, and they weren't just to do with the success of television. The most dangerous of them was the inflationary rise in production costs. Packagers and production companies like the Producing Managers Company simply passed on these costs to the theatres, so it was the playhouses themselves that were most threatened—and many of them eventually went under. It was not the actors who caused the

Maureen O'Sullivan, Walter McGinn and Chester Morris in Frank Gilroy's *The Subject Was Roses* (1966).

Miggs Burroughs, a graphic artist and sometime cable talk show host, designed the Playhouse's brochures for many years. He was also an apprentice in 1964:

I was shown over the Playhouse by Jim McKenzie personally. He talked a lot about "the magic of show business." Eventually, he flung open a door to reveal a toilet. He handed me a plunger. "Welcome to show biz, Miggs!"

problem—most of them were still working for not much more than $100 a week, though stars were getting a great deal more, of course. The much bigger problem was with the escalating costs of materials, on the one hand, and technical union personnel, on the other.

This tale of economic woe was the background against which all theatres worked in the 1960s and for most of the remainder of the century. It was worrying enough to Jim McKenzie and his fellow lessees at Westport that they made sure their audience was kept constantly aware of it. Writing in the playbill in the summer of 1967, they examined the problem: "Firstly, there is only one gambler in the theatre. That is the producer. The investor also gambles but his gamble is usually limited to the amount of money he invests. Everyone else connected with the theatre is guaranteed a salary or a fee. These salaries and fees are scaled at the prevailing rates that operate in the general business market. This is especially true with reference to other media of entertainment such as Television and Films. So the theatre is in constant competition with mechanized media for able talent even though it cannot afford to pay what these media can. Secondly, theatrical unions treat entrepreneurs as if they are all privately rich and are in an industry such as steel, cars or washing machines. They seldom care about the relationship between their demands and the general cost of production."[21]

Helena de Crespo, Lauren Gilbert and Joan Fontaine in Rachel Crothers's *Susan and God* (1960).

There would be no prize for guessing that that was written by producers (indeed, McKenzie and his colleagues were always careful to sign their playbill letters "The Producers"), but it was also a pretty accurate description of the system. For most of the 1960s and 1970s the Westport Playhouse's margin each season, after it had paid the Langner family for the lease, was between one and two thousand dollars either way—profit or loss.[22] The very slenderness of that margin highlights the importance of the theatre's subscription network, which reached out far beyond Fairfield County. Absent Ina Bradley and her subscription committees, Westport would likely have gone under, as so many summer theatres did. But Westport had the good sense not only to use its star power to the maximum to attract (and hold) subscribers, but also to keep the subscription price so low that it could clearly be seen as a bargain. In 1950, the price for a six-play subscription was $19.80; in 1967 it was still only $25.[23] To have pushed the price higher must have been tempting: it might have increased the slender profit margin, but it might just as easily have slashed the number of subscribers and brought disaster.

SEASONS WITHIN SEASONS

Given these difficulties, it is not surprising that the post-Langner managements at Westport strove to find new solutions—and it is equally unsurprising that the solutions with which they experimented often involved prescriptions that had been tried before.

The Playhouse had begun its existence in 1931 and 1932 as a repertory company—with the idea that the company would take the same plays to Broadway for the fall and winter season. In practice, it hadn't worked, but the repertory idea had an enduring attraction because, potentially (that is, if you could get away from the union problems on Broadway), it had an economy of scale that was not readily available elsewhere. Laurence Feldman was convinced he could make it work by creating a company that would rehearse (but not play) in New York, use Westport as its tryout, then tour the principal cities of Mexico and South America. The company he put together in 1961, the New York Repertory Theatre, was a distinguished one, led by the Swedish-born actress Viveca Lindfors, who had made a considerable reputation for herself on both sides of the Atlantic. It also included Rita Gam, Betty Field, Ben Piazza and Bill Daniels. They took five plays with them— Tennessee Williams's *Sweet Bird of Youth* and *Suddenly, Last Summer*, John Van Druten's *I Am a Camera*, Strindberg's *Miss Julie* and Edward Albee's *The Zoo Story*. En route to Mexico they duly stopped off at the Westport Playhouse for a week in July. Whether or not the South American tour made any money for the Laurence Henry Company is not known—the experiment was not repeated—but it certainly offered the Westport subscribers an upmarket week of theatre.

The New York Repertory Theatre had performed as part of the normal summer season, but the Playhouse was always anxious to find ways of extending the theatre's performing time into other seasons of the year. That was the rationale for the fall season of 1963—the one the Producing Managers Company staged within weeks of taking over the theatre's management. On paper it was a distinguished season—as it was on the stage, too, from the evidence of the local press—but it was a financial disaster. The simple truth was that, by the beginning of October, a large proportion of Westport's summer population was back in New York, and it saw no particular reason to pop back to Westport for an evening of theatre, however strong the billing.

In 1965 the Playhouse tried again, this time with a spring season, and once again with a repertory company. Like Lawrence Langner, Ralph Roseman had a passion for Shaw, and he persuaded Jim McKenzie that a showcase festival devoted entirely to Shaw, outside the main season, would work at the box office. He was almost right. It just about broke even financially, and it had the considerable bonus of being a very definite artistic and critical success. The company was built around four well-known actors—Michael Allinson, Dina Merrill, Bramwell Fletcher and Lois Nettleton—and they performed three plays—*Major Barbara*, *Pygmalion* and *Misalliance*—in productions by Jack Sydow and William Francisco. The sixty-one-year-old English actor Bramwell Fletcher, who had been appearing, almost uninterruptedly, on the American stage since 1929, also performed his one-man show *The Bernard Shaw Story*, which he had written and first performed at the Gate Theatre in Dublin the previous December.

The qualified success of the Shaw season led McKenzie and his colleagues to try another spring season the very next year. The American Conservatory Theatre, only one year old in 1966, came to Westport to give what was, artistically, the most distinguished season yet given at the Playhouse. ACT, which had been founded in Pittsburgh in 1964 by William Ball with the support of the Rockefeller and Mellon foundations, was both a performing company and a teaching and training academy. It would figure large in the future of Jim McKenzie and several other people who worked at Westport, then and later. McKenzie became one of its trustees in 1966, at the time of the Westport visit, and he would later become ACT's executive producer from 1969 to 1982, combining it with his Westport duties. Another Westport alumnus, Charles Dillingham, who was general manager of the Playhouse in the 1969 season, went on to be ACT's general manager throughout the 1970s. But in 1966 ACT was still a "gypsy" company, uncertain of its future and experimental in nature. From Westport it was to go on to the Stanford Summer Festival in Palo Alto, and then to the Ravinia Festival outside Chicago. Only after that would it find its permanent home at the Geary Theatre in San Francisco.

The Westport engagement was particularly important because it offered the New York theatre establishment a chance

The Westport Country Playhouse
Presents A Festival from the repertoire of the

American Conservatory Theatre

William Ball Director

Six Characters in Search of an Author
Luigi Pirandello (adaptation by Paul Avila Mayer)
Tiny Alice
Edward Albee
Beyond The Fringe
Jonathan Miller Peter Cook Dudley Moore Alan Bennett
Uncle Vanya
Anton Chekhov
Death of a Salesman
Arthur Miller
Under Milk Wood
Dylan Thomas

May 16 thru June 11

Westport Country Playhouse,
Westport, Conn. (203) 227-4177

to see what the conservatory could do. Unfortunately, it also offered Actors' Equity an opportunity to make sure that ACT—already a substantial company of seventy-five—was observing all the rules. Apparently, it wasn't. On opening night, May 16, with the audience seated and the company ready to begin Pirandello's *Six Characters in Search of an Author*, what was politely called "a heated discussion" erupted in the wings between William Ball and Equity officials. They had ruled that ACT was in violation of the union's rule book and they refused to allow the curtain to go up. The audience had to be informed. For a time it looked as though that would be the end of the matter—the performance, perhaps the whole season, would be cancelled—but a visitor to the theatre came up with an ingenious solution. Warren Caro of the Theatre Guild suggested that audience members should be asked to agree that they had "donated" their ticket price to ACT and that they were now going to remain in their seats to watch a "rehearsal" of *Six Characters*. The performance (er, rehearsal) went on, and accommodations were reached with the union to enable the rest of the season to take place.[24]

The plays ACT presented at Westport, in addition to *Six Characters*, were Chekhov's *Uncle Vanya*, Dylan Thomas's *Under Milk Wood*, Edward Albee's *Tiny Alice*, Arthur Miller's *Death of a Salesman* and the Oxford and Cambridge review from England, *Beyond the Fringe*. Such an eclectic selection gave the actors, who were mostly young, a chance to show off their potential—and not just the actors, for ACT was concerned with all the crafts of the theatre: it designed and built its own sets, props, costumes and wigs. The idea of the company was that its youthful members would have the support and help of veteran actors, directors and craftsmen, and that its public performances would be extensions of the continuous teaching and training that was at the heart of the organization.

By the time Jim McKenzie ended his association with ACT almost twenty years later, it would have a membership of 250, an annual budget of $7 million, and some 13,000 alumni. In retrospect, the 1966 season at Westport had a historic importance for ACT because it had been the proving ground—the coming out party in front of American theatre's establishment.

The more immediate concern of the Playhouse's management, however, was that the ACT season might have given a false boost to the idea on which Westport had originally been based—the idea of the repertory company, which is what ACT was. As The Producers were quick to remind their audience in a regular season playbill, "Please note that there are no repertory companies in the country at the present time that are set up as profit-making institutions. Producers and investors would probably quickly go bankrupt if they tried it."[25] The Playhouse had "been there/done that" and it wasn't going to do it again.

It was interesting, though, that what The Producers disparagingly called "The Non-Profit Device" was, at the very least, a subject for discussion. Another playbill letter from The Producers (they were beginning to sound very like editorials at this stage) denounced the whole system on the grounds that for-profit and not-for-profit organizations could be running identical operations, but only the not-for-profit was eligible to apply for government and foundation grants. "Something is very wrong when the official policy of the land, of the highest channels of the Federal government, of State and local governments, and even of the industrial complex of America, can openly renounce profit-making motives in this country. It can go further, even to helping destroy profit-making theatrical enterprises, by giving artificial impetus to the sacred competitive cow, not-for-profit."[26]

At that stage, although The Producers would never have believed it, the Playhouse's own conversion to a not-for-profit institution was less than six years away.

In retrospect, the 1960s and early 1970s can be seen as the last good years of the twentieth century for summer stock. The number of theatres in the Northeast was beginning to decline, at first gently, later precipitously, but, for the time being, there were still enough of them to share costs and keep the packagers in business—including, most especially, the Producing Managers Company. In the 1960s, at least, Westport still had the advantage of being used by the Theatre Guild for tryouts. This normally enriched the end of each summer season, sometimes quite dramatically. In 1960, for instance, the Guild brought three plays to Westport in August and September—Leo Lieberman's *Captains and Kings* with Zachary Scott, Langston Hughes's *Tambourines to Glory* with Hazel Scott, and the Italian playwright Ugo Betti's *Burnt Flower Bed* with a stunning cast that included Eric Portman, Signe Hasso, Gloria Vanderbilt and Alexander Scourby. And just in case that wasn't enough, the season ended with another Broadway tryout, *An Evening with Mike Nichols and Elaine May*.

Liza Minnelli in 1964, the year she appeared at the Playhouse in *The Fantasticks*

There were a lot of interesting debuts, most of them crowd pleasers. Twenty-three-year-old Jane Fonda, whose film career was still in the future, followed in her father's footsteps when she starred in Jeremy Kingston's *No Concern of Mine* in 1960 (her father, Henry, had appeared in *The Virginian* at Westport the year his daughter was born). In 1964, eighteen-year-old Liza Minnelli came to Westport to get her Equity card. She played The Girl in *The Fantasticks*, with Elliott Gould as her co-star. On opening night, in the words of the Playhouse's fiftieth anniversary brochure, "the rather gawky teenager . . . received a standing ovation."[27]

Also making her stage debut was one of the greatest film stars Hollywood had ever known. At the age of fifty-six, Myrna Loy went on the summer stock circuit as the professor's wife in Leslie Steven's play *The Marriage-Go-Round*—with the dapper French actor Claude Dauphin as the professor. Miss Loy liked it enough to come back next summer with *There Must Be a Pony*. This was one of the first plays by actor-turned-playwright Jim Kirkwood, who, fifteen years later, would win a Pulitzer prize for his contribution to *A Chorus Line*. Walter Pidgeon and Sammy Davis, Jr., made Westport debuts at either end of the 1962 season, Van Johnson and Joel Grey in 1964 and Cicely Tyson and William Shatner later in the decade. The appearance of Captain James T. Kirk of the U.S.S. *Enterprise* in successive years, 1969 and 1970, caused the theatre to be stormed nightly by *Star Trek* fans, but it was when Mr. Shatner paid another visit, in 1977, that the "trekkies" went mad. This may have been because Mr. Shatner and his co-star, Yvette Mimieux, were scheduled to do a nude scene in *Tricks of the Trade*—which Miss Mimieux did indeed do. Order was restored, amidst huge disappointment, when Mr. Shatner appeared in a flesh-colored body suit that covered him from neck to ankles.[28]

The Playhouse continued to list great box-office stars on its marquee. Gloria Swanson returned in 1961, this time with a more rewarding vehicle, Malcolm Wells's *Between Seasons*; Tallulah Bankhead was back with George Oppenheimer's *Here Today* in 1962; Carol Channing was

When Jane Fonda starred in Jeremy Kingston's *No Concern of Mine* at Westport in the summer of 1960, she was no stranger to summer stock. She had just made her film debut playing opposite Tony Perkins in *Tall Story*, but most of her experience up to that point (she was twenty-three) had been a combination of modeling and stage acting. She was a pupil of Lee Strasberg at the Actors Studio, and many people were already predicting she would follow in the footsteps of her father, Henry, by making a career between Hollywood and Broadway, with occasional excursions into summer stock.

"THREE FLOUNCES AND A BOUNCE": JANE FONDA GOES WESTPORT

Her first professional stage appearance had been in 1955 as the ingénue in Odets's *The Country Girl*, with her father and Dorothy Maguire. The following year she had been back on the summer circuit, again with her father, in *The Male Animal* by James Thurber and Eliot Nugent. Neither of these outings had taken her to Westport, but a good many Westporters would have seen her on Broadway in the fall of 1959 when she won the New York Drama Critics Circle award as "Most Promising Young Actress" for her performance in *There Was a Little Girl*.

Certainly, by the time she arrived at Westport in July 1960, she had an established reputation as a stage actress and—through the just released *Tall Story*—the beginnings of a reputation as a film star. No one doubted she was going places, and it was natural that she should be given top billing over her co-stars, Ben Piazza and Geoffrey Horne. Nor was it unexpected that Henry Weinstein, who was already involved with television drama when he wasn't at Westport, had announced plans for educational television's WNET-TV to tape the play later for its *Play of the Week*.

The local critics were dazzled by Jane—and a bit disappointed with the play, which had previously had a three-month run in London but had not been seen in the States. The *Danbury News-Times* described a "tremendously funny" first act, deteriorating into "a slow-moving, mediocre melodrama." The play, it said, "is not equal to the talents of Miss Fonda," who played the part of a young drama student "with great charm. She has poise, beauty, and a gracefulness of manner that is completely captivating."[29] The *Meridien Record* agreed about the play, and was both more fulsome and a tad more critical of the star: "Jane Fonda is . . . a doll; she has her father's charm, and her own junior version of his looks. She's still at the stage where she uses three flounces and a bounce where a single one would do, but she's got time to learn the art of understatement."[30]

WESTPORT
COUNTRY PLAYHOUSE
— PHONE CA 7-4177 —
JULY 11 Thru **JULY 16**
IN PERSON
JANE FONDA
IN HER WESTPORT DEBUT
NO CONCERN OF MINE
A New Play by Jeremy Kingston
Monday Thru Friday Evenings at 8:40 — Saturday Eves. at 6 and 9 — Wednesday Mats. at 2:40

Shaw's Millionairess in 1963; and Margaret O'Brien, the most talented child star of the 1940s, came to Westport to try and make it as an adult. In 1964, Helen Hayes made a memorable last appearance on the Westport stage in *The White House* by a local playwright, A. E. Hotchner (the author of *Papa Hemingway*); Joan Fontaine was back in 1965 and 1967 in Agatha Christie mysteries; Hal Holbrooke, Eva Gabor, Imogene Coca, Maureen O'Sullivan, Alan Alda and Joan Bennett all appeared near the end of the sixties, and Sid Caesar, Mickey Rooney and Eddie Bracken rang in the seventies.

Helen Hayes in A. E. Hotchner's *The White House* (1964).

But the heart and soul of Westport's summer seasons was now becoming readily identified as a group of fine and dedicated stage actors who came to the Playhouse—not regularly, but often—and who continued to come over several decades. A great Hollywood star might be greeted by an appreciative round of applause, but these actors were greeted with real warmth and affection. They were recognized for what they were—the American acting profession at its best. To list them is invidious and risks unwittingly passing judgment on other actors, but these men and women were so important to the theatre's success that it is a risk worth taking.

In the summer of 1970, George Gobel starred in Woody Allen's **Play It Again, Sam.** *Melinda Dickinson, who was an apprentice that summer, remembers that the curtain had to be brought down in the middle of one performance:*

George Gobel had found the raccoon family that used to live under the building, right off the ironing nook in the green room. There was a popcorn machine downstairs, and they loved popcorn, so everyone fed them. I came in one afternoon and found Mr. Gobel in the ironing nook, dipping pieces of popcorn into a glass of Scotch and feeding them to the mother and three babies, who were lined up on the ironing board, begging.

Later on, during the performance, the now drunk raccoons snuck past Lindsay Law, the stage manager, filed onstage in a little line, and went straight for Mr. Gobel.

Betsy Palmer and Arlene Francis were certainly two of them, and they actually appeared on the Westport stage more than any other actors. Francis had been on Broadway since 1936 and was a product of the Theatre Guild School, whereas Palmer, from Chicago, had got most of her early experience in summer stock in Wisconsin and Illinois before going to the Actors Studio and making her Broadway debut in 1955. Both actresses spread their talents across all the available media—film, television and the stage—and both owed their greatest fame to being television personalities in the great age of quiz shows. Francis made her first appearance at Westport in 1953 in Robert Sherwood's play about Hannibal, *The Road to Rome*, and her tenth and last (in 1988, in her eightieth year!) opposite David Birney in Andrew Bergman's *Social Security*. Palmer made her first Westport appearance only three years after Francis's, in 1956, starring with Jules Munshin and Hal Holbrooke in Molière's *Le Médecin malgré lui*, adapted and directed by James Lipton. In 1998 (in her seventieth year!), when she appeared in Ron Clark's *A Bench in the Sun*, she surpassed Arlene Francis's record number of appearances with eleven.

Betsy Palmer in the 1950s.

Eileen Heckart was another member of this special group. "Heckie" appeared in seven Westport shows between 1949 and 1995—a bigger spread than either Francis or Palmer, and she, too, was well into her seventies at the time of her last appearance. In her first, forty-six summers earlier, she had starred opposite Sarah Churchill in *The Philadelphia Story*.

As a Fairfield County resident and next door neighbor of

the Langners when they moved to Apple Hill, Gypsy Rose Lee's sister, June Havoc, had a closer relationship with the Playhouse than most actors. Her first appearance was in the play with which the theatre reopened after World War II—Sidney Howard's *They Knew What They Wanted*—and her last, in 1983, was as Miss Hannigan in *Annie*. In between she was Lysistrata, Anna Christie and Agnes in Albee's *A Delicate Balance*.

Eileen Heckart (*left*), Celeste Holm and Jack Yankee (Eileen Heckart's husband) at the Playhouse in the 1950s

Haila Stoddard was another fine actress (and another Fairfield County resident) who made regular sallies into summer stock, beginning in 1936. She first played Westport in 1940 as Julia in *Goodbye Again*, and her last appearance there was as Martha in Albee's *Who's Afraid of Virginia Woolf?* Of all the roles she played in her great career, this was the one she herself liked best (she had inherited it from its creator, Uta Hagen), and she brought it to Westport in the summer of 1964, right after the Broadway run.

Nick, the puzzled young professor of that first Broadway production of *Who's Afraid of Virginia Woolf?* was George Grizzard. He first played Westport in 1960 along with Arlene Francis in S. N. Behrman's adaptation of the Jean Giraudaux play *Amphitryon 38*. He was there twice more in the 1960s, and again in the 1980s and 1990s. Eli Wallach and Anne Jackson had a rather similar record between 1959 and 1982, though, as befitted one of the theatre's most famous married couples, their appearances were almost always together (with the single exception of the production of *Slightly Delayed* in 1979 in which Anne Jackson appeared with Geraldine Page). During all this time no one was more faithful to the Playhouse, especially in the 1960s, than Hans Conried. He was another of those actors who had been made familiar to millions of Americans by television—he was Uncle Toonoose in *The Danny Thomas Show*—and he was a perennial favorite with the Westport audience.

Shelley Winters in William Gibson's *Two for the Seesaw* (1960).

There were other regulars—actors who weren't really regulars at Westport (by definition, no one was), but who were nevertheless thought of by the Westport audience as their own. Celeste Holm, the bright-eyed blonde who created Ado Annie in *Oklahoma!* and who would always be remembered for "I Can't Say No," was there every year between 1957 and 1961. She did everything from Shaw (*Back to Methuselah*—mercifully, a much cut version) to her own musical review (*What A Day!*), and included, in between, a new play, *Third Best Sport*, with which she went to Broadway. Tammy Grimes belonged to the Westport audience in a more literal way—she had apprenticed at the theatre and been the hostess of its restaurant, and she was married to one of the town's theatrical luminaries, Christopher Plummer. She made five appearances between 1956 and 1978. And there was the much more unlikely Eva Gabor, younger sister of Zsa Zsa and a film star of note. Between 1953 and 1963, the Hungarian actress made five appearances in light comedies at Westport, enjoying her summers on the stock theatre circuit even while her film career was in full spate.

There were two actors who came to Westport only occasionally, but whom the audience treated as its own for a very different reason. Both Shirley Booth and Keir Dullea converted Playhouse try-outs into huge successes on Broadway. When Shirley Booth, the plump and bubbly star with the baby voice, came to Westport with William Inge's *Come Back, Little Sheba* in 1949 she was already a household name. She had been Elizabeth Imbrie, the photographer, in *The Philadelphia Story* back in 1939, and she had won her first Tony as Grace Woods, the impertinent secretary, in *Goodbye, My Fancy* in 1948. Lola, the slovenly housewife of *Sheba*, won her the second Tony two years later, and was probably the role that best exhibited her powers as an actress. Brooks Atkinson said of that portrayal that it had "the shuffle, the maddening garrulity and the rasping voice of the slattern," but also "the warmth, generosity and valor of a loyal and affectionate woman."[31] When Shirley Booth returned to Westport in 1959 in the title role of *Nina* she was billed by the local press as "The First Lady of the American Theatre,"[32] and she was greeted by the first night audience as a returning heroine—as she was again in 1968 and 1970 with *Desk Set* and *Best of Friends*.

Keir Dullea, whose most recent film when he came to the Playhouse in 1969 was *2001: A Space Odyssey*, was described in the *Bridgeport Post* as "a handsome young buck with some pretty impressive acting credits,"[33] but the fact was that he had not made a very favorable impression on the local critics the previous summer. On that occasion he had been playing the lead in a Neil Simon comedy, *The Star Spangled Girl*, and he had seemed "inept and woefully uncomfortable," according to the *Westporter Herald*.[34] In point of fact, he had had good reason to feel uncomfortable in the Simon play: the following week's playbill had allowed its columnist, "coni-prez greiner," to apologize for the production: "Many of the long-term first-nighters complained vehemently (departing after second act). Be assured the producers do their best to bring us an enjoyable season: it's impossible to have a perfect batting average."[35] Now, a year later, in the hugely demanding role of the blind boy in Leonard Gershe's play *Butterflies Are Free*, Dullea and Blythe Danner, with Maureen O'Sullivan as the mother, blew the audience away. And the critics could sense it—most of them hastened to predict a Broadway future for both the play and the cast. They were right: it ran for three years on Broadway, with the same cast except that Eileen Heckart took over the heaven-sent role of the mother from Maureen O'Sullivan.

These, then, were some of the most considerable actors at Westport in the sixties and early seventies, and it was probably sometime during that period that they became a more important factor in the success of the subscription scheme than the Hollywood stars who made flying visits.

At the same time, though it was neither sudden nor dramatic, there was a discernible change in the type of repertory the Playhouse offered its patrons. To a large extent, it represented a simple passing of time—the second half of the century was less connected to the inter-war years, barely connected at all to the nineteenth century, and the audience did not particularly want to see plays of those eras unless they were certifiable classics, and then only rarely, please. But it also had to do with the kind of audience it had become. It was in thrall to television. Its view of the world was largely governed by what it saw on television, and what it was mostly seeing in those years was an ugly and dispiriting chronicle of death and mayhem in a far-off country where its young people were being sent in ever increasing numbers.

Although some profound and important dramatic writing would ultimately come out of this era, it was not what the Playhouse sought to offer its audience. Jim McKenzie and his team were becoming uncomfortably aware of the tenuous position that summer stock now occupied in the theatrical firmament. Even if it wasn't directly threatened in Westport (though it soon would be),

Sometimes it happens without warning. *Butterflies Are Free*, with its neat title from *Bleak House*,[36] and its appealing story of a blind boy in love with a kooky actress, came to Westport in the last week of August 1969, dutifully labeled "prior to Broadway." A lot of plays got that label at Westport, and not many of them made it to Broadway. But *Butterflies* did—and more than that, it had an exceptionally long run there: three years and well over a thousand performances.

BUTTERFLIES ARE FREE

The play was a good one—Leonard Gershe's only real success on the stage—with "lots of laughs and a few tears," and a production that worked unusually well for a summer theatre. "The most memorable feature of the set," wrote the *Stamford Advocate*, "is a high loft-type bed reached by a ladder, directly under the skylight. The scene projects beyond the normal curtain line and blackouts are used rather than curtain closings to divide the scenes. An interesting background lighting effect of clouds in the sky was used to introduce each scene as the lights came up gradually."[37]

The stars were good, too—Keir Dullea as the blind boy Don, and Maureen O'Sullivan as his mother—but it was the other two actors, with their names below the title, who lit up the play. Michael Zaslow's was a small part—the hippie Off-Broadway producer who specializes in nude scenes—but it was also the most grateful so far as comedy was concerned: he reacts to a blind person in all the ways we hope we never will. Blythe Danner's role, on the other hand, was a big one: she played the actress Jill Tanner whose doubts and hesitations about falling in love with a blind boy mirror the concerns that anyone might have.

Danner was twenty-five and she wouldn't earn her star status until she appeared on Broadway with *Butterflies* in the fall, but the local press had no difficulty in recognizing a star in the making. The *Bridgeport Post* said unequivocally: "[I]t is Blythe Danner who serves as the main spring of the action. She is cute and shapely and eye-filling when she strips down to an abbreviated bra and brief panties. But it takes more than physical charm to make her role really count. She has the necessary talent and the know-how to display it to the best advantage."[38] The harder-to-please *Westport News* was equally unequivocal, but more thoughtful in the telling: "Miss Danner is somebody very special. . . . She is ingenious without being cute, pert without being phony, wistful without being coy. Her freedom-loving girl who falls in and out of bed like a leaf in autumn but who cannot let herself feel or love is very real, touching."[39]

Keir Dullea and Blythe Danner went to Broadway with the show when it left Westport and won all sorts of laurels. Maureen O'Sullivan didn't—the mother was played in New York by another Westport regular, Eileen Heckart. As for the film that followed in 1972, that was a vehicle for the young Goldie Hawn playing opposite the even younger Edward Albert, Jr.

Keir Dullea and Blythe Danner,
Butterflies Are Free, 1969.

they had an intimate view of the other summer theatres through their control of the Producing Managers Company, and what they were beginning to see in the early seventies were summer theatres falling almost like dominoes. Inflation was doing what it always did best—it was sorting the wheat from the chaff.

In these circumstances, a prudent theatre management (as opposed to one that was either immensely brave or else suicidal) offered its subscribers a diet of plays that took few risks and rarely challenged them. The Playhouse lessees had to pay their way. Unlike Lawrence Langner, they had no latitude for losses. They continued to present between ten and twelve productions a year, but it is evident from the play lists that the sort of thing Theresa Helburn had once derided as "floss" was no longer beyond the pale. Even in the heart of the Langner era there had always been a noticeable presence of light comedy—mostly romantic comedies and mysteries. That presence now became a good deal stronger with a lot of revivals from the 1940s and early 1950s and a succession of London imports from prolific playwrights like Alan Ayckbourn and William Douglas Home, as well as less current writers like Agatha Christie and Noël Coward. Along with them came the plays of Ionescu, Peter Shaffer and other Europeans of note. Euripides made the lists with a Michael Cacoyannis production of *The Trojan Women* in 1965, but otherwise the classics of the nineteenth century and all previous centuries were missing. There were one or two revivals of Shaw and Behrman as vehicles for artists the Playhouse particularly wanted to attract, but the greatest American playwrights of the twentieth century were in short supply (no O'Neill, no Arthur Miller and Tennessee Williams only rarely). To compensate, there was a fairly constant supply of good contemporary American work—Edward Albee, Jean Kerr, Woody Allen, William Inge, Leonard Gershe and, above all, Neil Simon, whose plays customarily came to Westport within a year or two

Ralph Roseman, who played a major part in the running of the Playhouse in the 1960s and 1970s, gives an informal acting class to the 1965 apprentices.

of their first production on Broadway and who quickly became the Playhouse's most frequently performed author.

A typical year shows how dependent the theatre was on packagers. For Westport, this was not as great a concern as it was for some other summer theatres because the principal packager was the Producing Managers Company, which was Jim McKenzie's day job, so to speak. In 1969 (as a sample year) Westport presented twelve shows. Two of them were Broadway tryouts—*The Chic Life* by Arthur Marx and Bob Fisher, and *Butterflies Are Free*, which would become a Broadway sensation—and one was a major musical, *South Pacific*, from the Starlight Music Theatre of Connecticut. The remaining nine shows all came from packagers—and six of them were from the Producing Managers Company.[40]

By the late 1960s the Theatre Guild was producing less and less, so another of Westport's regular sources of production—Theatre Guild tryouts—began to disappear. George Abbot's successful 1966 tryout of *Help Stamp Out Marriage* by the British writers Keith Waterhouse and Willis Hall was one of the last. But there were other Broadway producers besides the Theatre Guild who needed venues for tryouts, and Westport was not only convenient but it had the essential qualification of having the "bug" on all its scenery—that is, it had unionized workshops, whose scenery and other products could be transferred to Broadway without problems. So tryouts continued, though not in such reliable numbers.

The 1972 season ended with a succession of classy productions—Jean Kerr's *Poor Richard*, Neil Simon's *The Gingerbread Lady*, a Broadway tryout of *Remember Me* (with Robert Stack) and a production of *Hello, Dolly!*—but it was becoming clear to Jim McKenzie and Armina and Philip Langner (who were still the owners) that the theatre's finances could not withstand many more seasons of inflationary costs. However amazing the efforts of Ina Bradley and her subscription committee, the days when they could sell 85 percent of the season by subscription were long gone. By now, they were struggling to sell 35 percent, with the remainder depending on single-ticket buyers.

Something had to be done, and it would have to be fairly drastic.

On summer Fridays, Rocky struts his stuff around the theatre, playing host to hundreds of noisy, excited children and their bemused parents. The children have come to watch *Aladdin* or *Rumplestiltskin* or *The Just So Stories*, or perhaps, if they are very lucky, *Tom Chapin in Concert*—shows that have nothing to do with the evening entertainments that adults come to see, except that they have to be performed within the set of whatever is onstage that week. There's no striking and resetting—this is an invasion, pure and simple, and the Playhouse staff can like it or lump in. Generally, they like it, for what is happening around them on

ROCKY THE ROOSTER RULES! THE PLAYHOUSE CHILDREN'S THEATRE

Fridays is what pays for at least a part of the shortfall on their main productions. The Children's Theatre regularly plays to between 95 and 100 percent of capacity (and occasionally 105 percent), and it is almost always in profit for the season. There are two shows each Friday—at 10:30 or 11 a.m. and again at 1 p.m.—and the Playhouse staff then has less than five hours to make necessary repairs to the theatre and the grounds before the evening audience arrives.

Generations of Westport children have had their first taste of live theatre at these Friday performances, and many of them (even, by now, their children) have gone on to become members of the main subscription list—which was precisely the motivation for starting the Children's Theatre, in the first place.

There had been sporadic productions of children's entertainments at the Playhouse in the 1930s, but never a properly sustained program. After the war, it was not until 1955 that the idea was revived, and then it was a single experimental production of *Davy Crockett, Hero of the Backwoods.* Its success ("the stout wood walls of the Playhouse are still relatively intact," observed the playbill)[41] led to a "season-in-miniature" on four Friday mornings in 1956. It led off with a children's ballet, *The Story of Dancy Feet*, in which Judith Martin danced all the characters. Then came the hugely popular *Robin Hood's Treasure*, presented by the Mae Desmond Children's Theatre. Then *Fred Keating's Magic Show for Children* (Mr. Keating was appearing with Beatrice Lillie in *Beasop's Fables* for the adult audience that week). And finally a puppet show—*The Sleeping Beauty*, performed by the life-sized Suzari Marionettes.

Lawrence Langner's hand can clearly be seen in this (it was while he and Armina were still actively involved in running the Playhouse), and the rationale for children's theatre published in the playbill bears the unmistakable mark of his thinking: "Not very long ago it was generally felt that the increasing influence of radio and television would eventually spell the end of stage productions as a medium of entertainment for children, but it seems that the appeal of live theatre is built of sterner stuff than its critics imagined. Recently the trend has changed, and Children's Theatre groups have been luring back enthusiastic audiences from what one sinister reference terms 'this shadow world.' In keeping with this tendency, the Playhouse has embarked upon its larger venture; and, in so doing, is presenting productions which should serve as a balanced introduction to the sort of theatre entertainment which will interest young audiences in later life."[42]

By 1961, the repertoire was somewhat different (ballet didn't seem to work too well with Westport's youngsters) and a second performance was added each Friday (reserved seats $1.50; general admission $1). The Musical Theatre for Children brought a successful Off-Broadway production of *Tom Sawyer* that was about to go off on a national tour, and there was a "complete children's musical comedy" called *Topsy*

Turvy Town. But the big attraction (on which weeks of preparation had been lavished) was a production of Hans Christian Andersen's *The Tinder Box* by the Playhouse's apprentices, directed by one of its interns, associate press representative James Shearwood of Staples High and Amherst College, "where he will graduate next spring." It became a custom that the apprentices would put on one of the children's shows each summer.

In 1965, the six-week summer series (as it had now become) was augmented with a spring season of three Saturday shows in May (*The Wizard of Oz, Rumplestiltskin* and a puppet version of *Hansel and Gretel*), but that was soon merged into the summer series, which became, and has almost always remained, an eight- or nine-production series.

For the most part, the Playhouse has not produced its own children's productions—with the exception of the apprentice shows and very occasional local productions, such as June Walker Rogers's 1977 production of *Winnie the Pooh*, which starred a large and well known Westport radio personality, John LaBarca, as Pooh. The vast majority of shows have come from production companies that specialize in children's entertainment and that tour several different shows around New England and New York each year. For a time in the 1970s The Famous Prince Street Players, which was an arm of CBS Television, was the dominant provider. It was succeeded in the 1980s (and beyond) by The Gingerbread Players and Jack, the Traveling Playhouse, and the Fanfare Theatre Ensemble, with many more specialized companies such as The Pandemonium Puppet Company. Over the years, they have entertained the children with popular fairy tales, magicians, musicians, puppets and plays and stories of all kinds. Occasionally there have been more thought-provoking shows, like *Imagine If* with Jamie the Imaginologist—and no one has had a more enduring success with the children than the A&M recording artist Tom Chapin.

In the mid-1990s it was decided that the summer series wasn't enough—a holiday children's series was added in December (generally four shows), and then fall and spring series as well (generally two shows each—a Halloween show, an Easter show and so on).[43]

More recently, there has been more experimentation. In May 2003, the Playhouse commissioned Child's Play Touring Theatre to stage an original production, *Something of Our Own*. It was a collection of short original plays written by children aged 5 to 16 from the Westport area. As Hyla Crane, the Playhouse's education director, put it: "The project offers a unique opportunity for children's work to be given a voice by a professional theatre company and for other children to be inspired by the creativity of their peers. It may motivate a child to think, 'if they can do that, so can I.'"[44]

And always, there is the children's genial host, Rocky the Red Rooster. Originally, Rocky stood atop the old barn above the weather vane. Then he found his way to the side of the barn, where he resided for many years. At the dawning of the twenty-first century, he sought restoration to his former glory and prevailed upon Ms. Woodward to accept that a rooster cannot crow properly or effectively unless he is on top of the pile. He continues to be the Playhouse's official mascot, a status he assumed almost fifty years ago when the local artist Stevan Dohanos painted him and put him on the front of the playbill one summer (which, incidentally, is another place where he thinks he rightfully belongs).

The tradition of children's shows at the Playhouse dates back to 1934.

Announcing • • • • •
CHILDREN'S VARIETY SHOW

Saturday MORNING, Aug. 18, at 11 O'clock

Juggling Tricks • MAGIC Punch and Judy Puppets • Fun for Children from 6 to 60 • All to the Tune of a Rollicking Accordion •

Under the Direction of

ROBERT REINHART

PRESTIDIGITATOR PAR EXCELLENCE

PRICES: 50c, 75c, $1.00. SPECIAL REDUCTION TO SUBSCRIBERS

WESTPORT COUNTRY PLAYHOUSE

CHILDREN'S SUMMER SEASON

Fridays @ 10:30am & 1pm

June 23
TOM CHAPIN IN CONCERT
Tom Chapin & Michael Mark

June 30
ANANSI, SPIDERMAN OF AFRICA
Crabgrass Puppet Theatre

July 7
BEAUTY AND THE BEAST
Gingerbread Players & Jack

July 14
ALICE IN WONDERLAND
Bits & Pieces Puppet Theatre

July 21
THE REALLY GOOD & FUNNY SHOW
Child's Play Touring Theatre

July 28
TEDDY BEAR CONCERT
Gary Rosen

Aug. 4
PINOCCHIO
Yates Musical Theatre

Aug. 11
POP-UPS, PUPPETS & PARADES
Jim West/TheatreworksUSA

Aug. 18
THE MAGIC OF CINDERELLA
Arnie Kolodner Magic

The 2000 children's season.

All theatres need a good lawyer, and the Westport Playhouse had one of the best—J. Kenneth Bradley. But when Lawrence Langner invited Mr. Bradley to look after the theatre's legal affairs, he got more than he hoped for, for Mr. Bradley married a bright, blue-eyed Scottish lass, who was not just a stunning beauty but also a woman of matchless talent and energy. What's more, she knew about summer stock—she had acted in it professionally for a short time before her marriage. So when Francesca Lodge launched the Playhouse's subscription scheme in the spring of 1946, she took Lawrence Langner's advice and asked Ina Bradley to chair the Westport committee.

INA BRADLEY: A FORTY-YEAR STARRING ROLE

For forty years thereafter, Mrs. Bradley was intimately involved in the theatre's activities. In 1955 she became chairman of the Playhouse Committee, and added the presidency of the Connecticut Theatre Foundation in 1973 when the theatre became a not-for-profit institution. By that time, in truth, she was an institution herself, though an exceptionally unpompous one. Every Monday night, with the opening of each new play, she would appear "front of curtain" to say a few words of welcome and introduction—and in all the hundreds of times she did it, legend has it that she never appeared in the same gown twice, and all of them were gorgeous. There were those who claimed they would be willing to buy a Monday night subscription just to see Ina make her appearance—and there were actors who thought they were being upstaged (which they were), but no actor ever complained about the luncheons and parties Ina gave for them in her home, or the extra publicity they got when she interviewed them on her radio program or in her newspaper column. And if they were just a little bit nervous of being photographed with her—well, cameras have a way of focusing on their most glamorous subject.

But to know Ina was also to know that a great part of her beauty came from within. There was nothing artificial about her charm.

And why did she give so much of her time to the Playhouse? "The answer is easy," she wrote: "It's a labor of love. I've been involved all these years for three reasons: love of the theatre, a deep affection for Lawrence and Armina Langner—whose friendship my husband and I have held dear for many, many years—and finally, my dedication to the idea of the Westport Country Playhouse as an integral part of community life, artistically and socially."[45]

Other than painting the scenery, there was really no part of the theatre's activities she didn't get involved in. In 1954, she took a small part in *The Lady Chooses*, which starred Faye Emerson and Walter Abel (Lily Lodge, Francesca's daughter, also had a part). In the 1960s, she hosted the fashion shows that were held in the restaurant before Wednesday matinees—she usually modeled some of the gowns as well, and sometimes provided the commentary. She often did her radio program "live" from the theatre's lobby. She hosted first night parties, be they never so weird (for Shaw's *Caesar and Cleopatra* in 1959 Henry Weinstein made everyone wear togas). She once sat for four different artists who were commissioned to paint her by Leonid Kipnis of the Kipnis Gallery in Westport, with an exhibition in the Playhouse lobby. And always, of course, there was the day-to-day business of drumming up more subscriptions, of searching out grants and donors once it became a not-for-profit theatre, and (as the years went by) of helping Jim McKenzie fend off the ever increasing number of financial crises.

The Playhouse was only one of a score of Connecticut institutions Ina Bradley was involved with. She worked for women's clubs, mental health projects, Republican political committees, arts organizations and a host of others. And she combined them all with her radio and television work, her journalism and her family (she had three children).

She resigned her offices at the Playhouse in 1986, just forty years after she had begun to work there. She died in 1996.

In the 1950s, Ina often did her radio program live from the Playhouse lobby on Monday nights.

For almost sixty years, the Playhouse has relied on its apprentice program to provide the labor that is needed to maintain a summer stock theatre. It simply wouldn't work without its apprentices and interns, and they, in turn, owe the Playhouse a debt of gratitude for allowing them to spend a summer being introduced to so many different aspects of theatre life.

Martin Manulis began the apprentice scheme at Westport in 1946. There was nothing very new about it—similar schemes were already in operation in many summer theatres across the country—but it revolu-

"SUBMIT YOUR RÉSUMÉ, WITH A PICTURE": THE APPRENTICE AND INTERN PROGRAMS

tionized the way things were done at the Playhouse, and that included the budgeting process, for apprentices represented free labor. Originally (and for many years thereafter), they worked a fourteen-week summer for no pay at all, and even paid for their own housing. At least they weren't expected to pay "tuition" on top—an "ill-disguised racket" at some summer theatres, according to Ralph Lycett, the theatre's publicist, in 1949.[46] Only since the 1980s has the Playhouse provided a weekly stipend for apprentices, just big enough (in theory) to pay for board and lodging.

The idea of the apprentice scheme was that young people who were seriously contemplating a career in theatre should have a brief but intensive immersion in "the real thing." In the course of the summer they were meant to rotate through every major department of the theatre's operations—the scene shop, the paint shop, stage management, lighting, scene shifting, concession stands, box office, wigs and costumes, props, the parking lot and even occasional minor roles onstage. They were supervised by whichever department head they were working for at the time—the scenic designer, the chief electrician, the chief carpenter, the general manager. "Strike nights" and "set-up days"—exhausting 24-hour weekend stints when one production went out and another came in—involved everyone. Not the least important feature of the scheme as it was originally designed by Martin Manulis was that apprentices also got the chance to take part in at least one "show case." In reality, these were talent shows—with the very special cachet that Manulis and the Langners invited theatre people from New York and the Westport area to attend. Three of the 1949 apprentices landed jobs on Broadway or in touring productions

1995 interns Stacie Turner and Tony Ortega constructing new stage props

as a direct result of these "show cases."[47] Less important, perhaps, but just as much fun, were the children's productions that the apprentices sometimes (but not always) banded together to produce.

Over the years, the apprentice program has changed in emphasis and detail, but not in its fundamentals. Since the day of its introduction, it has been central to the planning and execution of every summer season, and it still is today. Gender has never been an issue—there have always been male and female apprentices in more or less equal numbers, and they have always been required to share the work between them, regardless of their sex. Until very recently, there was a fairly wide age range—from as young as sixteen to as old as twenty-three—and in the 1970s and 1980s it became customary to invite back a few of the best apprentices to work as interns the following season. Interns worked for department heads as full-time assistants and did not rotate, but, like everyone else, they were required to lend a hand on "strike nights."

If one purpose of the apprentice program is to provide the Playhouse with a major part of its workforce, then another (and equally important) purpose is to provide the young people with an introduction to the world of theatre—and more than that, with some genuine education. As long ago as 1949, Lawrence Langner was writing to Martin Manulis to insist that apprentices should "have one lecture per week either by one of the actors or a member of the staff. . . . I want the kids to get some educational experience from their apprenticeship."[48] More often than not, however, the pressure of getting a dozen or more productions on stage in fourteen weeks prohibited expansion of the education component beyond the (enormously valuable) acquisition of hands-on experience. This changed in 2001, under the leadership of Joanne Woodward, when the apprentice-intern program was remodeled along the lines of the much admired program at the Williamstown Theatre Festival in Massachusetts. Apprentices, mainly drawn from the ranks of high school juniors and seniors, now have regularly scheduled morning classes that give them a theoretical introduction to almost every aspect of theatre, followed by the opportunity to put that learning into practice as they rotate through the various departments of the Playhouse, where their work is supervised by professionals.

Alongside this new-style apprentice program is a separate one for interns. This is for college students, graduate students or recent graduates, and it offers a much more specialized experience. Successful applicants spend the summer in a single department—properties, wardrobe, electrics, administration, marketing and public relations, development, company management, stage management and artistic—and they are chosen because they are already planning a career in the professional theatre.

In the early days, when there were as many as a dozen productions to be mounted, there were generally twenty apprentices, sometimes as many as twenty-five, with most of them drawn from college drama departments.[49] The positions were very competitive—750 applications in 1949.[50] Later on, especially after 1987 when there were only six productions to be serviced, the number of apprentices was reduced to eight, applicants were down to 100, and the age range was now "16 or older."[51] The alumni list shows that apprentices have come from as far afield as Pakistan, Spain, France, Germany and England (travel expenses are not reimbursed), as well as all parts of North America, but the largest number, by far, have come from the Westport area.[52]

Lawrence Langner was sometimes doubtful about the wisdom of having an apprentice program at Westport, but he was frequently on hand to encourage the young people.

Lawrence Langner, it has to be said, was a reluctant supporter of the apprentice program. Both the parent and the lawyer in him warned that the Playhouse was taking on a responsibility it was ill equipped to carry out, and these misgivings were spectacularly ignited by a polio scare in Westport in 1950–51. One apprentice was taken ill and hospitalized (though whether polio had anything to do with it was never revealed) and one or two others had suspicious symptoms, though they shook them off quickly enough.[53] One afternoon the apprentices were called together in the yard and urged to seek medical help if they had even the slightest suspicion that they might be developing symptoms.[54] It was a scary atmosphere. Noting that the latest medical opinion held that polio was "usually latent in people" and that "fatigue is one of the greatest factors in helping it to break out," Lawrence Langner wrote a memo to his colleagues (Armina, John Wilson, Martin Manulis and Philip Langner) at the end of the 1950 season:

I strongly suggest that we drop the employment of apprentices at Westport. If, however, others disagree with me, then I must insist on the following:

Apprentices are engaged with the understanding that the work is fatiguing and that there will be no parties or gatherings which keep them up later than 12 at night, except one night a week, which should be Monday night and definitely not Saturday night.

That we will employ 20 apprentices, of which six will have

WILLIAMS

OK
arr 23
File
acc.

May 2, 1950

Dear Mr. Manulis:

I hope you will forgive my delay in answering your letter of April 19, but I was waiting for my parents' return from Europe in order to discuss my summer plans with them.

I am looking forward to work at Westport this summer. As far as I know, I will commute from my home at Stamford each day, so it will not be necessary to get a room at Westport.

My only problem is this: I won't get out of school until June 22nd, so it will be impossible for me to report on the 12th. Would it be all right with you if I reported on the 26th, which would give me a few days' rest before transferring from the ivory tower of education into the cold, cruel world? That would be the Monday exactly two weeks after the date you mentioned. If you deem it necessary, however, I could report on the 23rd. Can you advise me on this?

Thanking you for your consideration, and with hope that I am not causing you too much trouble, I am

Sincerely,

Stephen Sondheim

Stephen Sondheim,
Williams College,
Williamstown, Mass.

Fred Graham was a flyman and carpenter at the Playhouse for eight seasons in the 1990s. He saw many apprentices and interns pass through the program—some of them memorable, some less fortunate: We always had good interns, but there were some who didn't know what they were getting into. It was tough. One year, there was Lauren: she had a bad season. The first day she was here, we were loading a truck to drop off scenery to Ogunquit. We were putting platforms on the truck and she smashed her hand. And then after that, she was using the table saw and she cut her finger. I was standing outside and I can hear when something doesn't sound right, but before I could get in there it was already too late. Luckily she wasn't hurt really badly. Then she was supposed to drive to New York City with a 15-foot Ryder truck. Before she even made it out of the parking lot, she hit a car. And that wasn't the end of it. We had a lamp that was borrowed and was worth $800. It was used for *Jackie O's Glasses* when we had a turntable. After the run ended, we put the lamp in Dressing Room #1, the farthest back, and they were going to return it the following day. But there was a plumber coming in, so the props master decided to put the lamp up on the stage. Lauren was up there sweeping, and she swung the broom round and knocked the whole thing over. It just wasn't Lauren's summer!

to leave by the beginning of August. Then we should engage six more to start work at the beginning of August to take the place of the six who leave. This will put us in a much stronger position to weed out the sheep from the goats.

Furthermore, the work schedule for the apprentices must be such that they do not work more than eight hours a day. There should be three shifts, each of four hours. If an apprentice works mornings and afternoons, he should not work evenings.

There should be a strong personality in charge of . . . apprentices, and responsible for their health. There should be a Tennis Tournament and Swimming Tournament for apprentices, to be organized by the apprentices themselves. There should be a lecture each week for apprentices after the Friday matinee.

No apprentice should be engaged who is under 19 years old. I'd rather it be 20.[55]

Langner was clearly outvoted on the abolition of the apprentice program, and it is equally certain that not all his safeguards and recommendations were implemented—despite the fact that he repeated them in a very similar memorandum the next summer.[56] He was almost certainly right that the theatre put itself in a good deal of potential peril by employing the apprentices—in a legal sense, at least—but he would also have had to admit, had he been around to see it, that the Playhouse would not have survived very long after his death without the benefit of this free (or virtually free) workforce.

Jim McKenzie works with 1959 apprentices on a script they will perform in a showcase. On the left is Patricia Beckert; on the right, Lisa Whitman, granddaughter of Otis Skinner.

Of all the hundreds of apprentices who have passed through the program, a few have gone on to fame and/or fortune—Stephen Sondheim, Frank Perry, Tammy Grimes, Sally Jessy Raphael, Mary Rodgers, Christina Crawford. A great many more have come from famous showbiz families—the 1959 intake alone included Jan de Vries, daughter of Westport playwright Peter; Tim Zinnemann, son of Hollywood director Fred; and Lisa Whitman, granddaughter of Otis Skinner.[57] Correspondence and other evidence suggests that a remarkable number of Westport apprentices make careers in the theatre, or in related activities.

Besides being very hard work (and it's a rare summer that all the apprentices last the course), it's not all fun. If there's one job most of them dread, it's when their turn comes round to be Rocky the Rooster for the children's performances on Friday. As David O'Connell (1988) put it: "Every week one of the apprentices dresses up in a hot suit and greets the kiddies and tells them not to eat in the theatre. They shove Doritos down the bird's beak, while the mother tells them not to punch the chicken."[58]

After
the
muggers,
the hookers,
the heat
and
the noise...

Find
harmony*
at
**The
Westport
Country
Playhouse**

(203)
227-4177

*har•mo•ny (här′mə nē)
n., pl. -nies (ME. armony < OFr.
harmonie < L. harmonia < Gr.
harmonia < harmos, a fitting <
IE. base *ar-: cf. ART¹, ARM¹)
1. a combination of parts into a
pleasing or orderly whole.

CHAPTER NINE

1973–84 The Not-for-profit Theatre

The wealth, but not necessarily the health, of the American theatre can be measured in statistics. Take Broadway, which has been the yardstick of success for as long as anyone can remember. In the early 1920s, when Lawrence Langner and his colleagues were busy founding the Theatre Guild, there were eighty theatres on Broadway. Between them they originated 218 productions a year—of which about 150 were new plays and 45 were new musicals. By 1990 there were only thirty-five theatres left, and between them they were originating a paltry thirty productions a year.[1]

Yet Lawrence Langner, had he still been around, might well have reckoned the American theatre more healthy in 1990 than it was in the 1920s, because the real powerhouse of invention (with the possible exception of musicals) had moved from the commercial to the non-commercial theatre—an area that was almost non-existent in Langner's day.

Not-for-profit theatre began its remarkable growth after World War II. When the Ford Foundation started making substantial grants to regional and local theatres in the 1950s, it was able to do so because those theatres had been incorporated as nonprofit corporations under Section 501(c)(3) of the Internal Revenue code. In 1965 the federal government established its own agency, the National Endowment for the Arts, through which it was able to make grants to arts organizations, including theatres and theatre groups, for the first time.

The end result of all this made Broadway look puny. By 1990 there were more than 250 not-for-profit theatres operating outside New York, and they were mounting more than 3,000 productions a year.[2] The most remarkable results could be seen in places like Chicago (where there were 110 theatre companies operating in 1990, including Steppenwolf, Goodman, Wisdom Bridge, Victory Gardens, St. Nicholas and Body Politic) and Seattle (Intiman, Seattle Repertory, A Contemporary Theatre). Equally important were the individual theatres that made themselves famous for their excellence and innovation—the Guthrie in Minneapolis under Liviu Ciulei, the Mark Taper Forum in Los Angles under Gordon Davidson, the American Repertory Theatre at Harvard under Robert Brustein and the Yale Repertory Theatre under Lloyd Richards. There were many others.

In a much more modest way, it was evident that summer stock theatres, if they were to survive, would also have to go the nonprofit route. Westport's management, which had been philosophically opposed to it in the 1960s—even derisive of it—was forced to follow suit in 1973. The Connecticut Theatre Foundation, Inc., was formed "for the purpose of assuring the continuance of summer theatre at the Playhouse."[3] It did not make a great deal of difference to the actual running

The actor Frank Savino is featured on a Playhouse poster at the Westport train station.

171

of the theatre, or its repertory. What it meant in practice was that the theatre's owners, Armina and Philip Langner, leased the theatre to the foundation, which, in turn, employed Jim McKenzie and Spofford Beadle to run it (Ralph Roseman, having acquired so many interests and assets on Broadway, was no longer part of the on-site management, but his financial acumen was retained through his appointment as treasurer of the new foundation and through his presence in the Playhouse's New York office). The Connecticut Theatre Foundation, the management assured its patrons, "is a public foundation, which means that all its assets belong to the people, none will go to shareholders or investors."[4] The foundation's chairman was Ina Bradley.

There were two principal benefits of the nonprofit status. The first, which became effective immediately, was that the theatre became exempt from most taxes, including corporation taxes and Connecticut's "amusement tax" (which was 10 percent of gross takings). This put the Playhouse on the same level as museums, libraries, symphony orchestras and other cultural institutions. The second benefit was the ability "to look for financial health beyond the ticket buyer"—in other words, to seek grants from government agencies and independent foundations (corporate and otherwise).[5] This was the part of it Jim McKenzie did not like and was instinctively wary of. He feared taking money from government agencies or foundations, and then being cut off the next year or the year after. He was a commercial theatre producer to his fingertips—he would avoid taxes if he could do so honestly, but he was not going to become dependent on sources of income over which he had no control.

Nevertheless, McKenzie and the foundation's board were prepared to make use of the not-for-profit status for relatively small fundraising purposes. In 1978 the Connecticut Commission for the Arts was applied to, and a grant of $5,000 was received. The same amount was received the following year, though this time the foundation's request had been for $30,000.

The National Endowment for the Arts was also applied to in 1979, but unsuccessfully. At this time McKenzie suggested to the board that it should adopt a target of $50,000 a year in fundraising, and subscribers were encouraged to make voluntary contributions in addition to their subscriptions. The results were not very encouraging—$2,242 in voluntary contributions in 1978, not much more in 1979. The real problem, the board

Vicky Camargo ushering in 1960.

concluded, was that Westporters had always perceived their playhouse as a commercial entity: they found it difficult now to think of it as being in need of charity. Maybe the fiftieth anniversary in 1980 would be an occasion to change this perception? Board members were encouraged to come up with the names of companies that might become commercial sponsors. A raffle was tried in 1976 and eventually became an annual event following its huge success in 1980, but grants of any sort— government or commercial—remained scarce.[6]

McKenzie did not appoint a development director until 1983 when Julie Monahan added it to her already very full portfolio. She was on the theatre's staff for twenty-five seasons, beginning in 1976, rising from usher to general manager. For most of that time a development office was an expensive, and often unaffordable, luxury. When a specialist was taken on in 1990 she lasted only six months before the board was forced to conclude that it could no longer afford to pay her salary.[7]

THE AUDIENCE

The 1970 census had shown that Westport's population of 28,000 was extraordinarily fluid—there had been a 30 percent turnover since 1960. It was a well-heeled community with a median income well above the national average, and educational qualifications that suggested interests more catholic and wide-ranging than almost anywhere else in the country. 1,400 copies of the *New York Times* were delivered to homes each day, more on Sundays. The town had almost no industry—

"If we mention Broadway at all, we call it the Winter-Theatre."

unless shopping and eating could be classified as industries. It was still determinedly un-suave, culti-vating the casual look and bucolic surroundings. The country club was community-owned, and the latest innovation was the "Westport Mystique"—a local transportation service of Mercedes Benz mini-buses shaped like loaves of fresh-baked bread.

But who went to the theatre? And were they likely to go on going? In 1974 the new foundation decided to find out. It commissioned a survey of the audience and discovered (what it knew already) that its patrons' principal grouses concerned the ineffec-tual and quirky nature of the theatre's air condition-ing, the lack of sufficient parking space, the absence of a theatre restaurant following the closing of the Players Tavern that summer, and the failure to pro-vide better padding for the pews (a substantial major-ity of the audience nevertheless preferred the pews to the possibility of individual seats).

More worrying were the overall statistics. Where once, in the late 1940s, 85 percent of ticket sales had been sold by subscription, the figure was now down to 35 percent. In large part, this was because the capacity of the theatre had risen from 500 to over 700, but there were other contribut-ing factors. One was that subscriptions were now offered for twelve weeks rather than six—for most people that was a hefty commitment of time, if not of money. Another (which we can no longer quantify, but it is apparent from the numbers) was that a great many of the 2,000 subscribers in 1974 were subscribing for only one seat, whereas the vast majority of the almost 1,000 subscribers Francesca Lodge and Ina Bradley had accumulated twenty years earlier had been subscribing for multiple seats—even if they no longer took whole rows, as "Miss Annie" Burr Jennings had done in the 1930s.

All this meant that there was a tremendous onus placed on the box office to make single ticket sales—and single ticket sales depended, to a large extent, on the amount of advertising the theatre management could afford to buy in the local media. It was a vicious circle.

One person who had been around in the 1950s, at the zenith of the Lodge/Bradley subscription scheme, was Henry Weinstein. He had left the Playhouse in 1961 at about the time the legal problems of his partner, Laurence Feldman, had become public, but Jim McKenzie brought him back to the Playhouse as artistic director in the mid-1970s—as chubby as ever, though definitely more svelte ("In my lifetime I have lost over 1,200 pounds," he told the *New York Times*). He could compare the 1950s audience with that of the 1970s: "The one thing that has not changed since the beginning is the Monday opening-night audience. That is a very stable, society-oriented audience. Many of them have held the same seats year in and year out. But except for Monday night everything is changed here. We used to think of Fairfield County as a very staid community. The truth is that there is a big change in residents every three years, and that has affected our audience. Except for Monday nights we get what I think of as the new Fairfield and Westchester County people."[8]

The "new" people had yet to show how far they would go to preserve their playhouse, but the survey turned up some encouraging signs. For a start, it seemed that they would be loyal: in 1974 50 percent of the audience had attended the Playhouse for at least five seasons. Second, it seemed that the vast majority of them were local or fairly local—75 percent lived within twenty miles of the Playhouse, and 84 percent said they were year-round residents, not just summer visitors. An unexpectedly large number (64 percent) said they would like the theatre to offer more productions spread over a longer period of time, maybe including spring and fall seasons.[9] Proving that this last finding was good information or bad (in fact, it was bad) would await the 1976 season.

The Playhouse now billed itself as "America's Foremost Summer Theatre," but whatever its hopes and pretensions, it was sometimes rather brutally reminded that it was just a rural theatre in a rickety old barn, doing summer stock and living uncomfortably close to nature. Everybody who has ever worked at the Playhouse comes away with wild animal stories—and one or two even get to confront "nature in the raw"—but it is traditional that the audience is shielded from these stories, and especially from first-hand experience. Sometimes, however, Nature intrudes.

As a young girl, Jim McKenzie's daughter Amy used to work at the Playhouse after school and during the summer holidays:

My favorite times were spent working in the box office. I loved that funny little box office, the size of most people's closets, with just enough room for a phone, a desk, the tickets and someone to sell them. I was a tad short for the job as the counter was unusually high, so I found a tall stool and then, by stacking a phone book or two on top, I could see over the counter to wait on customers. One day I looked up and saw a nose and two eyes straining to see me over the counter. The man stood on his toes, and there before me was Dustin Hoffman. Truly, Dustin Hoffman!

Such was the case in 1977 during the two-week run of Neil Simon's *California Suite*, starring Lynn Redgrave. If ever there was a trouper, by birth and avocation, it was Lynn Redgrave. On her first visit to the Playhouse, in 1975, she had played no fewer than six roles in the four one-act plays that made up Michael Frayn's *Two of Us*—a virtuosic performance that few actresses could have carried off. Now, two years later, her return was eagerly anticipated, with producers and subscribers scenting another triumph. What they got was an altogether more pungent aroma. With untimely efficiency, the theatre's much-maligned air conditioning system succeeded in filtering a terrible smell into every corner of the building. There was nothing the management could do about it. A skunk was trapped in the air conditioning system, and every time it got frightened (as when the audience entered or left, or applauded) it sprayed its hideous stench into the tiny space where it was trapped, and the air conditioner did the rest. It took several days to find and remove the creature, during which time the audience suffered and Miss Redgrave, trouper to the last, soldiered on.

GRANDSTANDING

Jim McKenzie and his colleagues were well aware that inflation was their enemy, and that it was an enemy they could never defeat. The best they could do was to stay level with it, and even to do that would involve colossal effort and the taking of sizable risks.

The first risk of the nonprofit era turned out to be a mistake. For the 1973 season the Playhouse announced that it had frozen ticket prices at 1972 levels. As Jim McKenzie later admitted: "We found that it really hurt us since no one else wanted to do the same."[10] The lesson was learned, and (in typical McKenzie fashion) it was turned to advantage, for it was out of that experience that the Early Bird Subscription Scheme came into being. The purpose of Early Bird was to get patrons to renew their subscription before, or immediately after, the previous season was completed. If they were prepared to do that, then their new subscription would be at the previous year's price. It proved to be popular with the audience, which quickly realized that the savings would be substantial in the inflationary climate of the 1970s—by 1977 Early Bird subscribers were saving 16 percent on plays and 30 percent on musicals.[11] It also had immense advantages for the management—in the years to come it would be the Early Bird subscriptions that kept the theatre going from one season to another.

The theatre's bank account was a matter for private grief, and one into which it was best not to intrude unless, as a member of the Connecticut Theatre Foundation's board, one absolutely had to. What it came down to was that the Playhouse had no endowment and no reserves of cash: if something big had to be done in the way of maintenance or repair, outside help was needed. And this was when Jim McKenzie began to reap the benefits of his own personal standing and the trust in which he was generally held. What he called the "Great Parking Lot Venture" was a case in point. It was clear that the patrons would not much longer stand for the appalling condition and inadequate size of the theatre's parking lot. In the spring of 1973 McKenzie therefore went to "our protectors at the Westport National Bank" and persuaded them to back a large-scale refurbishment of the parking area, including paving it—on the grounds that subscriptions wouldn't be renewed unless patrons knew they could park in safety close to the theatre entrance.[12] It paid off, but it was by no means the end of the parking lot saga, which may have consumed more executive hours at the Playhouse than anything other than putting on plays (and even that is doubtful).

When it came to putting on plays, McKenzie was still prepared to challenge his audience on occasion, even when he suspected the economic consequences would be dire. He was usually right about the economic consequences. There was *The Poison Tree* by Ron Ribman: McKenzie included it in the 1973 season despite his own admission that it was not summer theatre fare. Indeed, so convinced of this was he that he used the previous week's playbill to forewarn the audience (which would have read it while attending a performance of *The Gershwin Years* with Barbara Cook) and to offer them the chance of getting their subscription tickets refunded in advance: "*The Poison Tree* is certainly a play of reality—it concerns itself with the cruelty of man, the oppression of prison life, the world of little hope, and the possibility of retaining human dignity at astronomical cost. We think it is a brilliant play and want to share it with you. We approach next week with great trepidation, however, because there are no holds barred to telling this violent story. The language of the streets of Harlem makes *Virginia Woolf* seem like tea-time talk, the cruelty of human relationship goes beyond Marat de Sade, and the harsh reality of prison is laid bare for your dramatic inspection."[13]

Six years later, in much the same way, McKenzie appealed to his audience on behalf of Mary O'Malley's *Once a Catholic*: "We feel the play is worth your evening, and ask only that you look at it as a play—not as propaganda for or against religion, sex, or social mores."[14]

By contrast, McKenzie was capable of what theatre purists doubtless considered gimmickry, at best, and pandering to the lowest of popular tastes, at worst—but the theatre's accountants liked him for it. Moreover, he could argue, with justice, that it was a necessary part of being a nonprofit. In 1973 he turned over a whole week of August to the Preservation Hall Jazz Band, a group of originals from the world of New Orleans jazz who would make return appearances to the Playhouse for years to come (though generally for one-night-only stands). In 1973 they gave a whole week of

concerts, but what was more eye-catching was the transformation of the Playhouse and its precincts into a giant riverboat gambling den got up for Mardi Gras at the turn of the century. As the playbill explained: "Whether your pleasure be blackjack, roulette, craps or horse racing, it's here for you to enjoy. You have the chance to win generous gift certificates from a selection of area businesses. And if you're not lucky enough to win, you can rest assured that you've contributed to an excellent charity, the Society to Advance the Retarded (STAR)."[15]

Connecticut had recently passed gaming laws that limited gambling at a theatre to three nights a week, but those who attended on other nights were bidden to return to the Playhouse (with their ticket stubs) when the party began at 10:30 p.m. on Monday, Wednesday or Friday. The result was that STAR got a nice contribution and the Playhouse drew a large crowd and a lot of pub-

A den of iniquity. The not-for-profit casino, 1973.

licity. It was successful enough, at any rate, that when it was next tried—during a week's run of *Guys and Dolls* in 1978—the charity was cut out and all the profits went to the Playhouse: "Proceeds from the floating crap game and other amusements, all run by our own Playhouse Committee hustlers, will help support the operation of the Connecticut Theatre Foundation, to bring more plays to Westport."[16] By the same token, the theatre took to holding an annual Country Fair and Antique Show and many other fundraising events.

Occasionally, like most theatres, Westport attracted publicity it would rather have avoided. One such occasion, which consumed more column inches of newsprint than it could ever have merited, was when an actress exposed her breasts in Lanford Wilson's *The Hot L Baltimore*. This was 1975, already eight years after *Hair* had opened on Broadway, but still too soon to commit such a deed in Westport. It wasn't as though Jim McKenzie was unaware of Westport mores: the previous year, 1974, when *Hair* itself had come to the Playhouse, the nude scene had been omitted.

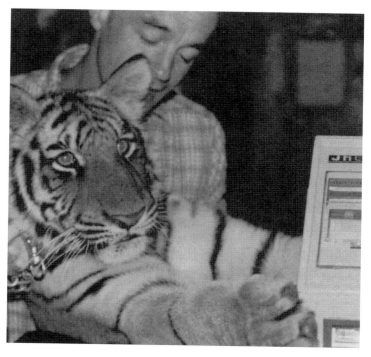

Jadu, the six-month-old Bengal tiger who had a starring role in the Stephen Schwartz–Doug Henning musical *The Magic Show* (1979). With him is his handler, Bill Sell.

There were other, more serious, innovations and experiments—a 1976 season of Sunday evening concerts in alternate weeks throughout the summer; a 1978 fall season of Guest Artists in Concert (people like Mischa Dichter, Pete Seeger, Eartha Kitt, Julie Harris and Carlos Montoya)—but none of them lasted very long. The "grandstanding" (or stunting) is proof that McKenzie and his team were working very hard to keep things going, but it also disguises the fact that they had what was, basically, a successful recipe. It consisted of between ten and twelve shows for a fourteen-week season—in other words, mostly one-week runs, but every season would include some that ran two weeks. The shows themselves were a mixture of old and new— "old" generally being defined as no earlier than the 1940s, and "new" being a category broad enough to include plays that had run successfully in London but had not yet been seen in the States. Every season would feature between two and four of these new plays.[17] In addition, there was always at least one musical, sometimes more, and the bulk of the season would be made up of packaged productions of plays that were not new but had already been successful on Broadway or elsewhere. Most prized of all were the Broadway tryouts, which got fewer as the years went by. The casting was not as starry as it had been in the past, but the regulars—the Eli Wallachs, Anne Jacksons, Betsy Palmers and George Grizzards—still came to Westport quite frequently, and every now and again a Vincent Price or a Douglas Fairbanks, Jr. descended from the clouds.

By and large, this recipe worked. Subscription booking remained at about 35 percent, and the box office did a brisk business in single ticket sales, so that the theatre generally played to 80–85 percent of capacity, and not infrequently to full houses. Selling seats was not the problem, though McKenzie and his staff worked hard at it and were wary of raising seat prices any more than was absolutely necessary. Unfortunately, it *was* necessary, and more or less every season. Yet the Playhouse's expenses continued to rise even more steeply, and this was the crux of the problem: it was caught in an inflationary spiral. Most of the cost increases were beyond its control—they were the costs of producing and presenting plays, and the costs of the very limited amount of union labor that was employed at the theatre (four posts, reduced to three—just enough to ensure there were two professional carpenters and an electrician to supervise the theatre's continuing supply of apprentices and interns).

It is hardly surprising, then, that the management was constantly on the lookout for new ideas that might cut costs or raise income. As Jim McKenzie put it in a 1977 interview: "There's no theatre that succeeds as well or fails as badly as this one. We're always doing something unusual here."[18]

And sometimes these experiments got them into really bad trouble, most notably in 1976—a year that ended with Jim McKenzie, Henry Weinstein and the general manager, Sharon Giese, having to waive their remuneration. What they had been doing was following up a suggestion (admittedly, a rather vague one) that had come out of the 1974 audience survey. People had been asked if, instead of a twelve-play season, they might prefer only six plays, each running for two weeks. About one-third of respondents had reacted quite favorably to the idea of two-week runs, but a lot of them had added the rider that they would then want a longer season (i.e., more than six plays). At any rate, there seemed to be enough encouragement there for McKenzie and Weinstein to make a radical switch in 1976. They presented a fourteen-week season with only seven plays. The mix was much the same as previous seasons, though a little more backward-looking, if anything—two musicals (Jerome Kern's *Roberta* with Patti Davis and Ruth Warrick, and John Kander's *Zorba* with Theodore Bikel); three plays from the 1930s and 1940s by Clifford Odets, George Kelly and Noël Coward; one very current offering—Eli Wallach and Anne Jackson in John Guare's black comedy *The House of Blue Leaves*—and a brand new play, Allen Swift's *Checking Out*, on a Broadway tryout. Each play was on stage for two weeks.

The management team in 1976—(*left to right*) Henry Weinstein, Jim McKenzie, Ralph Roseman.

The theatre's costs were considerably reduced by this schedule, of course, but it still didn't work. There was nowhere near enough box-office business to support the extended stays. What was worse was that patrons had been given a promise at the end of the previous season, when this new scheme was first revealed to them, that retail prices for tickets would be frozen at 1975 levels, and that subscriptions would be half the cost of 1975 since there would be half as many plays. In fact, there were more than half as many plays—there were seven, not six—so 1976 subscribers got six plays at the same per play cost as the previous year, and one that was completely free!

Markland Taylor, the acerbic and forthright critic of the *New Haven Register*, thought there was a much more fundamental problem to be solved. He laid it out in his review of the first production of the season, Jerome Kern's *Roberta* (a musical notorious for its book and famous for its wonderful songs, including "Smoke Gets in Your Eyes"). Under a bold headline "More in Anger Than Sadness," Taylor called on Jim McKenzie to resign: "It is time to call a halt to what Jim McKenzie . . . has done and is doing to summer theatre. For some years now he has made mockery of theatre at the Westport Playhouse." Taylor had originally applauded the new two-week schedule because he expected it to result in less "schlock summer stock." Instead, he wrote, on the evidence of *Roberta*, it seemed that what was happening was "the exact opposite of what McKenzie had led us to expect. [*Roberta*] was, in fact, the apotheosis of schlock summer stock. Ludicrously over-ambitious, it was dull, vulgar, completely lacking in style, poorly cast, poorly directed and poorly produced. To add insult to catatonic shock, it ran from 8:45 p.m. to 11:55 p.m." And of the performance of Ruth Warrick, the soap opera star in the title role, he had nothing good to say: "She has little or no stage presence, her acting is rudimentary, her speaking voice is uncontrolled, and her

In 1973, Jerry Orbach appeared in Bob Randall's play 6 RMS RV VW *with Marcia Rodd as his co-star:*

One night there was a major thunderstorm and we lost power in the theatre. We were given flashlights and shone them on each other for the whole second act. Talk about giving and getting focus!

The lights were always going out:

In 1991, during a performance of *A Few Good Men*, the power failed and the cast and audience sat in total silence, with no one making a sound. After several minutes, the lights came back on. The actor who was playing the young defense attorney said: "Well, I guess we paid the bill." The audience broke up for at least two minutes before the play resumed.

WESTPORT
COUNTRY PLAYHOUSE

BOX OFFICE NOW OPEN
ORDER YOUR TICKETS TODAY!

June 23 - July 2
BETTY COMDEN
ADOLPH GREEN
A PARTY WITH BETTY COMDEN &
ADOLPH GREEN

July 4 - 9
prior to Broadway
in association with the J. F. Kennedy Center
ELI WALLACH
ANNE JACKSON
LEE RICHARDSON
ABSENT FRIENDS
By Alan Ayckbourn

July 11 - 16
in association with the J. F. Kennedy Center
RICHARD KILEY
JANE ALEXANDER
TERESA WRIGHT
THE MASTER BUILDER
By Henrik Ibsen

July 18 - 23
*BUBBLING BROWN SUGAR
By Loften Mitchell

July 25 - 30
SANDY DENNIS
CATHLEEN NESBITT
THE ROYAL FAMILY
By George S. Kaufman & Edna Ferber

August 1 - 13
LYNN REDGRAVE
CALIFORNIA SUITE
By Neil Simon

August 15 - 20
a new pre-Broadway play
WILLIAM SHATNER
YVETTE MIMIEUX
TRICKS OF THE TRADE
By Sidney Michaels

August 22 - 27
a new pre-Broadway play
COLLEEN DEWHURST
REX ROBBINS
GEORGE HERN
AN ALMOST PERFECT PERSON
By Judith Ross

August 29 - September 10
a new pre-Broadway musical
*THE KING OF HEARTS
Book By Steve Tesich
Music By   Lyrics By
Peter Link   Jacob Brackman

CHOICE SEATS AVAILABLE NOW FOR SUBSCRIPTION
& SINGLE TICKET ORDERS
SUBSCRIBE & SAVE — 9 PLAYS FOR THE PRICE OF 8
For Subscription Information: (203) 226-0153
Single Ticket Information & Instant Charge: (203) 227-4177

singing voice is excruciating. Florence Foster Jenkins, where are you?" Finally, Taylor wrote that he understood McKenzie had been in Russia with American Conservatory Theatre (of which he was also executive producer) while *Roberta* was in rehearsal. "If this is so, it seems to me that he has failed to fulfill his obligations to Westport. If it is not so, his production of *Roberta* suggests that he is an incompetent, tasteless producer."[19]

The season got better after that, and included some distinguished work, notably Eli Wallach and Anne Jackson in John Guare's *The House of Blue Leaves*, but there was no argument that it was a catastrophe overall—commercially, for certain, and artistically, too much of the time.

When McKenzie and Weinstein finally sat down in September to examine what had gone wrong, they decided that the obvious reasons—frozen ticket prices, over-generous discounts, the extended two-week stays and one or two severe lapses in production standards—did not, by themselves, account for the disaster. There was another, more fundamental, reason, they thought, and it had to do with repertory—with the sort of shows they put on and the overall mix of the shows in the course of a season. "People in Westport and the surrounding communities," McKenzie said, "are not going to just be pleased with summer packages. They are too sophisticated. They can always go to New York. We must supply something more."[20]

THE SOMETHING MORE

In 1977, the Playhouse gave them "something more" and the resulting season was, in Westport terms, a sort of miracle. It had begun discouragingly in the early spring with the discovery that there was dry rot in the theatre—Bob Bass, the local builder, had performed prodigies of work to ensure that the building could be pronounced safe and the season could start on time. The cost of the work meant the indefinite postponement of one of McKenzie's pet projects—the building of an orchestra pit—but, as he explained it to the patrons, "safety before art!"[21]

After that, things got a lot better, and quickly. McKenzie and Weinstein turned out to have been right about the underlying problem—it *was* about repertory rather than extended runs. The Westport audience wanted more than the traditional summer stock packages, and, to prove it, they put their money on the table. In July Henry Weinstein told the *New York Times* just how big the financial turnaround had been: "Three years ago on opening day we had an advance of $2,000. Two years ago it was $1,500, and last year it was $900. But this year, with an Ibsen revial and four never-seen-before productions, our advance was $9,681 on opening day. And we are 40 percent subscribed this season" (the actual number of subscribers represented a new record for the theatre—the percentage had been substantially higher in the 1940s, but there were only 499 seats to fill in those days, compared to well over 700 now).[22]

Betty Comden and Adolph Green—two of Westport's favorite performers. They first appeared at the Playhouse as revue artists alongside Judy Holliday and Gene Kelly in 1939.

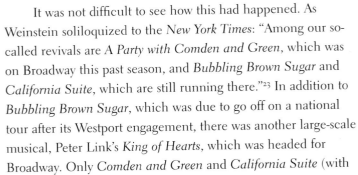

It was not difficult to see how this had happened. As Weinstein soliloquized to the *New York Times*: "Among our so-called revivals are *A Party with Comden and Green*, which was on Broadway this past season, and *Bubbling Brown Sugar* and *California Suite*, which are still running there."[23] In addition to *Bubbling Brown Sugar*, which was due to go off on a national tour after its Westport engagement, there was another large-scale musical, Peter Link's *King of Hearts*, which was headed for Broadway. Only *Comden and Green* and *California Suite* (with Lynn Redgrave and the skunk) had two-week runs, but there were at least two other productions that would have benefited from them. They were the Ayckbourn play *Absent Friends* with Eli Wallach and Anne Jackson, and Ibsen's *The Master Builder* with Jane Alexander and Richard Kiley. These two plays were special because they were the first fruits of a co-production deal between the Westport Country Playhouse and the John F. Kennedy Center for the Performing Arts in Washington, D.C. This is what Jim McKenzie devoutly hoped would be the "something more" of future seasons.

The Kennedy Center's Eisenhower Theatre needed to build a reputation as a house where fine productions of important plays could be seen. McKenzie, who had been a member of the Theatre Advisory Panel of the National Endowment for the Arts and therefore an occasional visitor to the capital, was aware of the Center's problem and he knew its chairman, Roger Stevens. Everyone in theatre knew Stevens. Since 1949 he had been one of the most distinguished producers on Broadway, and he had special links with Westport and the Langners—he had been a co-founder of the American Shakespeare Theatre at Stratford, Connecticut, with Lawrence Langner in 1954–55. Since 1971 he had been running the infant Kennedy Center with a special mission for the theatre side of it. No surprise, then, that he reacted positively to the idea of a Westport–Kennedy Center production partnership and agreed with McKenzie that Ed Sherin, a Broadway producer whom they both knew, should be artistic director for the exchange plays between the two theatres.

McKenzie and Sherin sat down together in the fall of 1976, while McKenzie was still getting over the terrible failure of his summer season. The idea they came up with was a variation on the old repertory company idea. "What we're trying to do is build upon a concept whereby a company of actors can earn their money while doing great plays. We're not trying to promiscuously cast thousands of stars. We're looking to find a leading group of actors, a star-resident company if you will, who can work together on a number of plays over an extended period."[24] For the 1977 season, they agreed on two plays, with one more to follow later (it never did). Each of the plays would have a one-week run at Westport and a four- or five-week run in Washington. They both did well.

The first to come to the Playhouse, right after the two-week run of *A Party with Comden and Green* that opened the season, was a production of Alan Ayckbourn's comedy *Absent Friends*. It had originated in London in 1974—a funny play on the surface, but also a fairly bleak exploration of dysfunctional marriages in the more wintry style that Ayckbourn adopted in the 1970s. This was not really a new production: it was an adaptation of the London staging that had been produced by the Long Wharf Theatre of New Haven and was now taken over by Westport, en route for Washington, with some cast changes and re-rehearsal.[25] Most importantly, it starred Eli Wallach,

Anne Jackson and Lee Richardson. It played a sold-out week at Westport and went on to Washington for its scheduled five weeks.

In the meantime, Ibsen's *The Master Builder* was completing its six-week Kennedy Center engagement and moving into the Playhouse for the week following *Absent Friends*. It was remembered by the audience as one of the finest productions ever staged at Westport, with stunning performances from Jane Alexander and Richard Kiley. The stage staff remembered it for a rather

Richard Kiley and Jane Alexander in the 1977 staging of Ibsen's *The Master Builder*—a collaboration with the Kennedy Center in Washington, D.C., directed by Edwin Sherin.

different reason—"how on earth did we get *Absent Friends* out and on its way to Washington, and *The Master Builder* in, lit, rehearsed and ready to go, in the 44½ hours between Saturday midnight and the 8:30 curtain on Monday evening?"

From Westport's point of view, the success of these productions was inestimable. Jim McKenzie and Henry Weinstein began planning an ambitious scheme for two companies, one playing Westport while the other played Washington, then each company mounting another play and the sequence being repeated. They hoped to be able to work with the same group of performers for five seasons.[26] But from the Kennedy Center's point of view, the relationship was nothing like so valuable. The fact that it was artistically successful was useful, but the summer months were not a time when Washingtonians (those who were still in the city) flocked to the theatre.

In the end, Westport had to be content with an occasional relationship. It was activated again in 1978, when Tammy Grimes starred in Samuel Taylor's play *Gracious Living*, but not often thereafter. So McKenzie continued to search for the "something more" he could bring to his audience. In 1979 he thought he had found it—in his own gift, in a way—at the American Conservatory Theatre in San Francisco. McKenzie had been executive producer of ACT since 1969—it was why he journeyed constantly across the country—and he had long wanted to bring the company back to Westport after its extraordinary spring season there in 1966. The opportunity came with Somerset Maugham's 1921 play *The Circle*, about a young

The American Conservatory Theatre brought Somerset Maugham's *The Circle* to Westport in 1979—with Marriann Walters and William Paterson. Executive producer of ACT was Jim McKenzie's "day job."

woman and her subversive relationship with her mother-in-law. Westport co-produced it and it played an impressive two-week run in the middle of the season, with stellar reviews from important critics. But that didn't prevent the second week being a disaster at the box office.[27]

In the meantime, the ever-inventive Henry Weinstein had been trying his hand at a winter season. What he sought to do in the fall and winter of 1978 was an eclectic season that included films as well as plays. He opened with a screening of *Gone with the Wind*, complete with a big

Douglas Fairbanks, Jr., in *Out on a Limb* (1978)—way out!

In 1978, Douglas Fairbanks, Jr., took his show Out on a Limb **by James Thurber on a tour of summer theatres, including Westport. Carole Claps was the Playhouse's press agent:**

He was a wonderful man, but he was ridiculed in that show. His entrance was in black tights, swinging on a vine, just like his father. It was awful. But you couldn't get a seat, of course—standing room only. Until after the intermissions, when there were free seats everywhere. So many people left!

Before the show arrived in Westport, I'd gone up to an East Hampton estate called The Clock House, where Mr. Fairbanks was staying. He did interviews and a photo shoot for us. On the way back, I went to the John Drew Theatre where the show was playing that week. I tried to buy a ticket for that night, but they wouldn't let me have one. I called Jim and told him "Something's afoot. They won't let me into the theatre!"

barbecue at which the Old South was represented by Colonel Sanders himself, along with a lot of Kentucky Fried Chicken. Later on there were children's films and a stage production of *Dracula* that starred Farley Granger (it was promoted with a blood drive!).[28] Estelle Parsons was also a part of the season: she brought a one-woman show, *Miss Margarita's Way*, wherein she played a school teacher with the audience as her class. Latecomers were given hell and gum chewers had their mouths washed out.[29] It was all good fun, but the winter season, as a whole, was not successful enough to merit repetition.

For the rest, the "something more" had to be manufactured in the old-fashioned way—with stars—and McKenzie put together a pretty good track record in the late 1970s. William Shatner was there in 1977, doing his decidedly non-nude scene with the very naked Yvette Mimieux in *Tricks of the Trade*, and causing the Playhouse to be stormed by hundreds of "trekkies" each night. Arlene Francis introduced *Side by Side by Sondheim* twenty-eight years after the author had himself

been a Westport apprentice. Colleen Dewhurst came with Judith Ross's *An Almost Perfect Person*, and she also brought Zoe Caldwell to direct it. Louis Jourdan brought the house down with a Feydeau farce, hot from Broadway. Dick Cavett brought a Simon Gray play, David McCallum a Michael Frayn play, and Kathryn Crosby a Bernard Slade play. Douglas Fairbanks, Jr., brought a great deal of scenery for what was billed as a light sketch and song review called *Out on a Limb*—alas, it was one of those (very rare) weeks when apprentices cast lots on the number of cars that left at intermission. And in 1979 came the man that everyone involved with the Playhouse at the time has always nominated as "the nicest man that ever came to Westport"—Vincent Price. He brought an excellent little show, John Gay's *Diversions and Delights*, but what people remembered most was the sight of him joyously shucking corn in the courtyard with the apprentices and interns at the traditional early evening party between shows on Wednesday.

The other, slightly risky, part of "something more" was finding new plays that could begin their lives (their American lives, at least) in Westport. In 1977, McKenzie and Weinstein could justifiably boast that the Playhouse audience was among the first to see Judith Ross's *An Almost*

"I sometimes feel that I'm impersonating the dark unconscious of the whole human race. I know this sounds sick, but I love it." The Master of Horror he may have been, but Vincent Price was remembered at Westport as one of the nicest, gentlest actors ever to play the theatre. In 1979 he was Oscar Wilde in *Diversions and Delights*.

Perfect Person and the Peter Link musical *King of Hearts* (with Robby Benson). Two years later they offered two brand new scripts—Cy Howard's *Have a Nice Day* and James Prideaux's *Slightly Delayed* (with Geraldine Page, Anne Jackson and Kevin McCarthy, directed by George Schaeffer, who took time out from the network television mini-series *Blind Ambition* to do it)—and they followed up with one of the most controversial plays to have been seen in London for several years, Mary O'Malley's *Once a Catholic* with Rachel Roberts. By no means all the plays that were tagged with the advertising legend "Prior to Broadway" pleased the audience, but enough of them did to keep the subscribers signing up from season to season. A hard core of 50 percent were long-term subscribers, and renewals were generally between 70 and 80 percent each year.

THE SUMMER PACKAGE—STILL GOING, BUT ONLY JUST

The great years of the summer circuit packagers were almost at an end. What was undermining them was not so much their own internal economics—for they simply passed on the costs to their clients, the theatres—as the steadily decreasing number of clients. The theatres could no longer endure the inflationary spiral and were going out of business. The Council of Stock Theaters (COST) reported in 1980 that it had twelve members remaining—out of the fifty-two Jim McKenzie had reported in 1964 when he was president of COST.[30] Twelve was still enough for one or two packagers to remain in business, but the Producing Managers Company was no longer one of them: it had ceased to operate as an entity when its three owners—McKenzie, Ralph Roseman and Spofford Beadle—had gone their separate ways in the mid-1970s, with only McKenzie staying at the Playhouse.

The principal packager in the early 1980s was Jack Booch, who was also "managing artistic director" of the Westport Country Playhouse. The title reflected the fact that (in 1980, for instance) he was packaging no fewer than six of the ten shows being presented at Westport in its fiftieth anniversary season. Having Westport as what amounted to a "pre-sold" market made it easier to get other theatres on the circuit to buy into his shows, and not just the COST theatres on the East Coast—the Neil Simon play *Chapter Two* went on to the Star Theatre in Flint, Michigan, capacity 2,800, and other shows went to places as distant as Denver and St. Louis.

In the history of American show business Henry Weinstein's peculiar fame was that he was the producer who tried, and failed, to help Marilyn Monroe complete her final film, *Something's Got to Give*. The task had fallen to him in 1962 when Twentieth Century Fox was advised by Monroe's therapist that "it would be better if Marilyn had someone who understood her and could deal with her."[31] Amongst the things Weinstein had to deal with was coming to her aid when she overdosed on barbiturates, and having her cry on his shoulder fairly constantly. After several weeks of filming, Fox eventually dismissed her for absenteeism, and she died of a drug overdose two months later. Years later, Weinstein told her biographer, Anthony Summers, "We all experience anxiety, unhappiness, heartbreaks, but that was sheer primal terror."[32]

HENRY T. WEINSTEIN
1924–2000

He was a Brooklyn boy, a graduate of City College with a master's degree in drama from Carnegie Institute of Technology, so there was never any doubt that he was going to make his career in the theatre. But by the time he came to do so, right after World War II, the film industry was exerting a powerful pull on ambitious people of his generation, and television was just beginning to be a serious medium for drama. Henry began in the theatre, with spells directing plays at the Falmouth and Norwich playhouses, and another as a stage manager of *The Innocents* on Broadway, but then he headed into television and became a director for several New York stations. By retaining his freelance status he was able to combine a television career with occasional theatre assignments, particularly in the summers. He stage-managed for the Theatre Guild, he directed at the Theatre in the Round in Houston and the Brattle Theatre in Cambridge, Massachusetts, he was managing director of the Falmouth Playhouse (where he staged the world premiere of Arthur Miller's *A View from the Bridge*), and he directed *Antigone* at the Carnegie Hall Playhouse.

He came to Westport for the first time in 1957–61 when he was co-managing director, first with Philip Langner, then with Laurence Feldman. He was thus the link between the Langner family's active management of the theatre and the new team that took over in 1959. It was a time when the Westport Playhouse was at its zenith, and when summer stock, as an American institution, was in the best of health. Weinstein and Feldman founded the Laurence Henry Company as a producer and packager of summer plays, and they seemed set fair to dominate that business. But Feldman was not the right partner for Weinstein (as later events were to make very clear), and after the 1961 season Weinstein departed for television and movies—and his unlooked-for experience with Marilyn Monroe.

It was fifteen years before he returned to Westport. In the interval he did his most substantial work—as producer of the award-winning television series *Play of the Week* and as executive-in-charge-of-production for the American Film Theatre (AFT). AFT made film versions of serious plays for subscription audiences in movie theatres, and Weinstein produced a number of major films for them, including *A Delicate Balance* with Katharine Hepburn, Paul Scofield and Joseph Cotton, and *The Three Sisters* with Laurence Olivier and Joan Plowright. He was also responsible for a number of studio movies, including F. Scott Fitzgerald's *Tender Is the Night* with Jennifer Jones and Jason Robards, Jr.

His reputation was for quality work in what was generally labeled "serious drama," and it was his unique good nature that made him such a good producer—everyone liked Henry and, for his part, he seemed to get along with everyone. But Hollywood was neither the most comfortable nor the most productive environment for someone of his temperament, which was always more artistic than it was commercial.

His return to Westport in 1976 (as artistic director) was as enjoyable for him as it was for everyone who worked at the Playhouse. Summer stock had changed drastically in his absence—of the twenty-five theatres for which he and Laurence Feldman had packaged productions in the early 1960s, only twelve were left—but he was still ebullient about the Country Playhouse and its future, and ideas for its development and expansion poured out of him in endless torrents, whether he was talking to members of the theatre staff, the board of directors or the press. The 1976 season, with its misjudgment about the audience's needs and expectations (it was the season when only seven productions were presented, each of them running two weeks), was an aberration, but the 1977 and 1978 seasons, both of them extremely successful, bore the true Weinstein marks of quality and diversity.

Those summers at Westport in the late 1970s were Weinstein's last contacts with summer stock and live theatre. He returned to movies and television—a spell as an executive producer on PBS's *American Playhouse*, and one truly successful movie, *Runaway Train*, which received three Oscar nominations—but these were probably not very happy years for him. David Thomson, the film historian, remembers meeting him in Hollywood—"living in a small apartment in Studio City, soaked in his own sadness. He was also very intelligent, unexpectedly tender in his feelings and insights, and nursing many secrets."[33]

What private demons Henry had to fight with, no one really knew. To the outside world he presented a cheerful, energetic face and he was widely recognized as an authority on literature, theatre and film lore. For the Westport Playhouse he had a particular importance, which was his presence there at two moments in the theatre's history that were pivotal, in both of which he provided leadership and inspiration that got the Playhouse over some awkward moments and moved it onwards.

Henry Weinstein, as the Playhouse's producer, visits Gloria Swanson in her dressing room before the curtain goes up (and the reviews come down) on *Red Letter Day* (1959).

Perhaps because she lived so much of her life in Weston, perhaps because she worked harder than anyone (harder even than Lawrence Langner) to realize the ideal of a repertory company, perhaps because her performances at the Playhouse covered a span of forty-five years, or perhaps because she was such a force in American theatre for such a long time . . . whatever the reason, Eva Le Gallienne was special to the Playhouse.

Like Langner, she began her life in Britain but made her career in America. She was the daughter of a

EVA LE GALLIENNE
1899–1991

talented English poet, Richard Le Gallienne, and a Danish journalist, Julie Norregaard. She was educated mainly in Paris and returned to London to study briefly at what was then the Beerbohm Tree Academy (it later became the Royal Academy of Dramatic Art). At the age of sixteen she had a major success on the London stage as the cockney girl in *The Laughter of Fools*. Soon afterwards, she and her mother crossed the Atlantic and she spent five difficult years trying to gain recognition in the American theatre. It finally happened in 1920 with Arthur Richman's play *Not So Long Ago*, and it led directly to her being cast as Julie in the Theatre Guild's 1921 production of Molnar's *Liliom*. This was a huge success for her: it made her one of the most sought-after actresses in America, and it began her long acquaintance with Lawrence Langner.

Le Gallienne was in perpetual need of new mountains to climb. She had no patience with the central ideal of the American theatre—"the long run"—and she quickly espoused the idea of repertory companies in which actors and production staff would present several plays at a time. It would be a cheaper way of presenting drama to the public, she thought, and would act as a counterforce in the American theatre, which "has fallen into the hands of real estate men and syndicates and those who have no love or interest in the stage."[34]

So, in 1926, she founded the Civic Repertory Company in a huge warehouse on Fourteenth Street in Manhattan, and there, for eight heroic seasons, she and her company presented high-class productions of Ibsen, Chekhov, Shakespeare and many other classic dramatists, at rock bottom prices, to generally sold-out houses. She accumulated a subscription list of 8,000, and she took the company on tour to other cities. She provided free classes for aspiring actors. The red ink with which financial statements were liberally spattered was wiped away each year by subsidies from wealthy backers. But

As Marguerite Gautier in Dumas's *Camille* in 1936, her first season at the Playhouse.

during the Depression the subsidies disappeared, and with them the company. It ended with the 1933–34 season and the venture was formally disbanded in 1935. Eleven years later Le Gallienne tried again, this time in partnership with Margaret Webster and Cheryl Crawford, but it lasted only one season. Later still, in 1961, she headed up a National Repertory Theatre for the American National Theatre and Academy, making a successful tour with Schiller's *Mary Stuart* and Maxwell Anderson's *Elizabeth the Queen*—but again, the financial facts of life dictated a speedy closure.

As a producer, director and translator (of Chekhov and Ibsen, in particular), Le Gallienne was always in demand, but it was as an actress that she was best known. She was capable of great passion—as Fanny Cavendish in *The Royal Family*, or earlier, as Elizabeth in *Mary Stuart* or Marguerite Gautier in *Camille* (which was one of the roles in which the Westport Country Playhouse saw her in 1936)—but her more typical acting style was cool, cerebral and intellectual, in roles like Rebecca West in *Rosmersholm* and Madame Ranevskaya in *The Cherry Orchard*. The critics were divided about her: some thought her emotionless, almost frigid, others saw how she was able to involve her audiences in the inner life of her characters —a rare gift. She had little time for acting schools and the academic teaching of drama—she believed you had to get up there and do it—and she had almost as little time for Method acting—she thought that was what actors had been doing for centuries, attempting to enter into the inner lives of their characters.[35]

She never really stopped. In addition to her activities within the theatre she wrote two volumes of autobiography and an authoritative book about the great Italian actress Eleanore Duse. She went on acting into her eighty-third year. She appeared at Westport as Grandie in Joanna Glass's *To Grandmother's House We Go* in 1981, forty-five seasons after her first appearance there in *The Way to Love*, which was Lawrence Langner's cunning adaptation of two of Congreve's plays.

Since her death in 1991, there have been two full-length biographies of her, both of which have explored quite fully her open lesbianism and speculated on how much of a disadvantage it was to her in the American theatre at a time when few others were brave enough (or rash enough, as they might have seen it) to follow her example of openness.[36]

Relaxing in the Playhouse grounds before playing Grandie in *To Grandmother's House We Go* (1981).

Carlton Davis was another well-known packager, a specialist in musicals. In 1980 he was offering three of them to COST theatres—*Carousel*, *Mame* and *The Student Prince*—though none was taken by Westport. Theatres had different capacities and different needs. Those that relied on tourist traffic, like Ogunquit in Maine and the Cape Playhouse in Dennis, Massachusetts, tended to like musicals and light frothy plays, preferably with stars (though the Dennis playlist is evidence that it has tackled a great deal of stronger fare in its time). Westport, along with some of the more suburban theatres, like the Paper Mill in Millburn, New Jersey, prided itself on going for a more upmarket repertory. But what they were all looking for, regardless of what their mission statements might say, was a show that sold out at the box office. In 1979 Charles Forsythe, who was one of the longest established independent packagers, had come up with a family comedy called *The Impossible Years*. It was reported to have broken house records at every theatre it played (Westport was not one of them). This success had little, if anything, to do with the play, but everything to do with the star, who was Ted Knight of *The Mary Tyler Moore Show*. As Mr. Forsythe told the *New York Times*: "If you have a hot star, they will come out of the bushes to see him."[37]

There just weren't enough hot stars to go round, and one of the reasons was that the television companies were in the process of moving their annual hiatus from the summer months to the spring. Increasingly, they wanted their stars back on the set in July, and that made it impossible for them to commit to a theatre tour with enough stops to make it viable. The packagers did their best to keep down their costs—it was not in their interest to kill off their clients, the theatres—but it was no longer possible. The growing mortality rate among theatres is easily explicable by a look at the statistics.

In 1959 the production cost of summer stock packages (that is, the cost of producing and rehearsing a show in New York before it went out on tour to the theatres) averaged around $3,300.[38] In 1980, the same kind of show came in between $10,000 and $15,000.[39] That basic cost would be shared between the theatres that took the show (normally four to six of them), but each theatre then had to pay the entire running costs of the show for the one or two weeks it was on its turf, and that is where inflation hit hardest. In 1959 most actors had been working for barely more than $100 a week, but by 1980 the Equity minimum in the COST contract was $284.50, plus a per diem of $7.50 when the actor was outside New York City, plus all transportation costs. Actors paid their own accommodation and meals—unless the only available accommodation came to more than 25 percent of their weekly salary, in which case the theatre paid the difference. And that was just the "basic" actor. Featured actors got $500–$600 a week, and stars anything from $2,500 to $5,000.[40] On top of all this, of course, the theatre had to pay its own overhead, and that, too, was inflating along with everything else.

In response, the theatres did their best to keep ticket prices down, and they were fairly successful to begin with. As late as 1967 Westport patrons could still get a six-play subscription in the best seats for $25, compared to the $19.80 it cost them in 1950.[41] But after that, prices began to climb steeply. By 1980, the price of a single seat in the front orchestra for one performance had risen to $13.50, and the cheapest seat in the house, at $4.90, was now about the same as the most expensive seat had been in 1967. But these prices were barely sufficient to cover the escalation in costs.

It was still the packagers who made the whole thing possible. Take them away and survival would be a desperate struggle. The trouble was that the packagers themselves could not survive without a minimum number of theatres on the circuit. What that minimum was, no one dared speculate—but everyone knew it was being approached at alarming speed.

In 1978, Louis Jourdan came to Westport as the star of a Feydeau farce called **13 rue de l'Amour. Dulcy Rogers was a twelve-year-old usher:**

Louis Jourdan was absolutely wonderful. In the last act of the play, he has locked himself in a boudoir and the police are trying to break down the door to arrest him. One night, just as the police were about to start their banging, the door fell off in Mr. Jourdan's hand. He froze for a fraction of a second, then he propped the door up in its frame, but in such a way that the audience could see through to the backstage area behind. He sighed audibly, and the audience broke up. Then he looked out to us, shrugged, and made a very Gallic type of gesture with his hand—as though to say, "C'est la vie." Then he turned back to the door, knowing full well what the next line was.

One of the young policemen, played by an apprentice who was trying to get his Equity card, had the line: "Open up this door or we will break it down!" Mr. Jourdan turned to the audience with a quizzical look on his face, and the play simply came to a halt for several minutes while they howled with laughter— they were in complete hysterics. Finally, as I remember it, Mr. Jourdan turned back to the policeman and said, "You are going to have to break down the door because I am not going to let you in." He really was a master of his craft, and I think a lot of people in the theatre that night thought that was exactly the way it was supposed to happen.

Carole Claps was the Playhouse press agent in 1978. She remembers that Louis Jourdan's trunk arrived about two months before he did:

It was locked, and for two months all these stories were circulating about what was in the trunk. . . . Finally, he showed up and I told him, "There's been speculation about what's in the trunk." "What do you mean?" he asked in his French accent. "Well, everything," I said, "from drugs to a body to . . . you name it." Well, he started to laugh, and he opened it up. It was filled with white T-shirts—nothing but white T-shirts. "When I do summer theatre, I'm on vacation, and I don't dress up," he explained. And he never wore the same white T-shirt twice. He thought all the speculation about the trunk was the funniest thing he'd ever heard!

What the trunk brought forth.

It was planned as a community celebration, not just a Playhouse event. Ann Rossell, a board member and long-time local broadcaster on WMMM radio, was appointed chairman and coordinator of the Fiftieth Anniversary, and the celebrations began at the end of May with two special events. First, the Lodges (the former governor and his wife Francesca, who had done more than anyone to create the subscription scheme and give the theatre its sure foundation) gave a garden party at their home on Easton Road with Armina Marshall Langner, a youthful-looking eighty-three-year-old, as the guest of honor. Then the town joined in by featuring the Playhouse on Memorial Day. The parade was headed by an American LaFrance Pumper fire engine that had been delivered to Westport the week the theatre opened in June 1931, and it was followed by a barn-red Ford convert-

Memorial Day parade, 1980.

ible complete with rumble seat to tow a bevy of "flappers" through the streets, all in appropriate costume. A few weeks later, at the end of June, with the season under way, a golden anniversary ball was held at the Inn at Longshore. Finally, the week before Labor Day, a great "reunion picnic" was planned to bring everyone together one final time.[42] And amidst all this, Ann Rossell organized a summer-long raffle as the main fundraising effort. There had been a raffle four years earlier, in 1976, but it was the size and success of the 50th anniversary raffle that persuaded the Playhouse to make it a regular (or almost regular) feature of subsequent years. Most seasons, it brought in around $25,000.

Around the Memorial Day holiday, as the town got ready to celebrate the theatre, the parade got rained on a bit, though not catastrophically. The local press dug up an "unpaid taxes" story (a story that had actually been public and transparent for several years) and succeeded in making it sound sinister, which it wasn't. Ina Bradley, in her role as president of the Connecticut Theatre Foundation, wrote to the *Westport News* to put the record straight: "The fact is that in 1973 when the Foundation was established, we were granted tax-exempt status by the IRS, starting with that year. However, the Connecticut State Tax Department disputed this (for the year 1973 only) and challenged us in court. In the lower court we won but on appeal by the Tax Department to the State Supreme Court, we lost. And the long court delays added considerable interest and penalties to the original tax."[43] The $55,000 in interest and penalties (on taxes of $16,000) would take the Playhouse years to pay off.

The season itself was a fairly typical one, though it did not begin well. Boucicault's *The Streets of New York* was brought back as a homage to the theatre's founders. Where fifty years ago it had been Dorothy Gish, Romney Brent, Moffat Johnston and Rollo Peters, it was now Farley Granger, Orson Bean and Katharine Houghton (the look-alike niece of Katharine Hepburn). On opening night, tiny Lillian Gish, "stately in a black evening suit accented by a neckline of sedate white ruffles,"[44] took a brief bow to honor the memory of her sister, who had died in 1968 — but opening night wasn't really the best time to see the play: rather a lot of lines were missed! Markland Taylor of the *New Haven Register* was still not over the shock when he returned to the theatre a week later, though he saw great improvement in the second play, which was Neil Simon's *Chapter Two*: "Professionalism has erased ineptitude. Merciful amnesia has relegated last week's horrendous *The Streets of New York* to the file-and-forget bin. A week late, the Westport Country Playhouse 1980 season has now begun."[45]

Anita Gillette played Jennie in *Chapter Two*, a part she had created on Broadway in 1977. And she was followed by another Broadway habitué in his big role — David Atkinson as Don Quixote, once more reunited with his Broadway Aldonza, Gerrianne Raphael, in the musical *Man of La Mancha*.

They, in turn, were followed by a couple of big television stars — Sada Thompson, best known as the star of *Family*, and Richard Thomas, forever beloved as John Boy in *The Waltons*. Both had done summer stock before, and both had played Westport — Miss Thompson seven years before when she appeared in George Furth's play *Twigs*, and Mr. Thomas way back in 1962 when he was nine years old and had played the son in Ira Levin's *Critic's Choice*. He ruefully recalled slamming the door as he made his entrance one night, causing the entire jerry-built set to collapse. "Hans Conried was on stage with me and after I did a couple of double takes we just continued the scene to the end, pretending not to notice."[46]

This time, Sada Thompson came with an A. R. Gurney play called *Children*. It was billed as a Broadway tryout, though it had already played in London and at the Manhattan Theatre Club. The *New Haven Register* didn't rate its chances: "[A]lthough *Children* is a considerable cut above much of what we're exposed to in summer theatre, I doubt if it will make it to Broadway."[47] Richard

Van Johnson and Annette Hunt in Bernard Slade's *Tribute*.

Thomas, on the other hand, arrived with a proven vehicle — Brian Clark's *Whose Life Is It Anyway?*, which had already won a Tony for Tom Conti as the sculptor Ken Harrison, paralyzed from the neck downwards in a car accident. Mr. Thomas, the *Wilton Bulletin* reported, gave a performance to remember — "a controlled, passionately positive performance that is totally believable and sparked by flashes of sheer unadulterated reality."[48]

Two more plays about invalids were separated from *Whose Life Is It Anyway?* by a stellar production of *My Fair Lady*. Starring Michael Allinson, one of Rex Harrison's stand-ins on Broadway, and Susan Watson, who had last played Westport as Gigi fifteen years earlier, it won all hearts and could easily have played two weeks rather than one.

Instead, it was back to invalids. Henry Denker's *Horowitz and Mrs. Washington* came from Broadway with Sam Levene as the elderly Jewish widower who is mugged in Central Park and looked after, much against his will, by a black nurse, played by another fine Broadway actress, Claudia McNeil. After that came what was, in many ways, the star turn of the summer, in prospect if not in actuality. Van Johnson, back at Westport after a ten-year absence, had a very personal statement to make. *Tribute* was Bernard Slade's play about a man dying of cancer, a man who has been a failure at everything except friendship, at which he has excelled. On Broadway, Jack Lemmon had played the dying man as a tragic figure, but Johnson, who had himself survived two bouts with cancer, wanted to make the point that it need not necessarily mean the end.[49] He clearly succeeded. Don Nelsen reported in the *Daily News*: "He's so damned buoyant and boyish, so *VanJohnsonish*, that death seems out of the question. He survived all those war movies with June Allyson and Spencer Tracy with the world's widest grin: how can he not beat this?"[50]

After so much illness, Hugh Leonard's *Da* must have come as something of a relief. It also came with outstanding credentials—no fewer than four Tony awards, including Best Play of 1978—

Jack Aranson as Da, looking back on fifty-four years as a gardener (1980).

and it got easily the best reviews of the summer. It had a cast of eight, a true ensemble, performing together "with the glorious interplay of an octet of top-flight chamber musicians," wrote Markland Taylor in the *New Haven Register*.[51] But it also had its star, for Da is a bigot of massive proportions, a man who hates the English as much as he hates Catholics, and seems to prefer Adolph Hitler to most other possible rulers. At Westport Jack Aranson gave Da a truly memorable performance—one that many long-time patrons of the Playhouse cite as one they will not easily forget, right down to the moment when Da stands alone on the stage and recites the names of all the roses he has tended in his lifetime.

The final week of the season was given over to one of the most glittering musicals the Playhouse had ever staged. *An April Song* was a true Broadway tryout—a musical adaptation of a Jean Anouilh play about life in a French chateau at a time when princes fell in love with shop girls and duchesses gave balls that lasted until dawn. It was, admittedly, a work in progress, but one on which a great deal of money appeared to have been expended. It boasted, said Jeanne Davis in the *Westport News*, "the most lavish sets and costumes, the most pertinent lighting and general over-all staging we have seen at the Westport Country Playhouse in quite some time. The scenery and the women's ensembles are elegant from start to finish, purely lovely to look at."[52] It came with a star to match—Britain's Glynis Johns, who had last been seen on Broadway singing "Send in the Clowns" in Sondheim's *A Little Night Music*—and a lot of songs ("some forgettable, some hummable, and most enjoyable") with lyrics by Sammy Cahn and music by Mitch Leigh, who was making his second appearance of the summer, for he was also the composer of *Man of La Mancha*.

It rounded off a season of ten shows, each playing a single week, that offered the sort of mix that was now becoming customary—a couple of big musicals; a hard core of plays that had recently been seen on Broadway, some of them with their original casts; a couple of tryouts, neither of which seemed likely to make it without radical revision; two or three major stars to keep the autograph hunters happy; and at least one truly great theatrical experience (in this case, Jack Aranson's performance as Da).

Run an eye down the theatre credits in the small print of the 1980 playbills and you find names like assistant general manager Todd Haimes and box-officer treasurer Vicki Reiss. Twenty-five years later they can be found on Broadway, running the Roundabout Theatre and the Shubert Foundation respectively.

In the 1930s the New School ran a playwriting seminar that was supervised by Theresa Helburn and John Gassner. It was one of the ways in which the Theatre Guild got early intelligence about the best new writers in the American theatre (Gassner was the Guild's official play-reader). At one stage, both Tennessee Williams and Arthur Miller attended the seminar and thereby came (potentially, at least) within the orbit of the Theatre Guild. In the end, with the war intervening, Miller went to different producers for his first successful plays, *All My Sons* and *Death of a Salesman*, and the Guild never achieved a relationship with him. Williams, on the other hand, was four years older than Miller and he had a script ready (or nearly ready) before America went to war. Terry Helburn passed it on to Lawrence Langner and Langner invited Williams to stay at his Connecticut farm while he rewrote it. What should have happened then was that the play—it was called *Battle of Angels*—was tried out at the Playhouse, where it could have been tested on what was at least an approximation of the New York audience. Instead, the Guild chose to try it out in Boston where audiences, critics and censors greeted it with shock and horror. A number of Guild subscribers expressed outrage at the language. The play was withdrawn and Langner and Helburn wrote a humbling letter of apology to their Boston subscribers: "The treatment of the religious obsession of one of the characters, which sprang from frustration, did not justify, in our opinion, the censor's action . . . *Battle of Angels* turned out badly but who knows whether the next one by the same author may not prove a success?"[53]

Prophetic words, but Tennessee Williams wasn't about to wait around and see. When *The Glass Menagerie* and *A Streetcar Named Desire* came out right after the war the Theatre Guild was not the producer. Nor was it invited to produce the rewritten version of *Battle of Angels* that finally came to Broadway (and failed) as *Orpheus Descending* in 1957.

In 1981, however, *Battle of Angels* finally came to Westport with a cast led by John Ritter. Jim McKenzie cannily dedicated the production to a long-time Westport resident, Audrey Wood, who had been Williams's agent and deserved a great deal of the credit for bringing him back from the appalling blow that the 1940 Boston withdrawal had been to him. Forty years later the play was still strong meat for summer theatre audiences, but it was the sort of gesture McKenzie enjoyed making—filling in the gaps in the Playhouse's history. It was, after all, a history of which he himself had now been a part for more than twenty years.

The 1981 season's biggest artistic success was Lanford Wilson's one-act play *Talley's Folly*. Gratifyingly, it was also a popular success, establishing a new box office record for a play. It was about anti-semitic prejudice and bigotry, and the two characters were played by the Birneys, David and Meredith (on Broadway the previous year, when *Talley's Folly* had won its Pulitzer, they had been played by Judd Hirsch and Trish Hawkins). The production that came to Westport had originated at Buck Hill Falls in Pennsylvania, and it was directed by Burry Fredrik, a Weston resident who would play a significant role in the Playhouse's artistic fortunes for the remainder of the century. She had made her debut in the house four years earlier with Judith Ross's *An Almost Perfect Person*. For the next twenty years, she would direct at Westport more often than anyone else, and with a remarkable record of success.

The 1981 season included another piece of history. The last production was Joanna Glass's *To Grandmother's House We Go*, and with it came Eva Le Gallienne in her eighty-second year—a long-time resident of Weston, a Tony nominee for *Grandmother's House*, and surely entitled to be called "the first lady of American theatre." She had first come to the Playhouse in 1936, and now, after her many adventures as actress, director, impresario and proprietor, she returned to make her last appearance in the old barn.

By and large, McKenzie managed to maintain the precarious balance between big names and challenging plays. Cybill Shepherd and Timothy Bottoms made Playhouse debuts in 1982—so did *Elephant Man* (with Bruce Davison behind the bandages) and Mark Medoff's controversial *Mass Appeal*. The next year, Donal Donnelly and Shelley Winters, whose Playhouse record went back further than McKenzie's (she first appeared there as an eleven-year-old), brought Helen Hanff's gentle and charming *84 Charing Cross Road*.[54] And June Havoc, another local resident, played the theatre one last time as Miss Hannigan in *Annie*.

In 1984, there were no fewer than three world premieres on the schedule—Leonard Gershe's *Snacks*, Lawrence Roman's *Alone Together* (which went on to Broadway), and Westport dramatist David Rogers's *Not for Keeps*—and that was in addition to *Agnes of God*, which was promoted by McKenzie in the previous week's playbill as another of those "difficult pieces"— "hardly the light fare usually associated with summer theatre"— yet it did very well at the box office with Geraldine Page and Sandy Dennis as its stars.[55] Frank Gorshin, Cloris Leachman and the ever-faithful Betsy Palmer made appearances during the season, and there was a slew of hugely popular stars from *The Love Boat*—Fred Grandy, Bernie Kopell, Lauren Tewes—all with their own vehicles, all packing the theatre.

One very welcome visitor during this time was Jean

June Havoc and her co-stars in *Annie* (1983).

The best little whorehouse in Westport (1983)—(*left to right*) Dulcy Rogers, Nina Fuentes, Blaine Hammer, Julie Monahan, Lisa Ambrose, Carole Claps.

Stapleton. Her last appearance at Westport had been almost thirty years before during the 1954 season, when she had been part of a large cast for William McCleery's *The Lady Chooses*, along with Faye Emerson and Walter Abel. No one knew more about summer theatre than Jean Stapleton: many years before, she and her husband, Bill Putch, had created their own playhouse in Fayetteville, Pennsylvania—the Totem Pole Playhouse—and they still ran it as one of the best resident summer theatres in the country. Stapleton returned to Westport in 1983 for *Clara's Play* by John Olive—an otherwise very local event since her co-star was Jon De Vries, son of Westport novelist Peter De Vries, and the producer and director both lived in Weston—Haila Stoddard and Burry Fredrik respectively.

Jim McKenzie's deep roots and long service in theatre occasionally enabled him to avert disaster. That was the case at the end of June in 1983. Three weeks earlier he had discovered that the season's new musical, *Luv Song*, was not going to be ready for its June 27 opening. Desperate to fill the gap, he remembered that his very good friends (and very loyal Westport supporters) Eli Wallach and Anne Jackson were enjoying a quiet summer prior to beginning a yearlong national tour with *Twice Around the Park*. "The telephone lit up from East Hampton to Texas to Los Angeles and back again in answer to our emergency pleas, and by Monday morning we had our show—an unscheduled week of *Twice Around the Park*."[56] People did that sort of thing for Jim McKenzie—a few years later George Grizzard and Karen Valentine would do something very similar, at even shorter notice.

And the "grandstanding" went on (why be a nonprofit if you weren't going to take advantage of its fundraising provisions?). Visitors to *The Best Little Whorehouse in Texas* in August 1983 found the theatre adorned as, well, just that. There were cowboys and fancy ladies on stage and off, and a lot of "voluntary contributions" in the form of dollar bills somehow got attached to parts of the ladies' clothing.

In the wider world of summer theatre, however, the signs were ever more ominous. By 1984, the number of COST theatres was down to six.[57] Jim McKenzie was very aware that the packaging system depended on there being at least a minimum number of theatres for productions to visit, and he reckoned that minimum number was probably three. They were getting perilously close to it. "The packaging system," he wrote, "is based on the practical fact that a one-week run cannot possibly pay for a two- or three-week rehearsal."[58]

Packaging aside, McKenzie had reason to worry about the economics of his own theatre. The Playhouse's annual budget had now passed the million dollar mark. It had a summer staff of fifty, encompassing members of five different theatrical unions. In addition, there were fifteen interns and apprentices who were unpaid but whose expenses were not inconsiderable. This staff was putting on 107 performances in an eleven-week season—eleven

In 1983, Shelley Winters starred in Helen Hanff's play **84 Charing Cross Road** *during a very hot week in July. Dulcy Rogers, who was House Manager at the time, recalls the Wednesday matinee:*

Rather than stay in her Westport hotel, Ms. Winters had decided to return to New York after the Tuesday night performance. The Wednesday matinee was due to start at 2 p.m., and at the half hour there was no sign of her. Two o'clock came and went—no one could find her. Inside the auditorium a very traditional Wednesday afternoon audience, mainly composed of ladies, was getting fidgety, then anxious, then angry. To make things much worse, the ancient air-conditioning system chose that moment to konk out—on one of the hottest days of the year. It was now fifty minutes past curtain time and an executive decision was made "upstairs" to throw open the doors and invite the audience to go into the garden for free Coke and Tab. There was a lot of murmuring and a good deal of perfectly justified outrage. Those of us behind the concession stand thought our lives might be in danger.

Then, tearing down the driveway, burning rubber, comes a car that pulls right up beside the garden. Out jumps Ms. Winters, who has now missed the entire first act. Her hair is in curlers and she is clutching what seems like fifty shopping bags. She dives into the center of the lynch mob, which has been silenced by her screeching wheels, and at the top of her lungs she screams out, as though these were all her best friends: "My dears, it was AWFUL. . . ."

She never did tell us what was so awful, or what made her late, nor did she apologize. She didn't need to, because in one fell swoop she had made them all her closest chums who had been let in on a secret. They were thrilled to be there on the afternoon when the "awful" thing happened to Shelley. So they all piled back into the theatre and were extremely happy to be starting the show over an hour late. That's star power!

Paul Osborn's *Mornings at Seven*
(1982)—(*left to right*) Carl Low,
Patricia Englund, Mimi Cozzens,
Robert Moberly, Shepperd Strudwick,
Patricia Morison, Frances Peter,
Barbara Berjer, Maurice Copeland. The
set was designed by Robert Thayer,
costumes by Constance Wexler. The
director, Burry Fredrik, is looking out of
the window on the right.

one-week shows, nine children's shows and occasional special events. A certain amount of income came from program advertising sales, concessions, the annual raffle (which had quickly become a reliable generator of dollars) and tax-deductible contributions, which were now running at about $15,000 a year, but the bulk of the million dollars had to be covered from box-office takings. Ticket prices were still less than two-thirds of Broadway prices and McKenzie reckoned he could break even if the theatre averaged 75 percent of capacity—that meant selling 550 tickets per performance. It helped to have 2,000 subscribers seeing all eleven productions, but that represented less than one-third of the audience—the remainder depended on single ticket sales.[59]

It was a knife-edge business, but it was made slightly easier by the fact that, by 1984, Lorraine Hansberry, the subscription director, was maintaining a 78 percent renewal rate from season to season.[60]

Everything changed on a bitter cold day in December 1984. Jim McKenzie was alone in his tiny, cramped office at the Playhouse when he took a phone call. He was told that the theatre was being sold from under him.

With the Connecticut Theatre Foundation's lease about to expire, Philip Langner had accepted an offer of $1.2 million from Playhouse Square, the shopping center that adjoined the theatre. McKenzie was told that although, technically, the foundation had a right to match the offer, Langner's lawyer hoped it would be waived so as to allow his deal to go through quickly and smoothly. It seemed very unlikely that the foundation would be able to match such a price.[61]

The Playhouse's famous olio curtain, its rooster logo, the covers of its playbills, even the menus at the Players Tavern—they were all designed by Steve Dohanos, "a Renaissance man," as Jim McKenzie called him, certainly Westport's most famous artist and illustrator. Indeed, you could hardly be an American in the middle decades of the twentieth century without being aware of Dohanos. In the forties and fifties he painted no fewer than 125 covers for the *Saturday Evening Post*, and in the sixties and seventies he designed 40 U.S. postage stamps—the Hall of Stamps in Washington, D.C., is named for him.

STEVAN DOHANOS
1907–1994

He had moved to Westport at the beginning of World War II and it was his home for more than fifty years. He called it "Any Town, U.S.A.," and it inspired many of the scenes he painted. When Lawrence Langner wanted a new program cover for the Playhouse in 1950, who better to go to than Dohanos? And that was the first of ten covers he produced over the next thirty years. "It is a way of saying thanks from my family and myself for the many evenings of good theatre we have enjoyed for so many years."[62]

He came from Hungarian stock, but he was born and brought up in Ohio, where he was fated to work in a steel mill. It was when he got an office job at the mill that he became entranced by the art calendars that arrived in the mail from clients and customers. He started making copies of them in colored crayons and selling the copies to his workmates for two or three dollars a time. One of his most successful efforts was a picture of a tramp roasting a hot dog over a fire built in a tin can, while a hungry dog eyes the cooking with anticipation. It was copied from a magazine cover by a man called Norman Rockwell.[63]

He began to attend night classes at Cleveland School of Art and eventually, in 1938, he began what he called his "*Post* graduate" work with a cover for *McCall's*. Within a very few years he was working alongside Rockwell and painting the pictures that most accurately defined America and Americans at the mid-century.

Three of the playbill covers designed by Stevan Dohanos (1959, 1970 and 1980).

BACKSTAGE IN THE SEVENTIES

The empty stage, seen from the wings. The hemp rigging was temperamental, liable to slackness in wet weather and tautness in dry. Stagehands wore gloves to operate it—or else carried tweezers to remove hemp splinters from their hands. The sandbags used to counter the weight of flying scenery and lighting instruments would often leak sand on the heads of actors waiting in the wings.

right: The barebones green room. Later, more comfortable furniture was installed.

center left: A dressing room. No mod. cons.

center right: The scene shop.

bottom left: Wardrobe.

bottom right: The catacombs—used as a storage area.

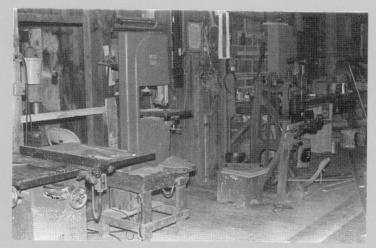

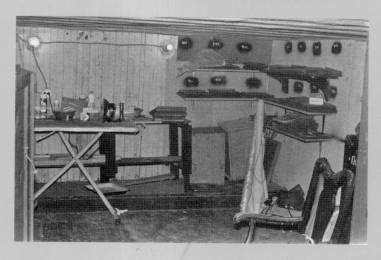

LORRAINE HANSBERRY
1918–1992

Lorraine was the Playhouse's indispensable subscription manager for thirty-seven years—"our Rock of Gibraltar," Jim McKenzie called her. When she arrived, in 1947, she was assigned to the box office and very soon took over the nuts and bolts of the grandiose (and immensely successful) subscription scheme that had been invented and implemented by Francesca Braggiotti Lodge in 1946. Mrs. Lodge was the public face of the scheme, but it was Lorraine who made it work.

Her secret was in the details she always had at her command. She created a file of subscriber cards, each one of them meticulously updated from year to year in her beautiful script. She knew the subscribers personally, she knew their likes and dislikes, and she was always available to handle their requests. If someone wanted to improve their seats, she would almost always find a way—her knowledge of the Playhouse and its auditorium was unrivaled. For most of her tenure, the subscription office was a little cubbyhole next to the Chorus Dressing Room, just off the Green Room area. A window faced out onto the courtyard, and it was at that window that Lorraine could generally be found during the season. In winter, she would take all the cards and ticket boxes home and they would sit on her piano until the following spring, being updated as occasion demanded.[64]

It wasn't just the nuts and bolts of the subscription scheme that concerned Lorraine. She felt she also had a responsibility to represent her subscribers in the Playhouse's planning, and most particularly in the selection of its plays. "She fought tenaciously to preserve quality theatre and protect the morals and language of the stage," Jim McKenzie said, and he would know: as the years went by, he frequently found himself in heated discussions with Lorraine after she had read a play he wanted to schedule—and she made sure she always read them.[65]

She had been born in Illinois, but the family came to live in Westport in 1939. Wanting to be independent, Lorraine rented a house for herself on Evergreen Avenue, and she lived there for fifty years. She always walked to work (she never learned to drive), instantly recognizable by the erect way in which she held herself, head held high. For many years, she spent her winters in Palm Beach, Florida, running the subscription scheme of the Royal Poinciana Playhouse with the same loving care she lavished on her Westport scheme.

In 1958, the last year the Langners themselves ran the theatre, they wrote in the playbill, "Not to embarrass her, but in genuine regard and admiration, the Playhouse wants to say that Lorraine's work and worth in creating a happy, regular audience for the theatre are of such caliber as to make her the most valued member of the Playhouse staff."[66]

A 1961 picture showing Lorraine Hansberry (*left*) with the Playhouse's 1,000th subscriber, Mrs. Sidney Lehrer.

Very early in the season, as soon as almost all the staff had arrived, Jim McKenzie would address them. Pizza and soda were served and everyone sat in a circle in the courtyard. Each person would have to say a few words about himself or herself, by way of introduction. Then Jim would make his speech—basically the same speech every year. The following version of it has been reconstructed from his notes and from the memories of those who heard it many times—and saw the effect it unfailingly had.

"WELCOME TO WESTPORT"

Welcome, everyone, to Westport. This should be a very good summer for us all. You could be anywhere in the world right now. Circumstances find us in this universe, on this planet of Earth and in this country. Beyond that we are, of our own free will, at this moment in Connecticut, in Westport, here at the Westport Country Playhouse—a tiny throwback of New England. There is a busy world at the end of this driveway. But back here is a tiny oasis. This place is paradise for each of us right now.

The summer will be a great experience if we all live with positation. What's positation? The opposite of negation. Some negative terms are: downer, down the tubes, slow down, sit down, fall down, it's the pits, rainfall and no way. How much better it would be to live and work with the positive thoughts of: speed up, stand up, go for it, can do, look up, up and coming, rise and shine, yes indeed.

We should all try to be yes-men and yes-women. NO kills while YES creates. Take a small flower—if it is stepped on it will be crushed and gone forever. But if we water it and nourish it suddenly there will be a wonderful bloom. When someone has an idea it is very important to say Yes—their first idea is the most important—it needs nourishing. It may not really be a workable idea but if it is nourished and allowed to grow, by the time the person's seventeenth idea comes along, it will be a genius idea.

Help each other. We all have our departments, but it comes together when we work together. If you see something on the ground, pick it up. If you see someone carrying something heavy, give them a hand.

We all have a chance to start a new life here—no matter what mistakes any of us may have made before now, here we start with a clean slate. It's your chance to create a new life, new personality, with a new scoreboard. You can be whoever you want to be. Have a positive outlook because you are perfect. Say to yourself, "I am perfect, I am wonderful, I believe in me."

The joke is "the work." The secret is we are the Players—the court jesters—we are paid to play. PLAY HARD—give 100 percent once—push yourself just to see how far you can go—then go for 80 percent. Keep your health. Keep your fun. YOU ARE PERFECT RIGHT NOW.

We are here to support actors. Actors are fragile creatures. They put themselves on the line every night. All the scenery, lighting, publicity and management in the world means nothing if the actors aren't out there. All of us, every department—our sole function is to support the actors. The first twenty-four hours that the actors are here, overwhelm them with kindness. They are in a strange place; many of them are shy; say hello and do whatever you can to help them feel at home. You will make lifelong friends in the theatre. Now let's all have a wonderful summer.

Jim's speech, 1998—a composite of three photographs.

CHAPTER TEN

1985–99 Saving the Theatre: The Playhouse Partnership

The shock generated at the end of 1984 by Philip Langner's decision to sell the land on which the theatre stood was very great—though it probably shouldn't have been since the size (three acres) and position of the theatre's plot (adjacent to Playhouse Square, one of Westport's shopping centers) made it a highly desirable piece of real estate.[1] The first thing Jim McKenzie and his board members did was to dig out the lease and read the small print.

Since 1959, when the Langners had ceased to be involved in the day-to-day running of the theatre, the lease had borne a number of different names. To begin with it had been Laurence Feldman and Henry Weinstein; then it had been the Producing Managers Company triumvirate of Jim McKenzie, Ralph Roseman and Spofford Beadle; and since 1973 it had been the Connecticut Theatre Foundation. But through all those twenty-six years the man who effectively ran the theatre was Jim McKenzie. So it had fallen to him to ensure that the basic conditions of the lease were met. The most important condition was that 10 percent of the theatre's gross had to be paid to the Langners (which, by 1984, meant Philip, for Armina, though still very much alive, was in her ninetieth year). The payments were still being made, though a little bit tardily on occasion.[2]

The small print of the lease contained another clause that now became vital, for it gave the lessee (the foundation) the right to purchase the theatre if it could match the offer within forty-five days. Without having any real idea of how they would raise $1.2 million Jim McKenzie and the trustees of the foundation immediately invoked that clause—and they did so in full awareness that $1.2 million would not be the end of their problems, for the foundation had an accumulated deficit of $100,000 and the theatre was in urgent need of major repairs that could no longer be put off— extensive new plumbing, electrical rewiring and drainage work in the courtyard, to name just a few.[3]

It took seven months, a lot of scrambling and some very creative thinking, but the Playhouse was saved. On July 2, 1985—right in the middle of the summer season—it was formally purchased from Philip Langner, not by the foundation, but by a group of twenty-eight local investors who, together, formed the Playhouse Foundation Limited Partnership, with Jim McKenzie as General Partner (see Appendix A). The Partnership promptly leased the theatre back to the foundation for a peppercorn rent, thus retaining its not-for-profit status. One of the new partners was Philip Langner

The Ghost Light. Theatre tradition dictates that whenever the stage is empty and the house has no audience, a single lamp must be kept alight. There are many different explanations, but the most universal is that the ghost light will keep spirits from inhabiting the theatre whilst it is empty.

himself, whose contribution was made in the name of his mother, Armina, as well as himself.[4] And it was certainly true that the deal would not have been possible without Philip's willingness to extend the original forty-five-day deadline on several occasions.

Much of the creative thinking had come from the foundation's president, Steve Monahan, and its lawyer, Vincent Tirola. When it was clear that neither corporate donations nor individual gifts were going to come close to raising the required sum, it was their suggestion that an "investment vehicle" should be created. They thought that if a small group of people who cared deeply about the Playhouse's survival was willing to invest enough for a down payment, then a local bank might be willing to provide the balance in the form of a mortgage loan, using the value of the property as collateral. They were right. Connecticut Bank & Trust Company agreed to a $900,000 mortgage, provided the Partnership could come up with the remainder (which was $450,000 by the time legal and other costs had been added in). Eric Friedheim, the publisher and philanthropist, who had long been one of Jim McKenzie's most loyal supporters, came up with the first $100,000. Thereafter, all the members of the Partnership chipped in until there was only $150,000 to find. At that stage James McManus, founder of the Marketing Corporation of America, offered $75,000 provided it was matched by further donations that had been pledged but not yet paid. In the last hours before the last extension of the option ran out, the last checks were gathered in. In a display of matchless optimism, the partners announced that they would limit the return on their investment to 7 percent "at best."

The Playhouse was saved, but there was a heavy price to pay—$10,000 a month, to be exact, which was the amount of the monthly payment to service the mortgage. There was no possibility that the theatre could generate that much money—indeed, the best that could be hoped for was that it might break even—so the burden would be placed squarely on the restaurant.

The Playhouse had had a restaurant on its premises since 1955 when the Players Tavern had first opened its doors. The Tavern had quickly become an important feature of the theatre complex, by day and by night, and it had run successfully for twenty years. In the mid-1970s it was succeeded by Backstage, which was popular and successful as a restaurant but was even more popular and successful as a disco when dinner was over. Theatre patrons were bothered by both the noise and the clientele. Backstage, for its part, was bothered by having to pay $10,000 a month in rent, and it folded its tent and left in 1987. But the successor, Neonz, turned out to be a much greater problem—it was a popular bar, a "joint," and it even began to feature "male stripper nights." In 1989 its failure to pay the monthly rent would precipitate the next great crisis in the Playhouse's uncertain existence.

THE SHOW MUST GO ON

However great the backstage drama (and Jim McKenzie used every opportunity to make the people of Fairfield County aware that their playhouse was in danger), the 1985 season had to be planned and produced—Early Bird subscribers had bought tickets for it long before it was known that the theatre was for sale. It may not have been a vintage season on paper, but it turned out to be a very successful one at the box office—whether because of the "theatre-in-peril" publicity blitz, or because of the presence of a number of well-known stars (Leslie Caron, David McCallum, Lucie Arnaz, John Ritter, Shelley Berman, James Whitmore). In August Jim McKenzie announced a 34 percent increase in attendance compared to 1984 and an 8 percent increase in subscriptions. *Evita* broke the box-office record for musicals, while Richard Culliton's *A Place to Stay* broke the record for plays (perhaps because it starred John Ritter and Lucie Arnaz).[5] And the last two weeks

Sandy Dennis and Eileen Heckart in
Marsha Norman's *'night, Mother*
(1985).

of summer featured an exceptionally classy production of Bob Fosse's *Dancin'*, which had originated in Chicago earlier in the year. But that was not all.

On the triumphant day in early July when he announced the purchase of the Playhouse,
Jim McKenzie also announced, on behalf of the foundation, what he called "ambitious long-term
goals." These were to include a six-month season with longer-running plays, as well as a number of
much-needed repairs to the building.[6] No one thought a six-month season was imminent, but, as
an earnest of its intentions, the foundation decided to commit itself immediately to extend the current (1985) season by three weeks. Instead of ending, as planned, with Marsha Norman's *'night,
Mother* in the week after Labor Day, two productions were added—a revival of Clemence Dane's
1920s play *A Bill of Divorcement*, and the tryout of a brand new musical (a rock opera, no less) on
its way to Broadway.

'night, Mother had won a Pulitzer prize in 1983 with Anne Pitoniak and Kathy Bates as
its two-woman cast. In Westport, Sandy Dennis and Eileen Heckart took on the roles, and a
Weston resident, Burry Fredrik, directed. Many more local residents appeared in *A Bill of Divorcement*: six of the nine roles were taken by members of the Westport Theatre Workshop, and another

In *Bill of Divorcement* (1985),
Katharine Houghton plays Margaret
Fairfield, a woman who is confronted
by her husband (Christopher Walken),
long thought to have been killed in the
war, on the eve of her remarriage to
someone else.

local—Christopher Walken
from Wilton—had the lead.
But most attention, inevitably,
was focused on Katharine
Houghton (from Old Say-
brook), who was recreating
the role in which her aunt,
Katharine Hepburn, had made
her film debut in 1932.

The rock opera was
not local at all. With lyrics
and music by Paul Schierhorn,
and with Jeff Conaway and
Anthony Crivello heading up
the cast, *The News* was an
unlikely show to come to
Westport, but it got a very
warm reception from a
remarkably young audience
at the Playhouse, where it ran
for two weeks. By contrast, it survived on Broadway for only four performances after its official
opening night.[7]

REALITY STRIKES

Roderick Cook, who directed *A Bill of Divorcement*, was soon back at the Playhouse. He opened
the 1986 season with Carole Shelley in an exceedingly popular show of his own devising, *Oh,
Coward!* Thereafter, Jim McKenzie announced that the theme of the season was "the study of
women." "Although it evolved somewhat inadvertently," he wrote, "fully half of our summer is
devoted to the mystique of the feminine mind." In pursuit of this, he cited four shows—Neil
Simon's *The Odd Couple* (in its revised form of 1985, with female rather than male proponents);

the American premiere of Louise Page's *Real Estate*, starring Colleen Dewhurst as a woman torn between career and family; Michael Learned and Eileen Heckart facing another dilemma (between love and loyalty to their country) in Hugh Whitemore's British thriller *Pack of Lies*; and Barbara Rush in Elizabeth Forsythe Hailey's period drama *A Woman of Independent Means*.[8] He might have added Sandy Dennis and Anne Meara in Paul Zindel's *And Miss Reardon Drinks a Little*. The production that came away with the best reviews was *Pack of Lies*, which was very much a homegrown affair with Burry Fredrik directing three current or former Connecticut residents— Michael Learned, Eileen Heckart and Charles Cioffi. Michael Learned, laden with Emmys from her years in *The Waltons*, was making her first appearance at the Playhouse, but she had been brought up in West Norwalk and vividly recalled the magic of her early visits to the Playhouse with her mother when she was very young.

Once more, it was intended that the season should be extended into the fall, but that plan was quietly abandoned as a new reality dawned.

This was the year, 1986, when the television companies finally and officially moved their hiatus (that is, the three months during which production teams take their annual vacations) from the summer months to the spring. It had long been pending, and in some cases effected, but from now on June-to-September theatres like the Westport Playhouse could not rely on the availability of *current* television stars—that is, the people who were almost always the biggest attractions. Even before he knew this for certain, Jim McKenzie had wondered out loud about the straw hat circuit's dependence on stars in an interview he gave at the beginning of the season: "There is a lack of legitimate theatre stars around today. Stars are now made by television and they will do a play only if there's no work on T.V."[9]

The 1986 season was thus the last of the ten- or eleven-production seasons that had been a tradition at the Playhouse since 1946. Henceforward, there would be only six productions in a season, each of them running two weeks—which was precisely the pattern that had failed so badly in 1976. Why should it work any better now?

In fact, it *did* work better, largely because the sales and marketing staff came up trumps. But another way of looking at it in 1987 was to ask if it was even remotely possible to continue operating in the old way, and the answer was No. Nationwide, there were probably fifty summer theatres left (compared to nearly 500 in the 1930s), but by the time the 1987 season began there were only six stock theatres still operating in the Northeast under the COST contract.[10] By 1989 there would be only four,[11] and in the early 1990s it was reduced to the three survivors— the Cape Playhouse in Dennis, the Ogunquit Playhouse in Maine and Westport. So few theatres sharing ten or eleven productions made neither logistical nor economic sense, even if one or two of the productions were also shared by theatres further afield, in places like Denver, Detroit and Chicago. Moreover, production, union and staff costs were continuing to rise much faster than ticket prices—inflation had already proved fatal to countless commercial theatres across America. In the case of Westport, there was an additional threat hanging over it: it had to make a $10,000 mortgage payment every month without fail.

Even if the Playhouse could survive inflation, its continued existence depended on the ability of the restaurant to pay its rent—because that was what paid the mortgage.

There was another source of income that was available to the foundation: it could take advantage of its not-for-profit status by seeking government and corporate grants. But Jim McKenzie had always been opposed to that sort of dependence. He believed that such grants were arbitrarily handed out and arbitrarily taken away—there one year, gone the next—and how did you then replace the revenue? He preferred not to get into it. Several of the other theatres in Connecticut took the opposite point of view—and lived to regret it in the 1990s when first government, and then corporate, funding dried up.[12]

The decision to change from eleven productions to six was not made until January 1987. By that time, the subscription manager Julie Monahan, who had succeeded Lorraine Hansberry in 1983, had already sold a great many Early Bird subscriptions for the regular eleven productions. The first hurdle, therefore, was to find out if these subscribers, many of whom had had their subscriptions for decades, would accept a smaller number of productions. It turned out that they would, and most of them welcomed it. In fact, many of them chose to accept Julie Monahan's offer to convert each of their eleven-production subscriptions into *two* of the new six-production subscriptions—at no extra cost.

Up to this time, Jim McKenzie had not known whether the reduction to six productions would be a positive or a negative move. He had known it was something he had to do and that it would dramatically reduce the theatre's expenses, but he had had no way of gauging the public's reaction. The memory of 1976 was still too recent to allow him to be optimistic. Now, however, there could be little doubt—it was positive. And as the spring progressed, and activity in the subscription office went from busy to frenetic, he came to realize that it was a very big positive. Eventually, the number of subscriptions almost *tripled*, from less than 2,000 to over 5,500![13] At half the price of the old ones, and requiring a commitment of only half as much time, they sold like hotcakes.

At the same time, the prospects for single ticket sales at the box office were enormously improved. The days when critics had regularly got their reviews into Tuesday's papers were long gone—most reviews weren't hitting until Thursday or Friday, and that meant that Saturday performances were the only ones to benefit in the one-week scenario. But now, with two-week runs, the whole of the second week could benefit from good reviews—and it almost always did.

Artistically, there were also gains. "The new policy," Jim McKenzie said when he announced the change in January, "will enable the theatre to double its available resources of time and energy for each production, including rehearsal time, production, promotion and audience development. In addition, the two-week run of each play will allow the foundation the luxury of producing plays by itself without having to rely on the booking of plays from other theatres. The effects of this policy will be that the Westport Country Playhouse can become more of a regional theatre, producing plays pointing towards its own audiences, its own area performers and its own artistic integrity."[14]

SIX AT A TIME

The subscribers having done their part, McKenzie and his creative colleagues now had to do theirs. As Markland Taylor of the *New Haven Register* remarked at the end of his preview of the 1987 season: "Whether WCP audiences respond positively or negatively will clearly have a lot to do with future plans and policies."[15]

Obba Babatunde in Judd Woldin's
musical *Little Ham* (1987).

Aside from the fact that each of the six productions ran for two weeks, the principal change from previous seasons was that all six productions were, as promised, homegrown.[16] Jim McKenzie, as executive producer, thus placed the burden of proof squarely on his own shoulders. And the local critics felt he had passed the test. By and large, they liked his choice of plays, they praised the casting and acting (noting that the principal roles were in the hands of fine stage actors like Frances Sternhagen, Lee Richardson, George Grizzard, Karen Valentine, Charles Keating and David Groh, rather than visitors from Hollywood), and they were especially positive about production standards.

Neil Simon's *Biloxi Blues* led off the season—his memoir of basic training during World War II—directed by the author's twenty-four-year-old daughter Nancy. She had been a production assistant on the original Broadway production, directed by Gene Saks, and it was Jim McKenzie who had given her her first opportunity to direct when he produced the play for the Peninsula Players at Fish Creek, Wisconsin, the previous summer (that was McKenzie's other summer theatre, the one that he owned and had been associated with ever since he was an apprentice there in 1947). During the winter, McKenzie and Nancy Simon had taken their production to Hawaii for a five-week run at the Honolulu Community Theatre. Now, here they were in Westport, with a new cast but a confident production—one that Miss Simon kept moving "at a fast clip," wrote Barbara Meyer of *The Advocate*: "Before you know it, several hours have passed in laughter and you leave the theatre feeling well entertained."[17]

The next play provided a much bigger test of the Playhouse's production standards (and not just because it had to compete with the real-life Iran-Contra hearings on television). It was Arthur Miller's *All My Sons* with a very fine cast that included Lee Richardson, Frances Sternhagen, Felicity La Fortune and Tracy Griswold. Originally, it was to have been a restaging of Arvin Brown's recent production at the Long Wharf Theatre in New Haven that had gone on to Broadway, but Brown had dropped out late in the day and McKenzie had persuaded Jose Ferrer to direct what was, in effect, a new production with a new cast—thus giving the critics a chance to compare Westport standards with New Haven/Broadway standards. The Playhouse came out of it very well. "Jose Ferrer . . . has staged the production with relatively little movement," wrote Robert Viagas of *Fairpress*, "but a finely tuned touch for the nuances and frequent double meanings of Miller's dialogue. Ferrer passes the test of this play: making each of the script's manifold revelations hit their emotional targets."[18] Alvin Klein of the *New York Times* noted that the Long Wharf production had been a "casualty of the commercial theatre's general apathy towards 'serious' plays," having closed after only three weeks on Broadway and even before it was awarded the Tony for the season's best revival. "The Westport production is truly the Westport production . . . ," he wrote; "Obviously, the point is the play, and it is herein well served. Poor Broadway. Lucky Westport."[19]

With these first two productions of the 1987 season Jim McKenzie might be said to have nailed his manifesto to the theatre's door. He was clearly saying that the Playhouse management intended to bring its nearly 6,000 subscribers high quality theatre that could stand comparison with anyone else's, even Broadway's. As Irene Backalenick somewhat grudgingly wrote in the *Westport News* after *All My Sons*: "In fairness to the Westport Country Playhouse, we must point out that the theatre has come a long way since its days of lightweight, shabby, careless productions. It is making a genuine attempt to bring solid offerings to its audiences this summer, judging by its first two shows."[20]

The other four productions in 1987 (all comedies except for *Little Ham*, the musical based on a Langston Hughes play that ended the season) were well received. The playwright David Wiltse had the satisfaction of seeing *Doubles* staged at his hometown theatre. *Doubles*, which was about male

David Wiltse's *Doubles* (1987). Jill Jones in the men's locker room.

One of Westport's most popular acting partnerships: Karen Valentine and George Grizzard in A. R. Gurney's *Perfect Party* (1987).

Charles Cioffi as Gould and Wayne Rogers as Fox in David Mamet's comedy *Speed-the-Plow* (1989).

As an addition to the 1989 season, the Playhouse hosted five performances of a production of the play Margaret Sanger: Unfinished Business **that had originated at Lucille Lortel's White Barn.** This was the only time the Playhouse was ever picketed. The play—about the founder of the birth control movement—was sponsored by Trojan, who sent boxes of condoms to be distributed free to the audiences. The title role was played by Eileen Heckart (*below*).

bonding in the locker room of a tennis club, had already played on Broadway, but it was truly a Westport creation because it had started life at the town's Theatre Artists Workshop. It was followed by an English bedroom farce, *Wife Begins at Forty*, in a slick and fast-moving production that proved an excellent vehicle for Charles Keating. But it was George Grizzard and Karen Valentine who gave the most pleasure with their celebration of A. R. Gurney's *The Perfect Party*, directed by Burry Fredrik. Writing in *The Ridgefield Press*, Fran Sikorski exclaimed that "the casting is perfect, as is the direction of the perfect cast in *The Perfect Party*."[21] That cast included David Rogers and June Walker, a real-life husband-and-wife team from Westport, as the couple who live next door. The Rogers family had already made major contributions to the Playhouse— and would be heard from again, collectively, in 1998.

The only real problem about setting high artistic standards is maintaining them, and Jim McKenzie's misfortune was that there were too many distractions. The 1988 and 1989 seasons did not live up to the 1987 prototype, though they both had memorable moments. A fine production of Herb Gardner's *I'm Not Rappaport* with Samuel Wright and Paul Soles was the highlight of 1988; and a strongly cast production of David Mamet's *Speed-the-Plow*, with Wayne Rogers, Charles Cioffi and Mia Dillon, directed by the prodigious Burry Fredrik, got a lot of well deserved attention in 1989 (McKenzie later admitted that they had "downplayed" the language, without actually changing it, so that "it wasn't as rough here, as offensive as it might have been in Chicago or New York").[22]

But, by this time, most of the drama was taking place offstage. Artistic considerations were no longer being given the priority they needed, and if you were privy to the worried meetings and conversations of those in the know—the members of the Partnership, the foundation trustees, McKenzie's senior management—then you could readily understand why.

THE FINANCIAL FACTS OF LIFE

A profile of the Playhouse in 1988 provided graphic evidence of just how tenuous the theatre's survival was in this new world where summer stock was largely a thing of the past, and where the difference between success and failure was the ability to pay the mortgage at the end of the month. For Jim McKenzie, after more than forty years of producing plays in American theatres, it was an alien and a scary business.

The profile showed that the Playhouse (or, more accurately, the foundation, since it was the employer) had 52 paid members of staff, 8 apprentices and more than 200 active volunteers who looked after all the unpaid jobs—ushering, opening night parties, the annual raffle, special benefit shows, administrative help, community relations and so forth.[23]

The theatre produced five plays and one musical, each of them having sixteen performances in a two-week run. The overall budget for rehearsing and staging these six shows was $975,000—of which $925,000 would be found from subscription and box-office revenues if the theatre played to 72 percent capacity, which was the estimate on which the annual budget was based.

In addition, and in order to sustain what had long ago become a Westport tradition, the Playhouse put on nine children's plays during the course of the summer, budgeting them (in total) at just over $60,000. The projections anticipated income of a little more than $47,000, so there was leeway to make up here, too—though, in practice, the children's series almost always ended up making money because it sold so well.

A much more recent development was the theatre's support of the Westport Country Playhouse School of the Theatre. This was one of the few "ambitious long-term goals" announced at the time of the Partnership's purchase of the theatre in 1985 that had actually come to fruition. It was a professional training program in the theatre arts that offered classes throughout the year at the Westport Center for the Arts. Run by a married couple, DeAnn Mears and Frank Savino, both of them fine actors and teachers, it taught everything from Acting Technique to Dramatic Writing, from Directing to Voice & Speech. Each of its four semesters a year was limited to 100 students because of space limitations. Budgeted at $77,000 a year, the 1988 projections showed that it would need $14,000 in grants to break even (in actual fact, it made a profit that year, as it did in most years of its existence—it had to be discontinued in 1989 when it lost its lease at the Arts Center and alternative space at comparable cost could not be found).[24]

Finally, there was the Apprentice Program. Where once there had been as many as twenty apprentices, there were now eight. While the theatre accepted no responsibility for their living accommodation or food, it did now give them a stipend of $60 for each of the fourteen weeks they were expected to be in Westport. In all, the program was costing almost $10,000 in 1988.

One advantage of doing only six plays in a twelve-week season was that it freed up the five Sunday nights when there were no sets to change. In 1988 they were used for a subscription series of one-night-only presentations called *Sundays at Eight*. The series included one-woman shows by Julie Harris (as Charlotte Brontë) and Piper Laurie (as Zelda in "The Last Flapper"), an evening with the comedy duo of Monteith and Rand, the ever-faithful Preservation Hall Jazz Band, and a "pianologue" by Stan Freeman (impersonating the irrepressible Oscar Levant—"a concert of high brow music and low brow conversation"). In subsequent years, there were occasional Sunday night presentations (most notably the Preservation Hall Jazz Band and, later on, the Doo-Wop shows), but the idea of a regular Sunday night series was deemed impracticable.

There were other activities from which the Playhouse made money, of which parking, concessions and the raffle were three of the most important. The raffle had begun in 1976 and although it had missed a few years since then, it was by now a Playhouse tradition, with its own permanent booth in the courtyard below the theatre.

Nevertheless, the bottom line of the 1988 budget included in the Playhouse profile of that year showed anticipated expenditures of $1.23 million against projected income of $1.17 million. At least $55,000 was required in unearned income (or unexpected revenue) to bridge the gap.[25]

None of this, of course, took any account of the mortgage. The assumption on which the Playhouse operated was that the $10,000 monthly payments would be taken care of by the restaurant's rent.

ALARUMS AND EXCURSIONS: 1989–90

Right up to the last moment it looked as though the 1989 season would have to be postponed. The barn was now 154 years old, and a hard winter followed by an incredibly wet spring had almost done it in. In April and early May the roof was leaking so badly that the auditorium was uninhabitable. At the same time, an urgent project to put in new power lines for safety considerations had to be stopped because the work was too dangerous to undertake in the continuing downpour. The scenery wouldn't dry; the grounds were a mess of mud. By the time the sun finally came out there was only just time to get the essential work done—the roof was actually completed at 8:23 p.m. on opening night.[26]

Storm clouds gathering over the diamond jubilee season.

And while all this was happening, Jim McKenzie and the members of the Playhouse Partnership were painfully aware that something much worse had gone wrong. Neonz, the noisy and unwelcome discotheque that had taken the place of the Backstage restaurant in 1987, had ceased to pay its rent in February. For several months the theatre's lawyers had been exerting themselves to get an eviction notice served, and they finally succeeded at the end of July. By that time $60,000 was owed in rent and that, in turn, meant that the mortgage was in serious danger of going into default. The Connecticut Bank & Trust Company, which was now part of the Bank of New England (which, in turn, was reporting major losses for the year), was unlikely to be flexible.

When Jim McKenzie held a press conference on November 8 to make the bad news official he was careful not to bat around too many figures—he merely stated that "the Playhouse is three months in arrears on mortgage payments . . . in addition, some $50,000 in taxes and payments to subcontractors are overdue." Describing the overall situation, he said: "Funds are insufficient to pay the mortgage, back taxes, subcontractors, and execute the renovations necessary to expand into fall and winter seasons. In addition, the Playhouse must . . . comply with recent revisions in the town's fire and safety codes including spacing between seats, new fire retardant materials, updated electrical services, etc."[27] Inevitably, the press eventually supplied much more alarming figures. The *Westport News* told its readers: "The Connecticut Theatre Foundation (CTF), which operates the Playhouse,

The Ceruzzi plan (1990): Had it been approved, the Playhouse would have been part of a stylish complex of offices and (*on the right*) a restaurant.

New offices, at left, proposed at Westport Country Playhouse, center, and restaurant in Westport, Conn.

owes over $250,000 for mortgage payments, taxes and payments to subcontractors. It also faces a loss of about $192,000 after making renovations to the Playhouse to meet fire and safety codes."[28]

The next eighteen months were a roller-coaster ride peopled with angels, bureaucrats (of the short-sighted kind) and world-class restaurateurs who disappeared at the shake of a tutu.

It began with Louis Ceruzzi, who was clearly heaven-sent. His company, Ceruzzi Mack Properties, Inc., was a successful local developer. His offer was, first, to make good the outstanding mortgage payments so as to prevent default; then to take over the Playhouse property, to assume the $900,000 mortgage, to renovate and winterize the theatre and its two adjoining buildings; then to lease the Playhouse back to the foundation for $1 a year for 99 years. In return, Mr. Ceruzzi would own the property, lease the restaurant to a new operator and construct a limited amount of commercial space, which he would rent out.[29] The plan was that another local drama company, the Boston Post Road Stage Company, with which Burry Fredrik was closely involved, would take up winter residence.[30]

A fully restored Playhouse, free of debt, at no cost and no risk, for 99 years! It sounded too good to be true. And, of course, it was.

In March 1990 the Westport Planning and Zoning Commission rejected the plan by a 5 to 2 vote on grounds that the limited office space would bring too much traffic to the area. "I'd like to save the playhouse," said one of the commissioners who voted to kill it, "but I feel that this is selling our soul."[31] Nancy Gilchrist, the chairman of the commission, who also voted against the proposal, ended the meeting with a pious expression of hope: "I have a dream we will have someone very enterprising in this community come forward to save the playhouse."[32]

Louis Ceruzzi (who quite justifiably thought *he* had been that "very enterprising" person) had spent $50,000 on mortgage payments, as well as a further significant sum on architectural plans. If he got any satisfaction out of the whole mess (which is doubtful) it might have been that his contribution to the mortgage enabled the Connecticut Theatre Foundation once again to put off closing the theatre. Five anonymous board members—whose names should be known: Walter Bergen (the newly elected President), Jim McKenzie, Eric Friedheim, Steve Monahan and Burry Fredrik—clubbed together to put up $75,000, and shortly after that another anonymous source came up with a loan of $45,000. Collectively, these donations enabled the foundation to make a substantial payment towards the theatre's delinquent mortgage payments, eliminating the immediate threat of foreclosure and allowing the 1990 season—the theatre's sixtieth—to go ahead.[33] It was a temporary fix, but it bought some much-needed time.

Amidst all the uncertainty and anxiety of the spring and summer of 1990, Jim McKenzie could comfort himself with the knowledge that the theatre's leadership team now included two tough-minded and efficient colleagues, both of whom were in it for the long haul. Walter Bergen, an Easton resident who owned a computer consulting business, had become president of the foundation in the midst of the 1989 crisis. Together with two other board members who were close to McKenzie—Eric Friedheim and Steve Monahan—Bergen became McKenzie's chief source of support and advice. In the meantime, Julie Monahan (Steve's daughter), who had been in and around the Playhouse for fourteen years, was appointed general manager at the beginning of the 1990 season. Julie had worked her way up from usher to subscription director—a post in which she had succeeded the legendary Lorraine Hansberry in 1983—and she had been largely responsible for the miracle of 1987, when subscriptions had tripled at the beginning of the six-plays-a-season era. McKenzie had reason to be grateful that he had these people beside him. What he could not have foreseen was that they would remain his principal colleagues and co-conspirators throughout most of the 1990s.

Two things needed to be done in a hurry. One was to put together a summer season suitable for the celebration of a diamond jubilee. The other was to find a new restaurant operator so that regular mortgage payments could be resumed.

Considering how little time there was to plan it, the season was a very creditable one. Its bookends were British—British plays led by British actors. In June, it was Tom Stoppard's *Rough Crossing*, with music by André Previn. It is a play that takes place on a transatlantic liner as an acting company approaches a Broadway engagement for which it is ill prepared. Charles Keating, British by birth and training, now a resident of Weston, Connecticut, played the role of Dvornichek, the cabin steward. Equally successful at the end of the season was Willy Russell's one-woman show *Shirley Valentine*. It had originally been planned that Ellen Burstyn would play it (she had taken the show on the road after Pauline Collins had created the role in London and New York), but she had dropped out when a film opportunity came up, and Jim McKenzie had asked Millicent Martin, the greatly talented British actress who now lived in Redding, Connecticut, to take over the engagement—which she did with stunning success.

Rosemary Prinz as Daisy and Ellis E. Williams as Hoke in *Driving Miss Daisy* (1990).

In between these very British evenings came three incontestably American plays—A. R. Gurney's *The Cocktail Hour*, Alfred Uhry's *Driving Miss Daisy* (with Rosemary Prinz and Ellis Williams, veterans of *Miss Daisy* road companies) and Robert Harling's *Steel Magnolias* with Anita Gillette. The most successful offering with the audience was another British import (the only musical of the season), Noel Gay's *Me and My Girl*, resurrected from the 1920s and a recent megahit in both London and New York. It introduced Westport to a young man called Jamie Torcellini, who had a huge success and would return the next season with *Where's Charley?*

The Gurney play brought to the Playhouse, at long last, an actress who had been a personal friend of the Langners and had spent many evenings in the theatre as their guest, but never performed there. Elizabeth Wilson had actually made her debut on Broadway in the Theatre Guild's 1953 production of William Inge's *Picnic* (she was the schoolteacher), and she was probably best remembered as Dustin Hoffman's unflappable party-giving mother in the film of *The Graduate*. Now she played Gurney's genteel society matron, Ann—and did so opposite Fritz Weaver, an actor with whom she had apprenticed at the Barter Theatre in Abingdon, Virginia, many years before.[34]

Unlike most other milestones in the Playhouse's illustrious history, all of which had been celebrated to the hilt, no one felt particularly inclined to hold a birthday bash in 1990. The future was too uncertain. But all the traditional elements of a Westport season were there—Monday night openings (only six of them now, but still quite glitzy occasions), an outstanding series of nine children's plays on Fridays, a number of benefits and galas scattered through the season and occasional Sunday night concerts.

Meanwhile, behind the scenes, Walter Bergen and his cohorts were still looking for a restaurant operator willing to take on a $10,000 a month rent.

They thought they had found one—a world class restaurateur with whom they negotiated an excellent deal. At the last moment he backed out when his ballerina girlfriend, who was to have managed the restaurant, ran off with one of his chefs.[35]

Jamie Torcellini "doing the Lambeth Walk" in Noel Gay's 1920s musical, *Me and My Girl* (1990).

Elizabeth Wilson and Fritz Weaver reunited in A. R. Gurney's *The Cocktail Hour* (1990).

As the winter of 1990–91 approached, there was still no resolution and the mortgage was once again endangered. But there was hope. Felton Weller, an accomplished manager of several New York City restaurants, together with his wife Diana, professed themselves willing to invest $800,000 in the restaurant building. They were also willing to sign a lease for the magic number of $10,000 a month. Once again, it seemed too good to be true.

But this time it was for real. Early in 1991 Weller opened a very fine Tuscan restaurant called Sole e Luna. The *New York Times* gave it an "excellent" rating and (more importantly) it paid its rent on time.[36]

WINTER QUARTERS

Despite all the good news, there seemed little chance that the Connecticut Theatre Foundation would be able to achieve the most ambitious goal Jim McKenzie had set for it on the day the theatre had been purchased in 1985—a six-month season. Twelve weeks was the most that could be managed, but that did not necessarily mean the Playhouse could only be used for twelve weeks of the year. In the summer of 1990 the building had been officially declared a landmark (this was its sixtieth birthday present from the state, which had it entered into the Register of Historic Places kept by the Connecticut Historical Commission), but it was still essentially a summer place—and sometimes a very leaky one, at that.

The Boston Post Road Stage Company had plans to change this state of affairs.

The company dated from 1981, though it had not begun producing plays until 1984, and it did so then in a Fairfield school. In six seasons it had produced twenty-four plays, mostly of the Off-Broadway variety, and it had attracted notice. The *New York Times* had called it "the pluckiest and fastest growing professional theatre in the state."[37] By 1990 it needed a home that wasn't a school, and preferably a place that would allow it to have an audience of more than a hundred. It was the company's literary manager, Burry Fredrik (later its artistic director), who came up with a neat way of reconfiguring the Playhouse's 707-seat auditorium into a more intimate setting that would seat 190 with a forestage and an interior winter lobby at the back of the orchestra. It meant replacing the traditional pews with individual seats covered in red velvet, but it was made clear that the pews would be back in place for the start of the Playhouse season the following summer.

The Playhouse auditorium reconfigured to seat a winter audience of 190.

The Boston Post Road Stage Company (which later changed its name to the Fairfield County Stage Company) performed at the Playhouse through the fall/winter/spring seasons of 1990–91, 1991–92 and 1992–93. It put on eighteen shows during that time, ranging from Shakespeare's *The Merchant of Venice* to Christopher Durang's *Sister Mary Ignatius Explains It All for You* (which gave predictable offence).[38] Its one undeniable hit was *A Christmas Carol* in an adaptation by the company's artistic director Doug Moser. But other plays did not sell as well: the fourth season, advertised for 1993–94, had to be cancelled before it began.

The company's move to Westport, which cost about $100,000 by the time it had reconfigured the auditorium and carried out essential winterizing repairs (such as ensuring that there was sufficient heat and that the dressing room windows were weatherproofed), had been premised on the promise of bonding money from the State of Connecticut. A succession of legislative postponements and bureaucratic hang-ups meant that the company did not receive its money on time and was always behind the curve, but that wasn't the "killer" problem. "We just didn't sell enough tickets," Burry Fredrik said.[39] And Marilyn Hersey, the company's managing director, pointed to another irony: "[W]e had a stronger following in Fairfield. With 100 seats we played 88 to 89 percent capacity over a season. But we were lucky if we sold 50 percent of the seats in Westport. I don't think people in Westport really want a winter theatre."[40]

And that, in the end, may have been the real problem.

THE NINETIES

Near the end of the 1991 summer season the Fairfield County newspaper, *Fairpress*, ran a headline that summed up the feelings of a lot of people: "Westport Playhouse Enjoys a Comeback." It noted that the six productions staged that summer were "fresh fare to many Fairfield County theatre-goers, who do not often make the trip to Broadway and Off-Broadway."[41] Jim McKenzie attributed the high quality of production to the fact that "the Playhouse Foundation is back into producing its own plays and has control over rehearsal time, staging, and where the play will go next."[42] All but one of the 1991 productions had gone on to at least three venues after Westport, one of them as far afield as Kansas City, and the last production of the season, *M. Butterfly*, was scheduled for a 35-city tour. The only "downer" had been a hurricane in August that caused a power outage to darken the theatre for two consecutive nights during the

Aaron Sorkin's *A Few Good Men* (1991), directed by Steve Karp, with (*from the left*) Patrick J. Kinsella, Marc Epstein, John Hickok and Rob Bogue.

run of *Dangerous Obsession*, a British thriller that starred Juliet Mills. Julie Monahan told the *Westport News* it cost the Playhouse $15,000.[43]

When regular patrons of the Playhouse were asked which Westport production of the 1990s made the greatest impression on them, they were apt to choose one of the productions from that 1991 season — Aaron Sorkin's *A Few Good Men*. It is a courtroom drama about the death of a young marine, and it was remarkable for the depth and quality of its ensemble cast — no great stars but a

A Chorus Line (1995).

group of very fine actors, led by John Hickok and Deidre Madigan, directed by Steve Karp of Stamford Theatre Works (who was also a teacher in the Westport School of Theatre). David Henry Hwang's *M. Butterfly*, which followed, was remembered for the performance of Allan Tung. As he put it himself, "Here I am, a Chinese actor playing a Japanese actor playing an actress who is actually a spy. Even within the role I have to be an ingénue, Garboesque, Dietrichesque . . ." Almost continuously on stage, he was required to change costumes sixteen times, and wigs six times—not to mention "his voice, his manner of walking, sitting, standing, turning his head, using his hands" as he transformed himself from the male spy into Song Liling, the female singer with whom the French diplomat Gallimard has fallen in love.[44]

The most memorable production of them all was Kander and Ebb's *The World Goes Round*. Coming from an Off-Broadway run of almost a year, it began its national tour at Westport at the end of August 1992, bringing with it no fewer than three Tony winners, including its star, Karen Ziémba. "The joyful news is that, here and now, the show is at its sparkling best," reported the *New York Times*. "Most impressive, [Scott] Ellis and [Susan] Stroman, who were the show's director and choreographer since its inception, have so refined their work that it honors the essence of the Kander-Ebb oeuvre in the purest way. . . . Finally, near its end, one can proclaim the summer's best musical production."[45]

Politicians at Westport: Laurence Luckinbill as LBJ (1995), Jean Stapleton as Eleanor Roosevelt (1998).

Three years later the season featured another much praised musical production. *A Chorus Line*, so recently a permanent presence on Broadway, seemed like a daring selection for summer stock, especially in a part of the country where the production would certainly be compared with the Broadway version. "[It] proves to be a highly satisfying entertainment for summer audiences," the *Westport News* reported. "[It] is so much an ensemble that it is difficult to note single performances for excellence, though each, and particularly the women performers, create memorable characters."[46] This was a production made specifically for the three remaining stock theatres in the Northeast—Ogunquit, Westport and the Cape Playhouse in Dennis—and it showed what they were capable of.

A month later, the *Westport News* was even more enthusiastic about Laurence Luckinbill's solo performance of *Lyndon* on a Sunday night, in which he delivered a remarkable impersonation of LBJ: "James B. McKenzie and his entire staff of professionals at the venerable 65-year-old theatre should be commended for mounting such an exquisite production. It's worth a full week, not just one night."[47] That lesson was learned by the time the next political/one-person show arrived at Westport in 1998. It was Rhoda Lerman's *Eleanor: Her Secret Journey*, with Jean Stapleton as Mrs. Roosevelt. It played two weeks before going off on a national tour, and it earned Miss Stapleton a fine reception and some excellent notices.[48]

Few people gave as much pleasure to the Westport audience as Stephanie Zimbalist. She first came to Westport in the unlikely guise of a dog called Sylvia, the star of A. R. Gurney's play that had

A dog's life: Stephanie Zimbalist in the title role of A. R. Gurney's *Sylvia* (1996), with Edmond Genest.

already enjoyed a considerable success Off-Broadway. "As the title mongrel, Stephanie Zimbalist is as flexible and bouncy as a new-born pup," wrote the *Norwalk Hour*. "Whether frisking off for a rendezvous with the neighborhood stud, Bowser, prancing into the kitchen to check 'le kibble du jour,' or rolling about in a half-hearted desire to please Greg, the actress is a physical charmer."[49] The audience loved her—and would have loved her even more had they known that her own beloved dog, Dippy, had been killed by a coyote in the yard of her California home just weeks before she set out for Westport.[50]

Many of the best productions at Westport in the 1990s (and later) were directed by David Saint. *After-Play* was one of them, the work with which the 1997 season closed. Coming off a New York run, it was notable for many things—not least that it was written by the actress Anne Meara, and that it had a fine cast that included Jane Powell, as well as Anne Meara herself and her hus-

Paul Benedict, Jane Powell, Jerry Stiller and Anne Meara in Ms. Meara's *After-Play* (1997).

band, Jerry Stiller, who was taking a break from *Seinfeld*. It was Jane Powell's first appearance at the Playhouse and one that brought out a lot of her admirers and Connecticut neighbors.

There were moments when things didn't go quite as planned. Opening the 1993 season, Millicent Martin led the cast in a slick and hilarious production of Michael Frayn's *Noises Off*—made somewhat harder to perform when one cast member lost her voice and walked through the production, doing all the stage action while someone else spoke her lines from the wings.[51] Equally unexpected was the reception Shakespeare got when he returned to the Playhouse in 1994 after a long absence. The play was *The Taming of the Shrew* with Victoria Tennant—but its interracial casting led to a number of audience complaints and some cancelled subscriptions.[52]

Gavin MacLeod and Millicent Martin in Ken Ludwig's comedy *Moon Over Buffalo* (1997), directed by Pamela Hunt.

And, of course, there were occasional disasters. In 1992 A. R. Gurney's *The Fourth Wall* broke the Playhouse's unofficial record (previously held by the 1978 production of *Out on a Limb* with Douglas Fairbanks, Jr.) for the number of patrons making early exits—not because it was a bad play but because they disliked its undoubtedly liberal bias in the midst of the Bush/Clinton election campaign.

And then there was the 1994 production of Alan Ayckbourn's *Intimate Exchanges* with Elaine May and Gene Saks. The reviews were not encouraging—and worse, Miss May suffered a shoulder injury during the first week. She cancelled on Labor Day, and the next two performances as well. On Wednesday morning, confronting horrible losses and realizing they were about to lose the Wednesday matinee, Julie Monahan, who was in charge (Jim McKenzie was on a plane to Wisconsin), called George Grizzard and Karen Valentine, who lived not far away, and asked if they would be willing to do a reading of A. R. Gurney's *Love Letters* that very afternoon. Great troupers that they were, they arrived at the Playhouse within two hours and performed for delighted matinee and evening audiences. Since Elaine May did not return, Gene Saks and Irene Worth performed *Love Letters* for the remainder of the week.

INTIMATIONS OF MORTALITY

There were important exceptions, of course, but as the decade wore on it became clear that the Playhouse had settled into a routine that more often flirted with mediocrity than it did with artistic triumph. Much of the interest during the last years of the century was sparked not so much by great theatre as by publicity gifts—such as Jerry Herman's Broadway show in 1997, or Fred Savage's stage debut in *Wendell & Ben* in 1998. The buoyancy of the 1990 and 1991 seasons had been dulled by the monotonous repetition of offstage problems, and also by the sheer difficulty of doing anything adventurous or innovative in the prevailing circumstances of summer stock. Subscription levels slipped back quite drastically. After the high point of 1987, when they had risen to 5,500 in response to the introduction of the six-play season, they had fallen back to under 4,000. It wasn't until the 1999 season, with a sudden 17 percent increase, that they once again passed 4,000.[53]

The fundraising outlook was no more optimistic. Back in the mid-1970s when Jim McKenzie and the foundation board had first experimented with fundraising under the theatre's nonprofit charter, they had encountered a very fundamental problem: Westporters continued to think of their Playhouse as a commercial entity—they did not particularly wish to see it as a mendicant organization, dependent on their charity. Nor, for that matter, did McKenzie want to be thought of in that light, but "needs must," and over the years, as the theatre's woes had become increasingly public, voluntary contributions had crept upwards—by the early 1990s they were running at about $35,000 a year, with annual appeals bringing in a further $7,000–$10,000. But it was still fairly minimal in a million dollar budget, and hopeful applications to the Connecticut Commission for the Arts and the National Endowment for the Arts were coming up empty, or (in the case of the Connecticut Commission) with occasional $5,000 grants in response to $50,000 applications. The only bright spots were the $25,000 grants regularly given by the Charles and Mildred Schnurmacher Founda-

tion (on which the Plotkin and Weinstein families were represented as directors and trustees) and the continuing ingenuity of the theatre's most committed supporters in organizing an array of galas, benefits and the annual raffle.

A 1994 audience survey had told McKenzie little he did not already know, but it painted a picture of an audience that was loyal (and likely to remain so) though not very enthusiastic—because it saw little to be enthusiastic about. Respondents complained that the plant was rundown and inefficient. They were especially critical

One of Richard Ellis's design drawings for *Blackbirds of Broadway (A Harlem Rhapsody)* (1997).

of the refreshments, the comfort of the seats, the parking arrangements and the decor. And they were critical of the shows. In general, they wanted more musicals and comedies, though subscribers specifically asked for "more contemporary dramas, including (in particular) a performance of *It's a Wonderful Life*."[54]

However bemused he might be by that particular finding, Jim McKenzie could not mistake the flat and uninvolved tone of most of the responses to the survey. It bespoke an institution that was badly in need of rethinking and remodeling. He could keep things going, partly because he commanded immense personal loyalty throughout the profession, partly because he was a cussedly determined man who was not going to give in, come what may. He proved that spectacularly in the winter of 1992–93 when he was diagnosed with lung cancer. He eventually had surgery in June of 1993—but not before he had put together the Playhouse's summer season. That was the sort of man he was!

Testament to the loyalty that Jim McKenzie inspired was the number of otherwise perfectly sane people who returned to work for him year after year. Never was this more so than in the 1990s. By the time the last year of the century came around, Julie Monahan, the general manager, was notching up her twenty-fourth season. Patricia Blaufuss, the press and marketing director, was into her eleventh. So was Richard Ellis, the theatre's greatly talented scenic designer. Susan Roth, the lighting designer, and Cathy Mulligan, the Ticket Czar who looked after both subscriptions and

To the extent that the Playhouse had a resident playwright in the last two decades of the twentieth century (which, of course, it didn't), it was Pete Gurney. From *Children* in 1980 to *Ancestral Voices* in 2000, Westport staged thirteen of his plays, two of them world premieres.

Gurney belongs to a tradition of American playwriting that flows directly from Philip Barry and S. N. Behrman. He is the wry observer of WASP society, its critic as well as its celebrant. "I don't write about rebels or dissenters or gangsters," he once told the London *Times*; "I write about my own people, the Americans you see haunting Harrods [the London department store] in midsummer, the Americans who call themselves Anglos now because WASP has become such a pejorative term."[55]

"PETE" A. R. GURNEY AND THE WESTPORT PLAYHOUSE

Although he has been writing plays since the late 1950s, it was not until 1987, with *Sweet Sue*, that Gurney reached Broadway. Until then almost all his plays had made their way via Off-Broadway and regional theatres, and almost all of them had been seen in summer stock. In many ways, they were ideal for the summer circuit, with small casts and sets that were easily reproduced—they were "doable." Moreover, their subject matter was the sort that generally interested and entertained summer audiences.

Gurney liked the summer circuit. He often followed his plays as they made their way from playhouse to playhouse. He knew that the best sets were generally designed at Dennis; that Ogunquit was stricter about bad language than other theatres; and that Westport was a useful "bellwether"—the reactions he got there were generally indicative of what he could expect from audiences in New York and other major cities. Moreover, Jim McKenzie was a man he liked personally and trusted professionally, so he often asked him to act as producer when one of his plays was being staged for the summer circuit. He knew this would assure him of a first-class director (most often, David Saint), an experienced and efficient stage manager, and— of the greatest importance—an excellent cast. Westport liked stars, of course, but he knew that McKenzie would always work with a professional casting agent and would offer his suggestions for the author's approval.[56]

Pete Gurney backstage at the Playhouse with Karen Valentine, 1987.

For many years Gurney taught literature and humanities at the Massachusetts Institute of Technology. His plays have a literary distinction that is rare in contemporary American theatre, as well as genuine wit, and emotions that are almost always restrained. Sheridan Morley, the leading British critic and theatre historian, has described him as the "most elegant and accomplished theatrical writer to have come out of America since the war."[57]

No theatre—let alone a country playhouse—could ask for a better friend and colleague.

In 1998, Jim McKenzie exercised an option to give the American premiere of *Perfect Wedding*, a bedroom farce by the English playwright Robin Hawdon. It was the sort of play that could only be performed effectively by a group of actors who knew each other well and could play off each other easily and naturally. Such teamwork is not easily come by in summer stock where rehearsal periods are necessarily brief. But McKenzie found a shortcut for this one. He offered the six principal roles to three married couples, all of whom were actors, and all of whom were related to each other.

THE ROGERS FAMILY OF WESTPORT

The dynasty was the Rogers family of Westport, and David was its patriarch. He was a playwright, two of whose plays had been performed at the Playhouse (*The Moments of Love* in the fall season of 1963, and *Not for Keeps* in 1984). He and his wife, June Walker Rogers, were also actors and had worked together on the Playhouse stage in 1987, playing a married couple in A. R. Gurney's *The Perfect Party*. Ten years earlier June had directed one of the few children's plays that Westport produced itself—*Winnie the Pooh*.

They had two daughters, Dulcy and Amanda. Aside from making their stage debuts in *Winnie the Pooh* (as rabbits), they had each spent a large portion of their teen years at the Playhouse—in fact, they'd more or less run it for several years. Both of them had become ushers when they were twelve. Dulcy was head usher at fifteen and house manager at sixteen, a job she continued to hold down throughout her four years at Yale ("she was the only house manager we ever had who knew where to kick the old air conditioner to get it started," McKenzie said of her).[58] Amanda followed in her sister's footsteps, but she had to wait to be house manager until she was eighteen and an undergraduate at Northwestern—she filled in with spells in concessions and the box office.

Hardly surprisingly, both girls had become actresses—an outcome about which David felt a certain amount of guilt: he feared they hadn't known there was anything else. And now they were both married to actors. Dulcy was Mrs. Diedrich Bader (*The Drew Carey Show*) and Amanda was Mrs. Frank Ferrante (*Groucho*).

Now the whole darn dynasty was playing Robin Hawdon's *Perfect Wedding* at the Playhouse—with Melissa King as the only "outsider" in the cast. Jack Going directed, and Jim McKenzie was proved to have been right—it worked. The reviews were overwhelmingly good, and the *Stamford Advocate* reported: "it brings waves of laughter back to the Playhouse, where coughs and errant hearing aids have dominated the airwaves this summer."[59]

The Rogers family—June, Amanda, Dulcy and David at the Playhouse, 1987.

Sisterly love—Dulcy (with the knife) threatens Amanda (unarmed) in Robin Hawdon's *Perfect Wedding* (1998).

single ticket sales, were working on their ninth seasons. And Philisse Barrows had been around longer than any of them—in fact, she had arrived the same year as Jim McKenzie, 1959, when she was a fourteen-year-old usher. She had gone on to run the box office at sixteen, and after that the business office. There weren't many jobs around the Playhouse Philisse hadn't done at one time or another—one season she had even been credited in the playbill as "Tree Dryad." From 1973 onwards she was generally billed as assistant to the executive producer, and that was certainly a true

Two of the Playhouse's employees in the 1990s—Caragh McGovern (house manager) and Tom Landry (box office)—held their wedding reception at the theatre, April 26, 2003.

description, for she had been Jim McKenzie's faithful companion in both his personal and professional lives for many years, and the mother of their much loved daughter Agatha.

At no other time in the Playhouse's history had there been such continuity behind the scenes, and it was the collective experience of this team that enabled McKenzie to keep going through the 1990s, despite his manifold health problems. It was also at this time—in the late 1990s—that personal and corporate giving began to be a factor in the theatre's finances. By 1999, with Erika Ellis now a part of Julie Monahan's team as development director, the playbill was able to list more than two hundred individuals, corporations and foundations who were making gifts of between $50 and $25,000, and a further 150 individuals and businesses who were donors to the annual benefit and auction.[60] Belatedly, fundraising had become a major part of the Playhouse's activities.

But it was not enough. There was a Sword of Damocles hanging over the theatre, and no amount of routine fundraising would make it go away. The Playhouse was haunted by its mortgage. The first order of business at any meeting of the foundation board or the management team was almost always to ask if the next monthly payment could be made. And it had to be made, without exception and without delay, because one of the minor repercussions of the savings and loans scandal that had rocked the nation in the late 1980s and early 1990s had been the takeover by the FDIC of the bank that had made the original mortgage loan in 1985. To make matters worse, when the FDIC took over the rate was adjusted to current interest rates and payments rose to more than $12,000 a month. Under federal regulation of the bank, the foundation knew it could expect no mercy: failure to pay would mean the automatic assignment of the mortgage to a government collection agency. And that would spell the end of the Playhouse.

The ability to make the mortgage payments continued to depend mainly on the restaurant paying its rent, though important contributions were made by a variety of community groups who used the theatre during the winter. Felton Weller had proved himself a fine restaurateur, and for several years Sole e Luna was a considerable ornament to Westport, enabling the theatre to make its mortgage payments regularly and on time. But success bred disaster. Thinking to duplicate his success, in late 1995 Mr. Weller opened a second restaurant in Westport—a "casual" restaurant with a French tone to it—but it did not do well. Sole e Luna had to be subleased to a succession of operators, none of whom could repeat its original success. By 1998 it seemed certain that it would have to close its doors. That would mean no rent, and no rent would mean no mortgage payments.[61]

MORE THAN JUST SURVIVAL—A STRATEGY FOR REVITALIZATION

This was the background to the change that came about in the Playhouse's affairs in the last two years of the century. In reality, the change took place on the board—in its membership and its thinking—and it took place without fanfare and without publicity. Janet Plotkin (who, with her husband, Fred, had been a very generous donor for many years) had succeeded Walter Bergen as president of the board at the end of 1991, and it was during her presidency that a group of board members got together to develop a strategy for the revitalization of the Playhouse. This strategy was greatly influenced by two new members of the inner circle. The first was Liz Morten, who joined the board in 1996 and, along with Walter Bergen, co-chaired a committee to launch a capital campaign to renovate the Playhouse. Liz's background was in music (she had been an opera singer) as well as arts administration and finance, and she quickly became the focal point of an informal group that laid the groundwork for what had to be done. Other members of the group were Catherine Herman, Barbara Stern, Janet Plotkin and Walter Bergen. They hired a consultant in 1998 to do a feasibility study, and he advised them that there would be support for a $5-million campaign to renovate the Playhouse and develop it as a year-round arts center—but only if board members were themselves seen to be major contributors, and if the foundation could guarantee that it would either own the theatre and its property or have a long-term lease on it.[62]

The other important new contributor to the board (even before he became a member of it) was Bill Haber. In 1975 he had been a founding partner of Creative Artists Agency in Hollywood; now he was a Fairfield County resident, a director of the Westport-headquartered Save The Children, and a Broadway producer as well. He visited the Playhouse in the summer of 1997 for a performance of *An Evening with Jerry Herman*, and he immediately saw the potential of the place. He knew from his friend Catherine Herman that the board was keen to get Joanne Woodward involved, and he knew instinctively that this was the right course. So he took it upon himself to go and see Ms. Woodward and convince her that she could play a pivotal role in saving the Playhouse if she was to become artistically involved. Armed with her cautious expression of interest, he let the board know, through Catherine Herman, that Ms. Woodward might be prepared to help under the right circumstances. It was not long before Bill Haber was himself a member of the board, and an exceedingly influential one.[63]

There was, then, a key group of supporters who became the driving force behind the dream of creating a revitalized Playhouse. They were Liz Morten, Catherine Herman, Walter Bergen, Ann Sheffer and Bill Haber, and they would later be joined by Steve Wolff. Jim McKenzie was very much a part of their discussions, for he was not just the theatre's executive producer and a member of its board; he was also the general partner of the Playhouse Foundation Limited Partnership and the landlord for the Playhouse and the foundation. As such, he accepted responsibility, and liability, for everything that happened on the property, even though he had virtually no ownership stake in it. On the other hand, his position as general partner gave him security—no one could remove him—and that was an important element in what followed.

This was the position in the spring of 1999 as Jim McKenzie readied his forty-first Westport season. At that stage, no one knew it would also be his last. In most ways, it was a typical McKenzie season, and a very creditable one.

James Naughton in his one-man show
Street of Dreams (1999).

The bookends were bravura shows by fine performers. The opener was *Street of Dreams*, James Naughton's much-praised one-man show of song standards and theatre anecdotes, which had twice been an Off-Broadway hit. Naughton, an accomplished director as well as a much decorated actor, would shortly be playing a major role in the Playhouse's future, but no one could foresee that when he opened the season in front of an unusually starry audience of his Westport and Weston neighbors. The season's closer, twelve weeks later, was Frank Ferrante's celebrated impersonation of Groucho Marx. It was written by Robert Fisher and Marx's son, Arthur, and Ferrante had first done it Off-Broadway in 1986. Now he repeated it, to enormous acclaim, on the stage where Groucho himself had given so much pleasure in 1958.

In between these bookends were two new plays and two tried and tested plays. The new plays were Kevin Rehac's *Chasing Monsters* (a first play) and Ron Clark's *A Bench in the Sun*. The established properties were A. R. Gurney's very successful *Far East*, straight from Lincoln Center, and Alfred Uhry's warm and funny *Last Night of Ballyhoo*. Gurney's special relationship with Westport went back many years, and Uhry, as the author of *Driving Miss Daisy*, could be assured of a hearty welcome.

The two new plays were guaranteed success at the box office by the casting of well-loved television stars in the principal roles. *A Bench in the Sun* boasted Betsy Palmer and Tim Conway—the former making her tenth appearance at the Playhouse in her seventieth year (a statistic few members of her audience would have credited), while Conway, after doing thirty-three *Carol Burnett Shows* a year for eleven years, was as well known a face as you could find in American theatre.

Chasing Monsters, to everyone's delight (including their own) reunited Olivia and John Walton in the forms of Michael Learned and Ralph Waite. The production was outstanding, but the play was not. As one of those involved later recalled, "it made *Moose Murders* look good."[64]

> **Tim Conway starred with Betsy Palmer and Paxton Whitehead in Ron Clark's play A Bench in the Sun in 1999:**
>
> There was so much to see at Westport . . . the audience sitting in pew style seating, the wooden rafters holding the ceiling together, the rake of the stage practically dumping you into the laps of the folks in the front row, the stage crew huddled just off the wings ready to spring into action at the drop of a curtain or the dim of a light, the reflection of the patrons' eye glasses as they captured the stage lights, the smiles of those in the first choice rows as they looked up at me. . . .
>
> These were all the things I had an opportunity to stare at whenever I went up on my lines. It was such a pleasant sight I went up on my lines with some frequency just to enjoy the view.
>
> Westport Country Playhouse was the best theatre in the country because there is so much to see during those awkward theatrical moments.

Groucho on I-95 (above) and Frank Ferrante as Groucho on the Playhouse stage (right) in 1999.

Stephanie Zimbalist was also back in Westport in 1999. To the American public at large she was probably best known as Pierce Brosnan's partner, Laura Holt, in the 1980s hit series *Remington Steele*, but to Westporters she was celebrated for her remarkable performance as the dog Sylvia in A. R. Gurney's play three years before. Now she was back with another Gurney play, *Far East*, as the wronged wife in a complicated set of relationships between a young Navy officer, his Asian love interest and his commanding officer.

By the time Frank Ferrante's Groucho rang down the final curtain in September, it could certainly be accounted a successful year. There was the usual round of fundraisers—a "Salute to Ol' Blue Eyes" at the Patterson Club in Fairfield in May, and a "Musical Murder Mystery Fundraiser" called *Stage Struck* in October ("A great way to kill an evening—dress casually in black and bring a mask"). Voluntary giving had increased very markedly, but it was still a comparatively small part of the budget. Subscriptions were far down from their high point in 1987, but 90 percent of the theatre's income was still coming from the box office, just as Jim McKenzie had always insisted it must.

True to his philosophy, McKenzie used his last "Dear Friends" letter in the Playbill to urge patrons to take out their Early Bird subscriptions for next season, and he ended it with his familiar "Thanks for being here."[65]

Early on, Jim McKenzie used to say that his career in the theatre had taken him through Flood, Fire and Famine—and he wasn't exaggerating much. Hurricane Hazel had been responsible for drowning the 3,000-seat tent in which he had been producing musicals at the Lake George Music Carnival in 1954; and shortly before that, the Evanston Showcase Theatre in Illinois had gone up in flames while he was its press agent. There had even been a time, in 1952, at the 172-seat Dobbs Ferry Playhouse, when Jim, his wife and two sons had had to live, eat, sleep and work literally "on the boards."[66]

THE ROAD LESS TRAVELED: THE UNORTHODOX CAREER OF JAMES B. MCKENZIE
1926–2002

Drama (of the theatrical kind) was the dominant feature of Jim's life from the moment he introduced his own one-act version of *Hamlet* to a startled audience in Appleton, Wisconsin, when he was eleven years old, but another kind of drama—real-life drama—was a frequent companion on his unorthodox journey through life. It most often involved the sea. When he was seventeen, he enlisted in the navy and spent two years in the smoke and slaughter of the South Pacific where he became a chief radioman and reckoned he covered 200,000 miles, most of it at 9 knots.[67] Later on, as he settled into his theatrical profession, he tried never to produce plays anywhere that was not adjacent to a large body of water, preferably an ocean, so that he could sail as often as possible. He boasted on his sailing résumé that he had been grounded more than one hundred times (which didn't look very good on a résumé, some might have thought, but he claimed it showed "experience" as well as "the overwhelming satisfaction of having refloated the boat each time"). And anyway, he was a very good sailor—one of the best. "Who else," asked his longtime friend and colleague Spofford Beadle, "can find Mama Rhoda Rock sailing into the Berry Islands in a raging storm off the Great Bahama Bank at midnight? And who else can generate a standing ovation sailing up to Christie's dock in Newport after a fog-bound passage from Block Island—so thick that the radar-equipped ferries couldn't make it?"[68]

On the water, as in the theatre, McKenzie was an outstanding navigator. He sailed in four Newport-to-Bermuda races; he completed the Southern Ocean Racing Circuit (of six races a year) five times; he sailed single-handed from Maine to the Bahamas most years in the 1960s; and at various times he was the proud owner of six boats (sloops, ketches and cutters). At one time, in the 1960s, he ranked among the top twelve ocean racing navigators in America. He once lost a 700-mile race by 18 seconds, and he won another by 11 seconds. He was no mean sailor![69]

But there were two things that were always more important—the theatre and his family. In his time, he worked at, and generally ran, a great many theatres, many of them simultaneously. Without exception, they all seem to have thought they ranked Number One in his affections, for he lavished his love and his energy on them without any apparent limitation. There was also sleight of hand involved, for with so many irons in the fire he could hardly be tending to them all at the same time—yet that was just what he appeared to be doing. Charles Dillingham, who was general manager of the Westport Playhouse in 1969 and went on to be one of McKenzie's closest colleagues at ACT for more than a decade thereafter, described how he would prepare himself to explain to the Langners that they'd "just missed Jim," when who should hop out of a car in the parking lot than Jim himself, just in from the airport.[70] But, in truth, there was one theatre that was dearest to him, and that was the little "Theatre in a Garden" in Fish Creek, Wisconsin. It was where he apprenticed; it was where he became the producer in 1960; and it was where he became the proud owner and proprietor in the late 1970s. It was also where his daughter Amy was the leading ingénue for several seasons.

Of his many achievements in the theatre, the most important, by far, was producing more than 1,500 plays in 49 states of the Union and 11 different countries. 419 of the plays were produced at Westport. He was many things in the theatre—from apprentice to proprietor, from stage manager to impresario—but above all things he was a producer. That was what excited him as an eleven-year-old with a vision of how to do *Hamlet*, and it was what still excited him on the day of his death. And the reason it excited him so much was that it was all about people—molding the diverse talents of many different people into one seamless production. How good at it he was can be judged from the way people thought of him. "With Jim, it was all about the actors," said the actors—and that was certainly true. Yet the staff and technicians who worked for him as regular employees, even if they knew in their hearts it wasn't all about them, worked for him with an extraordinary devotion. There were playwrights to whom he gave a first, blessed opportunity, and there were hundreds of apprentices and interns in whom he fostered a real love of the theatre. They all knew they were important to him—and they were all right, for one thing Jim McKenzie knew for certain was that making theatre was a cooperative enterprise. His job (and his delight) was to bring them all together.

If there was one single achievement for which McKenzie deserves a place in American theatre history, it is the saving of ACT. He first became involved with the American Conservatory Theatre in 1966, its very first year of existence, when he hosted a remarkable spring season for the young company at Westport. He became a trustee and watched from a distance as the company, now based in San Francisco, mired itself in debt and played to houses that averaged little more than 30 percent of capacity. In 1969 Bill Ball sent him an SOS—could he help? Most people, asked that question at such a late stage, might have said they would help to wind up the company, but McKenzie saw something else—a basis of civic and community pride that might turn it all around. He enlisted the aid of the Ford Foundation, and he used his skills and instincts as

With Dakota.

a commercial producer to bring in popular productions to fill the Geary Theatre between seasons (*Hair* was the most successful of them).[71] He not only saved ACT, but he became its executive producer for thirteen years that were among the most enjoyable of his career. He only left in 1982 because (as he recalled, without bitterness) they got a $4 million grant from the Ford Foundation and the board suddenly wanted to become involved in running the company. That ended the fun for him and he moved on.[72]

Aside from the Peninsula Players at Fish Creek, the Westport Playhouse was the longest commitment of McKenzie's career. In a sense, he took it over directly from Lawrence Langner, and he therefore saw it as a trust. During his first three seasons, when he was general manager but not yet in charge, he frequently encountered Langner in the theatre, and after Lawrence's death in 1962 Armina was a continuing presence. By that time McKenzie was pretty well a veteran of summer theatre himself; he knew that the system the Langners passed on to him—what was largely a star-driven system, but also relied on frequent Broadway tryouts and a fair sprinkling of brand new plays—was the right system for Westport. In subsequent years, as circumstances changed and summer theatre was forced to accommodate itself to the television industry and to fight off the insidious effects of inflation, McKenzie increasingly had to improvise. In the end, survival represented success, and he had the satisfaction not only of ensuring that the theatre survived but that he handed it over to a major artist whom he greatly respected.

In his personal life, as in his professional life, McKenzie was unorthodox. He was, as someone remarked after his death, "a philosopher of life."[73] With Robert Frost, he was proud to say:[74]

> Two roads diverged in a wood, and I,
> I took the one less traveled by,
> And that has made all the difference.

By his first marriage, to Jeanne Bolan, he had three children—David, Kevin and Amy—and later two grandchildren. After he became a widower, in 1976, he found happiness with a young woman he first met at the Playhouse when she was a fourteen-year-old usher. He and Philisse Barrows had a remarkable and enduring relationship which involved a great deal of cross-country travel—she by Jeep, he by plane, meeting up in the most unlikely places—and a remarkable system of mutual support and caring. They reviewed their relationship without fail every six months; they had a daughter, Agatha; and their last great adventure was to get married sixteen days before Jim's death.

People who knew Jim well tended to use the same words and phrases to describe him—"smart," "brave," "compassionate," "humorous," "a gentleman," "a man whose word was his bond." He was a dreamer, for sure, but he was also a realist who lived to make dreams come true.

In his office at the Playhouse, 1998.

IN HIS OWN WORDS

When Jim McKenzie died in 2002, his wife Philisse put together these autobiographical fragments from words that Jim had spoken or written on various occasions.

I started at the top—when I was 11 years old I produced, directed and starred in *Hamlet* in Appleton, Wisconsin, where I was born. I cut the play down to one act and got my friends to do it. My little brother was Ophelia, complete with half-lemons for breasts. I put the whole thing in Yorick's grave, so we only needed the top half of costumes. The local newspaper publisher fell off his seat laughing and gave us front-page coverage. I never stopped after that.

Life becomes simple when you know what you want, and I just wanted to produce plays. Everything I learned in jobs or courses—plumbing, piano, voice and diction, English literature, carpentry—was aimed at that. I became an actor, stage manager, manager and press agent. The only reason I learned anything was so I could use it as a producer.

I first worked at the Peninsula Players as an apprentice and after 55 years continue to take pride in the special ambience and goals of the theatre. It's a total resident company 60 miles north of Green Bay, Wisconsin. We have 20 acres, and 16 buildings where the 33 actors live and eat and never leave the place. It's always 33 because that's how many beds we have. We light bonfires outdoors and the customers gather round, and we give them marshmallows to roast.

Each theatre I've run has been very different. In Dobbs Ferry we had 172 seats. We lived in the scene shop—the whole company. We shared our meals. If we took a night off, we'd go broke.

The Royal Poinciana Playhouse in Palm Beach was the classiest theatre in the country. Black tie every night. We would have 54 chauffeurs waiting for our subscribers, and if more than 10 of them left at intermission, we knew we were in trouble! With the yachts and all nearby, it was a fantasy world we lived in.

In 1968 I joined the American Conservatory Theatre—I've never been the same since. I threw away my neckties and suits and became a child of the 60s. It was 17 years of total bliss. In our three theatres we did 10 plays a week in rolling repertory. It was a dream of a lifetime, 152 classics in repertory on a raked stage. It was Nirvana for me. Classical theatre, a huge company, 250 people, year-round, the largest theatre in the world in its time.

My life in Westport really is summer theatre and it is quite different from regional theatre or repertory or resident theatre. What we do here is essentially entertain people. We give them a reason to go out and have fun for an evening. If they happen to learn something, it is kind of by accident. Choosing a season is like buying a pair of shoes. You try them on until something fits. It has to fit what I think the public wants to see—I think of myself as the public, as the average theatre-goer.

(Above) As a teenager, on stage with the Peninsula Players at Fish Creek, Wisconsin.

(Below) "It's been a wonderful adventure." Handing over to Joanne Woodward at the end of his forty-one-year odyssey at Westport.

Every "first" is a highlight—first night, first tour, first stock show and first Broadway show. Every new play, new theatre, is a thrill, even though I've now produced more than 2,000 plays. I live the unknown and get turned on by doing something I've never done before. Just do it. I see no end to producing. It's just a thing I love doing. I'll do it anywhere. It's putting together a crossword puzzle.

It's been a wonderful adventure.

Throughout the spring, summer and early fall of 1999, a consensus developed that this was the moment when the disparate threads of the board's strategy had to be brought together and acted upon in unison. The symbolism of the fast approaching millennium was lost on no one. In early November, a new board was put in place, with Liz Morten as its president, Catherine Herman, Walter Bergen and Ann Sheffer as its principal officeholders, and Bill Haber and Anne Keefe among its members.[75] Anne Keefe, long revered as one of the finest stage managers in the business, and most recently associated with the Long Wharf Theatre at New Haven, was there by right as a Weston resident and a leading member of the American theatre, but she was also there as a friend and colleague whom Joanne Woodward greatly respected and who epitomized the board's intention to engage highly qualified theatre professionals in the running of the Playhouse.

Stephanie Zimbalist was one of the stars of A. R. Gurney's Far East when it played Westport in 1999:

We managed to complete barely half of the first act in our final dress rehearsal. The next night, opening night, Pete Gurney was in the audience. Throughout the play, we all soldiered on through a loud, distinct wheezing from the back of the audience (later determined to be someone's oxygen tank). At the end of the play, I recall my character Julia had some sort of emotional upheaval. So did the set. As I struggled with lines never before performed and beats never fully realized, my concentration continually pricked like a balloon by the wheeze of the oxygen tank, an under-rehearsed Japanese sliding door suddenly collapsed beside me. With the playwright in the audience! I recall trying to ignore it, little trouper that I am, which was undoubtedly much more distracting, or amusing, than bending down and picking the darn thing up.

There was something else about this new board that was very striking. It was a board of trustees, all of whose members were there to play a very specific role in the revitalization of the Playhouse. One or two were able to contribute their talents as theatre professionals, but most of them were there because they were willing to make significant financial contributions to the capital campaign that would be the principal business of the board. And they did—often on a very large scale, because it quickly became clear that the original target of $5 million was far too low. An organization and strategy consultant was contracted;[76] theatre consultants were commissioned to develop a master plan for building and renovation;[77] architects were engaged;[78] and experts on the running of capital campaigns were asked to draw up a fundraising strategy.[79] Finally, a target figure of just over $30 million was arrived at, and board members pitched in with the first, very substantial, donations.[80]

The painful decision to encourage Jim McKenzie to retire had been arrived at by the foundation board while it was still under the presidency of Janet Plotkin. Members of the board put together an extremely generous retirement package and it fell to Walter Bergen, who knew him best, to approach McKenzie to convince him that he should accept it—on grounds of ill health, if nothing else, because he was far from well. His immediate response was that he had suffered at least five life-threatening illnesses or traumas in the past five years, and (as he put it) "I'm still clinging to the wreckage."[81]

In the end, because he knew it was the only way he could ensure his family's future security, McKenzie accepted the package at the end of January 2000. Two weeks later, at a large and nostalgic gathering at the Inn at Longshore that included many theatre celebrities, the Playhouse bade him a formal farewell, and both the State of Connecticut and the Town of Westport presented him with proclamations that memorialized his achievement—which was nothing less than the leadership and preservation of Lawrence Langner's proud little theatre through four tumultuous decades, during which, all about it, other summer theatres had brought down their curtains and disappeared.

In these circumstances, Joanne Woodward agreed to accept joint responsibility for the Playhouse's artistic direction, with Anne Keefe as her colleague and partner. They declined to take formal titles at this stage: instead, they used their positions as co-chairs of the theatre's artistic advisory council. With less than four months to go, they set out to create a season that would uphold the great expectations with which they were inevitably burdened.

One thing remained before the Campaign for a New Era could be launched. The 1998 feasibility study had said that it would be difficult, if not impossible, to raise money unless it could be shown that the foundation owned the theatre, or (at the very least) had a long-term lease on it. So Walter Bergen consulted individually with the members of the Playhouse Partnership who had bought the theatre in 1985 to save it from the developers. In an extraordinary act of generosity, twenty-four members of the Partnership agreed to donate their shares so that the foundation could be the sole and outright owner of the theatre and its property. The $900,000 mortgage, which had sat like a millstone around the neck of the Playhouse for fifteen years, was finally paid off at the end of 2003.

With everything now in place, it was quickly agreed that the target date for the completion of the renovation project should be the seventy-fifth anniversary of the Playhouse in 2005.[82]

CHAPTER ELEVEN

2000–5 "A Doer, Not Just a Dreamer": Joanne Woodward Takes Charge

Joanne Woodward had known the Playhouse for a long time. In fact, they had grown up together, though at a distance, because they shared the same birth year. Since 1961 they had shared a town as well—that was the year when she and her husband had come to live in Westport.

When it came to theatre—the whole idea of theatre, of growing up in it and being a part of it—Joanne Woodward was passionate. Too many people thought of her as a film actress—which she was, of course, with an Oscar to prove it, but she was much more than that. "I like to work on stage," she said: "I was never terribly enamored of making movies. . . . I didn't make a lot of them."[1] Instead, her résumé showed that she had spent a goodly proportion of her career in the theatre, beginning with summer stock in Chatham, Massachusetts, when she was still in drama school, and continuing right up to the recent past when she had made a name for herself as a stage director, most notably at Williamstown, and most interestingly with the plays of Clifford Odets.[2]

Her earliest memory of the Playhouse was going there in 1956 to see a performance of *Anastasia*, but by that time she already knew the Langners from having worked for the Theatre Guild as an understudy in the 1953 production of *Picnic*. Over the years she had taken a considerable interest in the Playhouse—as a mother accompanying her children, as an actress seeing her friends perform, as a trustee who had played a pivotal role in ensuring that the theatre survived. She had done one or two benefits since the theatre had become a nonprofit in the 1970s, but she had never acted there as part of the regular season.

The artistic advisory council over which she and Anne Keefe presided in 2000 exuded Westport's star power—Jayne Atkinson, Maureen Anderman, James Naughton, Jane Powell, Christopher Plummer, Frank Converse, Lynne Meadow, Amy Nederlander, Jason Robards, Jr., Marlo Thomas, David Wiltse, Gene Wilder and Paul Newman were all members of it. Aside from her many qualifications as a theatre professional, Anne Keefe had occasionally worked at the Playhouse since the 1970s, so she understood, better than most, the theatre's technical abilities and

Joanne Woodward directing Richard Greenberg's play *Three Days of Rain* (2001).

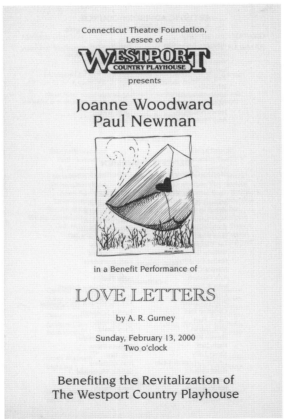

Connecticut Theatre Foundation,
Lessee of

WESTPORT
COUNTRY PLAYHOUSE

presents

Joanne Woodward
Paul Newman

in a Benefit Performance of

LOVE LETTERS

by A. R. Gurney

Sunday, February 13, 2000
Two o'clock

Benefiting the Revitalization of
The Westport Country Playhouse

disabilities. Elissa Getto, president of the Cincinnati Arts Association and a former head of Wolf Trap, was named CEO and executive director; and Janice Muirhead, a former director of production at the Long Wharf Theatre in New Haven, was named artistic manager. Together, the new team began work on the daunting task of putting together the 2000 season—"daunting" because there was so little time: it was almost March before they began work, and the season would have to be announced in early May.

Both Woodward and Keefe were volunteers that first season. Keefe became a part-time employee in 2001, while Woodward continued as a volunteer, and it was, to a large extent, those "voluntary" and "part-time" labels that enabled them to overcome the "terror" they both admitted to at the thought of running the Playhouse. There was an unreality to it all, they said (they have a habit of finishing each other's sentences): "Surely we're not in charge, we thought. . . . We just had a good time reading plays. We'd get together and read them out loud, and it was fabulous. . . . But ultimately, what happened was that it became clearer and clearer that there can be only one artistic voice."[3]

That realization was acted on at the beginning of the 2001 season, when Joanne Woodward agreed to accept the title of artistic director, with Anne Keefe as associate artistic director. The two of them formally assumed responsibility for the theatre, along with a new executive director, Alison Harris.

THE START OF SOMETHING NEW

The 2000 season was actually the Playhouse's seventieth anniversary season, but most people inevitably thought of it as the inaugural season of the Woodward era. So how different was it?

In shape and format, it was no different at all—five plays and one musical, each running for two weeks—but the content and presentation were markedly different. For a start, there was less reliance on star names, which is not to say that there were no stars around—there were!—but plays were billed in such a way that the featured names were those of authors and directors. Then there was the content. "We want to include provocative and controversial theatre in our season," Anne Keefe told the Waterbury *Republican*, and there was certainly less of the lighter fare that a McKenzie season had always featured.[4]

Overall, it was very successful. Subscriptions were up dramatically—to 5,700, which was as high as they had ever been—and, for the most part, the audiences liked what they saw.[5] Five of the six productions originated at Westport. Two were world premieres—*Triangles for Two* by Weston playwright David Wiltse, and a musical called *Nicolette and Aucassin* by Peter Kellogg and David

Friedman. They both did well with audiences and reviewers. Katherine Burger's comedy *Morphic Resonance* (about thirty-something Manhattanites confronting love and commitment) was directed by James Naughton with predictably good results, while Joanne Woodward herself directed the first play of the season.

Steve Loddo was a production intern in 2000, and later third carpenter in 2001–2:

The barn that housed the offices and scenery shop was long a home to woodland creatures. Birds, raccoons, and even feral cats made homes in the rafters of the building. During the 2000 season, a litter of kittens was born in the ceiling above the props area. One night, during a performance of *Orson's Shadow*, these tiny creatures literally began falling from the sky. Staff members, including Joanne Woodward and Annie Keefe, helped to gather up the kittens and arrange for them to be given to a local animal shelter.

The choice of that opening play was one of the earliest decisions Woodward was called upon to make. "It just happened that I went to the library . . . and the first book of plays I reached up for was Somerset Maugham, and it was the first play I read. And I literally said 'Oh, wonderful —a feminist play!'"[6] *The Constant Wife* was a perfect fit—it had been part of the Playhouse's historic past (Ethel Barrymore had starred in it during the 1938 season), and yes, it was a feminist play. It had escaped no one that the Playhouse's new management team was entirely feminine, in contrast to its patriarchal past, and no one was either surprised or offended by the choice of a twentieth century classic that just happened to be feminist.

The only play that did not originate at Westport in that first season was Austin Pendleton's *Orson's Shadow*, which focused on Orson Welles's reputation as it loomed over Laurence Olivier and his two wives,

Alison Mackie and Kali Rocha in Somerset Maugham's play *The Constant Wife*, directed by Joanne Woodward (2000).

Vivien Leigh and Joan Plowright. The production had originated at the Steppenwolf Theatre in Chicago and was presented in association with the Williamstown Festival—another statement of intent, perhaps, for Joanne Woodward had a long association with Williamstown.

Predictably, however, the biggest success of the season was the two-week run of A. R. Gurney's *Ancestral Voices*. It was not unlike his *Love Letters*, which had been performed at the Playhouse as recently as February, when Paul Newman and Joanne Woodward had done it as a fundraiser and netted $200,000 for the capital campaign in a single afternoon. In *Ancestral Voices* Gurney still allowed the actors to be armed with scripts, but this was much more a play than a reading. It required a larger cast than *Love Letters*, and it also had David Saint to direct it. Paul Newman, Joanne Woodward, James Naughton, Swoosie Kurtz and Paul Rudd made up one cast, while Jason Robards and Frank Converse were scheduled to head up the other one. As it happened, Robards took ill and Converse had to bow out, but that merely allowed the Playhouse to demonstrate the depth of talent it could call upon: Elizabeth Wilson, Fritz Weaver, Jane Curtin, Neil Patrick Harris and Sam Freed moved effortlessly into the void.

Artistically, there was no doubt that the new management had succeeded, just as it had at the box office, which played to almost 80 percent of capacity—an improvement of 15 percent on the previous seasons.[7] But there were lessons to be learned. One of them was that two-week runs did not really work. More rehearsal time was needed, particularly technical rehearsal, if the standards Woodward and Keefe insisted upon were to be realized. So it was decided that each 2001 production would run two and a half weeks—Sunday through Tuesday to load in set and lights; then Wednesday and Thursday previews, followed by a gala opening on Friday. In this way each production would get an extra weekend, with two performances (5 and 8:30 p.m.) on Saturdays. To compensate, there would be only five productions instead of six.

Another, more painful, lesson was that Joanne Woodward's ambition to develop the year-round activities of the theatre would have to be postponed—postponed but certainly not forgotten. For the time being, it was clearly necessary to focus everyone's energies on the summer season,[8] and it was equally clear that a great deal of work would have to be done to the theatre (weather-proofing and the overhaul of technical facilities being two of the highest priorities) before it would be feasible to start expanding the theatre's role and programs.

Luckily, there was one area—educational programming—that could be exempted from this postponement because its development and expansion did not depend on the theatre's physical plant.

The Playhouse's educational presence in the Westport area had generally been limited by lack of money and staff. At the beginning of the 2000 season it consisted of its two basic and traditional elements—the children's series of summer plays, and the program for apprentices and interns. Joanne Woodward wanted much more than this: she wanted to establish the Playhouse as a resource that all schools in the area could make use of. She wanted to engage students and teachers in creative writing programs, in workshops on theatrical production and in the study of individual dramatic scenes (from Shakespeare, for example). She wanted to provide programming that would complement classroom work and serve as a resource for more effective learning—in reading, writing and communication skills. She wanted to use theatre and drama to empower students through self-exploration and self-expression. And in many other ways she wanted to expand the theatre's outreach into the community.

These were not necessarily new ideas, but they were big ones. They would take time, money (mostly in the form of grants) and manpower if they were to come to fruition. The first three or four years of the century were used to develop them with area educators and to begin piloting them in schools. This was a part of the mission that began to make considerable, and very exciting, progress under the Playhouse's Education Coordinator, Hyla Crane.

In the meantime, of course, the overhead had been considerably increased. Whereas Jim McKenzie's "permanent" staff could be numbered at three (himself, Julie Monahan and his unpaid assistant, Philisse), the new management had quickly increased the regular staff to a dozen and then to fifteen. A significant part of this was the new Development Depart-

The Playhouse goes to school. *Cootie Shots* was invented by Norma Bowles's educational theatre company, Fringe Benefits. It celebrates diversity and promotes tolerance with an imaginative assortment of plays, poems and songs, which it takes into elementary schools. In 2003–4 the Playhouse produced a *Cootie Shots* show and took it to schools in Fairfield County and beyond.

ment, headed by one of the most accomplished professionals in the field, Lis Saxe, who came to the Playhouse fresh from her successful multimillion dollar campaign at the Stepping Stones Museum in Norwalk. A development department such as this was expensive, but the only way to raise money was to employ experts to raise it, and that was something the board—with a target of $30 million—knew it had to do. To oversee all this, Alison Harris, a former managing director of the McCarter Theatre in Princeton, was appointed executive director in November 2000, effectively taking the place of Elissa Getto, whose appointment as CEO had been premised on the immediate expansion of the Playhouse's activities into a year-round operation—something it now knew it would have to postpone until the renovation was completed.

The 2001 season was, in Anne Keefe's phrase, "a bit scatter-shot," but nonetheless interesting because it bore little resemblance to any previous season in Westport history.[9] "Hip" but antique woodcut graphics adorned the playbill, and the season reflected the same sort of contrasts. There was innovation and virtuosity and some good direction, but, overall, it was uneven and not really cohesive—and it ended in September, as did everything else in 2001, in a thoroughly depressing manner.

Gozzi's *Princess Turandot* in a scintillating staging by Darko Tresnjak (2001).

The Williamstown collaboration was the season opener—an entirely new version of Gozzi's *Princess Turandot*, written and directed by Darko Tresnjak. His fast-growing reputation as a director, based on his staging of Wilder's *The Skin of Our Teeth* at Williamstown and, more recently, Stoppard's *Rosencrantz and Guildenstern Are Dead* at Long Wharf, was increased yet again by *Turandot*. "It has all the bright physicality of the circus," wrote Shirley Mathews in the *Connecticut Post*, "the extravagance of low theatre, a testosterone-infused intensity and enough on the theatrical menu to keep everyone happy."[10] Which is what Gene Wilder did with the next show—an immensely ambitious evening, directed by Gene Saks, in which Wilder and his accomplices put together an unlikely trio of classic "shorts" by Shaw, Feydeau and Chekhov. This was actually Wilder's fourth appearance at the Playhouse—

In the early summer of 2001, Annie Keefe took the train back to Westport after spending the day at a rehearsal in New York:
It was while we were performing Darko Tresnjak's *Princess Turandot* at the Playhouse. I noticed several members of the cast on the train. Then we stopped—there was a cow on the line, or some unidentified problem, and there was no indication of when we would get under way again. I walked through the train and found nine of the fourteen members of the *Princess Turandot* cast, all of them commuting up to Westport for the evening performance! We got together and got on our cell phones. Then we waited and waited. Finally, the train started moving again, slowly. The moment it got into Stamford we jumped off and leapt into the flotilla of cars we'd arranged to have meet us there. We reached the theatre at ten before eight, and the curtain went up only five minutes late!

his first since the 1960s—but he had never before been a featured actor: he had performed with Walter Pidgeon, Helen Hayes and Carol Channing, "but nobody knew who I was then."[11] They knew well enough now, and he packed the Playhouse for what the *New York Times* called "summer frippery of a distinguished order."[12]

Joanne Woodward chose a contemporary play as her own vehicle to direct—Richard

Greenberg's *Three Days of Rain*, an intriguing piece that revolved around architecture and harvested the best reviews of the year. The season's classic offering was Henry Seagall's *Heaven Can Wait*, last performed at the Playhouse in 1955 with Richard Kiley (this time with Leslie Uggams and Bruce Weitz), and David Wiltse once again contributed a play—this one a thriller set on a Midwestern ranch. Since it both opened and closed with an explosion, the critics could hardly avoid the line about "ending the season with a bang"—but nor could they have foreseen the far greater explosion that would take place on 9/11, during the last week of the season, and the pall it would cast over Westport, the Playhouse and all America.

"THE PASSION TO KNOW WHAT LIFE MEANS TO US"

If ever there was a time to show what theatre could mean to a community, this was it. Woodward and Keefe recognized that instinctively, and they began to make plans within days of 9/11.

They knew they wanted to do something within the community, and they knew they needed to do it quickly. What they did was to put together a major benefit—"For The Children"—and to give two performances of it on one day at the end of October. In addition to Joanne Woodward, there was Paul Newman, James Naughton, Gene Wilder, Christopher Plummer, Kristin Chenoweth, Robin Batteau and Adam Battelstein (of Pilobolus). All seats were priced at $25 so as to make it as accessible as possible, and the benefit raised a total of $67,485 for the WTC Relief Fund of the Children's Aid Society of New York.[13]

The 2002 summer season would begin a full nine months after the day the twin towers fell, but Woodward and Keefe knew it would still be a jagged and painful memory in Westport and the

Paul Newman as the Stage Manager in *Our Town* (2002).

surrounding area—how could it not be? They therefore determined to begin the season with a play that would speak directly to the community. The play was ready to hand—it was already on their wish list—and they simply leapfrogged it to the top of the list.

There was no question that *Our Town* was the right play. In his preface, Thornton Wilder had written: "The climax of this play needs only five square feet of boarding and the passion to know what life means to us."[14] The Playhouse's new production was intended as a demonstration of what that passion meant to one small town in Connecticut. Because it came from the heart, and because it was so honest, it would ultimately play on a much larger stage than Westport's, and television would ensure that it was seen by several million Americans at a time when its emotional impact was most powerful. That, of course, was not planned—but it is what happened.

In its existence of little more than six decades, *Our Town* has been performed in hundreds, maybe thousands, of communities in America—by schools and colleges, drama clubs and church groups, professionals and amateurs. And of all these communities and small towns in America, Westport is probably capable of casting it from the greatest strength. The passion and lyricism of this production lay in that fact—that the residents of Grover's Corner were truly the residents of Weston and Westport and the surrounding area, and when the Stage Manager said "This is the way we were: in our growing up and in our marrying and in our living and in our dying," he spoke for a community that had a real and vital existence.

Maggie Lacey, Paul Newman and Ben Fox in *Our Town*.

The planning came together when no less an actor than Paul Newman contacted the artistic director and offered to audition for the part of the Stage Manager. This was the role that Thornton Wilder himself had played at Westport in 1946, and Newman's casting began the process of recruiting what proved to be a remarkable cast of colleagues and neighbors. Jayne Atkinson, Jane Curtin, Mia Dillon, Jeffrey DeMunn, Frank Converse and Stephen Spinella were just six members of the large cast that James Naughton directed.

There were, of course, reviewers who were critical, but not many, and they were certainly at odds with the audiences. The *Westport News* was much more typical when it eventually looked back on the Playhouse production, on its transfer to Broadway for a limited season in December/January, and on its eventual adaptation into a video for Showtime that was transmitted nationwide on public television (and won an Emmy nomination for Paul Newman). It noted the "illuminating clarity" of Naughton's direction, "the superb ensemble cast" and the "low-key, omniscient Stage Manager" of Paul Newman.[15] The stage production won both Tony and Drama Desk nominations.

BREAKING NEW GROUND

Though overshadowed by the success and the star power of *Our Town*, the remainder of the Westport season of 2002 was well received—in particular, a production of Athol Fugard's *Master Harold . . . and the Boys* directed by Walter Dallas, and the American premiere of *A Saint She Ain't*, a musical by Dick Vosburgh and Dennis King, which was co-produced with the Berkshire Theatre Festival. Another play from Westport's past—Sutton Vane's *Outward Bound*, in which Laurette Taylor had appeared in 1939—proved to be a popular revival.

By now, the artistic success of Woodward and Keefe's first three seasons was being reflected in the theatre's financial situation. The Campaign for a New Era had been launched with a target figure of $30.6 million. About 60 percent of it was earmarked for construction and refurbishment, but there would also be money for land purchase and planning, for artistic and educational programming and (very importantly) for endowing some of the theatre's activities. At the beginning of the 2003

Pamela Payton-Wright and Jefferson Mays in Sutton Vane's *Outward Bound* (2002).

season, only months into the campaign, $16 million had already been donated, including $5 million from the State of Connecticut.[16] Most of the remainder had come in a series of extraordinary gifts from individual members of the board and their families.

Everyone in Liz Morten's team contributed to this state of affairs, but two of them took on particularly high profile responsibilities. This was the husband and wife team of Robert and Suzanne Wright, whose home was in Fairfield. Suzanne, as a member of the board, took over the campaign events portfolio, while her husband, Bob, vice chairman of GE and chairman and CEO of NBC, became chairman of the campaign committee itself, with the financier Vince Wasik as his vice-chair. It was Suzanne's experience as a fundraiser and organizer of benefits and galas that brought about the astonishing success of the first campaign benefit in October 2003. Entitled *Breaking New Ground: A Celebration!*, it netted $1.7 million for the campaign. With her co-chairs Laurie Lister and Judd Burstein, and with Harvey Weinstein (of Miramax) and his wife Eve as corporate co-chairs, Suzanne Wright and her team brought together a star-studded cast of entertainers and celebrity auctioneers (not to mention ticket buyers and bidders) that included Paul Newman, Robin Williams, Christopher Plummer (himself a board member), James Naughton, Carole King and Sean Hayes. Other benefits featured Whoopi Goldberg, Susan Sarandon, Tim Robbins and Matthew Broderick. There was no shortage of stars willing to support the old theatre.[17]

Meantime, the board, divided into many committees, went ahead with the planning of the renovation. John Vaccaro's committee came up with a strategic plan; Harold Bailey's produced a marketing plan; Olof Nelson's oversaw the governance of it all; Steve Wolff's was responsible for finance; and, in a nice link to the Playhouse's past, Jim Bradley chaired the building committee, a task he was exceedingly well qualified for, having guided many similar, and larger, projects through the process. His father, Ken, had been the theatre's first legal adviser in the 1930s and 1940s, and his mother, Ina, had been the Playhouse's preeminent champion and spokesperson for forty years.

Obviously, a very major shift in the theatre's philosophy and practice had taken place since Ina's day—and even since Jim McKenzie's day, it might be said. The Playhouse was now unashamedly a not-for-profit institution, making maximum use of its status to raise money and solicit grants. It hoped that its summer season would break even, if at all possible, but it did not really expect it to make money. Occasionally, it did, and that was gratifying to all concerned. It happened with the 2002 season because of the enormous commercial success of *Our Town* on Broadway and on video.

Every year since 1997 the Playhouse has featured a Doo-Wop Show *for one night only during its season. Organized (and emceed) by board member Walter Bergen, the show is unfailingly sold out:*

Walter Bergen had an idea for a musical based on a 40-year reunion at the General Curtiss E. LeMay High School—with a real 1950s Doo-Wop singing group. Bergen commissioned a writer, and Jim McKenzie allowed the Playhouse to be used in 1996 for a reading in front of 200–300 guests. "During the first part of the play," Walter Bergen remembers, "the audience sat politely and laughed very occasionally (this was supposed to be a musical comedy). About twenty minutes in, it was time for the Doo-Wop group. Emil Stucchio and The Classics—a Brooklyn group who had had a No. 1 record that sold six million copies back in the 1950s—started up with their hit song 'Till Then,' and the place went nuts. The audience were on their feet, singing and dancing in the aisles. Then the group left the stage and the dialogue resumed. The audience virtually went to sleep. Each time the group reappeared, this process was repeated. By the end of the show, the poor author was totally depressed.

"But Jim McKenzie had watched all this, and he knew exactly what to do. 'Throw away the script, Walter: we'll do a Doo-Wop show. You get it together, I'll put in on the stage.' And that's what happened. The next year, 1997, I produced the show and it was a total sellout, as it has been every year since. We had local disk jockeys to emcee it the first two years because we got free promotion on their radio stations, but it soon became clear that this show could sell out on its own, so I took over the emceeing myself. Emil Stucchio and The Classics have been back for every show, but we've had many other groups as well—Leslie Gore ('It's My Party'), Johnny Maestro and The Brooklyn Bridge ('Sixteen Candles') and lots of others, all original Doo-Wop stars from the 1950s and 1960s."

Our Town's earnings amounted to $1.1 million, but not all of it went into the campaign fund. $200,000 was allocated to the annual operating budget and another $130,000 went into a capital reserve, for while *Our Town* had been sold out from first to last, the rest of the season had not done as well. The huge increase in subscriptions in 2000, when the new creative team took over, had been sustained and slightly increased in the subsequent years. In 2002 subscriptions were flirting with the 6,000 mark, but that was a figure to treat with caution because a significant number of people seemed to have bought relatively low-priced subscriptions in 2002 just to get tickets for *Our Town*, and even the greatest optimist had to recognize that there would not be a magnet production like *Our Town* every year. Even so, the subscription business was doing pretty well—and certainly a lot better than single ticket sales, which had become a cause for concern. Westport was not alone in this—the drop in single ticket sales was a common complaint of theatres across the country—and it was certainly one of the considerations that caused the board of the foundation to put aside

Hydrangeas R.I.P.

a part of its windfall from *Our Town* to support the summer program.[18]

More support for the summer program arrived in timely manner when a local company best known for its salad dressing announced that it would become the Season Sponsor for 2003—and that was in addition to individual sponsors for individual productions.

No one who visited the Playhouse—let alone those who worked there, and the fire marshals and safety officials who were responsible for giving it certificates of worthiness each year—could deny the urgency of the rebuilding project. And even though the rebuilding plan was remarkably faithful to the original, it was still a wrenching decision to order large parts of Kemper's old barn to be torn down. And it wasn't only the barn. For as long as anyone could remember, the display of hydrangeas at the front of the Playhouse had been a feature of the theatre's exterior. In the end, even they were adjudged to stand in the way of progress. Despite press interest, despite the artistic director's best efforts, the hydrangeas had to go.[19]

The plan to close down the Playhouse for eighteen months so that the necessary work could be done was approved in principle before the 2003 season began. It meant that an abbreviated 2004 season would have to be given off site—at the Ridgefield Playhouse, about fifteen miles away—but that, it seemed, was a small price to pay for such a massive, and much needed, makeover.

For a theatre that had been within a heartbeat of closing its doors three years earlier, it was now in remarkably good shape, and it was able to begin the 2003 season with the certainty that there would be many more seasons to come.

AN END . . . AND A BEGINNING

Part of the *Our Town* cast was reassembled in the winter of 2003—not for another go at *Our Town*, not even for a performance, but for a reading. Anne Keefe's husband, David Wiltse, had written a new play. His very successful *Doubles* had been performed at the Playhouse as long ago as 1987, and there had been two more since the Woodward-Keefe team took over in 2000. This one, *The*

Good German, was not intended for immediate performance—the reading was simply an opportunity for Wiltse to hear it out loud—but the effect it had on its audience and its readers was so great that Joanne Woodward asked if the Playhouse could give the world premiere that very summer.[20] James Naughton agreed to direct.

The Good German, set during World War II, was about a German household that harbored a Jewish publisher, and about the diverse reactions of members of the household and their neighbors. It was about ideas and emotions that were provocative—"we realized how timely and relevant it is for today," Joanne Woodward wrote in the playbill. The *Stamford Advocate* agreed: "The playwright definitely poses some interesting questions about human nature, leaving audience members to question what makes a person a good German, a good American, or just a good human being."[21]

The Good German was the sort of involving and demanding theatre that Joanne Woodward clearly favored, but it was by no means the only sort of theatre she included in her five-play cocktail. *The Good German* was sandwiched between *Hay Fever*, a Noël Coward comedy that was still a favorite of a certain generation, and *The Old Settler*, a 1997 play about a May-to-December romance in 1940s Harlem, written by John Henry Redwood, whose death was announced as the Westport production went into rehearsal. Both these plays got fine productions—in much-complimented sets and lighting—from leading directors who were now becoming a hallmark of Westport seasons: Darko Tresnjak returned with *Hay Fever*, and Tazewell Thompson with *The Old Settler*. They were followed into the Playhouse by Doug Hughes, who had directed *Outward Bound* the previous season, with a taut production of Arthur Miller's *All My Sons*, starring Richard Dreyfuss, Jill Clayburgh, Sam Trammell, Jenny Bacon and David Aaron Baker. "Sometimes it's difficult to remember that the action of this play is taking place in 1947 instead of 2003," wrote the *Ridgefield Press*.[22]

The action of the final play of the season took place in 1857, but it was hard to look at it and not think of 1931. That was when *The Streets of New York* had first been seen on the Playhouse stage—on the opening night of the opening season, starring Dorothy Gish, Rollo Peters, Romney Brent, Winifred Lenihan, Moffat Johnston and the members of the New York Repertory Company. In the seventy-third season (though only the sixty-ninth in which there had been performances because of the interruption of World War II), the production came from another repertory company—this one the Irish Repertory of New York City—and it was a staging that had first been seen two years before. It was the same Boucicault play, of course, but just as Lawrence Langner had had special

Richard Dreyfuss and Jill Clayburgh in Doug Hughes's production of *All My Sons* (2003).

music and songs written for it in 1931, so now did the director, Charlotte Moore, who adapted the play herself and wrote the thirteen splendid songs. Once again, just as they had in 1931, Westport audiences hissed the villainous banker Gideon Bloodgood and his hard-hearted daughter Alida, and sighed and cheered for the frail and beautiful heroine, Lucy Fairweather.

As the curtain came down on the final performance, there were doubtless those who remembered how Dion Boucicault had brought to an end the original run of the play in New York in 1857—he had burned down the theatre, by accident.

Westport was planning an altogether different fate for its theatre—one that would involve a measure of tearing out and tearing down, but one that would have at its end, not oblivion and obscurity, but resurrection, renaissance and a long life beyond.

The Streets of New York (2003) in Charlotte Moore's production with *(left to right)* Joshua Park, Danielle Ferland, Rebecca Bellingham, Greg Stone, Margaret Hall, Terry Donnelly, Donald Corren.

THE PLAYHOUSE REDUX

After nearly a hundred years as a tannery and more than seventy years as a theatre, the old barn was badly in need of renovation.

Its makeover (which used approximately $18 million of the $30 million raised in the capital campaign) was designed to retain the rustic character of the theatre while, at the same time, turning it into a state-of-the-art facility.

Typically, the underlying purpose of such a renovation would be to enlarge the building and increase the seating area—but not this one. Seating was actually reduced from just over 700 to 580, while the character of Cleon Throckmorton's original auditorium was faithfully preserved. The familiar red-covered pews are now inlaid with individual seats, their sightlines enhanced and the acoustics significantly improved.

Anyone familiar with the old theatre could spot the principal innovations easily enough—an orchestra pit capable of seating ten or a dozen musicians, and new lobbies big enough for the audience to gather in before the show or during intermissions on rainy days.

The rainy days themselves were no longer the ordeal they had generally been in the past, for the old barn was now weatherized. Heating and cooling plants were upgraded and the makeshift electric and plumbing systems, having more or less skipped the twentieth century, were remodeled for the twenty-first. For the first time the Playhouse could claim to be both winterized and summerized, and in many other ways it had been made audience-friendly—not least by a marked increase in the number of restrooms.

Backstage, the improvements were less obvious to the layman's eye, but actually more extensive. There was a new lighting grid, new stage rigging, a new sound system and a proper control booth (for the first time). For the actors, there was a brand new rehearsal hall in an adjacent barn, new dressing rooms and a refurbished green room, still decorated with posters of long-ago productions and redolent of the theatre's history.

With no families of raccoons to share the accommodations any longer, the ghosts of actors past were finally free to strut unmolested through these nether regions of their theatre—an American theatre beside the old Post Road in Westport, Connecticut.

ROBERT WRIGHT
CHAIRMAN OF THE CAMPAIGN FOR A NEW ERA

Bob Wright is Chairman of NBC Universal and Vice-Chairman of G.E. He and his wife, Suzanne (who is a member of the theatre's board), have lived in Fairfield for twenty years. He agreed to head up the $30-million campaign because he believes the Playhouse is "the most important and dynamic attachment that Fairfield County has to Broadway, to Hollywood and the whole entertainment industry—a truly American institution." The campaign succeeded because of the dedicated work of a great many people and some enormously generous gifts from board members and other supporters—but "the most impressive thing about the campaign was the local support, which is deep-rooted and of long standing. These are not necessarily wealthy people, but literally hundreds of them made small donations, and they really added up."

(above) Fall 2004: Stripped and made ready for rebuilding

(right) Architect's rendering of the refurbished interior, viewed from the stage

(below) Spring 2005: Scale model of the rebuilt Playhouse and its campus

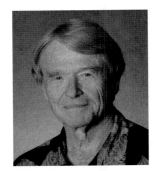

Bill Haber

Alison Harris, *Ex-Officio*

Anne Keefe, *Ex-Officio*

Roger Leifer

Laurie Lister

Sunny Neff

Olof S. Nelson

Janet Plotkin

Christopher Plummer

Steven Ruchefsky

Barbara Stern

Sharon Sullivan

Joanne Woodward

Suzanne Wright

Acknowledgments

They say that the Playhouse has a ghost, and those who have seen it generally describe it as bearing a close resemblance to Lawrence Langner.

I don't know if Lawrence's ghost really does haunt the theatre, but I do know that his spirit is very much present within and around it. Seventy-five years after he founded the Playhouse, it still possesses the singular quality he gave to everything he touched—class—and you cannot write about its history without being aware of that at every step along the way. It is as true in the time of Joanne Woodward and Liz Morten as it was in the time of Jim McKenzie and Ina Bradley, and as it most certainly was in the time of Lawrence and Armina Langner. To write about these great people of the theatre has been both a pleasure and a privilege.

Two people have guided me, encouraged me and somehow kept me on the rails throughout the endeavor. Walter Bergen, who has been a member of the theatre's board for more than twenty years, and who is second to none in his knowledge and love of the Playhouse and its history, conceived the idea of the book and then volunteered for the arduous task of being its godfather. He quickly became for me what he is to everyone associated with the Playhouse—a greatly trusted friend and adviser. That is a description I would also apply to Julianne Griffin of Yale University Press. She not only championed the project from the outset, but she brought to it her extensive experience and great expertise in dealing with deadlines, designers, recalcitrant authors and the Press itself.

If the book would never have happened without Walter and Julianne, then it could never have been written, illustrated and completed without Patricia Blaufuss. Pat was the theatre's press and marketing director from 1989 to 2000. She not only knows more about the Playhouse than anyone else, but she also cares for it greatly. Having her as picture editor was essential, but she did much more: she identified, found and interviewed a great many of the people quoted in these pages. Without her, a lot of the best stories would have remained untold. Prodigious research was also conducted by Alix Weisz, whose frequent sallies into libraries and cyberspace brought back much vital information about people and plays of bygone times.

Typically, the last person to join the book production team is the designer. This project, however, has enjoyed the luxury of having Katy Homans on board from early on. To work with someone of such experience is truly a joy.

Countless people have contributed their help, experience and anecdotes, and most of them are credited in the notes. Some, however, deserve special mention. Liz Morten, Joanne Woodward

THE PLAYHOUSE STAFF 2005

Joanne Woodward, Artistic Director

Anne Keefe, Associate Artistic Director

Alison Harris, Executive Director

Kathy Cihi, Development Manager

Meghan Coleman, Grants Manager

Hyla Crane, Education Coordinator

Donna Dollé, Bookkeeper

Erika Ellis, Board Relations Manager

Chance Farago, Marketing & Communications Manager

Jameson Gilpatrick, Business Manager

Christine Gilhuly, Audience Services Manager

Bruce Miller, Company/Operations Manager

Ruth Moe, Production Manager

Elisabeth Saxe, Development Director

Lyla Steenbergen, Annual Giving Manager

Robin Valovich, Database Manager

and Annie Keefe have given me not only their time and their thoughts but also their enthusiastic support. I am grateful to all the theatre's staff, but most of all to Alison Harris, Lyla Steenbergen and Chance Farago.

Special thanks are owed to Philip Langner and his wife, Marilyn, who recalled for me many of the people and happenings at the Playhouse during its first three decades. Philisse Barrows gave unstintingly of her memories of the forty-one years during which her husband, Jim McKenzie, ran the theatre. Paula Laurence and Richard Grayson were particularly helpful on the forties and fifties; Ralph Roseman and Charles Dillingham on the sixties and seventies; and Sharon Giese, Julie Monahan and Richard Ellis on the last decades of the century. Deborah Donnelly and Lily Lodge went to a great deal of trouble to find pictorial and documentary evidence of the important roles in the theatre's history played by their respective mothers, Ina Bradley and Francesca Braggiotti Lodge.

I also wish to record my thanks to the Westport Public Library, and especially to the Westport Historical Society, where most of the Playhouse's papers are stored. Ann Sheffer, a member of the Historical Society's board, is also a long-serving member of the Playhouse board; she was instrumental in ensuring that I had access to all the available documents. The papers of Lawrence Langner and the Theatre Guild are held by the Beinecke Rare Book & Manuscript Library at Yale University, where Ellen Cordes and her staff were unfailingly helpful.

Finally, I am indebted to the volunteers who worked so hard to compile the play listings in Appendix B—Audrey Conca, Mary Grace Dembeck, Wendy Tyler, Amy Potokar, Jeff Palmer, Linda Smith and Zita Casey.

Appendix A

Members of the Playhouse Foundation Limited Partnership 1985–2000

Westport Country Playhouse

Dr. Malcolm and Marjorie Beinfield

Walter and Paula Bergen

William and Christina Brown

Charles and Anne Cioffi

Brenda Lewis Cooper

Keir and Susie Fuller Dullea

Burry Fredrik

Eric and Edith Friedheim

Robert A. Graham, Jr.

June Havoc

Dr. Steven and Catherine Herman

John and Rachel Jakes

Geraldine Kennon

Philip, Marilyn and Armina Langner

Mortimer Levitt

Robert Ludlum

James B. McKenzie

James McManus

Stephen and Sara Monahan

Gloria Monty and Robert O'Byrne

Lee Richardson

Rita Salzman

John and Barbara Samuelson

Robert C. Schnitzer

William Sheffler and Ann Sheffer

Haila Stoddard

Robert Werme

Lori March Williams

Diane Seely Yohe

WESTPORT, CT '60

Appendix B

Westport Country Playhouse Play List, 1931–2004

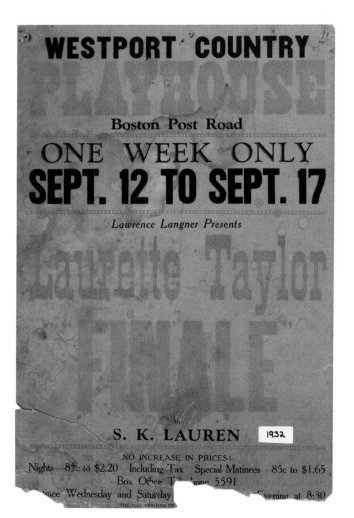

1931

The New York Repertory Theatre—with Dorothy Gish, Armina Marshall, Rollo Peters, Romney Brent, Moffat Johnston, Fania Marinoff, Jessie Busley, Tony Bundsman and Winifred Lenihan—in:

The Streets of New York, by Dion Boucicault, music arranged by Dr. Sigmund Spaeth, directed by Knowles Entrikin, designed by Rollo Peters with costumes by Eaves Costume Co.

Come What May, by Robert de Flers and G. A. Caillavet, translated by Ruth Langner, directed by Vassili Kouchita, designed by Rollo Peters

The Comic Artist, by Susan Glaspell and Norman Matson, directed by Moffatt Johnston, designed by Rollo Peters

The Bride the Sun Shines On, by Will Cotton, directed by Philip Loeb, designed by Rollo Peters

As You Like It, by William Shakespeare, music arranged by Dr. Sigmund Spaeth, directed by Charles Jehlinger and Lawrence Langner, costumes by Ronald Jones

The Pillars of Society, by Henrik Ibsen, directed by Winifred Lenihan, designed by Rollo Peters

1932

The New York Repertory Theatre, with June Walker, Osgood Perkins, Armina Marshall, Jane Wyatt, Kathleen Comegys, Elizabeth Risdon, Hugh Buckler, Blaine Cordner and Elisha Cook, Jr.—in:

Thoroughbred, by Doty Hobart, directed by Theresa Helburn, designed by Charles Stepanek

For Husbands Only, by Basil Lawrence (pseudonym for Lawrence Langner), directed by Winifred Lenihan, designed by Charles Stepanek

Chrysalis, by Rose Albert Porter, directed by Theresa Helburn

School for Lovers, adapted by Arthur Guiterman and Lawrence Langner from Molière's *L'Ecole des Maris*, music by Edmond Rickett, lyrics by Arthur Guiterman

Dear Mistress, by Kathryn McClure

The Man with a Load of Mischief, by Ashley Dukes, directed by Lawrence Langner, with Jane Cowl

Finale, by S. K. Lauren, directed by José Ruben, designed by Charles Stepanek, with Laurette Taylor

The Other One, by Henry Myers, with Helen Ford

1933

The Nobel Prize, by Hjalmar Bergman, adapted from the translation by Ingrid Smit and Herman Bernstein, directed by Antoinette Perry, designed by Charles Stepanek, with Otis Skinner

Understanding Women, by Frank Mandel, directed by Philip Loeb, designed by Charles Stepanek with decorations and furnishings by Earle B. Smith, with Dorothy Gish, Glenn Anders, Roger Pryor, Jesse Royce Landis

The Yellow Jacket, by George C. Hazelton & Benrimo, music by William Furst, directed by Charles Coburn, with Mr. & Mrs. Charles Coburn, Louise Groody, Rex O'Malley

The Pursuit of Happiness, by Alan Child and Isabelle Loudon, directed by Bela Blau, designed by Charles Stepanek, with Tonio Selwart, Peggy Conklin, Pedro de Cordoba

Present Laughter, by Charles Brackett, directed by Antoinette Perry, designed by Charles Stepanek, with Roger Pryor, Rose Hobart, Ilka Chase

Lady Godiva, by Lawrence Langner, directed by José Ruben and Lawrence Langner, designed by Charles Stepanek, with Violet Heming, Edmond O'Brien, Peggy Conklin

Rendezvous, by Edward Childs Carpenter, based on the Hungarian play by Paul Frank, directed by Julius Evans, designed by Charles Stepanek, with Rex O'Malley, Elena Miramova

How's Your Code? written and directed by Gene Lockhart, with Gene and Kathleen Lockhart

Heat Lightning, by Leon Abrams & George Abbott, produced and directed by Philip Dunning and George Abbot, with Jean Dixon, Robert Gleckler

Gaily I Sin, by Guido Nadzo, music by Fritz Loewe, directed by Antoinette Perry, designed by Charles Stepanek, with Helen Menken

Champagne Sec (Die Fledermaus), by Johann Strauss, book adapted by Alan Child, lyrics adapted by Robert A. Simon, staged by Monty Woolley, directed by Rudolph Thomas, with Peggy Wood, Kitty Carlisle, Helen Ford, George Meader, John E. Hazzard

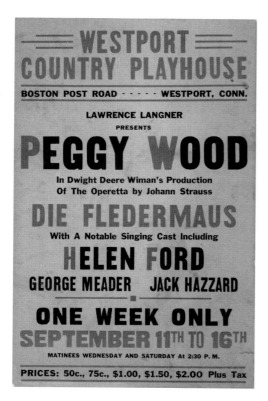

1934

The Chimes of Corneville, music by Robert Planquette, book and lyrics by Arthur Guiterman, staged by Lina Abarbanell, designed by Stewart Chaney, with Helen Ford, George Meader, Lucy Monroe, Phyllis Langner

The Bride of Torozko, by Otto Indig, translated and adapted by Thornton Wilder and Ruth Langner, staged by Herman Shumlin, designed by Stewart Chaney, with Jean Arthur, Sam Jaffe, Van Heflin

Tight Britches, by John Taintor Foote and Hubert Hayes, staged by Miriam Doyle, designed by Stewart Chaney, with Jean Dixon, Shepperd Strudwick

Love on an Island, by Helen Deutsch, staged by Alfred de Laigre, Jr., designed by Stewart Chaney, with James Rennie, Sam Zolotow, Betty Starbuck

Dream Child, by J. C. Nugent, staged by Eric North, designed by Stewart Chaney, with J. C. Nugent, Ruth Nugent, Alan Bunce, Shirley Booth

Hide and Seek, by Richard Macaulay and Lawrence Schwab, directed by Robert Sinclair, designed by Donald Oenslager, with Burgess Meredith, Jane Seymour

Kill That Story, by Harry Madden and Philip Dunning, staged by George Abbot, designed by Stewart Chaney, with James Bell, William Foran

Julie, by Frederic Arnold Kummer, music by Hugo Rubens, lyrics by Jules Loman and Allan Roberts, staged by Harry Wagstaff Gribble, with Lenore Ulric

For Love or Money, by Lawrence Langner and Armina Marshall, staged by Worthington Miner, designed by Stewart Chaney, directed by Lawrence Langner, with Phoebe Foster, Percy Kilbride

Lady Jane, written and directed by H. M. Harwood, designed by Woodman Thompson, with Frances Starr, Alan Marshal

1935

The Country Wife, by William Wycherley, directed by Lawrence Langner, designed by Tom Cracraft, with Ruth Gordon, Tom Powers, Ruth Weston, Frances Fuller, McKay Morris, Dwight Frye, Kathleen Comegys, George Meader, Daphne Warren-Wilson

Ode to Liberty, by Sidney Howard, adapted from Michel Duran's *Liberté Provisoire,* staged by Allen Fagan, designed by Tom Adrian Cracraft, with Ina Claire

The Coward, by Henri-Renée Lenormand, translated by D. L. Orna, staged by Worthington Miner, designed by Tom Adrian Cracraft, with Frances Fuller, Tom Powers, Robert Williams

The Long Frontier, by Mildred Knopf, staged by Robert B. Sinclair, designed by Tom Adrian Cracraft, with Alan Bunce, Nance O'Neil

If This Be Treason, by John Haynes Holmes & Reginald Lawrence, directed and staged by Harry Wagstaff Gribble, designed by Tom Adrian Cracraft, with McKay Morris, Tom Powers, Ruth Weston, Glenn Anders, George Coulouris, Armina Marshall

You Never Can Tell, by George Bernard Shaw, staged by Philip Loeb, designed by Tom Adrian Cracraft, with Florence Britton, John B. Litel

1936

The Way to Love, adapted by Lawrence Langner from William Congreve's *Love for Love* and *The Way of the World,* with Eva Le Gallienne, Dennis King

The Difficulty of Getting Married, by Louis Vernuil, with Grace George

Dr. Knock, by Jules Romains, adapted by Lawrence Langner and Armina Marshall, with Claudia Morgan, Richard Whorf

The Compromisers, by Armina Marshall and Lawrence Langner, with McKay Morris, Frances Fuller, Marcalo Gilmore

Fanny's First Play, by George Bernard Shaw, directed by Harry Wagstaff Gribbell, with McKay Morris, Claudia Morgan

The Would-Be Gentleman, by Molière, with Jimmy Savo

As We Forgive Debtors, by Tillman Breiseth, with Dorothy Hall, Ben Smith, Eda Heinemann

Russet Mantle, by Lynn Riggs, directed by Lawrence Langner, with Dorothy Gish, Jay Fassett, William Cragin, Viola Roache, Margaret Douglas, Phyllis Langner, Robert Bentley, Ben Smith, Claire Woodbury, He-ne-ah-ha-non-ton, Robert Williams

Camille, by Alexandre Dumas, with Eva Le Gallienne, Richard Waring, Averelle Harris, George Graham, Guy Moneypenney, Leslie Austen, Eva Leonard Boyne, Dorris Rich

1937

The Mistress of the Inn, by Carlo Goldoni, with Eva Le Gallienne

Retreat from Folly, by Amy Gould Kennedy, with McKay Morris, Margaret Anglin

Petticoat Fever, by Mark Reed, with Harry Ellerbe

Busman's Honeymoon, by Dorothy Sayers, with Mildred Natwick, Clarence Derwent, John Emery

Lysistrata, by Aristophanes, with Vera Allen, Myron McCormick, Elizabeth Love, Phyllis Welch

At Mrs. Beam's, by C. K. Munro, with Frances Farmer, Mildred Natwick

Princess Turandot, adapted by John Gerard and Lawrence Langner from the theatrical fable by Carlo Gozzi, with Anna May Wong

The Virginian, by Owen Wister, with Henry Fonda

Romance, by Edward Sheldon, with Eugenie Leontovich

Petrified Forest, by Robert E. Sherwood, with Frances Farmer, Philip Holmes

1938

Fool's Hill, by Robert Wetzel, with Rosemary Ames, Onslow Stevens, Theodore Newton

Accent on Youth, by Samuel Raphaelson, with Sylvia Sidney

Dame Nature, by Andre Birabeau, with Glen Anders, Onslow Stevens, Rosemary Ames, Theodore Newton

Ned McCobb's Daughter, by Sidney Howard, with Mildred Natwick, Van Heflin

The Inner Light, by Hugo Osergo, adapted by Worthington Miner, with Frances Fuller, Onslow Stevens

The Constant Wife, by W. Somerset Maugham, with Ethel Barrymore, Alice John, John Flynn, Audrey Ridgewell, Dorothy Francis, Madeleine Oliver, Boyd Davis, McKay Morris, Alfred Kappeler

Susannah and the Elders, by Lawrence Langner and Armina Marshall, with Uta Hagen, Onslow Stevens, Hugh Marlow, Theodore Newton, Edmond O'Brien, Theresa Helburn

Tovarich, by Jacques Deval, adapted by Robert E. Sherwood, with Eugenie Leontovich, McKay Morris, Mildred Dunnock, John Clarke, George Graham, Alfred Kappeler, Dorothy Francis, William David, Emma Wilcox, Don Stevens, Augusta Wallace, Alexander McDougall, Kathleen Comegys, Adora Andrews, Boyd Davis

The Millionairess, by George Bernard Shaw, directed by Harry Wagstaff Gribble, with Jessie Royce Landis, Onslow Stevens, Barry Thompson, Phillipa Bevans, Wilton Graff

A Mirror for Children, by Merrill Rogers, with Katherine Alexander, Onslow Stevens

Rain, by John Colton and Clemence Randolph (dramatized from a short story by W. Somerset Maugham), with Sally Rand, Theodore Newton, Richard Hale

1939

Anna Christie, by Eugene O'Neill, directed by Harry Wagstaff Gribble, with Glenda Farrell, Nance O'Neil, John Adair, Jack O'Connor, William B. Blood, Morgan James, Zachary Scott, Ralph Cullinan, Anthony Ross

Here Today, by George Oppenheimer, with Ruth Gordon

The Circle, by W. Somerset Maugham, with Florence Reed

Easy Virtue, by Noël Coward, with Jane Cowl

Arms and the Man, by George Bernard Shaw, with Jose Ferrer, Kent Smith, Claudia Morgan

Ghosts, by Henrik Ibsen, with Alla Nazimova

Outward Bound, by Sutton Vane, with Laurette Taylor, Kent Smith, Bramwell Fletcher

Private Lives, by Noël Coward, with Rex O'Malley, Eva Le Gallienne

Magazine Page, a musical revue, with Sheila Barrett, Gene Kelly and the Revuers (Betty Comden, Judith Tuvim, Al Hammer, Adolph Green, John Frank)

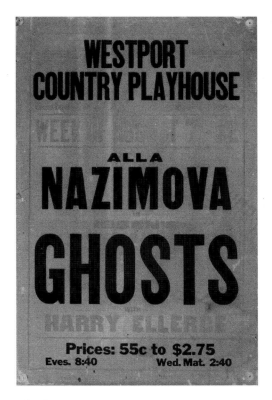

1940

Biography, by S. N. Behrman, directed by John Haggott, with Ina Claire, Forest Orr, Allan Hewitt, Charles Dingle, Mary Michael Dossett, Paul Ballantiyne, Beatrice Newport

Captain Brassbound's Conversion, by George Bernard Shaw, directed by Harry Ellerbe, with Jane Cowl, St. Clair Bayfield, Hale Norcross, Robert Chapman, Zachary Scott, Charles Newman, Robert B. Williams

Green Grow the Lilacs, by Lynn Riggs, directed by John Ford, with Mildred Natwick, Winston O'Keefe, Arthur Hunnicutt, Betty Field

The Bat, by Mary Roberts Rhinehart and Avery Hopwood, with Claudia Morgan, Kent Smith

The School for Scandal, by Richard Brinsley Sheridan, directed by E. M. Blythe, with Ethel Barrymore, Phyllis Joyce, Georgie Drew Mendum, Erna Rowen

The Emperor Jones, by Eugene O'Neill, with Paul Robeson

Good-Bye Again, by Allan Scott and George Haight, directed by John Cornell, with Haila Stoddard, Kent Smith, Morgan James, Harry Friedman, Wauna Paul, Elaine Anderson, Bethell Long, Mimi Doyle, Don Glenn, John O'Connor, William Bendix, Richard Babineau

Serena Blandish, by S. N. Behrman, with Greta Maren

1941

Her Cardboard Lover, by Jacques Deval and P. G. Wodehouse, with Tallulah Bankhead

La Belle Hélène, by Offenbach, in a swing version by Stewart Chaney, with Anne Brown, Hamtree Harrington

Meet the Wife, by Lynn Starling, with Mary Boland

Little Dark Horse, by André Birabeau, adapted by Theresa Helburn, with Walter Slezak, Evelyn Varden

Curtain Going Up! by Ivor Novello, with Constance Collier, Violet Heming, Gloria Stuart

Love in Our Time, by Leslie Reade, with Ilka Chase, Dennis King

Liliom, by Ferenc Molnar, directed by Lee Strasberg, with Tyrone Power, Annabella

Mis' Nelly of N'Orleans, by Laurence Eyre, directed by John C. Wilson, with Grace George

1942–1945

Theatre closed during war years

1946

They Knew What They Wanted, by Sidney Howard, with June Havoc, Kenny Delmar

Young Woodley, by John Van Druten, with Roddy McDowell

Design for Living, by Noël Coward, with Jean-Pierre Aumont, David Wayne, Marta Linden, Francesca Braggiotti

Night Must Fall, by Emlyn Williams, with Dame May Whitty

The Devil Take a Whittler, by Weldon Stone, with Patricia Neal, Carol Stone, John Conte, Tom Scott, Paul Crabtree

Our Town, by Thornton Wilder, with Thornton Wilder, Katherine Bard

Angel Street, by Patrick Hamilton, directed by John C. Wilson, with Frances Lederer, Bramwell Fletcher, Helen Shields, Pamela Gordon, Hazel Jones

Dream of Fair Women, by Reginald Lawrence, with Donald Cook, Anne Burr, Clarence Derwent, Nina Vale, Frank Milan

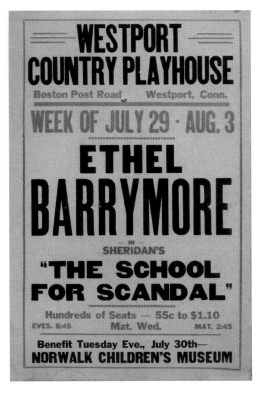

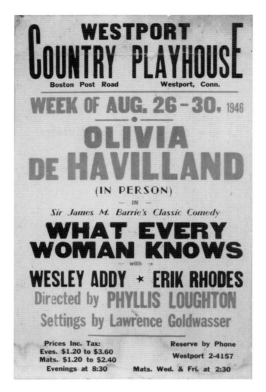

What Every Woman Knows, by James M. Barrie, directed by Phyllis Laughton, with Olivia de Havilland, J. P. Wilson, Erik Rhodes, Philip Tonge, Wesley Addy, Ted Smith, Peter Walker, Don Glenn, Josephine Brown, Elaine Stritch, Beverly Molot, Wyrley Birch, Alan Hodshire

It's a Man's World, by Hagar Wilde, directed by Martin Manulis, with Peggy Conklin, Carmen Mathews, Donald Cook

1947

The Girl of the Golden West, by David Belasco, directed by Armina Marshall, with June Havoc, Robert Stack, Murvyn Vye, Russell Collins, Paul Crabtree, Tom Scott, Lawrence Fletcher, Leo Chalzel, Philip Langner

French Without Tears, by Terence Rattigan, directed by John C. Wilson, with William Eythe, Erik Rhodes, Virginia Gilmore, Katharine Bard, Paul Crabtree, Lily Lodge, Don Peters

Private Lives, by Noël Coward, directed by Martin Manulis, with Tallulah Bankhead, Donald Cook, Buff Cobb, Phil Arthur, Therese Quadri

The Male Animal, by Elliott Nugent and James Thurber, with Buddy Ebsen, Katharine Bard, Lawrence Fletcher, Paul Crabtree, Doris Rich, William Degnan

The Man Who Came to Dinner, by George S. Kaufmann and Moss Hart, with Henry Morgan, Marta Linden, Paul Crabtree, Virginia Gilmore, Janet Fox

Ladies in Retirement, by Edward Percy and Reginald Denham, with Estelle Winwood, Fritzi Scheff, Zolya Talma, Elliott Reid, Elfrida Durwent, Frances Tannehill, Sally Brophy, Pat Sheridan

Papa Is All, by Patterson Green, with Jessie Royce Landis, Guy Spaull, Helen Carew, Emmett Rogers, Andree Wallace, John Larson

The Skull Beneath, by Richard Carlson, directed by Martin Manulis, with Fay Bainter, Hugh Marlowe, Alan Hewitt, Elliott Reid, Flora Campbell, Joan Shepard, Russell Collins

The Pursuit of Happiness, by Lawrence Langner and Armina Marshall, directed by Armina Marshall, with Alfred Drake, Mary Hatcher, Russell Collins, Katherine Raht, Seth Arnold, Dennis King, Jr., Chase Soltez

My Fair Lady, by Otis Bigelow, directed by John C. Wilson, with Alexander Kirkland, Marta Linden, Jane Seymour, Russell Collins, Kendall Clark, Maxine Stuart, Mendy Weisgald, John Larson, Alfrida Derwent

This Time Tomorrow, by Jan de Hartog, directed by Paul Crabtree, with Sam Jaffe, Ruth Ford, John Archer, Tyler Carpenter

1948

Lysistrata '48, adaptation by Gilbert Seldes, with June Havoc, Bibi Osterwald, Joan McCracken

Sundown Beach, by Bessie Breuer, an Actor's Studio Production, directed by Elia Kazan, with Steven Hill, Kim Hunter, Julie Harris, Robert F. Simon, Nehemiah Persoff, Martin Balsam, Treva Frezee, Jennifer Howard, Ellen Mahar, Vivian Firko, Ralph Cullinan, Don Hanmer, Joe Sullivan, Michael Lewan, Joan Copeland, Anne Hegira

The Beaux' Stratagem, by George Farquhar, with Brian Aherne, Carmen Mathews, E. G. Marshall, John Merivale, Maureen Stapleton, Richard Temple, Patricia Jenkins, Guy Spaull, Victor Beecroft, Lionelle Ince, Josephine Barnett, Mary Forbes, Milton Stiftel, King Sinanian

John Loves Mary, by Norman Krasna, directed by Martin Manulis, with Guy Madison, Katharine Bard, Paul Crabtree, E. G. Marshall, Matt Briggs, Elliot Reid, Margery Maude, Elizabeth Eustis, William F. Haddock, Robert Emmett

Anna Christie, by Eugene O'Neill, with June Havoc, George Mathews, E. G. Marshall, William F. Haddock, King Sinanian, Mark Sarel, Richard Hepburn, Chas Soltez, Florence Dunlap

Perfect Pitch, by Sam and Bella Spewack, directed by Martin Manulis, with Roland Young, Buddy Ebsen, Joyce Arling, Philip Coolidge, Daniel Ocko, Peter Lopouhin, Jonathan Marlowe, Harold Stone

Seven Keys to Baldpate, by George M. Cohan, directed by Paul Crabtree, with William Gaxton, Marianne Stewart, Martha Hodge, Kathleen Comegys, Lawrence Fletcher, Paul Crabtree, Guy Spaull, Eda Heinemann, Emmett Rogers, George Haggerty, E. G. Marshall, Edward Platt, Don Glenn

The Skin of Our Teeth, by Thornton Wilder, directed by John C. Wilson, with Thornton Wilder, Armina Marshall, Betty Field, Fania Marinoff, Richard Hepburn, Guy Spaull, Lois Braun, George Hersey, George Spelvin, Mark Sarel, Josephine Barnett

The Voice of the Turtle, by John Van Druten, directed by Edwin Gordon, with Joan Caulfield, Edwin Gordon, Jean Casto

The Silver Whistle, by Robert E. McEnroe, a Theatre Guild Production, directed by Paul Crabtree, with Jose Ferrer, E. G. Marshall, John Conte, Phyllis Hill, Kathleen Comegys, Jane Marbury, Stapleton Kent, Edward Platt, Charles Kuhn, Chas Soltez

1949

The Time of Your Life, by William Saroyan, directed by Paul Crabtree, with E. G. Marshall, Meg Mundy, Eddie Dowling, Lawrence Fletcher, Joe Sullivan, Leo Chalzel, Eddie Dowling, Paul Crabtree, Bob Emmett, Billy Taylor, Helen Chalzel, Lawrence Fletcher, John Randolph, Mary Anne Matson, Chilton Ryan, Allen Aldrich

Pretty Penny, by Jerome Chodorov, music and lyrics by Harold Rome, directed by George F. Kaufman, choreographed by Michael Kidd, with Peter Gennaro, David Burns, Carl Reiner, Marilyn Day, Barbara Martin, Lenore Lonergan, Bud Sweeney, George Keane

Yes, My Darling Daughter, by Mark Reed, directed by Herbert Brodkin, with Ann Harding, Muriel Hutchison, E. G. Marshall, Lawrence Fletcher, Phyllis Kirk

Accent on Youth, by Samuel Raphaelson, directed by Martin Manulis, with Paul Lukas, Katherine Bard, E. G. Marshall, Elaine Stritch, John Hudson

A Story for Sunday Evening, written and directed by Paul Crabtree, music by Walter Hendl, with Leora Dana, Laurence Fletcher, Paul Crabtree, Cloris Leachman

The Corn Is Green, by Emlyn Williams, directed by Edward McHugh, with Eva Le Gallienne, Richard Waring

A Month in the Country, by Ivan Turghenev, adaptation by Emlyn Williams, directed by Garson Kanin, with Ruth Gordon, E. G. Marshall, Howard St. John, Edmond Ryan, Scott McKay

Out of Dust, by Lynn Riggs, a Theatre Guild Production, directed by Mary Hunter, with Helen Craig, William Redfield, Berry Kroeger, Joan Lorning, Billy Redfield

Western Wind, by Charlotte Frances, directed by Martin Manulis, with Cornel Wilde, Patricia Knight, John Baragrey

The Philadelphia Story, by Philip Barry, directed by Herbert Brodkin, with E. G. Marshall, Jeffery Lynn, Sarah Churchill, Richard Derr, Oliver Thorndike, Tony Bickley, William Kemp, Peggy French

Texas Li'l Darlin', book by John Wheedon and Sam Moore, music by Robert Emmett Dolan, lyrics by Johnny Mercer, directed by Paul Crabtree, with Elaine Stritch, Kenny Delmar, Danny Scholl, Harry Bannister

Good Housekeeping, by William McCleery, a Theatre Guild Production, directed by Don Richardson, with Helen Hayes, Kent Smith, Mary MacArthur, Matt Briggs, Katherine Raht, Jack Manning, Mary Malone, Howard Stone, Shirlee Standlee

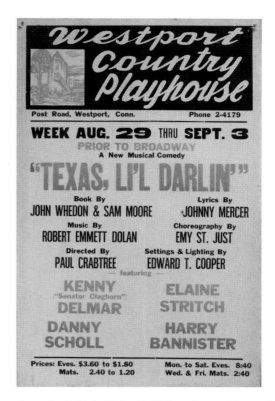

Come Back, Little Sheba, by William Inge, a Theatre Guild Production, directed by Daniel Mann, with Shirley Booth, Sidney Blackmer, Cloris Leachman, Lonny Chapman, John Randolph, Daniel A. Reed, Olga Fabian, Charles Hart, Wilson Brooks, John Larson

1950

The Second Man, by S. N. Behrman, directed by Martin Manulis, with Franchot Tone, Cloris Leachman, Walter Brooke, Margaret Lindsay

Angel in the Pawnshop, by A. B. Shiffrin, directed by Martin Manulis, with Eddie Dowling, Joan McCracken, Marie Murray Hamilton, Hugh Reilly, Robert Weber, Willie Lewis

The Devil's Disciple, by George Bernard Shaw, with Maurice Evans

The Life of the Party, by Lawrence Langner, with John Emery

The Winslow Boy, by Terence Rattigan, with Basil Rathbone, Meg Mundy

Within a Glass Bell, by William Marchant, with Mildred Dunnock, Don Hamner

The Long Days, by Davis Now, with John Baragrey, Florence Reed

Traveller's Joy, by Arthur Macrae, with Gertrude Lawrence, Dennis King

Miss Mabel, by R. C. Sherriff, with Lillian Gish

Over Twenty-One, by Ruth Gordon, with Eve Arden

My Fiddle Has Three Strings, by Arnold Schulman, with J. Edward Bromberg, Maureen Stapleton, MacDonald Carey, Betsey Blair, Fritzi Scheff, Steven Hill

Blind Alley, by James Warwick, with Zachary Scott

The Amazing Adele, by Pierre Barillet and Jean-Pierre Gredy, adapted by Garson Kanin, with Ruth Gordon

Head of the Family, by George Norford, with Frederick O'Neal

1951

The Animal Kingdom, by Philip Barry, directed by John Stix, with Nina Foch, Karl Malden, Kim Hunter, Scott McKay, Henry Hart, Louis Lytton, Gaby Rodgers, Anne Boley, Bernard Kates

Candida, by George Bernard Shaw, directed by Norris Haughton, with Olivia de Havilland, Edgar Kent, Katherine Squire, Kendall Clark, Frank Leslie, Richard Shepard

For Love or Money, by F. Hugh Herbert, directed by John Loder, with John Loder, Betsy von Furstenberg, Marta Linden, William Kester, Edith Gresham, Bert Bertram, Louis Lytton, Helen Donaldson

Love Revisited, by Robert Anderson, with Richard Kendrick, Helen Claire

The Philanderer, by George Bernard Shaw, directed by Romney Brent, with Tom Helmore, Claudia Morgan, Vanessa Brown

The Holly and the Ivy, by Wynyard Browne, directed by R. T. Ingham, with Leo G. Carroll, Anne Burr

The Little Screwball, by Walt Anderson, with Walter Abel, Edward Gargan

Island Fling, by Noël Coward, directed by John C. Wilson, with Claudette Colbert, Leon Janney, Edith Meiser, Reginald Mason

Glad Tidings, by Edward Mabley, directed by Melvyn Douglas, with Melvyn Douglas, Signe Hasso

Alice in Wonderland, music by John Charles Sacco, book and additional lyrics by Frances Pole, directed by Harold Hogan Fuquay, with Florence Forsberg, William Crach, Roy Raymond, John Henson, Bruce Adams, Anita Bolster

A Foreign Language, by S. N. Behrman, directed by Charles Bowden, with Edna Best, John Hoyt, Brenda Forbes, Howard St. John, James Lipton

A Case of Scotch, adapted by Philip Lewis from a play by Aimee Stewart, directed by Jerry Epstein, with Margaret Phillips, John Forsythe

Kin Hubbard, by Lawrence Riley, directed by John C. Wilson, with Tom Ewell, Josephine Hull, June Lockhart, John Alexander

1952

Pygmalion, by George Bernard Shaw, with Tom Helmore, Dolores Gray, Bramwell Fletcher

Lady in the Dark, by Moss Hart, a John Merrick Production, music by Kurt Weill, lyrics by Ira Gershwin, directed and choreographed by Elizabeth Gilbert, with Kitty Carlisle, Jackson Young, Lee Bergere, Russel Gold, Leta Bonygne, Addison Powell

Idiot's Delight, by Robert E. Sherwood, with Scott McKay, Luba Malina

Three to One, musical revue by Nancy Hamilton and Morgan Lewis, with Kaye Ballard, Alice Pearce

Heartbreak House, by George Bernard Shaw, directed by Basil Langton, with Beatrice Straight, Philip Bourneuf

Ballet Variante, with Mia Slavenska, Frederic Franklin, Alexandra Danilova

The Hasty Heart, by John Patrick, directed by John Patrick, with John Forsythe, John Dall, Mary Fickett

Right You Are, by Luigi Pirandello, with Alfred Drake and Mildred Dunnock

Jezebel's Husband, by Robert Nathan, with Claude Rains

Seagulls over Sorrento, by Hugh Hastings, with Rod Steiger

Dangerous Corner, by J. B. Priestley, with John Forsythe, Faye Emerson

Tin Wedding, by Hager Wilde and Judson O'Donnell, directed by John C. Wilson, with MacDonald Carey, Maureen Stapleton

"An Evening with Beatrice Lillie"

The American Lyric Theatre Presents: *California*, by Gordon Jenkins and Tom Adair; *The Old Maid and the Thief*, by Gian-Carlo Menotti; *Hey, You,* by Norman Meranus and June Caroll; *Down in the Valley*, by Kurt Weill and Arnold Sungaard

1953

Second Fiddle, by Mary Drayton, adapted from Ardyth Kennelly's novel *The Peaceable Kingdom*, directed by Elmer Rice, with Betty Field, Herbert Rudley, Paula Laurence, Dorothy Donahue, Amy Douglass

One Thing After Another, sketches and lyrics by Elizabeth Berryhill, music by Gordon Connell, directed by Elizabeth Berryhill, featuring the original California "Strawhatters"

Sailor's Delight, adapted by Lawrence Langner from Peter Blackmore's play *Miranda*, directed by Harry Ellerby, with Eva Gabor, Tom Helmore, Natalie Schaefer, Katherine Meskill, Chester Stratton, Philippa Bevans

What About Maisie? by Ruth and Francis Bellamy, adapted from Henry James's novel *What Maisie Knew*, directed by John C. Wilson, with Claudia Morgan, Beatrice Pearson

The Play's the Thing, by Ferenc Molnar, adapted by P. G. Wodehouse, directed by Ezra Stone, with Ezio Pinza, Frances Compton, Philip Loeb, Alexander Clark, Vilma Kurer, Michael Wager, Tye Perry

Once Married, Twice Shy, by Lawrence Langner, directed by Charles Bowden, with Elaine Stritch, Scott McKay, Clarence Derwent, Otto Hulett, Elizabeth Eustis, Catherine Doucet, Alice Buchanan, John Shay

Three Men on a Horse, by John Cecil Holm and George Abbott, directed by John Cecil Holm, with Wally Cox, Walter Matthau, Teddy Hart, Peter Turgeon, Fred Gwynne, Ann Whiteside, Sheldon Wile

The Road to Rome, by Robert E. Sherwood, directed by Charles Bowden, with Arlene Francis, John Baragrey, Ann Shoemaker, Ralph Sumpter, Tige Andrews, Michael Tolan, Evan Thomas, Henry Silver

The Starcross Story, by Diana Morgan, directed by Luther Kennett, with Eva Le Gallienne, Faye Emerson, Glenn Anders

Day of Grace, by Alexander Fedoroff, directed by Norris Houghton, with MacDonald Carey, Ben Gazzara, John Alexander, Katherine Squire

Comin' Thro' the Rye, by Warren P. Munsell, Jr. and Stephen DeBaun, music by Robert Burns, directed by Ezra Stone, with David Brooks, Anna Lee, Luella Gear

The Trip to Bountiful, by Horton Foote, directed by Vincent Donehue, with Lillian Gish, Eva Marie Saint, John Beal, Jo Van Fleet

A "New" School For Scandal, by Richard Baldridge and Albert Marre, directed by Albert Marre, with June Havoc, Hurd Hatfield

1954

The Lady Chooses, by William McCleery, directed by Luther Kennett, with Walter Abel, Faye Emerson, Hugh Reilly, Jean Stapleton, Lily Lodge, Arny Freeman, Beulah Garrick, Ellen Demming, Jeff Harris, Dennis Mahoney, Pat Mahoney, Ina Bradley, Claire Emory

The Apollo of Bellac, by Jean Giraudoux, adapted by Maurice Valency, directed by Joseph Anthony, with Zachary Scott, Ruth Ford, Gaby Rodgers

The Shewing-Up of Blanco Posnet, by George Bernard Shaw, directed by Joseph Anthony, with Gaby Rodgers, Jean Stapleton, Logan Ramsey, Norman MacKaye, Alexander Clark, Paula Laurence, Lou Gilbert, John Richards, Lily Lodge, Ellen Demming, Richard Hamilton

Happy Birthday, by Anita Loos, directed by Daniel Levin, with Imogene Coca, William Prince, Daniel Reed, Jack Diamond, Norman MacKaye, Lucille Benson, Fay Sappington

Court Olympus, by Richard Reardon, directed by John C. Wilson, with Rita Gam, Lee Grant, Josephine Brown, Nicholas Joy, Steven Hill, Tom Tryon

Candle-Light, by P. G. Wodehouse, directed by Charles Bowden, with Eva Gabor, Richard Kiley, Paula Laurence, John Baragrey, Monica Boyar, Gordon Nelson

Reunion 54, by Justin Sturm, directed by Lee Bowman, with Lee Bowman, Haila Stoddard, Tom Helmore, George Mathews, Carl White, Parker McCormick, James Hagerman, Drummond Erskine, William Hail, Wayne McIntyre, Ted and Ana Clark

Libel, by Edward Wooll, directed by Lexford Richards, with Peter Cookson, June Duprez, Fred Tozere, John Emery, Kenny Delmar, Don McHenry, Francis Bethencourt, Tammy Grimes

The Little Hut, by Nancy Mitford, adapted from André Roussin's *La Petite Hutte*, with Barbara Bel Geddes, Hiram Sherman, Howard Morton, John Granger, Kenneth Mays

Darling, Darling, by Anita Loos, adapted from a play by Pierre Barillet and Jean-Pierre Gredy, directed by John C. Wilson, with Gypsy Rose Lee, Richard Derr, Florence Sunstrom, Jill Kraft, Tom Tryon, James Nolan

My Aunt Daisy, by Albert Halper and Joseph Schrank, directed by Robert Ellenstein, with Jo Van Fleet, Leslie Nielsen, Rusty Lane, Winifred Cushing, Arthur Storch, Bern Hoffman

Home Is the Hero, by Walter Macken, a Theatre Guild–Worthington Miner Production, directed by Worthington Miner, with Peggy Ann Garner, Glenda Farrell, J. Pat O'Malley, Art Smith, Francis Fuller, Ann Thomas, Walter Macken, Christopher Plummer

Magic and Music, Cheryl Crawford's musical production of *Trouble in Tahiti*, music by Leonard Bernstein, directed by David Brooks, with Alice Ghostley, Richard Eastham, and *The Thirteen Clocks*, by James Thurber, stage adaptation by Fred Sadoff and Mark Bucci, lyrics by Thurber and Bucci, directed by Fred Sadoff, with Constance Brigham, Fred Sadoff, Martin Balsam, Alice Ghostley, Gene Saks, Janice Mars

1955

Brief Moment, by S. N. Behrman, directed by Peter Turgeon, with Betty Furness, Murray Matheson, Mark Roberts, Marc Lawrence, Robert Gallagher, Jan DeRuth, Hope Newell

Mother Was a Bachelor, by Irving W. Phillips, adapted from a story by Myna Lockwood, directed by Frank Carrington and Agnes Morgan, with Billie Burke, Tommy Halloran, Virginia Gerry, Suzanne Jackson, Barry Della Fiora, George McIver, Robert Baines

Detective Story, by Sidney Kingsley, directed by Windsor Lewis, with John Forsythe, Maria Riva, Kathy Nolan, Frank Campanella, Henry Silva, Henry Garrard, Jack Klugman

Star Light, Star Bright, by S. K. Lauren and Gladys Lehman, directed by John C. Wilson, with Terry Moore, Frank Albertson, Effie Afton, Cherry Hardy, Berry Kroeger, Jean Carson, John Vivyan, Howard Morton, Eileen Merry, Ralph Stantley, Eulabelle Moore

Wedding Breakfast, by Theodore Reeves, directed by Frank Corsaro, with Shelley Winters, Anthony Franciosa, Virginia Vincent, Martin Balsam

Blue Denim, by James Leo Herlihy and William Noble, directed by Arthur Penn, with Katherine Squire, Burt Brinckerhoff, Brandon Peters, Patricia Bosworth, Mark Rydell, Betty Lou Robinson

Heaven Can Wait, by Harry Segall, directed by Windsor Lewis, with Richard Kiley, Mercer McLeod, Howard Morton, Brook Byron, Stephen Gray, Jack Klugman

The Rainmaker, by N. Richard Nash, directed by Jeffrey Hayden, with Eva Marie Saint, Sidney Armus, Will Geer, Mark Richman, Arthur Storch, Jack Mullaney, Truman Smith

Gigi, by Anita Loos, adapted from the novel by Colette, with Estelle Winwood, Cathy O'Donnell, Josephine Brown, Bethell Long, Marion Morris, Ludmilla Toretzka, Angus Cairns

Hide and Seek, by Aurand Harris, directed by Windsor Lewis, with Jessie Royce Landis, Mark Roberts, Kathy Nolan, Tom Carlin, Deneen Gabler, Munro Gabler, Harry Stanton

The Empress, by Elaine Carrington, directed by William Bulter, with Geraldine Page, Paul Stevens, Michael Galloway, Leslie Barrett, Sally Jessy, Rod McLennan, Joseph Campanella, Judith Ives Lowry, Raymond St. Jacques

Oh, Men! Oh, Women! by Edward Chodorov, directed by Franchot Tone, with Franchot Tone, Betsy von Furstenberg, Patrick O'Neal, Lorette Leversee, Dana Elcar, Henry Sharp, June Hunt, Angus Cairns, Marshall Yokelson

The Great Waltz, book by Moss Hart, music by Johann Strauss, lyrics by Desmond Carter, with Mia Slavenska

Scandal at Montfort, by Hugh Mills, directed by Windsor Lewis, with Arlene Francis

A Palm Tree in a Rose Garden, by Meade Roberts, directed by Jose Quintero, with Alice Ghostley, Barbara Baxley, Betty Lou Holland, Herbert Evers, Belle Flower, Ron Harper, George Voskovec

1956

The Chalk Garden, by Enid Bagnold, directed by Charles Bowden, with Lillian Gish, Dorothy Gish, Neil Fitzgerald, Frances Ingalls, Charron Follett, O. T. Whitehead

Ballet Theatre, musical direction by Joseph Levine, with Nora Kaye, John Kriza, Lupe Serrano, Scott Douglas, Ruth Ann Koesun, Catherine Horn, Christine Mayer, Enrique Martinez

Posket's Family Skeleton, by Arthur Wing Pinero, adapted and directed by Peter Turgeon, with Bramwell Fletcher, Betty Sinclair, Ralph Sumpter, Frances Tannehill, Spencer Teakle, Alexander Clark, Charles Eggleston, Ellen Christopher, Charles Penman, Lily Lodge, Gorden Russell, Amy Douglas

27 Wagons Full of Cotton, by Tennessee Williams, directed by Peter Cass, with Maureen Stapleton, Jules Munshin, John Cassavetes; and *A Marriage Proposal*, by Anton Chekov, directed by Peter Cass, with Ed Heffernan, Jules Munshin, Maureen Stapleton

Welcome Darlings, A Revue, music direction by Peter Howard and Ted Graham, with Tallulah Bankhead, James Kirkwood, Sheila Smith, Don Crichton, Turnell Dietsch, Bob Bakanic, The Martins

The Gimmick, by Joseph Julian, directed by David Pressman, with Larry Blyden, Patricia Smith, Tammy Grimes, Gene Saks, Haywood Hale Broun, Amy Douglass, Robert Carricart, Ralph Bell, Hal Gerson, William Zuckert

The Doctor in Spite of Himself, by Molière, adapted and directed by James Lipton, with Jules Munshin, Betsy Palmer, Lawrence Fletcher, Marilyn Clark, Hal Holbrook, James Ambandos, Joe Campinella, Kenneth Mays, Hal Gerson, Gemze de Lappe

Beasop's Fables, A Revue produced and directed by John Philip, with Beatrice Lillie, Fred Keating, John Philip, Shannon Dean, Eadie and Rack at the pianos

Anastasia, by Marcelle Maurette, adapted by Guy Bolton, directed by Boris Tumarin, with Dolores Del Rio, Lili Darvas, Stephen Elliott, Boris Tumarin, Allan Shayne, Frank Marth, Clarice Blackburn, George Eberling, Paul Stevens

Knickerbocker Holiday, by Maxwell Anderson and Kurt Weill, directed by Frank Perry, with Will Geer, Susan Cabot, Biff McGuire, Clarence Hoffman, Rudolph Weiss, Marion Tanner, Dan Lincoln, Bob Burland, Hal Gerson, David Leland, Bill Bramley, Bryon Mitchell

Anniversary Waltz, by Jerome Chodorov and Joseph Fields, directed by Dan Levin, with Imogene Coca, Jules Munshin, Amy Douglass, Marilyn Clark, Peter Turgeon, Paul Lipson, Mary Lee Dearring, Rosetta Le Noire, Robert Galli, Hal Gerson, Raymond Burgin, Ralph Hoffman, Jr.

The Rhom Affair, by Larry Ward and Gordon Russell, directed by John Marley with Robert Pastene, Martin Brooks, Rudy Bond, Jack Weston, Thomas Carlin, Lois Nettleton, George Mitchell, David White

1957

Witness for the Prosecution, by Agatha Christie, directed by Michael McAloney, with Faye Emerson, Ronald Long, Will Hare, Neil Fitzgerald, Eva Leonard-Boyne, Michael Clark Laurence, Lily Lodge, Bryan Herbert, Peter Pagan, John Aronson

The Desk Set, by William Marchand, directed by Harry Ellerbe, with Nancy Walker, Evelyn Russell, Wayne Carson, Wesley Lau

The Reluctant Debutante, by William Douglas Home, directed by Walt Witcover, with Arthur Treacher, Sandy Dennis, Ruth Chatterton, Ralph Purdum, Harriet MacGibbon, Peter Craig, Helen-Jean Arthur, Ruth Estler

Mrs. Patterson, by Charles Sebree and Greer Johnson, directed by Mortimer Halpern, music by James Shelton, with Eartha Kitt, Nadia Westman, Terry Carter, Eric Burroughs, Ruth Attaway

With Respect to Joey, by Ernest Pendrell, directed by Darren McGavin, with Martin Balsam, Bertha Gersten, Jacob Ben-Ami, Frank Silvera, Zohra Alton, Milton Selzer, Robert Heller

The Man in the Dog Suit, by William H. Wright and Albert Beich, from a novel by Edwin Corle, directed by Melvyn Douglas, with Jessica Tandy, Hume Cronyn, Isobel Elsom, Tom Carlin, Mary Cooper, Betty Garde, John Griggs, Arthur Hughes, John McGovern, Elliott Reid

Janus, by Carolyn Green, directed by Donald Cook, with Joan Bennett, Donald Cook, George Voskovec, John C. Becher, Amy Douglas

Fever for Life, by Orin Borsten, directed by Henry T. Weinstein, with Fay Bainter, Rip Torn, Barbara Baxley, Ruby Goodwin, Jane Rose, John Randolph, Barbara Barrie

Showtime, A Revue composed and directed by Ben Oakland, with George Jessel, Tony Carroll, Susanne and the Escorts, Susanne Cansino, Dusty McCaffery, Michael Madill

Back to Methuselah, by George Bernard Shaw, adapted by Arnold Moss, directed by Philip Burton, with Celeste Holm, James Daley, Arnold Moss, Valerie Bettis, Michael Tolan, Felix Deebank

Minotaur, by Robert Thom, directed by Sidney Lumet, with Gloria Vanderbilt, Janice Rule, Philip Bourneuf, Betty Furness, Stefan Girasch, Gene Lyons, George Peppard, Madeline Sherwood, Ruth White

The Saturday Night Kid, by Jack Dunphy, directed by George Keathley, with Shelley Winters, Alex Nicol, Joseph Wiseman

1958

Picnic, by William Inge, directed by Scott Jackson, with Hugh O'Brian, Leora Dana, Susan Oliver, Yale Wexler, Virginia Payne, John C. Becher, Sylvia Stone, Lucille Benson, Anne Hennesy, Daryl Grimes, Joseph Dedda

Fallen Angels, by Noël Coward, directed by Bill Penn, with Hermione Gingold, Carol Bruce, Louise Hoff, Gordon Mills, G. Wood, Richard Blackmarr

Tonight at 8:30, by Noël Coward, directed by Christopher Hewitt, with Faye Emerson, Murray Matheson, Peter Pagan, Rita Vale, Jean Cameron, Charles Campbell

The Remarkable Mr. Pennypacker, by Liam O'Brien, directed by Frederick de Wilde, with Burgess Meredith, John McGiver, Iris Whitney, Wayne Wilson, Vera Lockwood, Arthur Lockwood, Jada Rowland, Terrence McGiver, Johnny Conrath, Brigit McGiver, Juleen Compton

He Who Gets Slapped, by Leonid Andreyev, directed by Robert Emhardt, with Alfred Drake, Boris Tumarin, Susan Kohner, Fredric Tozere, Marilyn Clark, Ben Yaffee, Karl Redcroff, Nicholas Pryor

Time for Elizabeth, by Norman Krasna and Groucho Marx, directed by Robert Dwan, with Groucho Marx, Harry Bannister, Katheryn Eames, Phoebe Bannister, Ed Wagner, Spencer Davis, Ruth Manning, Roland Wood, Elizabeth Tilton, Wyatt Cooper, J. Frank Lucas, Jim Kelly, Aileen Poe, Eden Hartford

Dulcy, by George S. Kaufman and Marc Connelly, directed by Robert S. Finkel, with Dody Goodman, Gene Lyons, Lawrence Fletcher, Perry Fiske, Gloria Barret, Howard Mann, Justice Watson, Brooks Rogers, Betty Rollin, Leo Bloom, Sanford McCauley

Triple Play (three short plays and a monologue)—*Bedtime Story*, by Sean O'Casey; *The Island of Cipango*, by Benn Levy; *Harmful Effects of Tobacco*, by Anton Chekov; *A Pound on Demand*, by Sean O'Casey—directed by Hume Cronyn, with Jessica Tandy, Hume Cronyn, Biff McGuire, Francis Sternhagen, Bryan Herbert

Visit to a Small Planet, by Gore Vidal, directed by Pat Chandler, with Bert Lahr, Kenny Delmar, Stanley Tackney, Kathern Shaw, Stratton Walling, Josephine Nichols, Jeff Davis, Grenadier Saadi, Curt Gibson, Bill Moise, Leonard Dalsemer, Jr.

An Inspector Calls, by J. B. Priestley, directed by Howard Stone, with Sir Cedric Hardwicke, Melville Cooper, Mary Scott, Howard Morton, James Valentine, Renee Gadd, Joyce Miko

Third Best Sport, by Eleanor and Leo Bayer, directed by Michael Howard, with Celeste Holm, Jane Hoffman, Andrew Duggan, Russell Gaige, Joseph Boland, Sally Gracie, James Karen, Tony Kraber, Irene Cowan, Stan Place, Milo Boulton

Sweet and Sour, by Florence Lowe and Caroline Francke, directed by Don Richardson, with Melvyn Douglas, Connie Sawyer, Ina Balin, Gerald Hiken, Martha Greenhouse, Leslie Woods, Theo Goetz, Alice Yourman, Daniel Reed, Alfred Leberfeld, John Zee

Holiday for Lovers, by Ronald Alexander, with Don Ameche, Irene Manning

1959

Once More with Feeling, by Harry Kurnitz, with Arlene Francis

Arms and the Man, by George Bernard Shaw, directed by Romney Brent, with Tony Randall, Joan Copeland

A Piece of Blue Sky, by Frank Corsaro, with Shelley Winters

Caesar and Cleopatra, by George Bernard Shaw, with Franchot Tone, Susan Strasberg

Red Letter Day, by Andrew Rosenthal, with Gloria Swanson, Buddy Rogers

Nina, by André Roussin, adapted by Samuel Taylor, with Shirley Booth

The Glass Menagerie, by Tennessee Williams, with Jo Van Fleet, Eli Wallach, Anne Jackson

What a Day, sketches by Max Wilk and Manya Starr, lyrics by Paul Rosner, music by Claire Richardson, with Celeste Holm

Bells Are Ringing, book and lyrics by Betty Comden and Adolph Green, music by Jules Styne, with Imogene Coca

A Party with Betty Comden and Adolph Green, with Betty Comden, Adolph Green

Marcus in the High Grass, by William Gunn, with David Wayne, Ben Piazza

Epitaph for George Dillion, by John Osborne and Anthony Creighton, with Ben Gazzara

Hilary, by Gerald Savory, with Joan Fontaine

1960

Amphitryon 38, by Jean Giraudoux, adapted by S. N. Behrman, directed by Martin Gabel, with Arlene Francis, Kent Smith, George Grizzard

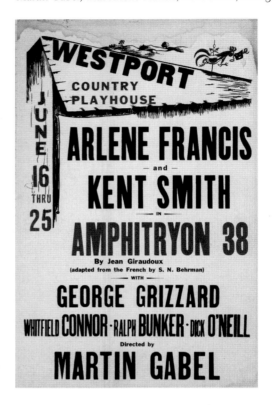

Two for the Seesaw, by William Gibson, with Shelley Winters

Make a Million, by Norman Barasch and Carroll Moore, directed by Sam Levene, with Sam Levene

No Concern of Mine, by Jeremy Kingston, directed by Andreas Boutsinas, with Jane Fonda

Not in the Book, by Arthur Watkyn, directed by Charles Olsen, with Hans Conried, Brook Byron, Francis Compton, Anthony Kemble Cooper, Arny Freeman, James Balentine, Norman Barrs, Carl Esser

Roar Like a Dove, by Lesley Storm, directed by Robert Ellis Miller, with Betsy Palmer, Brook Byron, Carl Esser, James Valentine, Norman Barrs, Hans Conried, Arny Freeman, Francis Compton, Anthony Kemble Cooper

Royal Enclosure, by Kieran Tunney, directed Romney Brent, with Celeste Holm, Cathleen Nesbitt

The Late Christopher Bean, by Sidney Howard, directed by Elaine Perry, with Shirley Booth

Burnt Flower Bed, by Ugo Betti, directed by Herbert Machiz, with Signe Hasso, Gloria Vanderbilt, Eric Portman, Alexander Scourby, Vincent Gardenia

Susan and God, by Rachel Crothers, with Joan Fontaine, Lily Lodge

The Captains and the Kings, by Leo Lieberman, directed by John Gerstad, with Zachary Scott, John Alexander, Walter Brooke, Sally Brophy, Donald McKee, Alexander Clark, Howard Freeman, John Boruff, Ben Yaffee, Phil Bruns, Charles McDaniel, Edmon Ryan

Tambourines to Glory, by Langston Hughes, directed by Herbert Machiz, music by Jobe Huntley, with Hazel Scott, Nipsy Russell, Ben Yaffee, Sally Brophy, Walter Brooke, Phil Bruns, Zachary Scott, John Alexander

An Evening with Mike Nichols and Elaine May, with Mike Nichols, Elaine May

1961

The Pleasure of His Company, by Samuel Taylor, directed by Charles Olsen, with Cornelia Otis Skinner, Hans Conried, Henry Sharp, Hilda Brawner, James Olsen, Guy Arbury, Bernard Wu

Once upon a Mattress, book by Jay Thompson, Marshall Barer and Dean Fuller, music by Mary Rodgers, lyrics by Marshall Barer, directed by Jack Sydow, with Pat Carroll, Joseph Bova, Kelly Brown, Irene Dean, Mort Marshall, Dan Resin, Harry Snow, Willy Switkes, Jane White, Tom Thornton, Myrna Galle, Gloria Stevens, Cheryl Killgren, Jean Palmerton, Bobbi Franklin, Ann Marisse, Richard Lyle

The New York Repertory Theatre—Viveca Lindfors, Ben Piazza, William Daniels, Betty Field, Rita Gam, Morgan Sterne, Nydia Westman—in: The Zoo Story, by Edward Albee, directed by Tad Danielewski; Miss Julie, by August Strindberg, directed by Tad Danielewi; I Am a Camera, by John Van Druten, directed by Michael Howard

Period of Adjustment, by Tennessee Williams, directed by John Lehne, with Dane Clark, Rosemary Murphy, Ann Wedgeworth, Adam Kennedy, Lester Mack, Ruth Hammond, Robert Wangler, Eleanor Andrews, Dutchess the Dog

Between Seasons, by Malcolm Wells, directed by Bill Penn, with Gloria Swanson, Charles Baxter, Ray Fulmer, Aileen Poe

A Majority of One, by Leonard Spigelgass, directed by Jacob Kalish, with Molly Picon, Martyn Green, James Karen, Zina Jasper, Esta Mann, Alvin Lum, Roger Morris

Invitation to a March, by Arthur Laurents, directed by Arthur Laurents, with Celeste Holm, Winifred Ainslee, Wesley Addy, Louise Latham, Nicholas Pryor, Claudette Nevins, Rees Vaughan, Jeffrey Rowland

Under the Yum Yum Tree, by Lawrence Roman, directed by James Monos, with Margaret O'Brien, Hugh Marlowe, James MacArthur, Monica Keating, Dan Elliot, Robert Wangler

The Marriage-Go-Round, by Leslie Stevens, directed by Wynn Handman, with Myrna Loy, Claude Dauphin, Siri, Moultrie Patten

Venus at Large, by Henry Denker, directed by Shepherd Traube, with Jan Sterling, Lionel Stander, William Prince, Martin Wolfson, Boris Tumarin, Larry Haines, Tom Carlin, Elsa Freed, Arnold Soboloff, Louise Allbritton

Journey to the Day, by Roger O. Hirson, directed by Boris Sagal, with Paul Hartman, William Redfield, Joan Hackett, Katherine Squire, Robert Simon, Nancy Marchand, Mario Alcalde, Charles Saari, Casey Allen

Ding Dong Bell, by Gurney Campbell and Daphne Athas, with Albert Dekker

1962

Complaisant Lover, by Graham Greene, directed by Del Hughes, with Walter Pidgeon, Martha Scott, Gene Wilder

Maggie, by Hugh Thomas, adapted from J. M. Barrie's What Every Woman Knows, directed by Ward Baker, with Betsy Palmer

Rhinoceros, by Eugene Ionesco, directed by Joseph Bernard, with Walter Slezak, Philip Bruns, David Hurst, Clifford Carpenter, Conrad Bain, Mary Carver, James Tolkan, Jean Barker, Miriam Phillips, Erica Slezak

Miracle Worker, by William Gibson, directed by Porter Van Zandt, with Eileen Brennan

Critic's Choice, by Ira Levin, with Hans Conried

Old Acquaintance, by John Van Druten, directed by Martin Gabel, with Arlene Francis

There Must Be a Pony, by Jim Kirkwood, directed by John Stix, with Myrna Loy, Donald Woods

Sunday in New York, by Norman Krasna, directed by Joe Brownstone, with Margaret O'Brien, Tommy Sands

Cradle and All (Never Too Late), by Summer Arthur Long, directed by Gene Lasko, with Paul Ford, Maureen O'Sullivan

The Happiest Man Alive, by Jerome Chodorov, directed by Darren McGavin, with Darren McGavin, Eva Gabor, Louise Latham

Here Today, by George Oppenheimer, directed by Jack Sydow, with Tallulah Bankhead

Desperate Hours, by Joseph Hayes, with Sammy Davis, Jr.

1963

Come Blow Your Horn, by Neil Simon, with Menasha Skulnik

H.M.S. Pinafore and The Mikado, by William Gilbert and Arthur Sullivan, produced by Laurence Feldman, directed by Martyn Green, with Martyn Green, Carol Bayard, Yvonne Chaveau, Paul Flores, Eugene Green, John Parella, Charlotte Povia, James Morgan Stuart

Mackeral Plaza, by William McCleery, adapted from the novel by Peter DeVries, with Hal Holbrook, Loring Smith

Tchin-Tchin, by Sidney Michaels, directed by Joseph Brownstone, with Teresa Wright, Dane Clark, Arlene Francis, Charles Grodin

The Millionairess, by George Bernard Shaw, with Carol Channing

Lord Pengo, by S. N. Behrman, directed by Malcolm Black, with Walter Pidgeon

God Bless Our Bank, by Mac Benoff, directed Ezra Stone, with Ann Sothern, Roland Winters

Take Her, She's Mine, by Phoebe and Henry Ephron, with Hans Conried

A Shot in the Dark, by Marcel Archard, directed by Malcolm Black, with Eva Gabor, Joan Wetmore

The Indoor Sport, by Jack Perry, directed by Gerald Hiken, with Darren McGavin, Shari Lewis, Patrick McVey, Kenneth Harvey, Louise Latham, Alice Beardsley

Seidman and Son, by Elick Moll, a Theatre Guild Production, directed by Sam Levene, with Sam Levene, Darren McGavin, Patrick McVey, Shari Lewis, Kenneth Harvey, Louise Latham

Fall of 1963

Oh Dad, Poor Dad, Mamma's Hung You in the Closet and I'm Feelin' So Sad, by Arthur Kopit, with Hermione Gingold

The Innocents, by William Archibald, adapted from Henry James's *The Turn of the Screw*, with Betsy Palmer

The Wind of Heaven, by Emlyn Williams, with Michael Evans, Nancy Coleman, Romney Brent

The Moments of Love, by David Rogers, directed by Herbert Machiz, with Ann Harding, Joanna Pettet, Nicholas Pryor, Leo Lucker, Roy Shuman, Dorothy Sands

The Strangers, by Andrew Rosenthal, with Cornelia Otis Skinner, Jane Wyatt, Constance Cummings, Peggy Conklin

The Threepenny Opera, book and lyrics by Bertolt Brecht, music by Kurt Weill, adaptation by Marc Blitzstein, directed by Joseph Leberman, with Scott Merrill, Christiane Felsmann, Robert Penn, Avon Long, Alfred Spindelman, Sharlie Shull, Barbara Louis, Nancy Andrews

Calculated Risk, by Joseph Hayes, directed by Howard Erskine, with Dana Andrews, Mary Todd, Jack Ramage, Philip Kenneally, Donal Hylan, Dana Hardwick, Harry Gresham, Charles Gaines, Allan Frank, Hal Burdick, Patricia Gilbert, Bert Thorn

1964

My Fair Lady, book and lyrics by Alan J. Lerner, music by Frederick Loewe, with George Gaines, Allyn Ann McLerie

Days of the Dancing, by James Bridges, directed and choreographed by Timmy Everett, with Shelley Winters, Robert Walker, Jr., Logan Ramsey, Vincent Beck, Louis Guss, Henry Madden, Bruce Roman, Bob Ennis, Anne Ramsey, Norma Donaldson, Sally Kirkland

A Thousand Clowns, by Herb Gardner, directed by Malcolm Black, with Van Johnson, Nancy Douglas, Doug Chapin, Robert Alvin, Richard Benjamin, Iggie Wolfington

The Fantasticks, book and lyrics by Tom Jones, music by Harvey Schmidt, with Liza Minnelli, Elliott Gould

A Girl Could Get Lucky, by Don Appell, with Betty Garrett, Pat Hingle

Kind Sir, by Norman Krasna, with Arlene Francis

The Wayward Stork, by Harry Tugend, with Hal March, Marjorie Lord

Heart's Delight, by Charles Robinson, directed by Brian Shaw, with Michael Rennie, Hiram Sherman, Nan Martin

Stop the World, I Want to Get Off, by Leslie Bricusse and Anthony Newley,

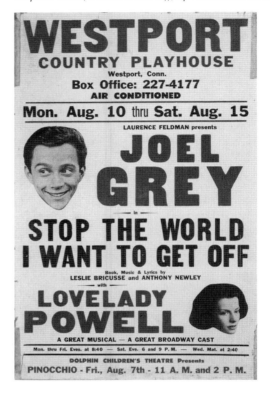

with Joel Grey

Who's Afraid of Virginia Woolf, by Edward Albee, with Henderson Forsythe, Haila Stoddard, Kendall Clark, Vicki Cummings

Thursday Is a Good Night, by Abe Einhorn and Donald Segall, with Tom Ewell, Sheree North

Dear Me the Sky Is Falling, by Leonard Spigelgass, directed by Herman Shumlin, with Gertrude Berg

The White House, by A. E. Hotchner, directed by Henry Kaplan, with Helen Hayes, James Daly, Gene Wilder

Spring of 1965

Shaw Repertory Festival: *Major Barbara* and *Pygmalion*, by George Bernard Shaw, both directed by William Francisco, with Michael Allinson, Lois Nettleton, Bramwell Fletcher; and *Misalliance*, directed by Jack Sydow, with Michael Allinson, Lois Nettleton, Bramwell Fletcher, Dina Merrill, Philippa Bevans, Dennis Cooney, Herbert Foster

1965

The Trojan Women, by Euripides, translated by Edith Hamilton, directed by Michael Cacoyannis, with Caroline Coates, Shirley Cox, Elaine Kerr, Dimitra Steris, Philip Sterling, George Morgan

Gigi, by Anita Loos, lyrics and musical adaptation by Jonathan Anderson, directed by William Francisco, with George Hamilton, Susan Watson, Anna Russell, Jan McArt, Dorothy Sands, Janet Fox, Jon Richards

Absence of a Cello, by Ira Wallach, directed by Charles Olsen, with Hans Conried, Ruth McDevitt, Michaele Myers, Fran Carlon, Robert Rovin, Pamela Dunlap, James Karen

Enter Laughing, by Joseph Stein, based on the novel by Carl Reiner, directed by Martin Freed, with Menasha Skulnik, Martin Huston, Richard Waring, Fayne Blackburn, Joe Young, Bonnie Bedelia, Jan LaPrade, David Rosenbaum, Rick Grayson, Burr Edson, Mimi-Garth Taub, Roger Madden, Anna Roman

The Private Ear and the Public Eye, by Peter Shaffer, directed by Leo Garen, with Tammy Grimes, Eric Berry, Stefan Gierasch, Tom Martin, James Douglas

Family Things, by William Inge, directed by Morton Da Costa, with Hiram Sherman, Dorothy Stickney, June Harding, Beau Bridges, Yolanda Bavan, Mary Farrell, Al Freeman, Jr.

A Funny Thing Happened on the Way to the Forum, book by Burt Shevelove and Larry Gelbart, music and lyrics by Stephen Sondheim, directed by Danny Dayton, with Danny Dayton, Eddie Phillips, Avril Gentles, Irving Harmon, Ed Preble, Edmund Gaynes, Linda Donovan, Evan Thompson, Jerry Lycee, Mark Stone, Douglas Norwick, Don Deleo

Unexpected Guest, by Agatha Christie, directed by Michael Kahn, with Joan Fontaine, Dennis Patrick, James Coco, Myra Carter, Guy Spaull, Eleanor Phelps, Stephen Scott, Herbert Foster, Ian Wilder

A Remedy for Winter, by Leonard Spiegelglass, directed by Charles Forsythe, with Dana Andrews, Susan Oliver

Madame Mousse, by Jean Pierre Aumont, adapted by Erich Segal, directed by Ward Baker, with Molly Picon, Jean Pierre Aumont, Estelle Winwood, Pierre Olaf, Marcia Rodd, Tony Musante

Nobody Loves an Albatross, by Ronald Alexander, directed by Perry Bruskin, with Dane Clark, Sherry Britton, Katherine Justice, James Dukas, Joy Stark, Isabelle Sanford, William Shust, Leonard Ross, Edmund Williams, Michael Enserro, Ina Miller, Norman Makaye, Evelyn Russell

So Much of Earth, So Much of Heaven, by Henry Denker, adapted from Ugo Betti's play, directed by Edward Parone, with Claude Rains, Leueen MacGrath, Larry Gates, Lester Rawlins, Joanna Miles, Harris Yulin, Howard Honig

Mrs. Dally Has a Lover, by William Hanley, with Arlene Francis, Ralph Meeker

Spring of 1966

American Conservatory Theatre in Repertory, William Ball, director

Six Characters in Search of an Author, by Luigi Pirandello, directed by Byron Ringland, with Scott Hylands, Austin Pendleton, Jacqueline Coslow, Charlene Polite, Harry Frazier, Tom Dement, Judith Mihalyi, Clarence Morley, Robin Gammell

Uncle Vanya, by Anton Chekhov, directed by Allen Fletcher, with Joan Croydon, Ray Reinhardt, Richard Gysart, G. Wood, Carol Teitel, Harry Frazier, Janice Young, Ramon Bieri, Jay Doyle, Jacqueline Coslow, Deann Mears, Josephine Nichols, Clarence Morley

Under Milk Wood, by Dylan Thomas, original conception by William Ball, with Ray Reinhardt, Robin Gammell, Paul Shenar, Theodore Sorel, Richard A. Dysart, Carol Teitel, Deann Mears, Joan Croydon, Judith Milhalyi, Janice Young, Rene Auberjonois, Jay Doyle, Scott Hylans

Beyond the Fringe, by Jonathan Miller, Peter Cook, Dudley Moore and Alan Bennett, directed by René Auberjonois, with René Auberjonois, Robin Gammell, Austin Pendleton, Charles Siebert

Tiny Alice, by Edward Albee, directed by Mark Megin, with Harry Frazier, Ray Reinhardt, Paul Shenar, Al Alu, Deann Mears

Death of a Salesman, by Arthur Miller, directed by Allen Fletcher, with Richard A. Dysart, Carol Teitell, Scott Hylands, Ted Sorel, Austin Pendleton, Janis Young, Harry Frazier, G. Wood, Paul Shenar, Judith Mihalyi, Thomas Dement, Al Alu, Jacqueline Coslow, Carlene Polite

1966

The Owl and the Pussycat, by Bill Manhoff, directed by Alan Alda, with Alan Alda, Cicely Tyson

Life with Father, by Howard Lindsay and Russell Crouse, adapted from the book by Clarence Day, directed by John Drew Devereaux, with Tom Ewell, Ludi Claire, Holly Hill, John McGovern, Adelle Rasey, Bonnie Boland, Kevin Conlon, Alan Cabal, Shawn McGill, John Madden, Karl Nielsen, Kitty Barling, Margaret Raphael, Marlene Ash, Laurie Crews, Harry Packwood

The Midnight Ride of Alvin Blum, by Donald Honig and Leon Arden, with Christina Crawford, Tony Roberts, Fred Clark

The Thinking Man, by John Tobias, directed by Richard Altman, with George Grizzard, Rita Gam, Roy Poole, Barbara Mattes, John Braden, Jerry Mickey, Lance Cunard

Mary, Mary, by Jean Kerr, directed by Scott McKay, with Betsy Palmer, Scott McKay, Paul McGrath, Richard Clarke, Judy Lewis

Riverwind, by John Jennings, with Lisa Kirk, Robert Alda

The Subject Was Roses, by Frank D. Gilroy, with Maureen O'Sullivan, Chester Morris

The Coffee Lover, by Stefan Kanfer and Jess Korman, directed by Morton daCosta, with Alexis Smith, Gabriel Dell, Vincent Gardenia, Truman Gaige, Gene Wood, Tony Lo Bianco, Linda Eskenas, Tracy Newman, Sandie Lessin, Saeed Jaffrey

Send Us Your Boy, by Jack Douglas, with Paul Ford

The Persecution and Assassination of Jean-Paul Marat as Performed by Inmates of the Asylum at Charenton Under the Direction of Marquis De Sade, by Peter Weiss, directed by Ben Janney and Nell Nugent, with Peter Bromilow, Ralph Clanton, Harvey Jason, Jack Ramage, Tom Rosqui, Stephen Scott, Barbara Stanton, Dorothy Tristan, Cherry Davis, Josip Elic, Peter Johl, James Sullivan, Lee Kissman, Richard Lundin, Yvonne Vincic

The Best of Burlesque, directed by Jack Vaughan, with Sherry Britton

Help Stamp Out Marriage, by Keith Waterhouse and Willis Hall, directed by George Abbott

1967

Generation, by William Goodhart, with Hans Conried

Spider's Web, by Agatha Christie, directed by Eric Berry, with Joan Fontaine, Eric Berry, Richard Clarke, Peter Pagan, Michael d'Forrest, Jean Bruno, Herbert Foster, Frank Macintosh, Kathryn Baumann, John Cameron, John Stewart

Any Wednesday, by Muriel Resnik, directed by Don Porter, with Don Porter, Rosemary Prinz, Peggy Converse, Ryan MacDonald

What Did We Do Wrong? written and directed by Henry Denker, with Paul Ford, Flora Campbell, Bruce Hyde, Gregory Rozakis, Caroline Kemp, Roy Providence, John Buckwalter

The Impossible Years, by Bob Fisher and Arthur Marx, with Tom Ewell

Luv, by Murray Schisgal, with Betsy Palmer

A Delicate Balance, by Edward Albee, directed by June Havoc, with June Havoc, William Prince, Jane Hoffman, Wendell K. Phillips, Lucille Patton, Salome Jens

Barefoot in the Park, by Neil Simon, directed by Harvey Medlinsky, with Joan Bennett, Charles Korvin, Christina Crawford, Angus Duncan, James Beard, Morris Kalman

The Seven Deadly Arts, by Harold J. Kennedy and Robert Koesis, with Caesar Romero, Carole Mathews, Lon Gardner, Elaine Giftos, Robert Koesis, Donna Pearson, Harold J. Kennedy

Wait Until Dark, by Frederick Knott, directed by Porter Van Zandt, with Barbara Bel Geddes, James Tolkan, Joseph Mascolo, Leslie Grega, Beeson Carroll, Barry Hoffman, Beau James, Michael Baseleon

She Loves Me, book by Joe Masteroff, adapted from a play by Miklos Laszlo, music by Jerry Bock, lyrics by Sheldon Harnick, directed by Milton Lyon, with Jeanie Carson, Biff McGuire, Ray Allen, Robert Mesrobian, Ray Fry, Steve Kraft, John Mintun, Tracey Phelps, Tom Shields, Larry Kurt

A Singular Man, by J. P. Donleavy, directed by Leo Garen, with E. G. Marshall, Sally Kellerman, Dick Schaal, Millie Slavin, Barbara Barrie

1968

The Little Foxes, by Lillian Hellman, original stage production by Mike Nichols, with Geraldine Page, Richard Dysart, Betty Field, John Beal, Jack Manning, Franklin Kiser, Russell Gold, Mary Sullivan, Gertrude Jeanette, André Womble

Desk Set, by William Marchant, directed by Gus Schirmer, with Shirley Booth, Paul McGrath, Ray Fulmer, Evelyn Page, Yolande Bavan, Alice Spivak, Liz Sheridan, Betty Linton, Peter Shawn, Alan James

The Star Spangled Girl, by Neil Simon, directed by Frank Corsaro, with Keir Dullea, Terry Kiser, K. C. Townsend

Black Comedy/The White Liars, by Peter Shaffer, directed by Paul Melton, with Dick Shawn, Joan Darling, John Horn, Diana Walker, Paul Benedict, Jerry Terheyden, Florence Tarlow, John O'Leary

Don't Drink the Water, by Woody Allen, directed by Ross Bowman, with Hans Conried, Dody Goodman, Joan McCall, Peter Helm, John Hallow, Roy Monsell, Don Draper, Luke Andreas, Joe Endes, J. Frank Lucas

The Odd Couple, by Neil Simon, directed by Mike Kellin, with George Gobel, Mike Kellin, Nathaniel Frey, Don Simms, Charles Randall, Harry Eno, Lois de Banzie, Diane de Lorian

The Lion in Winter, by James Goldman, directed by Larry Arrick, with Arlene Francis, Martin Gabel, Ron Leibman, Micheal Hawkins, Anne Draper, Douglas Travis, Alan Howard

Private Lives, by Noël Coward, directed by Richard Barr, with Joan Fontaine, Peter Pagan, Patricia Cutts, Georgia Healsip

Everybody's Girl, by John Patrick, with Vivian Vance

Cactus Flower, by Abe Burrows, adapted from a play by Pierre Barrillet and Jean-Pierre Gredy, directed by George Sherman, with Craig Stevens, Alexis Smith, Philip Cusack, Jenny O'Hara, Rudolph Willrich, Marcella Martin, Laura Miller, Errol Selsby, Arn Weiner

1969

You Know I Can't Hear You When the Water's Running, by Robert Anderson, directed by Eddie Bracken, with Eddie Bracken, Robert Anderson, Michaele Myers, Robert Elston, Susan Bracken, Sherman Lloyd

The Show Off, by George Kelly, directed by John McQuiggan, with George Grizzard, Jessie Royce Landis, Joseph Bird, Monica Lovett, Martha Bundy, Drew Snyder, Donald Gantry, Harley Hackett, Robert Paget

The Chic Live, by Arthur Marx and Robert Fisher, directed by George Sherman, with James Whitmore, Audra Lindley, Patricia McAneny, Tom Urich, Milo Bolton

There's a Girl in My Soup, by Terence Frisby, directed by William Shatner, with William Shatner, Jill Haworth, James Valentine, Anne Murray, Linda Simon, John Eames, Paul Collins

Why I Went Crazy, by Charles Dizenzo, a David Merrick production, directed by Joshua Logan, with Imogene Coca, Arnold Stang, Richard Castellano, Candy Azzara, Armand Assante, Mort Marshall

Spofford, by Herman Shumlin, adapted from the novel *Reuben, Reuben* by Peter DeVries, directed by Gordon Hunt, with Hans Conried, Annette Hunt, Mary Cooper, Eileen Letchworth, Hansford Rowe, Martha Miller, Phillip Schopper, Kathleen Morrison, Ralph Drischell, Fred Miller, Linda Parrish

The Prime of Miss Jean Brodie, by Jay Allen, adapted from the novel by Muriel Spark, directed by Porter Van Zandt, with Betsy Palmer, Douglas Watson, Paddy Croft, Remak Ramsay, Jane Hallaran, Robert Blackburn, Janice Mars, Judy Dowd, Maureen Mooney, Swoosie Kurtz

The Sound of Murder, by William Fairchild, directed by Porter Van Zandt, with Jeannie Carson, Biff McGuire, Hurd Hatfield, Olive Deering, Swoosie Kurtz

Janus, by Carolyn Green, directed by Burry Fredrik, with Myrna Loy, Caroline Green, William Roerick, Charles Braswell, Earl Montgomery, Lizabeth Pritchett

A Place for Polly, by Lonnie Coleman, directed by Arthur A. Seidelman, with Joan Hacket, Darryl Hickman, Evelyn Russel, Betsy von Furstenburg, Michael Hadge, Leona Maricle, Gordon B. Clarke, Humbert Allen Astredo, Walt Wanderman

Butterflies Are Free, by Leonard Gershe, directed by Milton Katselas, with Keir Dullea, Maureen O'Sullivan, Blythe Danner, Michael Zaslow

South Pacific, music by Richard Rodgers, lyrics by Oscar Hammerstein II, book by Oscar Hammerstein II and Joshua Logan, adapted from James A. Michener's *Tales of the South Pacific*, directed by Leslie Hornby, with Paul Ukena, Sandra Deel

1970

Dames at Sea, by George Haimsohn and Robin Miller, music by Jim Wise, with Julie Newmar, Marian Mercer

The Tender Trap, by Max Shulman and Robert Paul Smith, with William Shatner

The Boys in the Band, by Mart Crowley

Best of Friends, by James Elward, directed by Eugene O'Sullivan, with Shirley Booth, Donald Woods, Patrick McVey, Joe Henderson, Jacque Lynn Colton, Tom Brannum, Jennifer Warren, David Rosenbaum, Michaele Myers

Boeing-Boeing, by Marc Camoletti, English adaptation by Beverly Cross, with Van Johnson

The Secretary Bird, by William Douglas Home, directed by Porter Van Zandt, with Edward Mulhare, Inga Swenson

Signpost to Murder, by Monty Doyle, directed by Charles Maryan, with David McCallum, Tanny McDonald, Peter Rogan, John Leighton, Shawn McAllister, Jerome Raphael

Blithe Spirit, by Noël Coward, with Noel Harrison

Relatively Speaking, by Alan Ayckbourn, directed by Ben Janney, with Joan Fontaine, Ian Martin, Miranda Fellows, Neil Hunt

An Evening of Laughter and Music, conductor/Norman Geller, with Phil Ford, Mimi Hines

Play It Again, Sam, by Woody Allen, with George Gobel

Light Up the Sky, by Moss Hart, directed by Harold J. Kennedy, with Kitty Carlisle, Jan Sterling, Sam Levene, Kay Medford, Mark O'Daniels, Harold J. Kennedy, Michael Goodwin, Peter Adams, Jack Collard, Peggy Winslow

The Price, with Joseph Buloff, Douglass Watson

1971

Plaza Suite, by Neil Simon, directed by Jeremiah Morris, with Barry Nelson, Dorothy Loudon, Carol Mayo Jenkins, Epy Baca, Richard Alleman

Forty Carats, by Jay Allen, adapted from a play by Barillet and Grede, directed by Charles Maryan, with Barbara Britton, Robert Darnell, Nancy Cushman, Gil Rogers, Barbara Stanton, Tracy Brooks Swope, Ed Fuller, Robert Dannenberg, Minette Hirsch, Christopher Czukor, Greg Callahan

The Mousetrap, by Agatha Christie, directed by Noel Harrison, with Noel Harrison, Paul Collins, Cara Duff-MacCormack, Rudolph Willrich, Daryn Kent, Ivan Smith, Allan Frank, Marie Paxton

I Do! I Do! book and lyrics by Tom Jones, music by Harvey Schmidt, adapted from the play *The Four Poster* by Jan De Hartog, originally produced by David Merrick, originally directed by Gower Champion, musical direction by Leonard Oxley, with Patrice Munsel, Stephen Douglas

Marriage & Money, directed by Rip Torn, with Geraldine Page, Rip Torn, Muni Seroff

Promenade, All! by David V. Robison, directed by William Francisco, with Hume Cronyn, Anne Jackson, Eli Wallach, Richard Backus

And Miss Reardon Drinks a Little, by Paul Zindel, directed by Jerry Adler, with Sandy Dennis, Salome Jens, Mel Dowd, Helen Page Camp, Walt Wanderman, Yvonne Vincic, David Friedman

The Right Honourable Gentleman, by Michael Dyne, directed by Roderick Cook, with Edward Mulhare, Beatrice Straight, Carolyn Lagerfelt, John High, DeAnn Mears, Guy Spaull, Edward Holmes, Joan Croydon, Ellen Tovatt, Rex Thompson, George Taylor, Mary Alan Hokanson, Laurinda Barrett

The Warm Peninsula, by Joe Masteroff, directed by Jack O'Brien, with Tammy Grimes, Jan Sterling, Jeoffrey Scott, Theodore Sorel, Edith Meiser, Michael Prince, James Whittle

Norman, Is That You? by Ron Clark and Sam Bobrick, directed by Charles Olsen, designed by John Pitts, with Hans Conried, Charlotte Rae, Alec Murphy, Peter Simpson, Judith Jordan

The Big Coca-Cola Swamp in the Sky, by Jay Broad, directed by Jose Quintero, with Colleen Dewhurst, Chris Sarandon

Fiddler on the Roof, book by Joseph Stein, lyrics by Sheldon Harnick, music by Jerry Block, directed and choreographed by Frank Coppola, with Mike Kellin, Susan Willis, Avril Gentles, Fyv Finkel, Lee Horwin, Madeline Miller, Stuart Howard, Christopher Carroll, Elizabeth Hale, John Bentley, Fred Weiss, Dallas Alinder, George Axler, Peter Bosche

1972

1776, book by Peter Stone, music and lyrics by Sherman Edwards, directed and choreographed by Edward Roll, with Don Perkins, Bruce Mackay, Peter Lombard, Walter Charles, Jerry Lanning, Joneal Joplin, Ann Clements, Ben Rayson, James Cade, Leslie Miller, Brad Tyrrell, Skedge Miller, Keith Perry, Tom Sinclair, K. C. Wilson, Mervin Crook, Rick Perry

Last of the Red Hot Lovers, by Neil Simon, directed by Tom Porter, with Sid Caesar, Mimi Kennedy, Jill O'Hara, Doris Roberts

See How They Run, by Phillip King, directed by Christopher Hewett, with Mickey Rooney, Joan Bassie, Paddy Croft, George Pentecost, Benjamin H. Slack, Ariel Sebastian, Steve Parris, Jon Barry Wilder, Geoff Garland

The Girl in the Freudian Slip, by William F. Brown, directed by Herbert Machiz, with Eddie Bracken, Lewis J. Stadlen, Leora Dana, Donald Hotton, Elizabeth Perry, Cindy Hannah

Who Killed Santa Claus? by Terence Feely, directed by Stockton Briggle, with Arlene Francis, Ed Zimmerman, George Gitto, George Backman, Louis Edmonds, Caroline Lagerfelt, Michael Tolaydo, W. K. Stratton

Conflict of Interest, by Jay Broad, directed by Jery Adler, with Barry Nelson, Walter Abel, Scott McKay, William Prince, Dan Frazer, Iris Brooks, Lee Doyle, Gary Gage, William Gibberson, Paul Haney, Anna-Marie McKay, Donegan Smith

Dial M for Murder, by Frederick Knott, directed by Eric Berry, with Joan Fontaine, Richard Clarke, Eric Berry, Norman Barrs, Bob Brooks

Jacques Brel Is Alive and Well and Living in Paris, music by Jacques Brel, lyrics and additional material by Eric Blau and Mort Shuman, directed by Bill Francisco, with Jean Pierre Aumont, Eileen Barnett, Sidney Ben-Zali, Alan Brasington, Alice Evans

Poor Richard, by Jean Kerr, directed by Charles Maryan, with Noel Harrison, Robert Darnell, Nancy Pinkerton, Saylor Creswell, Kathleen Miller

The Gingerbread Lady, by Neil Simon, directed by Jeremiah Morris, with Nancy Kelly, Maureen Silliman, Neil Flanagan, Frank Savino, Manuel Sebastian, Lois Markle

Remember Me, written and directed by Ronald Alexander, with Robert Stack, Eileen Heckart, Marian Seldes, Hugh Reilly, Frances Helm, Barbara Stanton, Nicolas Surovy, Barbara Worthington, Linda Martin

Hello, Dolly! book by Michael Stewart, music and lyrics by Jerry Herman (adapted from the play *The Matchmaker* by Thornton Wilder), directed by Lucia Victor, with Anne Russell, Tanny McDonald, Paul Keith, Ed Goldsmid, Roseann Palma, Ted Bloecher, Estelle Tyner, Melody Gale, Jay Foote, Arnott Mader, Coley Worth

1973

A Song for Cyrano, by J. Vincent Smith, music and lyrics by Robert Craig Wright and George Forrest, directed by Jose Ferrer, with Jose Ferrer, Willi Burke, Don McKay, Edmund Lyndeck, Keith Kaldenberg, Marshall Borden, Helon Blount, Adam Petroski

6 RMS RIV VW, by Bob Randall, directed by Jerry Adler, with Jerry Orbach, Marcia Rodd, Jennifer Warren, Nancy R. Pollock, Randall Robbins, Alex Colon, Madeleine Fisher, Edmund Day

Twigs, by George Furth, staged by Bud Coffey, with Sada Thompson, Herbert Nelson, Jack Murdock, Mark Dawson, James Noble, Macintyre Dixon, Walter Klavun, Ned Farster

Suddenly at Home, by Francis Durbridge, directed by Peter Levin, with Jack Cassidy, Scott McKay, Valerie French, Kathryn Walker, Laurinda Barrett, Veleka Gray, Anthony Palmer, Edward Holmes

The Jockey Club Stakes, by William Douglas Home, directed by Cyril Ritchard, with Wilfred Hyde-White, Ronald Drake, Dillon Evans, Caroline Lagerfelt, Michael Lewis, Rudolph Willrich, Norman Barrs, Christopher Bernau, Ethel Drew, Chet Carlin, Douglas Norwick, Enid Rodgers, Roy Cooper

The Gershwin Years, music by George Gershwin, lyrics by Ira Gershwin, directed and choreographed by Bob Herget, with Barbara Cook, Nancy Dussault, Helen Gallagher, Harold Lang, Steve Ross, Edward Morris

The Poison Tree, by Ronald Ribman, directed by Arthur Sherman, with Al Freeman, Jr., Ron O'Neal, Moses Gunn, Richard Jordan, Daniel Barton, Charles Bergansky, Gerry Black, Howard Green, Parker McCormick, Don Plumley, Martin Shakar, Arlen Dean Snyder, Dennis Tate, Charles Turner

Preservation Hall Jazz Band—presented by arrangement with Stephen Baffrey, with DeDe Pierce (trumpet), Billie Pierce (piano), Josiah Cie Frazier (drums), Big Jim Robinson (trombone), Willie Humphrey (clarinet), Allan Jaffe (tuba)

Summer & Smoke, by Tennessee Williams, directed by Jeffrey Hayden, with Eva Marie Saint, Ronny Cox, Linda Kelsey, Harry Ellerbe, Jon Lormer, Amzie Strickland, Christine Avila, Mark Herron, Ethel Dugan, Howard Brunner, Ben Jones, Darrell Hayden, Sharon Beard, Oswaldo Calvo

The New Mount Olive Motel, by Steven Gethers, directed by Burt Brinckerhoff, with James Whitmore, Audra Lindley, Alan Manson, Maureen Silliman, Adam Arkin, William Duell, Josip Elic, Harry Eno, Rene Enriquez, Sam Gray, Robert Kya-hill, Alek Primrose, Shev Rogers

Prisoner of 2nd Avenue, by Neil Simon, directed by Tom Porter, with Art Carney, Barbara Carney, Ruth Jaroslow, Jane Courtney, Elsa Raven, Willard Waterman

Butley, by Simon Gray, directed by James Hammerstein, original London production by Harold Pinter, with Brian Bedford, Paul Jott, Barbara Lester, Sharon Laughlin, James Hummert, Saylor Creswell, Linda Charet

1974

Sleuth, by Anthony Shaffer, directed by Warren Crane, with Patrick MacNee, Jordan Christopher, Stanley Rushton, Robin Mayfield, Liam McNulty

The Sunshine Boys, by Neil Simon, directed by James Bernardi, with Jack Guilford, Lou Jacobi, Jeremy Stevens, Lee Meredith, Rosetta LeNorie, John Newhouse, Mark Rodman

Godspell, music and lyrics by Stephen Schwartz, directed by Larry Whiteley, original New York production directed by John-Michael Teblak, with Claudine Cassan, Randy Martin, Judy Congess, David Michaels, Bruce Connelly, Melinda Tanner, Barbara Deutsch, Michael Tucci, Michele Mais, James G. Vaughan

Finishing Touches, by Jean Kerr, directed by Wayne Carson, with Barbara Bel Geddes, Laurence Hugo, Gene Rupert, Caroline Groves, Jeanne Lange, Edward Clinton, Andrew Ian McMillan, Richard Backus

Crown Matrimonial, by Royce Ryton, directed by Ben Janney, with Eileen Herlie, David McCallum, Patrick Horgan, Paddy Croft, Marie Paxton, Enid Rodgers, Cynthia Hopkins, Elizabeth Swain, Donald Bishop

Born Yesterday, by Garson Kanin, directed by Stephen Porter, with Sandy Dennis, Gary Merrill, Peter Brandon, Eugene Stuckmann, Raymond Cole, Guy Spaull, Joan Croydon, James Carnelia, Sally Birckhead

That Championship Season, by Jason Miller, directed by John Mahon, with Broderick Crawford, Danny Aiello, Martin Cassidy, Jack Collard, Peter Maclean

Oh Coward! words and music by Noël Coward, directed by Roderick Cook, with Constance Towers, Michael Allinson, Joe Masielo

One Flew over the Cuckoo's Nest, by Dale Wasserman, adapted from the novel by Ken Kesey, directed by John Mahon, with Pernell Roberts, Manu Tupou, Louisa Horton, James Lonigro, Aleta, John Mahon, Scott Bruno, Patti Miller, Eugene Hobgood, Leonard Parker, Ken Konopka, Shelia Russell, Thomas J. Kubiak, Barry Vigon, John McPeak

Shay, by Anne Commire, directed by Edward Hastings, with Sada Thompson, Robert Gerringer, Tresa Hughes, James Sutorius, Barbara Dirickson, Dallas Greer, Edward Fuller, Polly Holliday

Absurd Person Singular, by Alan Ayckbourn, directed by Eric Thompson, with Richard Kiley, Sandy Dennis, Geraldine Page, Larry Blyden, Carole Shelley, Tony Roberts

No, No, Nanette, book by Otto Harbach and Frank Mandel, music by Vincent Youmans, lyrics by Irving Caesar and Otto Harbach, director–choreographer Bill Guske, with Helen Gallagher, Jerry Antes, Marsha Bagwell, Kevin Daly, Sara Louise, Jeannine Moore, Carol Swarbrick, Marilyn Seven, Marilynn Scott, Thomas Ruisinger

Hair, book and lyrics by Gerome Ragni and James Rado, music by Galt MacDermot, musical direction by Margaret Harris, with Jeffrey Hillock, Denise Delapenha, Larry Marshall, Shelley Plimpton, Gloria Goldman, Arnold McCuller, Tom Schuyler

Tobacco Road, written by Jack Kirkland, adapted by Haila Stoddard from the novel by Erskine Caldwell, music by Don Elliott, lyrics by Haila Stoddard and Joan Wilde, directed by Thomas Gruenewald, with Jeanne Bolan, Ed Bryce, Dorothy Bryce, Edward Donlan, Bert Gibson, Jo Henderson, George Hillman, Gene Lindsey, Joseph Pichette, Jill Rose, Gary Silow, Howard Sims, Diane Stilwell, Bobra Suiter, Joan Wile, Bob Wittenstein, Richard Yarnell

1975

Something's Afoot, book, music and lyrics by Davis Vos, James McDonald and Robert Gerlach, directed by Tony Tanner, musical direction by Milton Setzer, with Pat Carroll, Gary Beach, Gary Gage, Jack Schmidt, Willard Beckham, Barbara Heuman, Liz Sheridan, Boni Enten, Marc Jordan, Sel Vitella

God's Favorite, by Neil Simon, directed by Tom Porter, with Godfrey Cambridge, Ricard Kuss, Anna Berger, Philip Cusack, Minnie Gentry, Nick LaTour, Ellin Ruskin, David McDaniel

My Fat Friend, by Charles Lawrence, directed by Ben Janney, with John Astin, Patty Duke Astin, Peter McRobbie, Bruce Gray

Cat on a Hot Tin Roof, by Tennessee Williams, directed by Porter Van Zandt, with Sandy Dennis, David Selby, Ronald Bishop, James Murtaugh, Peggy Cosgrave, Don Draper, Gertrude A. Smith, Larry Swansen, Geraldine Kay

The Hot L Baltimore, by Lanford Wilson, directed Jeremiah Morris, with Jan Sterling, Larry Carr, Stan Edelman, Ray Edelstein, Clement Fowler, Sylvia Gassell, Susan Harney, Albert M. Ottenheimer, Donald Warfield, Erica Weingast

For My Last Number, by Steven Gethers, directed by Tony Tanner, with Paul Sorvino, Caroline Lagerfelt, Carol Mayo Jenkins, William Duell

Culture Caper, by Jerome Chodorov, directed by Edward Chodorov, with Gabe Dell, Jill O'Hara, Harold Gary, Pat Englund, Jacqueline Bertrand, Jim Jansen, Judith Lesley, Jean Gross, Jean Pierre Stewart, James Tolken

The Two of Us, by Michael Frayn, directed by John Clark, with Lynn Redgrave, David Leary, Carlos Carrasco, John Tillinger

In Praise of Love, by Terence Rattigan, directed by Michael Bawtree, with Tammy Grimes, Michael Allinson, Sam Gray, Gary Tomlin

The Good Doctor, by Neil Simon, adapted from stories by Anton Chekhov, directed by Ronald Roston, with Theodore Bikel, David Hurst, Lynn Milgrim, Rose Arrick, Lee Golden

Irene, book by Hugh Wheeler and Joseph Stein, adapted from original play by James Montgomery, music by Harry Tierney, lyrics by Joseph McCarthy, choreographed by Gwen Hillier, directed by John H. Love III, with Jack Fletcher, Jane Connell, Pamela Peadon, Peter Lombard, Terry Saunders, G. Wayne Hoffman, Barbara Erwin, L. J. Rose

A Little Night Music, book by Hugh Wheeler, music and lyrics by Stephen Sondheim, directed by Ruth Mitchell, with Patrice Munsell, John Michael King, Edith Meiser, Marti Morris, Rod Loomis, Karen Zanker, Jay Lowman

1976

Roberta, book and lyrics by Otto Harbach, music by Jerome Kern, choreographed by Leo Muller, directed by Leslie Cutler, with Ruth Warrick, Roderick Cook, Vicki Velmonte, Patti Davis, Carol Zwarbrick, Bill Hunt, Rick Gardner, Lola Kramer, Danny Carroll

Noël Coward in Two Keys, by Noël Coward, directed by Richard Barr, with Richard Kiley, Jan Ferrand, Teresa Wright, Spain Logue

The Fatal Weakness, by George Kelly, directed by Jeffrey Hayden, with Eva Marie Saint, John McMartin, Charlotte Moore, Mary Ann Chin, Howard McGillin, Regina David

Awake and Sing, by Clifford Odets, directed by Henry T. Weinstein, with Howard da Silva, Tresa Hughes, Lynn Milgrim, George Axler, Bruce Adler, Tom Capps, Carl Don, William Jaeger, Mitchell Jason

Zorba, book by Joseph Stein, music by John Kander, lyrics by Fred Ebb, directed by Jay Harnik, choreographed by George Bunt, originally produced and directed by Harold Prince, adapted from *Zorba The Greek* by Nikos Kazantzakis, with Theodore Bikel, Taina Elg, Marsha Tamaroff, Jana Robbins, Dennis Birchall, Arne Gundersen, Gary Middleton, Sal Provenza

The House of Blue Leaves, music and lyrics by John Guare, directed by Brian Murray, with Eli Wallach, Anne Jackson, Nancy Franklin, Ted Beniades, Margaret Whitton, Jacob Milligan, Elsa Raven, Laurie Copeland, K. T. Baumann

Checking Out, by Allen Swift, directed by Jerry Adler, with Allen Swift, Joan Copeland, Michael Gorrin, Hy Anzell, Larry Bryggman, Jonathan Moore, William Jaeger, Norman Barrs, Tazewell Thompson, Kurt Garfield

1977

A Party with Betty Comden and Adolph Green, directed by John Fitzpatrick

Absent Friends, by Alan Ayckbourn, directed by Eric Thompson, with Eli Wallach, Anne Jackson, Lee Richardson, Meg Wynn Owen, Jacob Brooke,

Dale Hodges

The Master Builder, by Henrick Ibsen, directed by Edwin Sherin, with Jane Alexander, Richard Kiley, Teresa Wright, Thomas Toner, Joel Stedman, Mary Catherine Wright, Shepperd Strudwick

Bubbling Brown Sugar, book by Loften Mitchell, concept by Rosetta Le Noire, directed by Ron Abbott, with Richard Brown, Mable Lee, Ned Wright, Marjorie Barnes, Jan Birse, Terri Lindsey, Francine Claudia Moore, Glover Parham, Jai Oscar St. John, Thomas Tofel

The Royal Family, by George S. Kaufman and Edna Ferber, directed by Burry Fredrik, with Sandy Dennis, Gale Sondergaard, Curt Dawson, Ellen Fiske, Maurice Copeland, Edward Earle, Peggy Cosgrave, Gene Rupert, Terry Layman, Urylee Leonardos, Nicholas Martin, Mark Fleischman, Kathleen Costello, Val Roy Gerisher, Tom Capps, Jerry Rodgers

California Suite, by Neil Simon, directed by John Clark, with Lynn Redgrave, Joe Silver, Paul Shyre, Chevi Colton, Pat Trott

Tricks of the Trade, by Sidney Michaels, directed by Morton Da Costa, with William Shatner, Yvette Mimieux

An Almost Perfect Person, by Judith Ross, directed by Zoe Caldwell, with Colleen Dewhurst, Rex Robbins, George Hearn

King of Hearts, book by Steve Tesich, music by Peter Link, lyrics by Jacob Brackman, choreographed by Miguel Godreau, directed by A. J. Antoon, with Robby Benson, John Braden, Abigail Haness, Kurt Knudson, Tony Kraber, Michael McCarthy, Allison McKay, Judith Anna Roberts, Elliott Savage, Gordon Weiss, Martin Zagon

1978

Side by Side by Sondheim, music and lyrics by Stephen Sondheim, additional music by Leonard Bernstein, Mary Rodgers, Jules Stein, directed by Ned Sherrin, with Arlene Francis, Carol Swarbrick, David Chaney, Bonnie Schon

Gracious Living, by Samuel Taylor, directed by Edwin Sherin, with Tammy Grimes, Paul Hecht, Patricia Rutledge, Jamie Ross, Pierre Epstein

Guys and Dolls, book by Jo Swerling and Abe Burrows, music and lyrics by Frank Loesser, choreography by George Bunt, directed by Charles Gray, with Jo Sullivan, Julius LaRosa, Ben Kapen, Laura Kenyon, Thomas Lee Sinclair, Carl Nicholas, Fran Stevens, Lee Sandman, Arthur Ostrin, Robert Barry, David Berk

Out on a Limb, by James Thurber, adapted by Haila Stoddard, music by Fred Hellerman, lyrics by Fran Minkhoff, directed by Stuart Vaughan, with Douglas Fairbanks, Jr., Meg Wynn Owen, Charlotte Fairchild, Edward Crowley, Steve Riley, Diana Lynne Drew, Tim Cassidy, Ginger Prince

13 Rue de L'Amour, by George Feydeau, adapted by Mawby Green and Ed Feilbert, directed by Basil Langton, with Louis Jourdan, Taina Elg, Bernard Fox, Kathleen Freeman, Laurie Main, James Cook, Stephen Stout, Sherry Skinker

Same Time, Next Year, by Bernard Slade, original New York production by Gene Saks, directed by Warren Crane, with Kathryn Crosby, Tony Russell

The Play's the Thing, a comedy by Ferenc Molnar, adapted by P. G. Wodehouse, directed by Stephen Porter, with Patrice Munsel, Edward Mulhare, Ronald Bishop, James Greene, Anthony Manionis, Dennis McGovern, James Valentine

Donkey's Years, by Michael Frayn, directed by Tony Tanner, with David McCallum, Carole Shelley, Richard Clarke, John Clarkson, Frank Latimore, John Michalsky, Leon Shaw, William Shust, Edward Zang

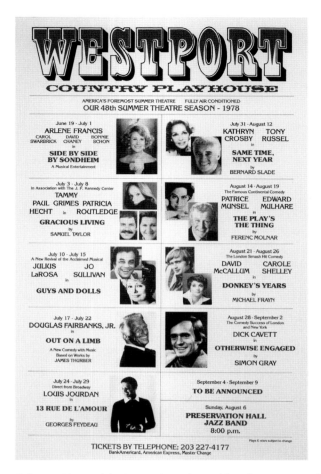

Otherwise Engaged, by Simon Gray, directed by John Horton, with Dick Cavett, Christine Baranski, Louis Edmonds, Jonathan Hogan, John Horton, Carol Mayo Jenkins, Philip Kerr

The Goodbye People, by Herb Gardner, directed by Jeffrey Bleckner, with Louise Lasser, Sam Levene, F. Murray Abraham, Michael Tucker, John K. Carroll, Sammy Smith

1979

The Crucifier of Blood, by Paul Giovanni, directed by Paxton Whitehead, with Paxton Whitehead, Christopher Curry, Timothy Landfield, Tuck Milligan, Cynthia Carle, Robin Chadwick, Joel Colodner, Philip LeStrange

Diversions & Delights, by John Gay, directed by Joseph Hardy, with Vincent Price as Oscar Wilde

The Magic Show, book by Bob Randall, lyrics and music by Stephen Schwartz, adapted for Broadway by Doug Henning, with Joseph Abaldo, Tudi Roach, Donna Lee Marshall, Cindy Cobitt, Robin Wesley, Ron Schwinn, Christopher Lucas, Les Johnson, Ben Felix, Tom Mardirosian

Have a Nice Day, by Cy Howard, directed by Martin Fried, with Darren McGavin, Christine Estabrook, Audra Johnston, Ellen Maxted, Stephen Pearlman, Harold Stuart

Present Laughter, by Noël Coward, directed by Milton Moss, with Louis Jourdan, Lois Markle, Carol Mayo-Jenkins, Lois Diane Hicks, Mark Fleischman, Jamie Ross, Donald Warfield, Laurie Franks, Susan Greenhill, Kermit Brown

The Circle, by W. Somerset Maugham, a co-production with the A.C.T. Company, directed by Stephen Porter, with Daniel Kern, Thomas Oglesby, DeAnn Mears, Barbara Dirickson, Randall Smith, William Paterson, Gerald Lancaster, Marriann Walters, Sydney Walker

The Voice of the Turtle, by John Van Druten, directed by Henry T. Weinstein, with David Cassidy, Kay Lenz, Ann Sachs

Camelot, book and lyrics by Alan Jay Lerner, music by Frederick Loewe, direction by Richard Natkowski, original production directed by Moss Hart, with David Holliday, Jeanne Lehman, Michael J. Stone, Irwin Pearl, Patrick Beatty

Slightly Delayed, by James Prideaux, directed by George Schaefer, with Geraldine Page, Anne Jackson, Kevin McCarthy, Michael Higgins, George Bamford

Once a Catholic, by Mary O'Malley, directed by Michael Ockrent, with Rachel Roberts, Peggy Cass, Roy Poole, Joseph Leon, Pat Falkenhain, Charlie Lang, Terry Calloway, Bill Buell, Virginia Hut

On Golden Pond, by Ernest Thompson, directed by Craig Anderson, with Frances Sternhagen, Tom Aldredge, Ronn Carroll, Barbara Andres, Stan Lachow, Mark Bendo

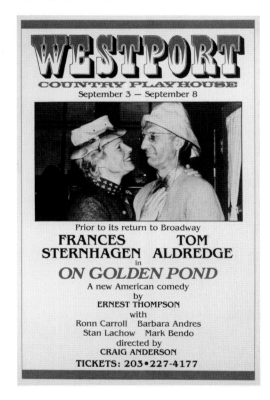

1980

The Streets of New York, by Dion Boucicault, directed by Tony Tanner, with Orson Bean, Farley Granger, Katharine Houghton, Mark Capri, Charles Ryan, Sel Bitella, Lance Davis, June Squibb, Rose Roffman, Jack Schmidt, Paul Hoover, Kathleen Gaffney

Chapter Two, by Neil Simon, directed by Jack V. Booch, with Anita Gillette, David Hedison, Susan Browning, Sal Viscuso

Man of La Mancha, book by Dale Wasserman, music by Mitch Leigh, lyrics by Joe Darion, directed by Gregory Allen Hirsch, with David Atkinson, Gerrianne Raphael, Jack Dabdoub, Walter Blocher, Ted Pejovich, Frances Roth, Marceline Decker, Doug Moore, Ted Forlow, Bob Miressi

Children, by A. R. Gurney, Jr., adapted from a story by John Cheever, directed by John Going, with Sada Thompson, Daren Kelly, Monica Merryman, Gisela Caldwell

Whose Life Is It Anyway? by Brian Clark, directed by Martin Herzer, with Richard Thomas, Catherine Burns, James Higgins, Edmond Genest, Catherine Gaffigan, John Straub, John Berstrom, Mary Boucher, Suzanna Hay, Emil Herrera, Christopher Nelson, Bruce Sterman

My Fair Lady, adapted from George Bernard Shaw's play and Gabriel Pascal's motion picture *Pygmalion*, original production by Moss Hart, book and lyrics by Alan Jay Lerner, music by Frederick Loewe, directed by Bob Herget, with Susan Watson, Michael Allinson, Gary Gage, James Hawthorne, Ada Brown Mather, Eleanor Phelps, Richard White

Horowitz and Mrs. Washington, by Henry Denker, directed by Jack V. Booch, with Sam Levene, Claudia McNeil, Denise Lor, David Rosenbaum, Bernie Passeltiner, Christopher Blount

Tribute, by Bernard Slade, directed by Warren Crane, with Van Johnson, John Carpenter, Annette Hunt, Anita Keal, Laura Beattie, Peggy Cosgrave, Timothy Askew

"Da," by Hugh Leonard, directed by J. Ranelli, with Jack Aranson, Ian Stuart, Virginia Mattis, Kevin O'Leary, George Feeney, Cyntia Carle, Mavis Ray, Curtis J. Armstrong

An April Song, adapted by Albert Marre, from Jean Anouilh's *Leocadia*, music by Mitch Leigh, lyrics by Sammy Cahn, with Glynis Johns, Sam Tsoutsouvas, Julie Boyd, Ruben Singer, Ronald Bishop, Ian Sullivan, Carl Don

1981

Tintypes, a new musical created by Mary Kyte, Mel Marvin and Gary Pearle, directed by Wayne Byron, with Nedra Dixon, Timothy Jerome, Marie King, Mary Catherine Wright, Jerry Zaks

Play It Again, Sam, by Woody Allen, directed by Robert Morse, with Robert Morse, Elaine Ritter, Pamela Sousa, Patrick Tovatt, Lynda Ferguson, Mark Shapiro

Battle of Angels, by Tennessee Williams, directed by Rob Shipp, with John Ritter, Nancy Morgan, Jill O'Hara, Virginia Gibson, Ellen Fiske, Richard Young, Harris Shore, Earl Christopher Williams, Jack Koenig, Rob Shipp, Jenny Sullivan

Talley's Folly, by Lanford Wilson, directed by Burry Fredrik, with David Birney, Meredith Baxter Birney

I Ought to Be in Pictures, by Neil Simon, directed by Frank Marino, with Lawrence Pressman, Deborah Offner, Mimi Cozzens

Romantic Comedy, by Bernard Slade, directed by Tom Troupe, with David McCallum, Dawn Wells, Peggy Cosgrave, Lauar Beattie, Aida Berlyn, Tom Troupe

Images, by David O. Frazier and Joseph J. Garry, music by Serge Lama, Alice Dona, Eve Gilbert, Nachum Heiman, Jean Morlier, Jacques Datin, Emil Stern; lyrics by David O. Frazier, directed and choreographed by Bill Guske, with Joe Masiell, Charles Repole, Jana Robbins, Don Hare, Jarrod Lund, Anne Parks

Sand Castles, by Bob Larbey, directed by Frederick Rolf, with Betsy Palmer, Peter Bergman, Forrest Compton, Elizabeth Hess, Anthony Weaver

Merry Widow, by Victor Leon and Leo Stein, music by Franz Lehar, lyrics by Adrian Ross, directed by Robert Baker, choreographed by Richard Natkowski, with Nancy Shade, Mark Jacoby, Harold Wilcox, Harry Danner, Woody Romoff, Richard Kinter

Educating Rita, by Willy Russell, directed by Mike Ockrent, with Lucie Arnaz, Laurence Luckinbill

To Grandmother's House We Go, by Joanna M. Glass, directed by Burry Fredrik, with Eva Le Gallienne, Lori March, John Beal, Ruth Neslon, Leslie Denniston, Harriet Harris, Alex Wipf, Caroline Lagerfelt

1982

Mornings at Seven, by Paul Osborn, directed by Burry Fredrik, with Shepperd Strudwick, Patricia Morison, Barbara Berjer, Maurice Copeland, Mimi Cozzens, Patricia Englund, Carl Low, Frances Peter, Robert Moberly

The Supporting Cast, by George Furth, directed by Tom Troupe, with Sandy Dennis, Barbara Rush, Peggy Cosgrave, June Dayton, Tom Troupe

The Elephant Man, by Bernard Pomerance, directed by Kevin Conway, with Bruce Davison, Mila Burnette, Stephen D. Newman, William Carden, Edward Gallardo, James Greene, George Guidall, Marilyn Rockafellow, Hansford Rowe

They're Playing Our Song, book by Neil Simon, music by Marvin Hamlisch, lyrics by Carole Bayer Sager, choreographed by Andrea Green, directed by Peter B. Mumford, with Timothy Bottoms, Marsha Skaggs

Gertrude Stein, written by Marty Martin, directed by Milton Moss, with Pat Carroll

Ain't Misbehavin', the Fats Waller musical, musical direction by Arthur Faria, directed by Richard Maltby, Jr., with Deoborah Byrd, Adriane Lenox, Ken Prymus, Eric Riley, Roz Ryan

The Subject Was Roses, by Frank D. Gilroy, directed by Jack V. Booch, with Shaun Cassidy, John McMartin, Betsy Palmer

Lunch Hour, by Jean Kerr, directed by Jack V. Booch, with Cybill Shepherd, James MacArthur, Lynn Milgrim, Patrick Tovatt, Michael Lipton

What I Did Last Summer, by A. R. Gurney, Jr., directed by Melvin Bernhardt, with Barbara Feldon, Eileen Heckart, Mark Arnott, Eve Bennett-Gordon, Ellen Parker, Todd Waring

Mass Appeal, by Bill C. Davis, directed by Geraldine Fitzgerald, with Gavin MacLeod, Charley Lang

Children of a Lesser God, by Mark Medoff, directed by Gordon Davidson, with Rico Peterson, Freda Norman, Mary Beth Barber, Mimi Bensinger, Herbert Duval, Joe Farwell, Charles Jones

1983

Deathtrap, by Ira Levin, directed by John Cullum, with Frank Gorshin, Steve Bassett, Austin Colyer, Emily Frankel Cullum, Doris Belack

Twice Around the Park, by Murray Schisgal, directed by John Vivian, with Anne Jackson, Eli Wallach

Clara's Play, by John Olive, directed by Burry Fredrik, with Jean Stapleton, Jon DeVires, Dave Florek, Paul Perri

I'm Getting My Act Together and Taking It on the Road, music by Nancy Ford, book and lyrics by Gretchen Cryer, choreographed and directed by Word Baker, with Nancy Dussault, Howard Platt, Betty Aberlin, Alan Axelrod, Martin Axelrod, Mark Buchan, Robin Cryer, Dewey Dellay, Gerard Mule, Boonie Strickman

Beyond Therapy, by Christopher Durang, directed by Jerry Zaks, with Fred Grandy, Melanie Chartoff, Jeff Brooks, Jeffrey Hayenga, Melodie Somers, Ian Blackman

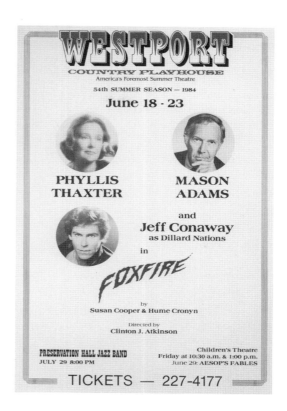

Crimes of the Heart, by Beth Henly, directed by Jack V. Booch, with Lauren Tewes, Marsha Skaggs, Don Howard, Timothy Askew, Amy McKenzie, Janet Newberry

84 Charing Cross Road, by Helene Hanff, directed by Edward Hastings, with Shelley Winters, Donal Donnelly, Fran Barnes, Richard Lederer, Thomas Nahrwold, Susan Pellegrino

The Housekeeper, by James Prideaux, directed by Joe Tillinger, with Cloris Leachman, Noel Harrison

Annie, book by Thomas Meehan, lyrics by Martin Charnin, music by Charles Strouse, choreographed and directed by Robert Fitch, with June Havoc, Alyson Kirk, Tom Avero, Robert Fitch, Judith Bro, James Todkill, Dorothy Stanley, Edmond Dante, Dana Dewes, Sherri Lynn Leidy, Monica Miller, Maura Erin Sullivan, Kimi Parks

The Dining Room, by A. R. Gurney, Jr., directed by Porter Van Zandt, with Bernie Kopell, Reed Birney, Heather Macrae, Stephen Bradbury, Peggy Cosgrave, Mimi Cozzens

The Best Little Whorehouse in Texas, book by Larry L. King and Peter Masterson, music and lyrics by Carol Hall, choreographed by Patti D. Beck, directed by Jack V. Booch, with Edie Adams, Douglas Easley, Mary Yarbrough, Jennifer Butt, Steven Earl-Edwards, Susann Fletcher, Patrick Hamilton, Denise Kellen, Sam Kressen

1984

Foxfire, by Susan Cooper and Hume Cronyn, music by Jonathan Holtzman, directed by Clinton J. Atkinson, with Phyllis Thaxter, Mason Adams, Jeff Conaway, George Cavey, Thomas D. Mahard, Nan Wade

Agnes of God, by John Pielmeier, directed by Frank Marino, with Geraldine Page, Sandy Dennis, Deirdre O'Connell

The Middle Ages, by A. R. Gurney, Jr., directed by Ron Lagomarsino, with Joseph Bottoms, Maeve McGuire, Valerie Mahaffey, Carl Bensen

A "Luv" Musical, book by Jeffrey Sweet, adapted from LUV by Murray Schisgal, music by Howard Marren, lyrics by Susan Birkenhead, choreographed by Jerry Yoder, directed by Jack V. Booch, with Gary Sandy, Marcia Rodd, Stephen Vinovich

Snacks, by Leonard Gershe, directed by Robert Drivas, with Linda Purl, Thomas Calabro, Andrew Bloch, Ray Virta

Joseph and the Amazing Technicolor Dreamcoat, by Tim Rice and Andrew Lloyd Webber, choreographed and directed by Tony Tanner, with Davis Gaines, Liz Larsen, David Ardao, Dennis Courtney, Timmy Fauvell, John Ganzer, Stephen Hope, Robb Hyman, Bryant Lanier, Lorene Palacios, Gordon Stanley, Tom Carter

Breakfast with Les and Bess, by Lee Kalcheim, directed by William Woodman, with Betsy Palmer, Keith Charles, Mark Henderson, John Leonard, Lori Lowe, Frank Maraden

Alone Together, by Lawrence Roman, directed by Arnold Mittelman, with Janis Paige, Kevin McCarthy, Dennis Drake, Alexandra Gersten, Don Howard, Kevin O'Rourke

Not for Keeps, by David Rogers, directed by Burry Fredrik, with Frank Gorshin, Carole Shelley, Sarah Chodoff

Pump Boys and Dinettes, by John Foley, Mark Hardwick, Deoborah Monk, Cass Morgan, John Schimmel and Jim Wann, choreographed and directed by Peter Glazer, with John Foley, Mary Gutzi, Jim Lauderdale, Fern Radov, William Swindler, John Schimmel

The American Dance Machine, by Lee Theodore, produced by Lee Theodore, musical direction by James Raitt, with Tinka Gutrick, Aja Kane, Harold Cromer, Harrison Beal, Newton Cole, Jennifer Dempster, Dan Fletcher, Luba Gregus, Kenneth Hughes, Eric Kaufman, Kelby Kirk, Kenji Nakao, Kim Norr, Mimi Quillian, Ralph Rodriguez, Camille Ross, Claudia Shell, Donna Smythe, Peter Wandel, Donald Young

1985

One for the Tango, adapted by Mawby Green and Ed Feilbert from a comedy by Maria Pacone, directed by Pierre Epstein, with Leslie Caron, Joseph Adams, Tresa Hughes, Lezlie Dalton, Marc Epstein

Harvey, by Mary Chase, directed by Dennis Erdman, with Joel Higgins, Mary Jo Catlett, Jane Gallaway, Richard McKenzie, Elizabeth Berridge, Ethan Phillips, Harvey Vernon and David Keith as Wilson

A Place to Stay, by Richard Culliton, directed by Rob Shipp, with Lucie Arnaz, John Ritter

Evita, lyrics by Tim Rice, music by Andrew Lloyd Webber, directed by Frank Marino, originally directed by Harold Prince produced on Broadway by Robert Stigwood in association with David Land, with Donna Marie Elio, James Sbano, David Brummel, Hal Maxwell, Amy Niles

Upper Broadway, by James Prideaux, directed by Porter Van Zandt, with Nanette Fabray, Woody Romoff, Haviland Morris, James Schilling, Kate Wilkinson

Handy Dandy, by William Gibson, directed by Arthur Storch, with James Whitmore and Audra Lindley

Run for Your Wife, by Ray Cooney, directed by Tony Tanner, with David McCallum, Stephen Temperley, Sybil Lines, Elaine Rinehart, Tom Flagg, I. M. Hobson

On the Level, by Ben Starr, directed by Joseph Bernard, with Shelly Berman, Danielle Brisebois

The Foreigner, by Larry Shue, directed by David Saint, with Bob Denver, Jane Connell, Victor Slezak, Leah Doyle, Granville Ames, Sam Stoneburner, Rick Lawless

Bob Fosse's Dancin', produced by Tom Mallow and James Janek, music and lyrics by Ralph Burns, George M. Cohan, Neil Diamond, Jerry Leiber, Mike Stoller, Bob Haggart, Ray Bauduc, Gil Rodin, Bob Crosby, Johnny Mercer, Harry Warren, Louis Prima, John Phillip Sousa, Barry Mann,

Cynthia Weil, Felix Walker, choreographed by Linda Smith-Polvere, directed by Thomas Sivak, with Celeste Carlucci, Linda Cholodenko, Vincent Cole, Kenneth Comstock, Jim Corti, John Crutchman, Dominique Decaudain, Tina DeLeone, Diana Laurenson

Fall of 1985

'Night Mother, by Marsha Norman, directed by Burry Fredrik, with Eileen Heckart, Sandy Dennis

A Bill of Divorcement, by Clemence Dane, directed by Roderick Cook, with Christopher Walken, Katharine Houghton, Lori March, Richard Council, Kate Hopkins, Marvin Greene, Frank Savino, Ken Parker, Mary Dunne

The News, by Paul Schierhorn, music and lyrics by Paul Schierhorn, choreographed by Wesley Fata, directed by David Rotenberg, with Jeff Conaway, Anthony Crivello, Cheryl Alexander, Frank Baier, Michael Duff, Jonathan Gerber, Anthony Hoylen, Patrick Jude, Lisa Michaelis, Charles Pistone, John Rineheimer, Peter Valentine, Billy Ward

1986

Oh Coward, words and music by Noël Coward, directed by Roderick Cook, with Carole Shelley, Roderick Cook, Patrick Quinn

The Odd Couple, by Neil Simon, directed by John Going, with Rosemary Prinz, Fannie Flagg, Mimi Cozzens, Diane J. Findlay, Michael Fiorella, Rita Gardner, Estelle Kemler, Kirk Thornton

Pirates of Penzance, by Sir W. S. Gilbert and Sir Arthur Sullivan, the ASF production choreographed by Jayne Luke, directed by Larry Carpenter, with George Ede, Jeff McCarthy, Polly Penn, Max Robinson, Cheryl Ann Rossi, Sal Viviano

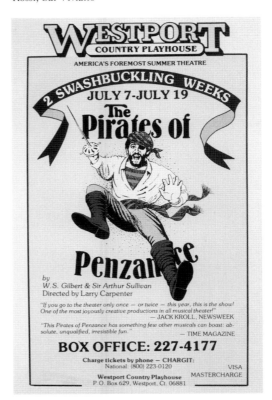

Real Estate, by Louise Page, directed by Andre Ernotte, with Colleen Dewhurst, Peter Michael Goetz, Maureen Anderman, Frank Converse

Pack of Lies, by Hugh Whitemore, directed by Burry Fredrik, with Michael Learned, Eileen Heckart, Charles Cioffi, Edmond Genest, George Taylor, Juli Cooper, Geraldine Court, Elaine Rinehart

Country Cops, by Robert Lord, directed by Tony Tanner, with Conrad Bain, Dennis Bailey, David Harum, Allen Kennedy, Holly Barron

A Woman of Independent Means, by Elizabeth Forsythe Hailey, directed by Norman Cohen, with Barbara Rush

And Miss Reardon Drinks a Little, by Paul Zindel, directed by Larry Arrick, with Sandy Dennis, Anne Meara, DeAnn Mears, Frank Savino, Rosalyn Farinella, Richard K. Johnson, April Shawhan

Brighton Beach Memoirs, by Neil Simon, directed by John Going, with Barbara Andres, Barbara Caruso, Rudy Goldschmidt, Robert Leonard, Alan Mixon, Joyce O'Brien, Sherry Stregack

Never Too Late, by Sumner Arthur Long, directed by Tony Tanner, with Gavin MacLeod, Marion Ross, Michael Countryman, Cynthia Dozier, Patti Macleod, Jan Peters, Richard Voigts

El Grande De Coca Cola, a musical revue by Ron House, Diz White, Alan Shearman, John Neville-Andrews, starring and directed by Ron House, Diz White, Alan Shearman, with Roger Bumpass, Cecilia Arana

1987

Biloxi Blues, by Neil Simon, directed by Nancy Simon, with Robert Cain, Kevin Hardesty, Steve Sherwin, Becky Gelke, Jeri Leer, Brian Tarantina, Marvin Greene, Rob Morrow, Richard Ziman

All My Sons, by Arthur Miller, directed by Jose Ferrer, with Lee Richardson, Frances Sternhagen, Dan Butler, Dawn Didawick, Tracy Griswold, Felicity La Fortune, Liann Pattison, Guy Paul, Stephen Root, Alex Ruchelman

Doubles, by David Wiltse, directed by Peter Flint, with David Groh, George Maharis, Donald Most, Jack Arron, Gavin Troster, Jill Jones

Wife Begins at 40, by Arne Sultan, Earl Barret and Ray Cooney, directed by Leslie Lawton, with Charles Keating, Louise Sorel, Ian Stuart, Alexandra O'Karma, Dennis Kennedy, William Russo

The Perfect Party, by A. R. Gurney, Jr., directed by Burry Fredrik, with George Grizzard, Karen Valentine, Debra Mooney, June L. Walker, David Rogers

Little Ham, adapted from the play by Langston Hughes, book by Daniel Owens, music by Judd Woldin, lyrics by Richard Engquist and Judd Woldin, choreographed by John Parks, directed by Billie Allen, with Obba Babatunde, Edye Byrde, Pi Douglass, Ann Duquesnay, Ellia English, Cary Gant, John Lagioia, Michael Leslie, Michael Mulheren, Natalie Oliver, Dick Sabol, Melodee Savage, Jeffrey V. Thompson, John-Ann Washington

1988

Return Engagements, by Bernard Slade, directed by Tom Troupe, with Reed Birney, Mia Dillon, David Hedison, Jill Larson, Ben Middleman, Louise Sorel, Tom Troupe, Marsha Waterbury

Beehive, originally directed by Larry Gallagher, adapted by Leslie Dockery, with Deborah Davis, Vicki Hubly, Molly McGee, Jessie Janet Richards, Letha V. Walker, Cookie Watkins

I'm Not Rappaport, by Herb Gardner, directed by John Going, with Paul Soles, Samuel E. Wright, Daren Kelly, Liann Pattison, John Connelly, Ken Forman, Anne Gartlan

My One and Only, book by Peter Stone and Timothy S. Mayer, lyrics by Ira Gershwin, music by George Gershwin, choreographed by Patti T'Beck, directed by Richard Casper, with George Dvorsky, Tia Riebling, Jan Mickens, Jan Neuberger, Bob Arnold

Social Security, by Andrew Bergman, directed by Peter Lawrence, with Arlene Francis, David Birney, Christine Healy, Jack Aaron, Laurie Heineman, Paul Lipson

A Walk in the Woods, by Lee Blessing, directed by Maureen F. Gibson, with Lawrence Pressman and Michael Constantine

1989

Broadway Bound, by Neil Simon, directed by Dick Latessa, with Barbara Caruso, Rudy Goldschmidt, Salem Ludwig, Bernice Massi, Alan Mixom, Marc Riffon

Ain't Misbehavin', the Fats Waller Musical Show (concept by Murray Horwitz and Richard Maltby, Jr.), directed by Richard Maltby, Jr., with Terri White, Eric Riley, Peggy Alston, Evan Vell, Rosemarie Jackson

All the Queen's Men, by John Nassivera, directed by Edgar Lansbury, with Elizabeth Ashley, Robert Burr, David Lansbury, Michael Graves, Cathy Reinheimer, Nicholas Sadler

Woman in Mind, by Alan Ayckbourn, directed by Larry Hecht, with Sally Kirkland, Richard Butterfield, Rick Hamilton, Lawrence Hecht, Ed Hodson, Fredi Olster, Ray Reinhardt, Jennifer Roblin

Speed-the-Plow, by David Mamet, directed by Burry Fredrik, with Wayne Rogers, Charles Cioffi, Mia Dillon

Words and Music, by special arrangement with Paul Blake and Marvin Cole, music and lyrics by Sammy Cahn, directed by Paul Blake, with Sammy Cahn, Kevin Anderson, Alisa Gyse, Anne Tofflemire

1990

Rough Crossing, adapted from the play by Ferenc Molnar, music by André Previn, lyrics and story by Tom Stoppard, directed by Alex Kinney, with Charles Keating, Richard B. Shull, Jack Koenig, Renee Rae Norman, Gavin Reed, Ian Stuart

Driving Miss Daisy, by Alfred Uhry, directed by Franklin Keysar, with Rosemary Prinz, Ellis E. Williams, Patrick Mickler

The Cocktail Hour, by A. R. Gurney, directed by David Saint, with Fritz Weaver, Elizabeth Wilson, Reed Birney, Ann McDonough

Steel Magnolias, by Robert Harling, directed by Elliott Woodruff, with Anita Gillette, Margo Martindale, Marilyn Cooper, Rae Lankford, Anne O'Sullivan, Patti MacLeod

Me and My Girl, book and lyrics by L. Arthur Rose and Douglas Furber, music by Noel Gay, revised by Stephen Fry, directed and choreographed by Tony Parise and William Alan Coats, with Jamie Torcellini, Sheri Cowart, Gary Gage, Lenka Peterson, Barbara Passolt, Lee Chew, Bill Nabel

Shirley Valentine, by Willy Russell, directed by Jeff Lee, with Millicent Martin

1991

Lend Me a Tenor, by Ken Ludwig, directed by David Saint, with George Grizzard, Jack Gilpin, Jane Connell, Jean De Baer, Fran Brill, Laura Hughes, Rick Lawless, Keith Curran

Rumors, by Neil Simon, directed by Peter Lawrence, with Stephen Berger, Catherine Campbell, Suzanne Dawson, Heather Macrae, Kathleen Marsh, Michael Minor, Wiley Moore, Reno Roop, Stephen Scott

Dangerous Obsession, by N. J. Crisp, directed by Kenneth Frankel, with Juliet Mills, Alex Hyde-White, Richard Poe

Where's Charley, based on Brandon Thomas's *Charley's Aunt*, book by George Abbott, music and lyrics by Frank Loesser, choreographed and directed by Tony Parise, with Jamie Torcellini, Gary Gage, Emily Loesser, Don Stephenson, Deborah Graham, Peter Walker, Tom Boyd, Joe Sullivan

A Few Good Men, by Aaron Sorkin, directed by Steve Karp, with John Hickok, Michael O'Hare, Deirdre Madigan, Marc Epstein, Tracy Griswold, Michael Hartman, David Harris, Joseph Rose, Omar Augustus Cooper, Rob Bogue, William Perry, Steven Dominguez, Patrick J. Kinsella, Stan Cahill, Christopher Burns, Paul Furey, David Greer, Dan Kelly, Gary McNeill, Jed Sexton

M. Butterfly, by David Henry Hwang, directed by Bob Borod, with Graeme Malcolm, A. Tung, Ian Stuart, Alexandra O'Karma, Craig Wasson, Lyn Wright, Ann Harada, Man Wong, Erika Honda, Alan Muraoka

1992

Lettice and Lovage, by Peter Shaffer, directed by Lonny Price, with Carole Shelley, Doris Belack, Daniel De Raey, Joanna Morris

Don't Dress for Dinner, by Marc Camoletti, directed by Pamela Hunt, with Karen Valentine, Caroline Lagerfelt, Reno Roop, Alexandra O'Karma, Max Robinson, Timothy Wheeler

Breaking Legs, written and directed by Tom Dulack, with Gary Sandy, Joseph Mascolo, Vince Viverito, Susan Denaker, Stephen Mendillo, Eddie Zammit

The Fourth Wall, by A. R. Gurney, directed by David Saint, with Tony Roberts, Kelly Bishop, Jack Gilpin, E. Katherine Kerr

The World Goes 'Round, music by John Kander, lyrics by Fred Ebb, choreographed by Susan Stroman, directed by Scott Ellis, with Joel Blum, Shelley Dickinson, Marin Mazzie, John Ruess, Karin Ziémba

Park Your Car in Harvard Yard, by Israel Horovitz, directed by Austen Pendleton, with E. G. Marshall, Mary Ann Plunkett

1993

Noises Off, by Michael Frayn, directed by David Saint, with Millicent Martin, John Rensenhouse, Richard Bekins, Keith Curran, James Carruthers, Deirdre Lovejoy, Anne Swift, Laura Hughes, Brooks Ashmanskas

The Decorator, by Donald Churchill, directed by Ian Stuart, with Charles Keating, Mary Kay Adams, Madeleine Potter

Dancing at Lughnasa, by Brian Friel, directed by Robert Bennett, with Alma Cuervo, Sean G. Griffin, Graeme Malcolm, David Herlihy, Gretchen Crich, Bernadette Quigley, Christina Rouner, Caryn West

Phantom, adapted from the novel *Phantom of the Opera* by Gaston Leroux, book by Arthur Kopit, music and lyrics by Maury Yeston, directed and choreographed by Pamela Hunt, with Brad Little, Kim Lindsay, Jay Stuart, Robert Frisch, Peter Marklin, James Van Treuren, Tom Boyd, Suellen Estey

The Substance of Fire, by Jon Robin Baitz, directed by Nicholas Martin, with Charles Cioffi, T. Scott Cunningham, Neal Huff, Wendy Kaplan, Kelly Bishop

Nunsense II, book, music and lyrics by Dan Goggin, choreographed and directed by Nancy E. Carroll, with Pat Carroll, Nancy E. Carroll, Caroline Droscoski, Donna M. Ryan, Lyn Vaux

1994

Song of Singapore, book by Allan Katz, Erik Frandsen, Robert Hipkens, Michael Garin, Paula Lockheart, music and lyrics by Erik Frandsen, Robert Hipkens, Michael Garin, Paula Lockheart, directed by Ron Nash, with Loretta Swit, Cathy Foy, Erik Frandsen, Michael Garin, Robert Hipkens, Frank Kane, Jon Gordon, Brian Grice, Joel Helleni, Earl May

Beau Jest, by James Sherman, directed by David Saint, with Jerry Stiller, Estelle Harris, Amy Stiller, Howard Samuelsohn, Paul Cassell, T. Scott Cunningham

Later Life, by A. R. Gurney, directed by David Saint, with Maureen Anderman, Frank Converse, Carole Shelley, John C. Venema

Forever Plaid, written, choreographed and directed by Stuart Ross, with David Benoit, Robert Lambert, Ryan Perry, Cliff Thorn

The Taming of the Shrew, by William Shakespeare, directed by Josephine R. Abady, with Victoria Tennant, Jonathan Peck, Tom Beckett, Ralph Buckley, Ronn Carroll, James Carruthers, Robert Colston, Mark W. Conklin, Peggy Cosgrave, Alexander Draper, Ron Frazier, Cheryl Gaysunas, John La Gioia, Eric Swanson, Ray Ford, W. Aaron Harpold, Joshua Knudson, Gerrit Vooren, Jason Tyler White, Joe Wyka

Intimate Exchanges, by Alan Ayckbourn, directed by David Saint, with Elaine May, Gene Saks

Love Letters, by A. R. Gurney, with George Grizzard, Karen Valentine, Gene Saks, Irene Worth

An Evening with Liza and Friends (November 13, 1994), benefit for "Bread & Roses" and "The Mid-Fairfield AIDS Project," music and lyrics by John Kander and Fred Ebb, with Liza Minnelli

1995

Camping with Henry and Tom, by Mark St. Germain, directed by Allan Miller, with Frank Converse, Nicolas Coster, David Huddleston, Tom Harris

A *Chorus Line*, originally directed and choreographed by Michael Bennett, book by James Kirkwood and Nicholas Dante, music by Marvin Hamlisch, lyrics by Edward Kleban, directed and choreographed by Sam Viverito, with Denise Ashlynd, James Beaumont, Marty Benn, Stephanie Bishop, Kenneth Boyd, Jarrod Cafaro, Kelly Cole, Paul Cole, Andy Ferrara, Barbara Folts, Tim Foster, Matthew Johnson, Anne Kulakowski, Paul Liberti, Shannon McGough, Tricia Mitchell, Kari Nicolaisen, Gavan Pamer, Mark Allen Pfeiffer, Nick Rafello, Rob Reynolds, Arleen Sugano, Sarah Timms, Peggy Trecker, Kelly Wade

The Supporting Cast, a comedy by George Furth, directed by Pat Carroll, with Rosemary Prinz, Marcia Wallace, Alexandra O'Karma, Laura Esterman, Ralston Hill

The Cemetery Club, by Ivan Menchell, directed by Margaret Booker, with Eileen Heckart, Estelle Harris, DeAnn Mears, Frank Savino, Betty Jinnette

A Cheever Evening, by A. R. Gurney, adapted from stories by John Cheever, directed by Nicholas Martin, with Karen Valentine, Laurence Luckinbill, Dana Ivey, Jack Gilpin, Jennifer Van Dyck, Jonathan Walker

The Woman in Black, adapted by Stephen Mallatratt, from a novel by Susan Hill, directed by Robin Herford, with Roy Dotrice, Maxwell Caulfield

Lyndon, by James Prideaux, based on the book by Merle Miller, with Laurence Luckinbill (performed August 27, 1995)

An Elegant Holiday Celebration, directed by Laurence Luckinbill, with Maureen Anderman, Lucie Arnaz, Maxwell Caulfield, Stephen Chapin, Frank Converse, Hume Cronyn, Charles Keating, Laurence Luckinbill, E. G. Marshall, Marin Mazzie, Juliet Mills, Karen Valentine, Julie Wilson (performed December 10, 1995)

1996

Love, Julie, by Patrick Edgeworth, directed by Jeff Lee, with Helen Reddy, Millicent Martin, Graeme Malcolm

Angel Street, by Patrick Hamilton, directed by Marcia Milgrom Dodge, with David McCallum, Jean LeClerc, Peggy Cosgrave, Libby Christophersen, Mia Dillon

Brigadoon, book and lyrics by Alan J. Lerner, music by Frederick Loewe, original choreography by Agnes DeMille, choreographed by James Horvath, directed by Ted Kociolek, with George Dvorsky, Edwardyne Cowan, Stephanie Douglas, Michael O'Steen, Robert Randle, Rebecca Sherman, Alan Bennett, Debby Kole, Don Perkins

Men in Suits, by Jason Milligan, directed by Joe Cacaci, with Charles Durning, James Handy, Dan Lauria

Sylvia, by A. R. Gurney, directed by John Tillinger, with Stephanie Zimbalist, Edmond Genest, Mary Beth Peil, Tim Donoghue

Snapshots, by Michael Scheman and David Stern, music and lyrics by Stephen Schwartz, directed by Michael Scheman, with Cass Morgan, William Parry, Erin Leigh Peck, Ric Ryder, Julia K. Murney, Don Goodspeed

1997

Blackbirds of Broadway (A Harlem Rhapsody), by David Coffman, choreographed and directed by Marion J. Caffey, musical direction by Danny Holgate, with Cheryl Alexander, Larry Hines, Andi Hopkins, Tracey Lee, Kimberly Michaels, Dennis Stowe, Eyan Williams, H. Clent Bowers

Jackie O's Glasses, by Tracey Jackson, directed by Dennis Erdman, with Alison Fraser, Tim Donoghue, John Hickok

Spider's Web, by Agatha Christie, directed by John Going, with Evalyn Baron, Jeff Breland, Thomas Carson, Munson Hicks, Alfred Hyslop, Des Keogh, Melissa King, Samuel Maupin, Christy Carlson Romano, Frank Runeon, Dennis Ryan

An Evening with Jerry Herman, directed Lee Roy Reams, produced by Jim Semmelman, with Jerry Herman, Lee Roy Reams, Florence Lacey, Jered Egan

Moon over Buffalo, by Ken Ludwig, directed by Pamela Hunt, with Gavin MacLeod, Millicent Martin, Ann Kittredge, Larry Cahn, Steve Routman, Jay Stuart, Becky Watson, Jane Connell

After-Play, by Anne Meara, directed by David Saint, with Jerry Stiller, Jane Powell, Anne Meara, Paul Benedict, Maureen Anderman, Peter Maloney, Lance Reddick

1998

Lawyers, by Henry G. Miller, directed by John Berry, with Kevin Conway, Ford Austin, Laura Dash, Sam Freed, Tom Ligon, Henry G. Miller

Wendell & Ben, by W. M. Whitehead and Warren Press, directed by Richard Zavaglia, with Dan Lauria, Fred Savage

La Cage Aux Folles, adapted from the play by Jean Poiret, book by Harvey Fierstein, music and lyrics by Jerry Herman, choreographed and directed by Tony Parise, with Walter Charles, Harvey Evans, Kenneth H. Waller, Linda Poser, Susan Cella, James Patterson, Tracy Generalovich, Michael J. Farina and Tim Johnson

Perfect Wedding, by Robin Hawdon, directed by John Going, with Diedrich Bader, Frank Ferrante, Melissa King, Amanda Rogers, David Rogers, Dulcy Rogers, June L. Walker

Something's Afoot, book, music and lyrics by James McDonald, David Vos and Robert Gerlach, additional music by Ed Linderman, choreographed and directed by Pamela Hunt, with Liz Sheridan, Tony Aylward, Maureen Brennan, Joy Franz, Gary Gage, Bill Kocis, John Sloman, Jay Stuart, Steve Wilson and Pamela Winslow

Eleanor, Her Secret Journey, a Theatre Guild production by Rhoda Lerman, directed by John Tillinger, with Jean Stapleton

1999

Street of Dreams, by James Naughton, produced by Mike Nichols, with James Naughton

A Bench in the Sun, by Ron Clark, directed by John Tillinger, with Tim Conway, Betsy Palmer, Paxton Whitehead

Chasing Monsters, by Kevin Rehac, directed by Sabin Epstein, with Michael Learned, Ralph Waite, Victor Slezak, Jenna Stern

Far East, by A. R. Gurney, directed by David Saint, with Stephanie Zimbalist, Geoff Pierson, Tim Williams, Sonny Brown, Momoe Nakamura, Angelika Sielaff, Barnaby Carpenter

The Last Night of Ballyhoo, by Alfred Uhry, directed by Isa Thomas, with Carolyn Michel, Sharon Spelman, Bradford Wallace, Rebecca Baldwin, Stacy Barnhisel, Matthew Tavianini, Erik R. Uppling

Groucho—A Life in Revue, written by Arthur Marx and Robert Fisher, directed by Frank Ferrante, with Frank Ferrante, Roy Abramsohn, Marguerite Lowell, Scott Greer

2000

The Constant Wife, by W. Somerset Maugham, directed by Joanne Woodward, with Mikel Sara Lambert, Donald Corren, Sharron Bower, Denise Lute, Jessie Cantrell, Allison Mackie, Kali Rocha, Daniel Gerroll, Armand Schultz, John Rothman

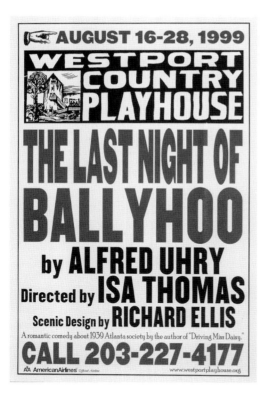

Morphic Resonance, by Katherine Burger, directed by James Naughton, with John Cunningham, Claire Lautier, Keira Naughton, Stephen Barker Turner, Tony Ward

Nicolette & Aucassin, book and lyrics by Peter Kellogg, music by David Friedman, directed by Seth Barrish, with Bronson Pinchot, Jennifer Allen, Darlesia Cearcy, James Judy, Jeremy Webb, Bill Buell, Richard White, Nancy K. Anderson, Chuck Cooper, Michael Wiggins

2001

"An Evening With Whoopi Goldberg," benefit for the Westport Country Playhouse, March 2, 2001

Princess Turandot, written and directed by Darko Tresnjak, based on the theatrical fable by Carlo Gozzi and on *The Arabian Nights*, with Anna Belknap, Jeffrey Binder, Wes Day, Jack Ferver, Matthew Gasper, Roxanna Hope, Christopher K. Morgan, Darrell Grand Moultrie, Ron Nahass, Gregor Pasalawsky, Caroline Pasquantonio, Josh Radnor, Maria Elena Ramirez, Mark Shunock, Dan Snook, James Stanley

Don't Make Me Laugh: "The Music Cure," by George Bernard Shaw; "Caught with His Trance Down," by Georges Feydeau, adapted by Norman R. Shapiro; "The Proposal," by Anton Chekhov, adapted by Gene Wilder; "The Dangers of Tobacco," by Anton Chekhov, adapted by Gene Wilder; directed by Gene Saks, with Gene Wilder, Carol Kane, Bob Dishy, Vivienne Benesch, David Costabile, Bill Buell

Three Days of Rain, by Richard Greenberg, directed by Joanne Woodward, with Alyssa Bresnahan, David Conrad, Alex Draper

Heaven Can Wait, by Harry Seagall, directed by Joe Grifasi, with Leslie Uggams, Ray Weiderhold, William A. Barry, Jessie Lynn Cantrell, Tristina Duarte, Sharde Edwards, Jerry Finnegan, Stephen McKinley Henderson, Virginia Lity, Andrea Magenheimer, John Tiscia, Keith Reddin, Peter Rini, Dean Nolen, Phoebe Jonas, Mary Fogarty, Mia Barron, Bruce Weitz, John Bowman

Orson's Shadow, by Austin Pendleton, concept by Judith Auberjonois, directed by David Cromer, with David Warren, Dominic Conti, Jeff Still, John Judd, Sarah Wellington, Lee Roy Rogers

Ancestral Voices (A Family Story), by A. R. Gurney, directed by David Saint. First Cast: Neil Patrick Harris, Jane Curtin, Frank Converse, Elizabeth Wilson, Fritz Weaver. Second Cast: Paul Rudd, Swoosie Kurtz, James Naughton, Joanne Woodward, Paul Newman

Triangles for Two, by David Wiltse, directed by Joe Grifasi, with Jayne Atkinson, Jeffrey Jones

Temporary Help, by David Wiltse, directed by Gordon Edelstein, with Jeffrey DeMunn, Karen Allen, Sam Freed, Chad Allen

"A Word or Two, Before You Go," an afternoon with Christopher Plummer, October 14, 2001

"For the Children," a special benefit performance to aid the families affected by the devastation of 9/11/01, Sunday, October 28, 2001, with Robin Batteau, Adam Battelstein, Kriston Chenoweth, Chris Coogan, James Naughton, Paul Newman, Christopher Plummer, Gene Wilder, Joanne Woodward

2002

Ancestral Voices, by A. R. Gurney, directed by Arvin Brown, with Matthew Broderick, Susan Sarandon, Tim Robbins, Joanne Woodward, Paul Newman (performed April 6, 2002)

Our Town, by Thornton Wilder, directed by James Naughton, with Paul Newman, Jayne Atkinson, Frank Converse, Jane Curtin, Jeffrey DeMunn, Jake Robards, Andy Friedland, Kristen Hahn, Harry Cooper, Maggie Lacey, Ben Fox, John Braden, Cynthia Wallace, Susan DeVaney, Jim Lones, Stephen Spinella, Mia Dillon, Robert Burian, Walter Kosner, Chris Wood, Danny Williams, Carter Jackson, Bill Barry

The Voice of the Turtle, by John Van Druten, directed by Connie Grappo, with Katie MacNichol, Sarah Zimmerman, Stephen Barker Turner

Master Harold . . . and the Boys, by Athol Fugard, directed by Walter Dallas, with Ray Anthony Thomas, Leon Addison Brown, Joshua Park

Outward Bound, by Sutton Vane, directed by Doug Hughes, with Tari Signor, Dennis Holmes, Garret Dillahunt, Jefferson Mays, Pamela Payton-Wright, T. Scott Cunningham, Patricia Conolly, Henry Strozier, Edward Hibbert

A Saint She Ain't, co-produced with Berkshire Theatre Festival, book and lyrics by Dick Vosburgh, music by Dennis King, directed by Eric Hill, with P. J. Benjamin, Joel Blum, Allison Briner, Lovett George, Jason Gillman, Christina Marie Norrup, Roland Rusinek, Jay Russell

2003

Hay Fever, by Noël Coward, directed by Darko Tresnjak, with Sarah Hudnut, Austin Lysy, Denny Dillon, Amy Van Nostrand, Jack Gilpin, Timothy Carter, Tessa Auberjonois, Robert Stanton, Arden Myrin

The Good German, by David Wiltse, directed by James Naughton, with Kathleen McNenny, Victor Slezak, Boyd Gaines, Casey Biggs

The Old Settler, by John Henry Redwood, directed by Tazewell Thompson, with Brenda Thomas, Tina Fabrique, Edward O'Blenis, Cherise Boothe

All My Sons, by Arthur Miller, directed by Doug Hughes, with Richard Dreyfus, Jill Clayburgh, Tom Hammond, David Costabile, Katie MacNichol, Caroline Baeumler, Sam Trammell, Conor Donovan, Jenny Bacon, David Aaron Baker

The Streets of New York, an Irish Repertory Theatre Production by Dion Boucicault, written, adapted and directed by Charlotte Moore, with David Staller, John Keating, Ciarán O'Reilly, John Bolton, Donald Corren, Greg Stone, Margaret Hall, Joshua Park, Nancy Anderson, Rebecca Bellingham, Terry Donnelly, Danielle Ferland

2004

Someone Who'll Watch Over Me, by Frank McGuinness, directed by Ethan McSweeny, with Sterling K. Brown, Michael Emerson, Ciarán O'Reilly

Trumbo, by Christopher Trumbo, directed by Peter Askin, with Gordon MacDonald, Paul Newman

The School for Husbands, by Molière, translated by Richard Wilbur, directed by Doug Hughes, with Mia Barron, Paul Blankenship, Joe Delafield, Danielle Ferland, Wayne Kasserman, Maggie Lacey, Louis Rosen, Henry Strozier, Andrew Weems

Notes

Chapter One: The Prologue

1 Sari Bodi, "Dion Boucicault: Upstanding Citizen and Passionate Scoundrel," WCP Playbill, September 13, 2003.
2 Gerald Bordman, *The Oxford Companion to American Theatre* (New York: Oxford University Press, 1992), 97.
3 Ibid.
4 Charlotte Moore, quoted in Bodi, "Dion Boucicault."
5 Oscar G. Brockett and Franklin J. Hildy, *History of the Theatre*, 9th ed. (Boston: Allyn and Bacon, 2003), 344.
6 Ibid., 345.
7 Norman Nadel, *A Pictorial History of the Theatre Guild* (New York: Crown Publishers, 1969), 89.
8 Ibid., 106.
9 Lawrence Langner, *The Magic Curtain* (New York: E. P. Dutton, 1951), 250.
10 Brockett and Hildy, *History of the Theatre*, 458.
11 Lillian Ross, "Onward and Upward with the Arts," *New Yorker*, August 20, 1949, 30.
12 Patricia Granjean, "A Summer Place," *Connecticut/Bravo*, July 1999, 12.
13 Author conversation with Sharon Giese, November 10, 2003.
14 Fenmore R. Seton, sales engineer, J. P. Salmini Company, to Lawrence Langner, September 8, 1948.
15 Gala Ebin to Lawrence Langner, July 24, 1952.

Chapter Two: Westport, circa 1931

1 Joanna Foster, "The Way Westport Was," *Westport News*, July 17, 1985.
2 Woody Klein, *Westport, Connecticut: The Story of a New England Town's Rise to Prominence* (Westport: Greenwood Press, 2000), 46.
3 Ibid., 89.
4 Ibid., 153.
5 *Westporter Herald*, May 31, 1932.
6 Klein, *Westport, Connecticut*, 181.

Chapter Three: The Barn Becomes a Theatre

1 Helen Higgins, *Fairpress*, June 18, 1980.
2 Lawrence Langner, *The Magic Curtain* (New York: E. P. Dutton, 1951), 251.
3 Joanna Foster, *Westport News*, 1987.
4 WCP Playbill, August 20, 1973.
5 Langner, *Magic Curtain*, 247.
6 WCP Playbill, August 20, 1973.
7 Ibid.
8 Langner, *Magic Curtain*, 297.
9 See UNCAT MSS ZA Theatre Guild, Box 78, Beinecke Rare Book & Manuscript Library, Yale University.
10 Langner, *Magic Curtain*, 297.
11 *Fairpress*, June 18, 1980.
12 Langner, *Magic Curtain*, 297.
13 See UNCAT MSS ZA Theatre Guild, Box 146, Beinecke Rare Book & Manuscript Library, Yale University.

Chapter Four: In Repertory, 1931–32

1 *New York Sun*, September 10, 1931.
2 WCP Playbill, August 24, 1931.
3 *Norwalk Evening Sentinel*, June 1956.
4 Poem V, "From a Very Little Sphinx," in *Collected Poems, Edna St. Vincent Millay* (New York: Harper and Row).
5 Daniel Mark Epstein, *What Lips My Lips Have Kissed* (New York: Henry Holt, 2001), 138.
6 Norman Nadel, *A Pictorial History of the Theatre Guild* (New York: Crown Publishers, 1969), 5.
7 *New York Times*, January 22, 1967.
8 Lawrence Langner, *The Magic Curtain* (New York: E. P. Dutton, 1951), 298.
9 *Bridgeport Times Star*.
10 *New York American*, October 7, 1931.
11 *New York American*, October 15, 1931.
12 *New York Evening Journal*, October 15, 1931.
13 *Evening Post*, October 15, 1931.
14 Letter to Theatre Guild subscribers and ticket buyers, October 20, 1931.
15 "Dear Friend": Letter from Philip Langner and Peter Turgeon to WCP subscribers, September 1956.
16 Information for this section was derived from Dennis Kennedy, ed., *Oxford Encyclopedia of Theatre and Performance*, vol. 1 (Oxford: Oxford University Press, 2003), 519; and Gerald Bordman, *The Oxford Companion to American Theatre* (New York: Oxford University Press, 1992), 295.
17 *World Telegram*, July 6, 1932.
18 *World Telegram*, October 7, 1931.
19 *World Telegram*, July 6, 1932.
20 Theresa Helburn, *A Wayward Quest* (New York: Little Brown, 1960), 137.
21 Langner, *Magic Curtain*, 301.

Chapter Five: "Doing the Plays We Really Want to Do," 1933–41

1 *New York Times*, July 1935.
2 Robert Garland, *World Telegram*, September 1933.
3 "Westport Country Playhouse": undated memo in Lawrence Langner's personal files, probably 1947.
4 *New York Times*, July 1935.
5 "Westport Country Playhouse": undated Langner memo, probably 1947.
6 *Bridgeport Sunday Post*, July 9, 1950.
7 Langner, *Magic Curtain*, 308.
8 *Bridgeport Sunday Post*, July 9, 1950.
9 UNCAT MSS ZA Theatre Guild, Box 78, Beinecke Rare Book & Manuscript Library, Yale University.
10 "Westport Country Playhouse": undated Langner memo, probably 1947.
11 Langner, *Magic Curtain*, 307.
12 *World Telegram*, July 30, 1935.
13 Ogler Quiller, *Ship, Rail and Air*, September 1935.
14 *Bryn Mawr* magazine, May 1945, 17.
15 Patricia Granjean, *Connecticut/Bravo*, July 1999, 4.
16 Tom Wolf, *Amarillo Daily News*, August 15, 1941.
17 "Gene Kelly Looking for Old Playhouse Programs," *Westport News*, September 6, 1991.
18 *Norwalk Hour*, June 27, 1940.
19 *World-Telegram*, December 13, 1932.
20 Gerald Bordman, *The Oxford Companion to American Theatre* (New York: Oxford University Press, 1992), 146.

21 *Bridgeport Post*, July 8, 1940.
22 *Variety*, July 24, 1940.
23 *Norwalk Hour*, July 16, 1940.
24 Max Wilk, *OK! The Story of Oklahoma!* (New York: Applause Theatre and Cinema Books, 1993), 23.
25 Ibid., 25.
26 Ibid., 30.
27 *Town Crier*, August 15, 1940.
28 *Bridgeport Star*, June 26, 1941.
29 Tom Killen, *Westport Country Playhouse 50th Anniversary*, 1980, 2.
30 *New York World Telegram*, July 2, 1941.
31 Tom Wolf, *Amarillo Daily News*, August 15, 1941.
32 Ibid.
33 *New York World Telegram*, August 12, 1941.
34 Quoted by Joanna Foster, *Stories From Westport's Past*, 1988, 38.
35 Philip Hoare, *Noël Coward—A Biography* (New York: Simon & Schuster, 1995), 281.
36 Information about Wilson is hard to come by and much of it is Coward-centric since it is obtained from Coward's diaries and biographies. However, the author is indebted to Wilson's great nephew, Jack Macauley, who provided the quotation from Wilson's unpublished memoir as well as much of the factual information about him.

Chapter Six: Lawrence Langner, 1890–1962

1 "Autobiographical Sketch, Lawrence Langner," undated carbon copy in Philip Langner's possession.
2 Robert Rice, "Business and Show Business I," *New Yorker*, October 1, 1949, 35.
3 Lawrence Langner, *The Magic Curtain* (New York: E. P. Dutton, 1951), 356.
4 "Founding Father of the Guild Credits It to a Girl and a Book," *New York Herald Tribune*, April 27, 1941.
5 "Lawrence Langner's Theatre Success Parallels Patent Law Career," *Bridgeport Sunday Post*, July 9, 1950.
6 Dennis Kennedy, ed., *The Oxford Encyclopedia of Theatre and Performance*, vol. 2 (Oxford: Oxford University Press, 2003), 1349.
7 Quoted in Norman Nadel, *A Pictorial History of the Theatre*

Guild (New York: Crown, 1969), 276.
8 Theresa Helburn, *A Wayward Quest* (New York: Little Brown, 1960), 313.
9 Nadel, *Pictorial History*, 3.
10 Rice, "Business and Show Business I," 35.
11 S. N. Behrman, "Farewell to Lawrence," *Sunday Herald*, February 10, 1963.
12 Author conversation with Richard Grayson, personal assistant to Lawrence Langner from 1953 to 1954, January 22, 2004.
13 *New York Herald Tribune*, April 27, 1941.
14 John C. Green to Lyla Steenbergen, December 2003.
15 Gloria Cole, "For Armina Marshall Life Is Theater," *The Advocate*, June 21, 1980.
16 Langner, *Magic Curtain*, 217.
17 UNCAT MSS ZA Theatre Guild, Box 78, Beinecke Rare Book & Manuscript Library, Yale University.
18 Lawrence Langner, "Eugene O'Neill," in Nadel, *Pictorial History*, 87.
19 Ibid., 86.
20 Ibid., 89.
21 Helburn, *Wayward Quest*, 275n.
22 Nadel, *Theatre Guild*, 97.
23 Helburn, *Wayward Quest*, 278.
24 Langner, *Magic Curtain*, 423.
25 Nadel, *Theatre Guild*, 44.
26 Ibid., 61.
27 Langner, *Magic Curtain*, 130.
28 Nadel, *Theatre Guild*, 47.
29 Langner, *Magic Curtain*, Appendix II, 454.
30 Ibid., 128.
31 Ibid., 134.
32 Nadel, *Theatre Guild*, 53.
33 Ibid., 44.
34 Gloria Cole, "For Armina Marshall Life Is Theater," *The Advocate*, June 21, 1980.
35 Ibid.
36 Ibid.
37 Thomas A. DeLong, "Westport Playhouse Celebrating 'Golden' Season," *Bridgeport Sunday Post*, June 22, 1980.
38 Ibid.
39 Ibid.
40 Cole, "For Armina Marshall Life Is Theater."

Chapter Seven: Happily Losing a Little Money, 1946–58

1 K. S., memo to Lawrence Langner, January 4, 1944, UNCAT MSS ZA Theatre Guild, Box 78, Beinecke Rare Book & Manuscript Library, Yale University.
2 Langner, *Magic Curtain*, 314.
3 WCP Playbill, August 12, 1974.
4 WCP Playbill, August 22, 1955.
5 *New York Herald Tribune*, July 17, 1949.
6 Quoted by Irene Backalenick, "Survival of the Fittest," *Westport Herald*, August 28, 1977.
7 Contract letter from Martin Manulis to the Theatre Guild, May 6, 1948.
8 "When It Was Good It Was Very, Very Good," *Broadcasting*, February 17, 1986, 95.
9 New York Times News Service, published by *Chicago Tribune*, November 2, 1990.
10 Patricia Grandjean, "A Summer Place," *Connecticut/Bravo*, July 1999, 6.
11 "Memorandum of the Westport Country Playhouse," signed by Armina Marshall Langner, January 26, 1949.
12 Letter and enclosure from Leslie A. Hoffman to Lawrence Langner, September 6, 1947.
13 See handwritten letter "Dear Dad," signed "Phil," May 24, 1948.
14 Lawrence Langner to Edwin Howard, February 18, 1952.
15 Lawrence Langner to Fenimore R. Seton of J. P. Salmini Company, Bridgeport, October 13, 1948.
16 Lawrence Langner to Philip Langner, August 28, 1951.
17 Grandjean, *Connecticut/Bravo*.
18 Patron letter dated May 14, 1949.
19 1931–50 tryouts listed in Appendix III, Langner, *Magic Curtain*, 461.
20 Lawrence Langner to Robert Garland, July 27, 1949.
21 *Bridgeport Sunday Post*, July 9, 1950.
22 *Bridgeport Post*, July 12, 1950.
23 Ibid.
24 *Variety*, July 15, 1950.
25 Conard Fowkes (secretary/treasurer, Actor's Equity Association: apprentice 1950) to Chance Farago, 2004.
26 Quoted in Audrey Wood, *Represented by Audrey Wood* (New York: Doubleday, 1981), 222.

27 In 1957 Inge rewrote *Farther Off from Heaven* as *The Dark at the Top of the Stairs*. With Pat Hingle, Teresa Wright and Eileen Heckart in the principal roles, it was well received by critics and the public, running for almost five hundred performances on Broadway.
28 Wood, *Audrey Wood*, 225.
29 *Norwalk Hour*, September 13, 1949.
30 *Bridgeport Post*, September 13, 1949.
31 Wood, *Audrey Wood*, 227.
32 "The 1951 Summer Season," undated subscription flyer.
33 Brendan Gill, preface to *The Collected Plays of Philip Barry*, quoted in Gerald Bordman, *The Oxford Companion to American Theatre* (New York: Oxford University Press, 1992), 30.
34 *The Stratford News*, June 15, 1951.
35 *Greenwich Time*, July 31, 1951.
36 *Town Crier*, August 23, 1951.
37 *Norwalk Hour*, September 4, 1951.
38 "Dear Folks" letter from Philip Langner to Mr. and Mrs. Lawrence Langner at Hassler Hotel, Rome, June 30, 1952.
39 WCP Playbill, August 11, 1958.
40 WCP Playbill, June 30, 1958.
41 Letters from Lawrence Langner to Alec Guinness, April 21 and May 4, 1953; letter from Guinness to Langner, April 26, 1953.
42 "Dreaming Big Dreams in Westport," *New York Times*, January 30, 2000.
43 WCP Playbill, June 23, 1958.
44 WCP Playbill, July 30, 1956.
45 WCP Playbill, June 12, 1955.
46 *Norwalk Hour*, July 26, 1957.
47 Norman Nadel, *A Pictorial History of the Theatre Guild* (New York: Crown Publishers, 1969), 211.
48 Armina Marshall, "The Theatre Guild on Radio and Television," in Nadel, *Pictorial History*, 213.
49 Ibid., 214.
50 Langner, *Magic Curtain*, 362.
51 *New York Herald Tribune*, June 2, 1959.
52 Frederic Morton, "Straw Hat Circuit," *Holiday*, July 1959, 68.
53 WCP Playbill, June 12, 1958.
54 Langner, *Magic Curtain*, 252–55.
55 Ibid., 256.
56 M. Mannes, "Behind the Throne," *New Yorker*, December 6, 1930, 31.
57 Theresa Helburn, *A Wayward*

Quest (New York: Little Brown, 1960), 86.
58 Ibid., 18.
59 Ibid., 104.
60 Mannes, "Behind the Throne," 33.
61 Helburn, *Wayward Quest*, 103.

Chapter Eight: Under New Management, 1959–72

1 Author conversation with Philip Langner, December 12, 2003.
2 WCP Playbill, July 18, 1960.
3 *New York Times*, March 11, 1967.
4 Ibid.
5 *The Town Crier*, June 14, 1959.
6 *New York Times*, March 11, 1967.
7 *The Norwalk Hour*, March 5, 1959.
8 *Stratford News*, July 23, 1959.
9 Marcia J. Monbleau, *The Cape Playhouse* (South Yarmouth, Mass.: Allen D. Bragdon, 1991), 18.
10 Arthur Gelb, "Summer Theatre, F.O.B. Broadway," *New York Times Magazine*, July 12, 1959.
11 Frederic Morton, "Straw Hat Circuit," *Holiday*, July 1959, 66.
12 Gelb, *New York Times Magazine*, July 12, 1959.
13 Ibid.
14 See Gelb, *New York Times Magazine*, July 12, 1959.
15 "The Whys of Hits and Turkeys," *The Town Crier*, June 14, 1959.
16 Leo B. Meyer (resident scenic designer at WCP, 1963), memo and letter to Chance Farago, January 5, 2004.
17 Ralph Lycett, "Off the Cuff," *Fairfield County Guide*, June 16, 1964.
18 Oscar G. Brockett and Franklin J. Hildy, *History of the Theatre*, 9th ed. (Boston: Allyn and Bacon, 2003), 501.
19 Patricia Grandjean, "A Summer Place," *Connecticut/Bravo*, July 1999.
20 Brockett and Hildy, *History of the Theatre*, 501.
21 WCP Playbill, August 7, 1967.
22 Author conversation with Ralph Roseman, December 16, 2003.
23 See mailing flyer: "Last 8 weeks of the 1950 summer schedule," and WCP Playbill, July 31, 1967.
24 Jim McKenzie, "Producer's Corner," WCP Playbill, July 1979.
25 WCP Playbill, August 14, 1967.
26 WCP Playbill, July 3, 1967.
27 Tom Killen, "Westport Country Playhouse 50th Anniversary," 1980, 3.

28 Dulcy Rogers e-mail to author, January 5, 2004.
29 *Danbury News-Times*, July 13, 1960.
30 *Meridien Record*, July 13, 1960.
31 Quoted in Gerald Bordman, *The Oxford Companion to American Theatre* (New York: Oxford University Press, 1992), 94.
32 *Westporter Herald*, July 26, 1959.
33 *Bridgeport Post*, August 26, 1969.
34 *Westporter Herald*, July 27, 1969.
35 WCP Playbill, July 15, 1968.
36 "I only ask to be free. The butterflies are free. Mankind will surely not deny to Harold Skimpole what it concedes to the butterflies!"
37 *Stamford Advocate*, August 26, 1969.
38 *Bridgeport Post*, August 26, 1969.
39 *Westport News*, August 26, 1969.
40 Author conversation with Charles Dillingham, 1969 WCP general manager, January 2, 2004.
41 WCP Playbill, June 30, 1956.
42 Ibid.
43 Julie Monahan, memo to author, February 2004.
44 "Something of Our Own," *Good Living, Minuteman Newspapers*, May 1, 2003.
45 WCP Playbill, June 17, 1968.
46 "Playhouse Apprentices' Performances Range from Foot to Parking Lights," *Town Crier*, August 1949.
47 Ibid.
48 Lawrence Langner to Martin Manulis, June 28, 1949.
49 "It's been a Hard Job," *Westport News*, August 1988.
50 "What Makes a Summer Theatre Tick?" *New York Herald Tribune*, July 17, 1949.
51 *Westport News*, August 1988.
52 "Behind Every Good Show," 1994 WCP press release from David McMahon.
53 Conard Fowkes (secretary/treasurer, Actors' Equity Association: apprentice 1950) to Chance Farago, 2004.
54 Pat Blaufuss interview with Phoebe Hopkins Burston (1950–51 apprentice), March 5, 2004.
55 Lawrence Langner, memo to Armina Marshall, John Wilson, Martin Manulis and Philip Langner, September 19, 1950.
56 Lawrence Langner memo, May 29, 1951.
57 "Fresh Talent Comes to Westport," *Bridgeport Sunday Post*, August 23, 1959.

58 "It's Been a Hard Job," *Westport News*, August 1988.

Chapter Nine: The Not-for-profit Theatre, 1973–84

1 Oscar G. Brockett and Franklin J. Hildy, *History of the Theatre*, 9th ed. (Boston: Allyn and Bacon, 2003), 569.
2 Ibid., 539.
3 WCP Playbill, June 17, 1974.
4 Ibid.
5 Ibid.
6 Sharon Giese, memo to author, March 21, 2004.
7 Author conversation with Julie Monahan, January 22, 2004.
8 *New York Times*, July 17, 1977.
9 The Connecticut Theatre Foundation, *A Survey of Audience Opinion*, August 1974.
10 WCP Playbill, August 27, 1973.
11 WCP Playbill, September 1977.
12 WCP Playbill, June 18, 1973.
13 WCP Playbill, July 23, 1973.
14 WCP Playbill, August 27, 1979.
15 WCP Playbill, August 6, 1973.
16 WCP Playbill, July 1978.
17 "For My Last Number," WCP Playbill, August 1975.
18 New York *Daily News*, July 10, 1977.
19 *New Haven Register*, June 13, 1976.
20 New York *Daily News*, Sunday, July 10, 1977.
21 WCP Playbill, June 1977.
22 *New York Times*, July 17, 1977, Sunday Arts Section.
23 Ibid.
24 New York *Daily News*, July 10, 1977.
25 WCP Playbill, June 1977.
26 New York *Daily News*, July 10, 1977.
27 Carole Claps interview with Pat Blaufuss, February 14, 2004.
28 Ibid.
29 Sharon Giese e-mail to author, April 11, 2004.
30 Ralph Tyler, "The Fine Art of Packaging a Summer Show," *New York Times*, June 15, 1980.
31 *New York Times*, September 24, 2000.
32 Ibid.
33 David Thomson in an article about Marilyn Monroe, reproduced on http://dir.salon.com.
34 "Eva Le Gallienne," Biography

Resource Center (http://galenet.galegroup.com/servlet/BioRC).
35 Ibid.
36 Robert A. Schanke, *The Lives of Eva LeGallienne: Shattered Applause* (Carbondale: Southern Illinois University Press, 1992); and Helen Sheehy, *Eva Le Gallienne: A Biography* (New York, Knopf, 1996).
37 Ralph Tyler, *New York Times*, June 15, 1980.
38 Arthur Gelb, *New York Times Magazine*, July 12, 1959.
39 Ralph Tyler, *New York Times*, June 15, 1980.
40 Ibid.
41 Mailing flyer: "Last 8 weeks of the 1950 summer schedule," and WCP Playbill, July 31, 1967.
42 *Norwalk Hour*, June 17, 1980.
43 *Westport News*, June 6, 1980.
44 *Boston Herald*, June 26, 1980.
45 *New Haven Register*, July 1, 1980.
46 Ralph Tyler, *New York Times*, June 15, 1980.
47 Markland Taylor, *New Haven Register*, July 15, 1980.
48 *Wilton Bulletin*, July 23, 1980.
49 Ralph Tyler, *New York Times*, June 15, 1980.
50 New York *Daily News*, August 13, 1980.
51 *New Haven Register*, August 20, 1980.
52 *Westport News*, August 27, 1980.
53 Quoted in Norman Nadel, *A Pictorial History of the Theatre Guild* (New York: Crown Publishers, 1969), 172.
54 *Norwalk News*, August 3, 1983.
55 WCP Playbill, June 1984.
56 WCP Playbill, June 1983.
57 WCP Playbill, *Joseph and the Amazing Technicolor Dreamcoat*, August 1984.
58 Ibid.
59 WCP Playbill, *Breakfast with Les and Bess*, August 1984.
60 WCP Playbill, *Foxfire*, June 1984.
61 Walter Bergen, memo to author, October 2003.
62 WCP Playbill, September 3, 1973.
63 "Stevan Dohanos: Cover to Cover," *Saturday Evening Post*, March 1991.
64 E-mail from Ginny Bolla to Pat Blaufuss, February 10, 2004.
65 "Westport Playhouse Remembers Longtime Staffer," *Westport News*, March 27, 1992.
66 WCP Playbill, July 21, 1958.

Chapter Ten: Saving the Theatre: The Playhouse Partnership, 1985–99

1 Philip Langner told the *Westport News* (December 14, 1984) that he was selling the Playhouse on the advice of his attorney, who was drawing up a new will for him. It was, he told the paper, "an estate planning matter . . . at a certain time in one's life one realizes that one doesn't live forever."
2 Sharon Giese e-mail to author, March 23, 2004.
3 "Westport Playhouse May Be Sold," *New York Times*, January 6, 1985.
4 *Westport News*, July 5, 1985.
5 WCP Playbill, *Run For Your Wife*, August 1985.
6 *Westport News*, July 5, 1985.
7 E-mail from Anthony Crivello to Chance Farago, February 10, 2004.
8 WCP Playbill, *The Odd Couple*, June 1986.
9 *Westport News*, June 1986.
10 "Playhouse Changes Scheduling Policy," *The Advocate*, January 28, 1987.
11 "Our Playhouse," WCP Playbill, August 1989.
12 Author conversation with Julie Monahan, January 22, 2004.
13 Ibid.
14 "Major Policy Changes for the Westport Playhouse," WCP press release, January 1987.
15 *New Haven Register*, June 21, 1987.
16 Ibid.
17 *The Advocate*, June 24, 1987.
18 *Fairpress*, July 9, 1987.
19 *New York Times*, July 12, 1987.
20 *Westport News*, July 3, 1987.
21 *The Ridgefield Press*, August 26–27, 1987.
22 *Fairpress*, June 1, 1990.
23 "The Connecticut Theatre Foundation, Inc.," undated paper in uncatalogued WCP papers for 1988, held by Westport Historical Society.
24 Julie Monahan, e-mails to author, March 10, 2004, and May 12, 2004.
25 "The Connecticut Theatre Foundation, Inc."
26 General Manager Paul Lambert, writing in the WCP Playbill, June 1989.
27 "Playhouse Future Threatened," WCP press release, November 8, 1989.

28 *Westport News*, December 1, 1989.
29 Walter Bergen, memo to author, November 2003.
30 "Pushing 60 and Hoping for the Best," *Westport News*, March 7, 1990.
31 Commissioner Ted Mueller, quoted in *Westport News*, March 21, 1990.
32 Ibid.
33 "Westport Playhouse Season Saved by Donors," *Westport News*, March 23, 1990.
34 *Fairpress*, July 6, 1990.
35 Walter Bergen, memo to author, January 2004.
36 Ibid.
37 Quoted in "Stage Company to Close Its Doors," WCP press release, September 14, 1993.
38 "Westport Company Drops Curtain," *New York Times*, September 26, 1993.
39 Ibid.
40 Ibid.
41 Betty Tyler, *Fairpress*, August 29, 1991.
42 Ibid.
43 *Westport News*, July 26, 1991.
44 "Transformation," *Fairpress*, August 22, 1991.
45 *New York Times*, August 23, 1992.
46 *Westport News*, July 14, 1995.
47 *Westport News*, August 30, 1995.
48 See *Greenwich Times*, August 28, 1998.
49 *Norwalk Hour*, August 24, 1996.
50 S. Zimbalist e-mail to Chance Farago, February 25, 2004, and Pat Blaufuss, memo to author, February 5, 2004.
51 Pat Blaufuss e-mail to author, January 2004.
52 Ibid.
53 WCP Playbill, August 2, 1999.
54 "Westport Country Playhouse Study," Guideline Research Corporation, October 1994.
55 Quoted in "A. R. Gurney, Jr.," Biography Resource Center, Contemporary Authors Online, Gale, April 15, 2004.
56 Author conversation with A. R. Gurney, December 16, 2003.
57 Quoted in "A. R. Gurney, Jr."
58 WCP Playbill, July 17, 1998.
59 *Stamford Advocate*, August 2, 1998.
60 WCP Playbill, June 21, 1999.
61 Walter Bergen, memo to author, January 2004.

62 The consultant was David Mallison.
63 Liz Morten: notes to the author, April 15, 2004; and author's conversations with Catherine Herman and Liz Morten, November 8 and November 13, 2004.
64 "A Celebration of Jim's Life," April 7, 2002.
65 WCP Playbill, August 30, 1999.
66 "Invisible Navigator," *In the ACT*, May 1980.
67 "James B. McKenzie, Sailing Experience to 01/01/00," sailing résumé.
68 Ibid.
69 *In the ACT*, May 1980; and "James B. McKenzie, Sailing Experience to 01/01/00."
70 Charles Dillingham in personal video recording, "A Celebration of Jim's Life," April 7, 2002.
71 *In the ACT*, May 1980.
72 "Jim McKenzie's Wild and Wacky Theatre Adventures," *Westport News*, June 18, 1993.
73 Peter Freedman in video recording "A Celebration of Jim's Life," April 7, 2002.
74 Robert Frost, *The Road Not Taken*, quoted in Elizabeth Knowles, ed., *The Oxford Dictionary of Quotations*, 5th ed. (Oxford and New York: Oxford University Press, 2001), 326
75 "Playhouse Creates New Board to Aid Renovation," *Norwalk Hour*, November 14, 1999.
76 Steve Wolff of AMS Planning & Research Corp, Fairfield, who subsequently became a board member himself and chaired the finance committee.
77 Fischer/Daks.
78 Ford Farewell Mills and Gatsch.
79 Payne Forrester & Olsen.
80 Liz Morten, April 15, 2004.
81 Walter Bergen, memo to author, January 2004.
82 "A Summer Veteran Gets New Life," *New York Times*, July 30, 2000.

Chapter Eleven: "A Doer, Not Just a Dreamer": Joanne Woodward Takes Charge, 2000–5

1 "Actress Adds Cachet to Playhouse," *Christian Science Monitor*, June 16, 2000.
2 "Joanne Woodward Draws on Theatre's Past to Plan Its Future,"

Greenwich Time, May 31, 2002.
3 Author interview with Joanne Woodward and Anne Keefe, March 17, 2004.
4 Waterbury *Republican*, October 1, 2000.
5 "A Summer Veteran Gets New Life," *New York Times*, July 30, 2000.
6 Author interview with Joanne Woodward and Anne Keefe, March 17, 2004.
7 Waterbury *Republican*, October 1, 2000.
8 "Westport Serves Up Seasonal Changes," *Variety*, October 2, 2000.
9 Author interview with Joanne Woodward and Anne Keefe, March 17, 2004.
10 *Connecticut Post*, June 13, 2001.
11 With Walter Pidgeon in Graham Greene's *The Complaisant Lover*, a role for which Wilder had won the Clarence Derwent Award for Best Actor on Broadway in 1962; with Carol Channing in Shaw's *The Millionairess* in 1963; and with Helen Hayes in A. E. Hotchner's *The White House* in 1964. See also "Westport Theater Readies for a Sizzler of a Season," *The Sunday Republican-American*, May 13, 2001.
12 "Courtship Follies from Chekhov, Shaw and Feydeau," *New York Times*, July 6, 2001.
13 Anne Keefe e-mail to author, April 7, 2004.
14 Thornton Wilder, preface to *Three Plays by Thornton Wilder* (New York: HarperCollins, 2003), 28.
15 *Westport News*, May 23, 2003.
16 "Woodward Tends Theatrical Garden," *Hartford Courant*, May 11, 2003.
17 Liz Morten, notes to author, April 15, 2004; and Walter Bergen, e-mail to author, July 11, 2004.
18 "Woodward Tends Theatrical Garden," *Hartford Courant*, May 11, 2003.
19 Ibid.
20 "German Play Asks Questions of Basic Decency," *The Advocate*, June 20, 2003.
21 *Stamford Advocate*, July 6, 2003.
22 *Ridgefield Press*, August 14, 2003.

Sources of Anecdotes

page 26
Excerpted from Sharon Giese e-mail to author, December 8, 2003.

page 46
Lawrence Langner, *The Magic Curtain* (New York: E. P. Dutton, 1951), 299.

page 53
top: Philip Langner in a conversation with the author, April 14, 2004.
bottom: Langner, *The Magic Curtain*, 309.

page 58
Langner, *The Magic Curtain*, 299.

page 61
Excerpted from Kitty Carlisle Hart to Joanne Woodward, undated note.

page 69
Westporter Herald, September 23, 1938; and Philip Langner, conversation with the author, October 29, 2003.

page 75
Langner, *The Magic Curtain*, 310.

page 106
See Langner, *The Magic Curtain*, 312; and *Westporter Herald*, August 26, 1946.

page 128
left: Excerpted from record of Paul Heller, interview with Pat Blaufuss, January 6, 2004.
top right: Lillian Ross, "Onward and Upward with the Arts," *New Yorker*, August 20, 1949, 33.
bottom right: Chilton Ryan, interview with author, November 11, 2003.

page 129
Phoebe Hopkins Burston, interview with Pat Blaufuss, March 5, 2004.

page 130
top left: Patricia Neal, *As I Am* (New York: Simon and Schuster, 1988), 69.
middle left: Edited version of undated note from June Havoc to the Playhouse, describing some of her memories.
bottom left: John Braithwaite, interview with Pat Blaufuss, January 2, 2004.
middle right: Author's conversation with Paula Laurence, April 6, 2004; and e-mail from Baboo Smiles to Chance Farago, January 7, 2004.

bottom right: Peter Levin, letter to Chance Farago, February 4, 2004.

page 131
left: Excerpted from June Lockhart, interview with Pat Blaufuss, January 6, 2004.
right: Adapted from Tammy Grimes fax to Joanne Woodward, January 14, 2004.

page 132
left: Conard Fowkes, undated letter to Chance Farago.
top right: Lily Lodge, interview with author, January 1, 2004.
middle right: Sally Jessy Raphaël with Pam Proctor, *Sally: Unconventional Success* (New York: William Morrow, 1990), 58.
bottom right: Christina Crawford, *Mommie Dearest* (New York: William Morrow, 1978), 229.

page 145
Jim McKenzie, quoted by Tom Killen, "The Show Must Go On," *Connecticut Magazine*, July 1982, 77.

page 149
Leo B. Meyer to Chance Farago, January 5, 2004.

page 150
Miggs Burroughs, phone conversation with the author, November 14, 2003.

page 156
Melinda Dickinson, e-mail to Chance Farago, October 13, 2003.

page 168
Excerpted from Fred Graham, interview with Pat Blaufuss, January 9, 2004.

page 172
WCP Playbill, *The Middle Ages*, July 1984.

page 174
Amy McKenzie, e-mail to author, April 15, 2004.

page 178
top: Jerry Orbach, undated letter to Joanne Woodward.
bottom: e-mail from Walter Bergen to the author, April 12, 2004.

page 182
Excerpted from Carole Claps, interview with Pat Blaufuss, February 14, 2004.

page 189
top: Excerpted from Dulcy Rogers, "Playhouse memories": e-mail to the author, January 5, 2004.
bottom: Excerpted from Carole Claps, interview with Pat Blaufuss, February 14, 2004.

page 195
Excerpted from Dulcy Rogers: "Playhouse memories": e-mail to the author, January 5, 2004.

page 201
Philisse Barrows and Julie Monahan, e-mails to the author, April 2004.

page 207
Pat Blaufuss, memorandum to the author, February 5, 2004.

page 213
Burry Fredrik, interview with Pat Blaufuss, February 9, 2004.

page 221
Excerpted from Fred Graham, record of interview with Pat Blaufuss, January 9, 2004.

page 224
Pat Blaufuss, memorandum to the author, February 5, 2004; and A. R. Gurney, interview with the author, December 16, 2003.

page 230
Tim Conway to Chance Farago, December 29, 2003.

page 236
Stephanie Zimbalist, e-mails to Chance Farago, February 5 and February 12, 2004.

page 241
Steve Loddo, e-mail to Chance Farago, December 19, 2003.

page 244
Anne Keefe, e-mail to Walter Bergen, April 14, 2004.

page 248
Excerpted from Walter Bergen e-mails to the author, March 18, 2004.

page 252
Author's interview with Bob Wright, November 11, 2004.

Index

Page numbers in italic type refer to photographs and other illustrations and information in the captions. "WCP" refers to Westport Country Playhouse.

Credits

JOHN EMERY
MILDRED NATWICK
CLARENCE DERWENT
In Dorothy Sayers' New Detective Comedy
"BUSMAN'S
HONEYMOON"
(American Premiere)

Weekday Evenings at 8:40
Matinee Wednesday at 2:30
Prices: .55 to $2.75

Benefit Night, Tuesday, July 20th
CHURCH OF HOLY TRINITY OF WESTPORT

WESTPORT
COUNTRY PLAYHOUSE
Boston Post Road   Westport, Conn.

WEEK OF JULY 29 - AUG.

ETHEL
BARRYMORE
— IN —
SHERIDAN'S
"THE SCHOOL
FOR SCANDAL"

Hundreds of Seats — 55c to $1.10
EVES. 8:45   Mat. Wed.   MAT. 2:45

Benefit Tuesday Eve., July 30th—
NORWALK CHILDREN'S MUSEUM

THE MAN WHO
CAME TO DINNER"
— WITH —
REX O'MALLEY
MARTA LINDEN   PAUL CRABTREE
RUTH FORD   JANET FOX
Staged by   Setting & Lighting by
MARTIN MAN   HERBERT BRODKIN

Prices: Reserve by Phone
$1.20 to $3.60 inc. tax   WESTPORT 2-4179
Evenings at 8:40   Mats. Wed. & Sat. at 2:40

WESTPORT
COUNTRY PLAYHOUSE
PHONE CA 7-4177
AIR CONDITIONED

UGUST 24 Thru 29

HENRY T. WEINSTEIN & LAURENCE FELDMAN
— PRESENT —

A PARTY"
— WITH —
BETTY   ADOLPH
OMDEN and GREEN

XCLUSIVE WESTPORT ENGAGEMENT

AS ORIGINALLY PRODUCED IN NEW YORK
By Gus Schirmer, Jr. and The Theatre Guild

NEXT WEEK: AUG. 31 - SEPT. 5
THEATRE GUILD TRYOUT
DAVID WAYNE
in "MARCUS IN THE HIGH GRASS"

MONDAY thru FRIDAY EVENINGS AT 8:40
DAY EVES. AT 6 and 9   WEDNESDAY MATS. AT 2:40

WESTPORT
COUNTRY PLAYHOUSE
-Phone CA- 7-4177
AIR COOLED
WEEK OF JULY 30 - AUG. 4 1956
MUSIC ★ SONGS ★ DANCES
JULES MUNSHIN - BETSY PALMER
— IN —
'THE DOCTOR IN SPITE OF HIMSELF'
— with —
LAWRENCE FLETCHER
MARILYN CLARK   HAL HALLBROOK
JAMES AMDANDOS   GEN7E DeLAPPE   JOE CAMPANELLA
SETS AND LIGHTING
MARVIN REISS
INEE ONLY at 2:40 P.M.
ATS. at 6 P. M. and 9 P. M.

WESTPORT
COUNTRY PLAYHOUSE
America's Foremost Summer Theatre
June 27 - July 2
EXCLUSIVE WESTPORT ENGAGEMENT
★ ★ PRIOR TO NATIONAL TOUR! ★ ★

ANNE JACKSON & ELI WALLACH
TWICE AROUND THE PARK

By Murray Schisgal
Directed by